Mexico, Slavery, Freedom

A Bilingual Documentary History,
1520–1829

Mexico, Slavery, Freedom

*A Bilingual Documentary History,
1520–1829*

Compiled, Translated, and Edited,
with an Introduction, by
Pablo Miguel Sierra Silva

Hackett Publishing Company, Inc.
Indianapolis/Cambridge

Copyright © 2024 by Hackett Publishing Company, Inc.

All rights reserved
Printed in the United States of America

27 26 25 24   1 2 3 4 5 6 7

For further information, please address
    Hackett Publishing Company, Inc.
    P.O. Box 44937
    Indianapolis, Indiana 46244-0937

    www.hackettpublishing.com

Cover design by E. L. Wilson
Interior design by Laura Clark
Composition by Aptara, Inc.

Library of Congress Control Number: 2023942296

ISBN-13: 978-1-64792-150-7 (pbk.)
ISBN-13: 978-1-64792-151-4 (PDF ebook)
ISBN-13: 978-1-64792-152-1 (epub)

The paper used in this publication meets the minimum requirements of American National Standard for Information Sciences—Permanence of Paper for Printed Library Materials, ANSI Z39.48–1984.

∞

To Molly, for everything

Contents

Acknowledgments	xii
Preface	xiv
Timeline	xvii
Glossary	xix
Maps of Colonial Mexico with Referenced Locations	xxii
Introduction: A Brief History of Slavery and Freedom in Colonial Mexico	1

Chapter 1—Conquest, Slavery, and Physical Dominion — 29

Document 1	1520—The conquistadors and the branding iron	30
Document 2	1528—Bernal Díaz del Castillo destroys the branding iron in Coatzacoalcos	32
Document 3	1530—Cortés and his extended family receive slave licenses	34
Document 4	circa 1553—Puebla's slave registry, *La Caja de Negros*	35
Document 5	1579—Viceroy Enrriquez calls for castrating Black runaways	38
Document 6	1587—Chichimec captives from Nuevo León displaced	40
Document 7	1600—Indigenous people held as slaves in bakeries	41
Document 8	1607—Forced labor for draining Lake Texcoco	42
Document 9	1610—Bishop Alonso de la Mota y Escobar's inventory	44
Document 10	1616—Textile barons demand Native workers and reject Black workers	48
Document 11	1621—Inventory of Pedro Gomez's textile mill	51
Document 12	1645—Enslaved labor and reproduction in the Fresneda textile mill	55

Chapter 2—The Transatlantic and Caribbean Slave Trade — 59

Document 13	1560—Mexico's archbishop on the illegitimacy of the slave trade	60
Document 14	1561—The Crown licenses trafficking 1,000 African captives to Mexico	63
Document 15	1602—Pharmacists, slave traders, and debts	64
Document 16	1615—Bill of purchase for twenty-one Arara captives	66
Document 17	1620—A slave trader's petition to the Puebla municipal council	67

Document 18	1621—Illicit arrival of slave ships on the Isla de Cabezas	69
Document 19	1621—Fraudulent officials in the slave trade	70
Document 20	1621—The royal slaves of the San Juan de Ulúa fortress	72
Document 21	1624—The slave trade from Santo Domingo to Campeche	75
Document 22	1630—A Portuguese slave trader's ledger	77
Document 23	1635—Jesuit College of Puebla purchases four African youths	82
Document 24	1664—The arrival of the *San Juan Bautista* slave ship	85
Document 25	1664—Condition of the survivors of the *San Juan Bautista* slave ship	86
Document 26	1675—The governor of Nueva Veracruz recalls the old slave trade	88
Document 27	1681—Sale of six recently arrived Africans	89

Chapter 3—Transpacific Slave Trade — 91

Document 28	1570—Arrival of enslaved Muslims from the Philippines	92
Document 29	1598—Sales taxes on five enslaved people from the Philippines	94
Document 30	1607—The slave trade through the port of Acapulco	95
Document 31	1650—Lázaro de la Cruz and Nicolás sold to a textile mill	96
Document 32	1672—The Queen of Spain abolishes Asian and Chichimec slavery	98
Document 33	1685—A bill of sale for a Mozambican *cafre* in Cavite	99
Document 34	1685—Legal title to enslaved *cafres* from the East Indies	100
Document 35	1708—Arrival of the Black *esclavos de pasa* from Manila	102
Document 36	1714—Investigation into enslaved Blacks arriving in Acapulco	104

Chapter 4—Rebellion and Marronage — 108

Document 37	1537—Black rebellion in Mexico City and the mines of Amatepec	109
Document 38	1549—The ruler of Nochistlán allies with Black fugitives	114
Document 39	1609—Two accounts of the maroons of Amatlan	116
Document 40	1619—Yanga, King of the Black Maroons	119
Document 41	1622—A bounty hunter and the maroons of Río Blanco	123
Document 42	1645—Francisco de la Cruz, enslaved *chino*, escapes	128
Document 43	1659—Precautions against the Black maroons of Chietla	130
Document 44	1665—A wet nurse and her daughter escape	132
Document 45	1669—Two eyewitness accounts of Crax Bomba's rebellion	134

Document 46	1760—María Manuela escapes from the Hacienda Santiago	142
Document 47	1760—María Josefa, Gertrudis Simona, and Captain Matute's politics	144
Document 48	1790—Freedom for Black fugitives in Chihuahua	148
Document 49	1799—Apache women fight and escape from La Rinconada	149
Document 50	1804—Escaping territorial Louisiana for Spanish Texas	151

Chapter 5—Afro–Indigenous Interactions — **153**

Document 51	1538—On Black-Indigenous unions and claims to freedom	154
Document 52	1563—Complaint regarding Black and Indigenous laundresses	156
Document 53	1582—Black women and mulattas dressed as Indigenous women	156
Document 54	1590—A mulatto interpreter of Spanish and Nahuatl in Coatepec	157
Document 55	1590—Labor, value, and death by *cocoliztli*	158
Document 56	1603—Native men kidnapped on textile mill owner's orders	161
Document 57	circa 1624—Lucas Olola and the religious beliefs of the Huasteca	162
Document 58	1628—Juana and Diego Pablo charged with trespassing	165
Document 59	1631—Marriage license for Juan Francisco and Juliana de la Torre	166
Document 60	1639—Religious syncretism and *nahuales* in Tehuantepec	168
Document 61	1662—Criminal charges against Gregorio for attacking Diego de la Cruz	169
Document 62	1682—Domingo de la Cruz establishes his son's free status	171
Document 63	1693—Charges against Juan de Medina, governor of Huaquechula	172

Chapter 6—Navigating Religion and Politics — **175**

Document 64	1587—Toluca friars warned to not intercede for textile mill workers	176
Document 65	1596—Juan Carrasco and the Inquisition	177
Document 66	1606—Pedro takes communion	180
Document 67	1606—Lucía takes communion	182
Document 68	1609—Charges of cohabitation against Esperanza and Lorenzo Loriga	184
Document 69	1625—Charges of blasphemy against Antonia	185

Document 70	1631—Will of Marta Rodríguez, a free Black woman	187
Document 71	1640—Dance Performed by the Black Creole Women of Mexico City	190
Document 72	1642—The life story of Sebastián Domingo, alias Munguía	204
Document 73	1655—The *chino* confraternity of Our Lady of Guadalupe	207
Document 74	1691—Marriage license for Magdalena de Santiago, White mulatta	210
Document 75	1698—The brotherhood of Santa Efigenia and its constitutions	211
Document 76	1710—Prayers in Mexico City to San Benito de Palermo	216
Document 77	1725—Nicolás Palomino Arias responds to accusations of bigamy	219
Document 78	1731—Lázaro del Valle's marriages in Acámbaro and Chihuahua	224
Document 79	1787—Priest of Huazolotitlán, Oaxaca demands obedience	228

Chapter 7—Freedom Papers — 231

Document 80	1581—A royal decree for the freedom of Benito	232
Document 81	1621—Conditional manumission for baby Constansa	233
Document 82	1625—Cathedral council manumits Juana de la Cruz's children	235
Document 83	1626—María Salomé sues for her freedom	237
Document 84	1630—Temporary freedom for Ana de la Cruz and her children	239
Document 85	1641—Huexotzingo natives demand not to be treated as slaves	240
Document 86	1650—María receives her freedom papers	242
Document 87	1650—Gabriel frees his wife and infant son	244
Document 88	1668—Clara de la Cruz, free *china*, ratifies her liberty	246
Document 89	1696—Manumission promise for Catarina de San Juan	247
Document 90	1714—Freedom for Micaela de la Cruz, of the Caravalí nation	249
Document 91	1780—María Antonia Mariscal finds an owner for her daughter	250

Chapter 8—Debt and Belonging — 253

Document 92	1590—Simón de Mesa, free and imprisoned	254
Document 93	1605—An indebted Afro-Indigenous family from Cholula	256
Document 94	1621—A free Acapulco woman pawns Juana de Terra Nova	258

Document 95	1626—Will of Gaspar Hernandez, free man from the Canary Islands	260
Document 96	1640—Francisco López's many, many debts	264
Document 97	1640—Lorenzo del Puerto's examination	266
Document 98	1675—Lázaro Rodríguez de la Torre, free master printer, leases a house	268
Document 99	1681—Will of Agustina Mónica, free *parda*	269
Document 100	1690—Burial arrangements for José de Peralta and his descendants	274
Document 101	1728—Antonio de Amaya accused of adultery with María de la O	276
Document 102	1734—Genealogy and education of a philosophy student	278
Document 103	1735—Inventory of a merchant in Zacatecas	279
Document 104	1788—Gertrudis Caballero's husband taxed unfairly	285
Chapter 9—Fragile Freedoms		**288**
Document 105	1612—Restrictions on Black socialization in Puebla	289
Document 106	1615—Controlling *Carnestolendas* or Mardi Gras	290
Document 107	1618—Ordinance against Black gatherings, dances, and games	292
Document 108	1623—Charges against Francisco Manzanedo, mulatto interpreter	294
Document 109	1646—Juan Martín and Luisa Hernández accused of cohabitation	295
Document 110	1658—Investigation into men who loved other men	296
Document 111	1658—List of men executed for and suspected of having sex with other men	306
Document 112	1686—A royal scribe and his family defect	315
Document 113	1783—Music, violence, and corruption in Colima	316
Document 114	1784—An Izúcar family demands its freedom	320
Document 115	1812—Restrictions lifted for qualified people of African descent	322
Document 116	1813—José María Morelos and "The Sentiments of the Nation"	323
Document 117	1826—A mass manumission in Teotitlán del Camino, Oaxaca	328
Document 118	1829—President Vicente Guerrero abolishes slavery	332
Essay on Sources		*334*
Bibliography		*339*
Index		*346*

Acknowledgments

I would first like to thank the students of the history department at the University of Rochester. Over the past ten years I have been fortunate to teach and learn from your insights, queries, challenges, and research projects. In truth, this documentary history would not have been possible without you. *Mil gracias*. So many students have contributed to this project that it would be a disservice to name them individually. I will simply express my profound gratitude for all who participated in The Other Atlantic, History of Captivity, and Black Mexico seminars. For those brave souls who ventured into the Mexico through Time and Digital Paleography experiments, I hope you will see and value the immense potential of your skill set. Finally, for the students in the African Diaspora in Latin America and the Colonial Latin America survey courses, thank you.

A healthy obsession with the archive and the secrets of paleography began during my graduate studies at UCLA. Claudia Parodi offered a wonderful and collegial evening course on paleographic techniques that brought in students of Spanish, linguistics, history, and other disciplines. Though she is no longer with us, this book is also for her. On the lower level of UCLA's Young Research Library, I found a home and haven in Special Collections and the Center for Primary Research and Training. Kelly Bachli and the entire CFPRT team allowed me to further practice my paleography and to learn cataloguing skills working with rare Peruvian and Mexican materials. Many, many thanks to them and to the entire staff of the UCLA libraries. Kevin Terraciano, my esteemed doctoral advisor, consistently encouraged me to hone these skills in the colonial archives of Puebla and Mexico City. A true believer in the power of the primary source, Kevin developed fantastic source readers (with their iconic red and blue cardboard covers) for the students of HIST 8A. Had it not been for his methods, support, and encouragement, I could never have imagined this book.

Over the years, my colleagues in the history department at the University of Rochester have unwaveringly supported my academic interests. Matt Lenoe, Stewart Weaver, Laura Smoller, and Ruben Flores, thank you for your friendship, generosity, and willingness to entertain my obsession with the primary source. I have never felt restricted in the courses I have taught at Rochester, and for that intellectual freedom I am so very grateful. This book is also a testament to the collegiality and mentorship of my peers. Tanya Bakhmetyeva, Molly Ball, Tom Devaney, Tom Fleischman, Joseph Inikori, Mike Jarvis, Elias Mandala, Jean Pedersen, Mical Raz, Joanie Rubin, Tom Slaughter, Laura Smoller, Brianna Theobald, you have all contributed to this book and archival journey. I am in your debt. Two phenomenal doctoral students at the UofR, Jeffrey Baron and Claire Becker, have also contributed insights to this project.

My dear *colega*, Ryan Prendergast, from the Spanish program in Modern Languages and Cultures, has always been a supportive and generous spirit. We have now co-taught various iterations of the History-Spanish collaborative course 1492 and Beyond, and I look forward to several more. Vialcary Crisóstomo also contributed valuable feedback during the workshop session held at the University of Rochester. To the fantastic researchers of Grupo, the Latin Americanist faculty group at the UofR, thank you for your camaraderie and very helpful comments in our workshops. Finally, I wish to express my heartfelt gratitude to the many faculty members of the Department of Black Studies and all those affiliated with the Frederick Douglass Institute for African and African-American Studies. Your conversations and insights throughout the years have made this documentary history possible. I also thank Anne MacPherson, Isabel Córdova, Ryan Jones, and all the Latin Americanists in the Rochester area for their generous workshops and candid suggestions over the years.

It has been an absolute pleasure to work with Rick Todhunter, Laura Clark, and the entire editorial team at Hackett. Thank you for entertaining the initial concept for this book (at the height of the COVID-19 pandemic!) and seeing it through. Many thanks to the initial readers of my book précis. Matthew Restall and an anonymous reader offered constructive criticism and suggestions for the manuscript revision. This book is undoubtedly the better for your comments. Andrés Reséndez graciously contributed insights and suggestions for this book's introductory essay. Tim O'Brien crafted the four wonderful maps that inform this book, and Tucker Million produced the useful index that follows the text. To all of you, *mil gracias, colegas*.

Finally, this project is also indebted to a new generation of scholars who are redefining the contours of Mexicanist scholarship. Five generous colleagues contributed documents to this book. Sabrina Smith (University of California-Merced) provided the high-resolution images of the 1825 mass manumission in Teotitlán del Valle, Oaxaca. Miguel Valerio (Washington University in St. Louis) generously offered the transcription and arduous translation of the 1640 "Feast of the Creole *morenas* of the very noble and loyal Mexico City." Norah Gharala (University of Houston) kindly contributed photographs for the fascinating 1735 inventory of Pascual de Vela from the Zacatecas archives. Adela Amaral (William & Mary) generously shared images from her research on Amapa for the deposition of two maroon women in 1760. Rafael Castañeda García (UNAM) contributed the photographs for a groundbreaking document: the founding constitutions for the Santa Efigenia confraternity of Toluca. To all five of you, thank you for trusting me with your sources and for your support through the years.

Rochester, New York   May 2023

Preface

This book is an invitation to conduct research on Mexico. To be more precise, this documentary history has been designed to provide you with primary sources on the free and enslaved people who lived in Mexico over the past five centuries. This includes the early years of the military phase of the Spanish conquest, formal colonial rule as the viceroyalty of New Spain (1535–1821), and the first eight years after independence. For some, this will be a first glimpse into the deep history of the African diaspora in Mexico. For others, this book will speak to the complexity of Native history and its long entanglement with freedom and enslavement. The experiences of bondage, displacement, and community formation for Asian people, generalized as *chinos*, are also central to this project. Over the past thirty years, scholars have published dozens of books, articles, and dissertations on the African, Native American, and Asian populations who experienced enslavement in what is today Mexico. Along the same lines, historians have studied these groups and their descendants as they resisted, adapted to, and transcended slavery from the sixteenth through the nineteenth centuries. The establishment of interracial alliances, the navigation of Catholicism, and the strategies used to secure freedom papers have all become essential elements for the study of Asian, Black, and Indigenous populations in Mexico.

This volume offers archival documents in their Spanish or Portuguese originals and in modernized English translations. At times, the original is necessary to make sense of idiomatic expressions or complex constructs, and may prove helpful to those interested in comparative projects on other Spanish- or Portuguese-speaking societies. The English translation intends to provide clarity and transparency on difficult topics and verbose statements. For the most part, I have translated key concepts into English as faithfully as possible to the original, so as not to alter the meaning of the primary source. I follow current capitalization practices in the introductory essay, but not in the document translations and transcriptions.

I have decided to retain the emendations, marginal comments, underlining, and other elements that indicate how a text was debated, censored, revised, or otherwise edited. I contend that this messiness is productive, as it often betrays an author's or scribe's hesitations. Capturing these corrections, then, is also an essential element of our work as researchers. (See the 1813 "The Sentiments of the Nation," attributed to José María Morelos y Pavón, for an especially powerful example of these tensions.) Any translation, however, necessarily distorts the original source; this volume is certainly not exempt from that reality. To improve comprehension, I have at times inserted periods or commas to allow the English reader a pause where the Spanish original continues for several more lines without any such pause. I have also modernized certain names—such as "Xpoual" to "Cristóbal" or "Jhoan" to "Juan"—in the English translation. I take full responsibility for any mistranslations or unintentional anachronisms.

The book's bilingual format is explicitly intended to reach a vast English- and Spanish-language readership. As a graduate student, I constantly found inspiration in Robert Conrad's *Children of God's Fire: A Documentary History of Black Slavery in Brazil* and Gloria García Rodríguez's *Voices on the Enslaved in Nineteenth-Century Cuba*. Lisa Sousa, Matthew Restall, and Kevin Terraciano's *Mesoamerican Voices: Native Language Writings from Colonial Mexico, Yucatan, and Guatemala* provided a priceless model for analyzing translated sources. Over the years, I have also found Leo J. Garofalo and Kathryn Joy McKnight's *Afro-Latino Voices* to be an essential companion for teaching African diaspora courses.

The present documentary history differs slightly from the titles above in that I do not introduce the reader to the context of every document. Instead, I have penned an introductory essay that discusses key topics and developments on slavery and freedom in Mexico from the early colonial period to the first years after independence. Each thematic chapter also features a short introduction to situate readers, but I do not offer leading questions or arguments, so as not to influence the reader's interpretations or research interests.

The documents in this bilingual history range from 1520 to 1829 and have been drawn from a wide variety of regional, national, and imperial repositories. I have transcribed documents from the Archivo General de la Nación in Mexico City, the Archivo General de Indias in Seville, the Bibliothèque nationale de France, and the Archivo General de Notarías del Estado de Puebla, among others. Some of these documents I studied in person; others I consulted in digitized form. I have also attempted to explore some of the variations that one encounters when studying experiences of freedom and enslavement in an immense viceroyalty. This documentary history features cases from Louisiana to Chiapas, from Oaxaca to Chihuahua, and from Veracruz to Manila. There is, admittedly, a geographical bias in the overrepresentation of cases from Puebla, the city that served as the setting for my first book. I have opted to use some of these documents (published here for the first time) for two reasons. First, because Puebla dynamics often mirrored urban interactions elsewhere in the viceroyalty, but also because the city's notarial archive contains priceless transactions, or copies of transactions, from Acapulco, Campeche, Mexico City, Tlaxcala, Veracruz, Zacatlán, and other locations.

Ultimately, I hope this documentary history will generate debate, counterpoints, and dialogue. I am especially optimistic that you, the reader, will take these documents beyond the classroom or research paper. The dialogues generated by these documents should be shared in the private and public spaces where they are most urgently relevant. We need to have these (admittedly) difficult conversations within our families, with those we trust the most. Despite considerable achievements in extending human and civic rights to marginalized populations over the last twenty years, there is much work to do in redressing the long legacy of slavery in Mexico and in the Western Hemisphere in general. Slavery was abolished, in theory, three times in Mexican history. Those momentous years were 1542, 1672, and 1829. And yet, the aftermath of slavery and the undeniable burden of racism and colorism in Mexico are still with us well into the third decade of the twenty-first century. I am under no illusion that this volume will cure those ills. I am hopeful, however, that this modest project will contribute to the construction of new educational models, the development of a memory of inclusion and empathy, and a clearer understanding of the roots of our present-day inequities.

Timeline

1519	Arrival of conquistadors in the Gulf Coast and Central Mexican highlands
1521	Fall of Mexico-Tenochtitlan to Iberian, Tlaxcalan, and other Native forces
1520s	Expansive Iberian slaving campaigns against Native populations
1535	Viceroyalty of New Spain formally established, Mexico-Tenochtitlan as capital
1537	Repression of Black rebels in Mexico City and the mines of Amatepec
1540–1542	Chichimec nations fight Spaniards in the Mixtón War
1542	Passage of the New Laws abolishing Native slavery
1565	Galleon route established between Acapulco and Manila
1570	Arrival of enslaved Muslims from the Philippines
1581	Beginning of the Iberian Union, King Philip II claims throne of Portugal
1590s	Transatlantic slave trade from West Central Africa intensifies
1612	Repression and execution of thirty-five Black men and women in Mexico City
1620s–1630s	Peak years of transatlantic slaving from West Central Africa to Mexican ports
1631	San Lorenzo de los Negros established by maroon population
1640	Transatlantic slaving networks disrupted by Portuguese independence
1658	Investigation, raids, and executions of men who had sex with other men
1669	Crax Bomba leads rebellion at La Rinconada, Veracruz
1672	Abolition of Asian and Chichimec slavery by Queen Mariana's decree
1680–1692	Pueblo Rebellion, Spaniards expelled from New Mexico for twelve years
1683	Mass abduction of Veracruz's African-descent population by buccaneers

1700	House of Bourbon ascends to the Spanish throne, ends Habsburg rule
1701–1713	French Compaignie de Guinée acquires *asiento* slaving monopoly
1713–1739	The English South Sea Company acquires slaving monopoly to Spanish America
1762–1769	Louisiana incorporated into the viceroyalty of New Spain
1792	Abolition of New Spain's African-descent militias
1803–1804	Spanish Louisiana transferred to France, then to the United States
1810	Beginning of the war for Mexican independence
1813	José María Morelos y Pavón proclaims "The Sentiments of the Nation"
1821	Mexican war of independence ends
1829	President Vicente Guerrero abolishes slavery, exempts Texas

Glossary

aguardiente   an alcoholic beverage produced by mixing sugarcane, fruits, spices, and other ingredients

alcabala   sales tax applied on purchases during the colonial period

alcalde   a local magistrate. Typically, *alcaldes* operated as judges or court justices and were appointed by the Crown or viceroy.

alma en boca huesos en costal   a term used in bills of sale to describe recent African survivors of slaving voyages; literally translates to "soul in mouth, bones in a sack"

armazón   a group of captives in a transport, by sea or overland. Concept frequently used by ship captains, overland slave traders, or their intermediaries. Appears as *armação* in Portuguese documents.

arriero   the person responsible for transporting all sorts of products by mule. These highly mobile men were also hired to transport enslaved people.

bachiller   generally referred to a person that held a university degree. *Bachilleres*, however, could specialize in medicine, law, or religion. *Bachiller* was commonly used as an honorific title that preceded the degree holder's name.

bozal   an enslaved person recently brought from Africa. Also used as an adjective to describe someone unfamiliar with Iberian languages, Catholicism, or Spanish legal systems.

cafre de pasa   a physical descriptor, derived from the term *kafir*, to identify people of African descent. It was often used to describe enslaved people with tightly coiled hair, especially in the transpacific slave trade of the late seventeenth century.

calidad   a social category that took into account a person's physical appearance, standing in society, reputation, and ancestry. As such, it was a complex and highly subjective category of identification that could be contested in tax disputes, town council elections, and debates about political privileges.

carimbo   a branding iron, often also the mark left by a branding instrument. In New Spain, *carimbos* were used to mark cattle, war captives, fugitive slaves, and Africans trafficked through Atlantic and Caribbean slaving routes.

casta   general term used to describe mixed-race people and to differentiate them from Natives and Spaniards. Occasionally, especially in the late colonial period, *casta* could include Black people.

castellano   the commander of a fortress, typically one in a port city. During the colonial period, *castellanos* could be found in San Juan de Ulúa and Acapulco.

china or ***chino***   a person of Asian descent. Typically a reference to a free or enslaved individual who arrived in Mexico via the Philippines, or a descendant of such an individual.

cocha or ***cocho***   a physical descriptor of skin color, often paired with the term *mulata* or *mulato*. In practice, this was a subjective reference to a light-skinned person of African descent. Taken literally, the term referred to the color of cooked quince (*color de membrillo cocho*).

cocoliztli   a Nahuatl term for various pestilential diseases, especially smallpox. In Spanish, *cocoliztli* was often associated with *viruela*.

corregidor   a direct royal representative at the local level. The *corregidor* presided over municipal councils, heard appeals cases, and remained a powerful figure until the late colonial period.

encomenderos   Spaniards who held grants of Native tribute and labor (not land itself). The Crown initially awarded these grants, or *encomiendas*, to former conquistadors and their descendants.

in facie ecclesia   a marriage celebrated by a priest according to the instructions of the church, literally "before the church"

licenciado   a holder of a university degree, typically indicating a higher level of studies (three or four additional years) than that of a *bachiller*. *Licenciados* often held law degrees in Spanish America, even if they did not practice law. *Licenciado* was used as an honorific title to denote social status.

morena or ***moreno***   label used to identify a dark-skinned person of African descent, especially associated with free-born or freed people. Commonly found in reference to men in the militias (*milicias de morenos*).

mulata or ***mulato***   label used to describe a person of African-Spanish descent or African-Indigenous descent. Depending on context, it often carried pejorative connotations. Increasingly used in the late colonial period with color modifiers to describe a variety of skin tones (*mulata blanca, mulato prieto*, etc.).

nahual or ***nagual***   a person with the ability to invoke and take on the physical form of an animal. Present throughout the Mesoamerican region, *nahuales* were associated with witchcraft and sorcery during the colonial period.

nahuatlata or ***nahuatlato***   a speaker of the Nahuatl language. Often used to refer to an interpreter who spoke both Nahuatl and Spanish for official and political purposes.

negra or ***negro***   label used to describe a dark-skinned person of African descent, free or enslaved. Strongly associated with enslavement in the sixteenth century.

palenque   a community composed of maroons, mostly people of African descent, who had escaped slavery. Equivalent to a *mocambo* or *quilombo* in other parts of Spanish America and Brazil.

parda* or *pardo   label used to describe a light-skinned person of African descent. Often used for free people and those in the free-colored militias (*milicias de pardos*).

primicia   a religious tax on first fruits that was supposed to be paid to the Catholic church, in addition to the tithe (*diezmo*)

vecina* or *vecino   a tax-paying individual in a city, village, or town. The term was often used to signal permanence in a location, as opposed to temporary residents and travelers. *Vecina* or *vecino* status marked belonging in a community.

yten   used to mark the next item on a list, commonly seen in inventories

zambaiga* or *zambaigo   a term for a person of African and Indigenous descent. Used more frequently in Peru than in colonial Mexico.

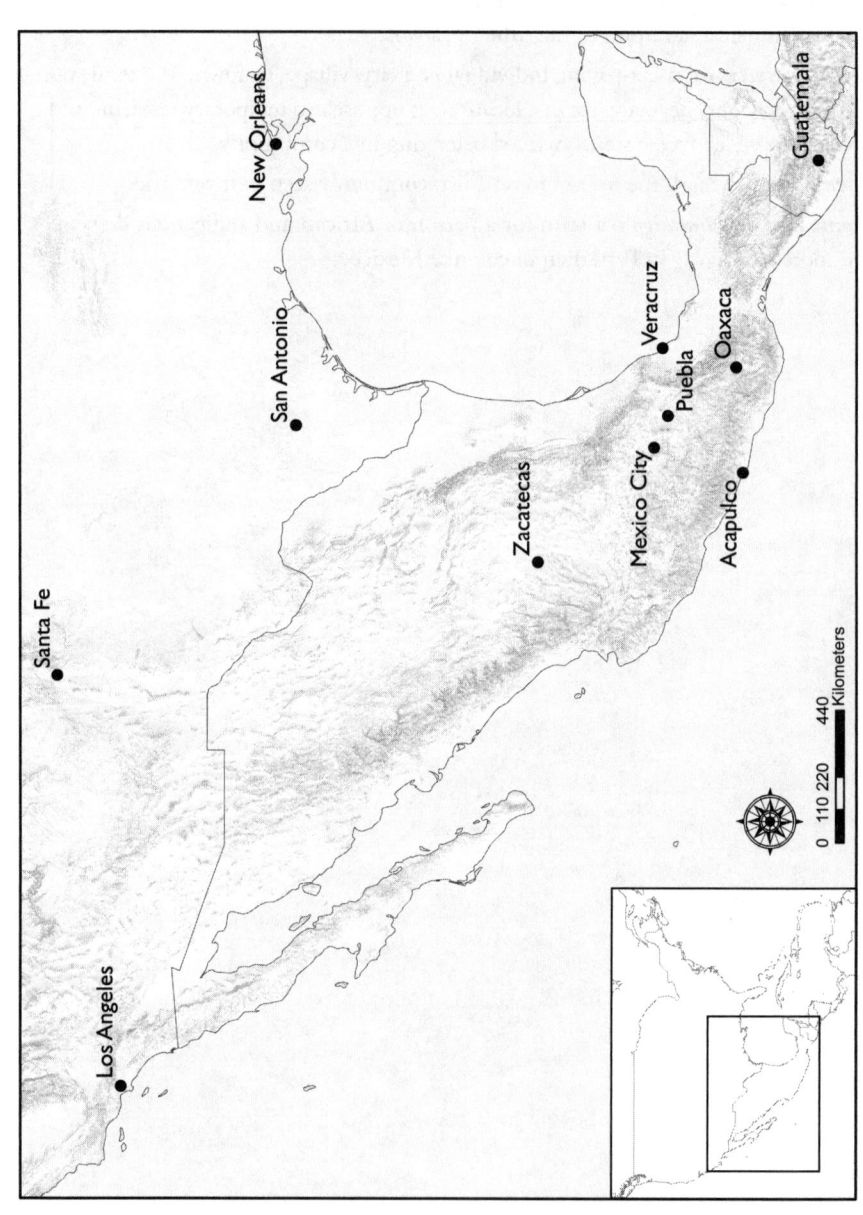

Map 1. Viceroyalty of New Spain

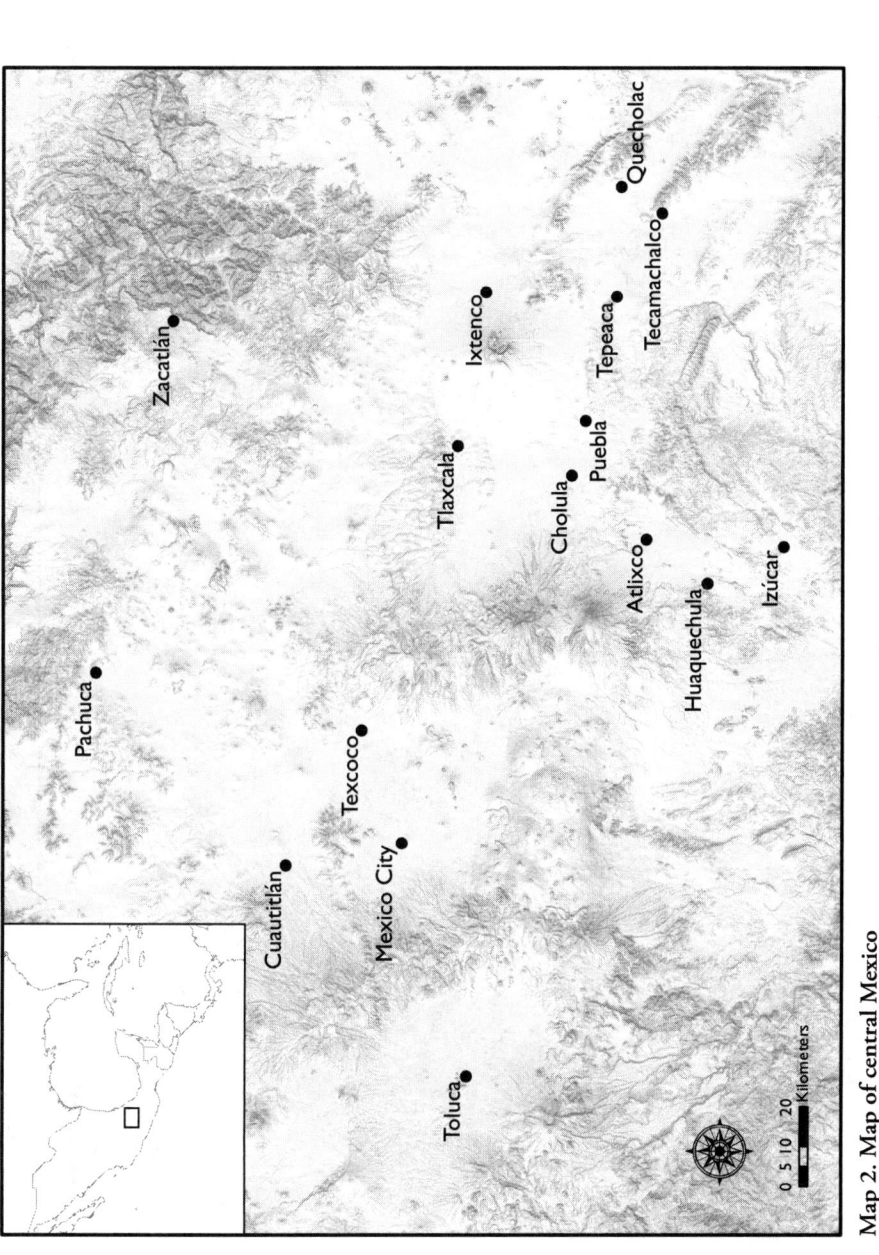

Map 2. Map of central Mexico

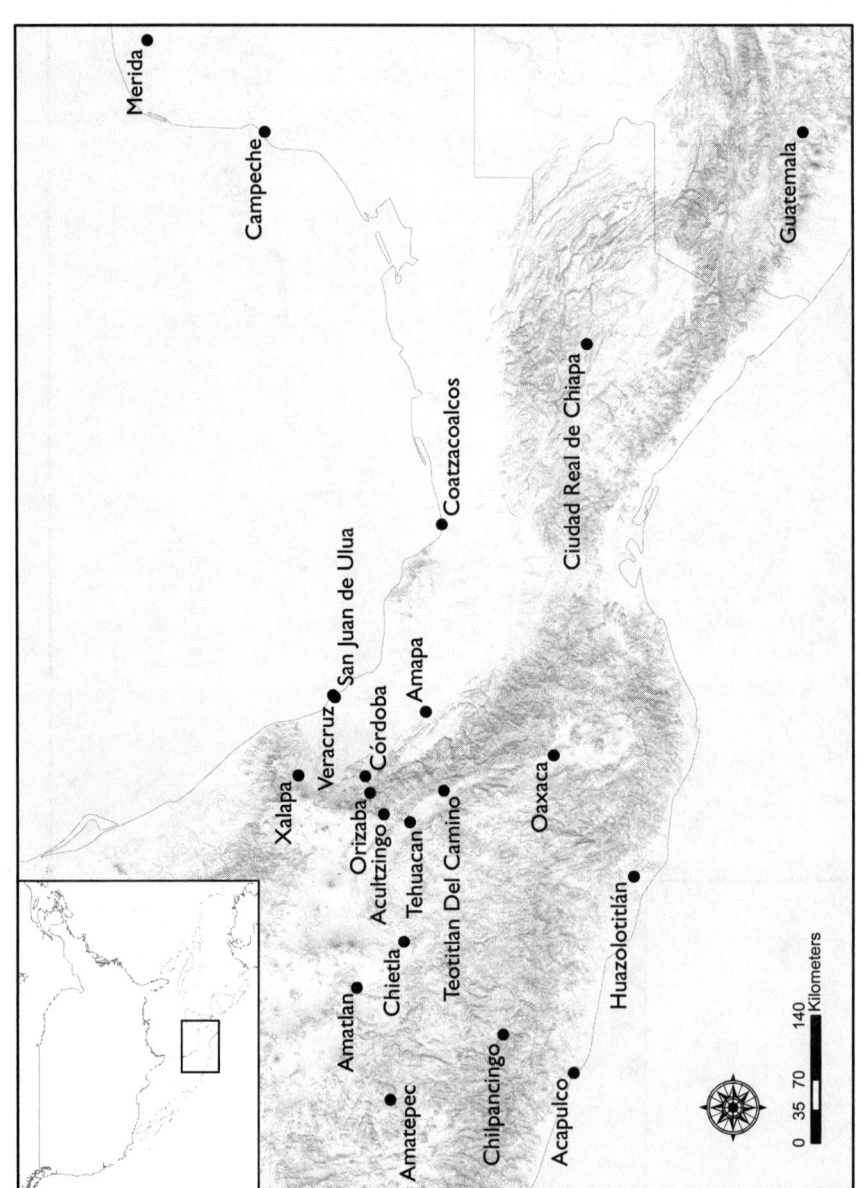

Map 3. Map of southern Mexico

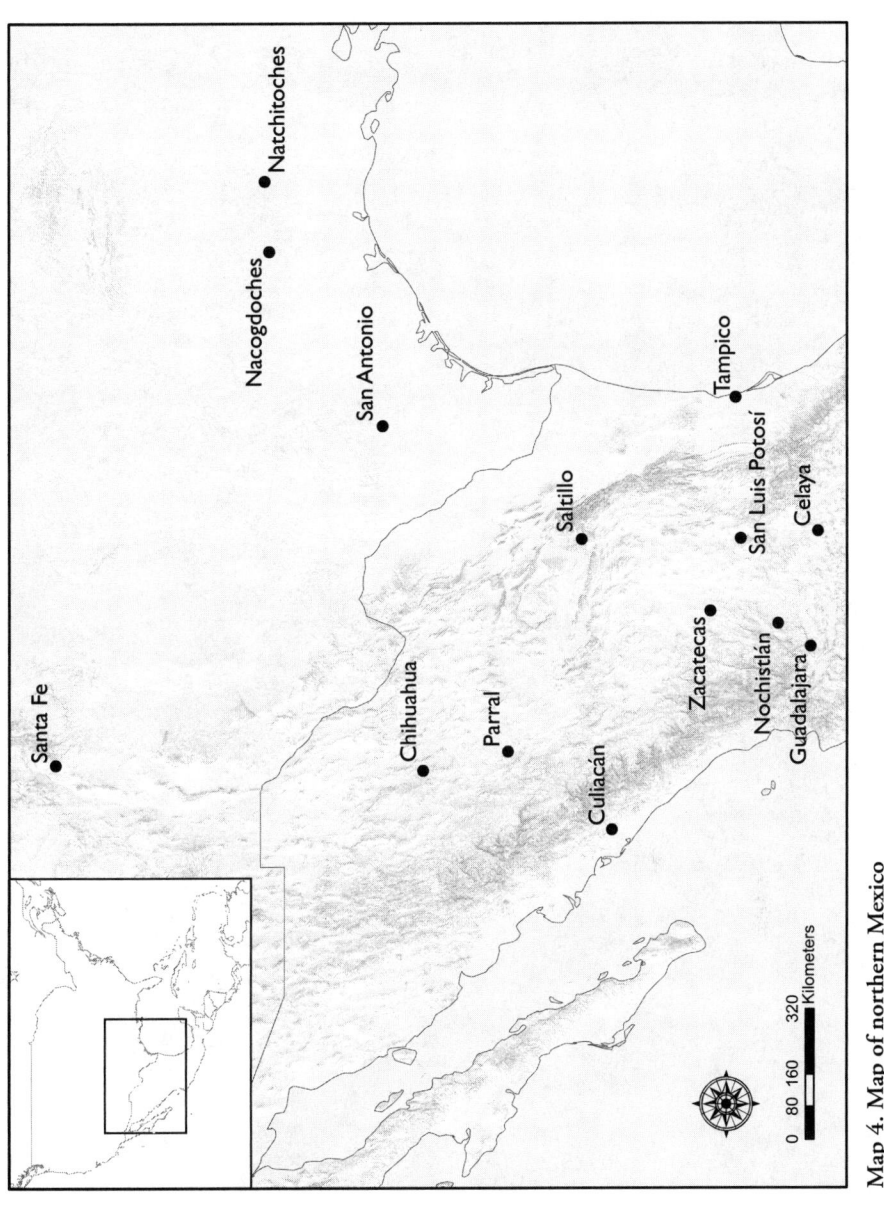

Map 4. Map of northern Mexico

Introduction:
A Brief History of Slavery and Freedom in Colonial Mexico

In the dawn of October 4, 1669, the enslaved Africans held at La Rinconada, Veracruz, rebelled against Don Agustín Lomelín, one of his servants, and two muleteers.[1] Breaking out of the long room where they had spent the night, the 300 captives took over the travelers' inn and sought out the man in charge of selling their bodies. They quickly found and killed him. Thus, on that Thursday morning, the factor for the slave trade to New Spain was dead; Crax Bomba, the leader of the rebellion, and his followers were no longer captives. In a deeply symbolic act, the rebels then destroyed Lomelín's litter and tore apart a train of mules that was transporting sugar to the port.[2] Under Bomba's authority, the Africans organized themselves into companies and appointed captains. In some accounts, there were three captains, while other accounts describe five, "one for each caste," an indication that the men, women, and children who had been shipped to Mexico belonged to different ethnic groups and spoke several languages. Regardless, they hailed Crax Bomba as their king. In this regard, an eyewitness was explicit: the leader "was called The Crax, which this witness has learned in their language means King, and he knew that they called him this to obey him, as he saw that all the Blacks did so."[3] Other witnesses corroborated this information, and one added that the leader was also called "Vomba Grande."

This stunning episode may seem out of place in a book on Mexican history. Slave ships, rebellions, and African kings? In fact, Crax Bomba and the other men, women, and children who rebelled that dawn were the survivors of at least two slaving voyages. On September 7, 1669, the *San Vicente* slave ship made port in Veracruz with 501 enslaved Africans aboard.[4] They had survived the month-long Caribbean voyage from Dutch Curaçao, to say nothing of their first Atlantic crossing from Lower Guinea and West Central Africa. When the rebellion broke out at the travelers' inn, they had been en route to the highlands or, more precisely, to the slave markets of central and southern Mexico. Crucially, the little that we know of their lives before and after the rebellion comes from eyewitness testimony, much of it from people who themselves lived somewhere along the spectrum of enslavement and freedom. How

---

1. Archivo General de Indias (hereafter, AGI), México, 45, N.57.
2. AGI, México, 45, N.57, 7v–9v.
3. AGI, México, 45, N.57, 24r–27v.
4. AGI, Contaduria, 893, N.1, R. 3, 6r–7r.

did people (of African, Spanish, Asian, and Indigenous descent) born into freedom think of Crax Bomba and the rebellion? What of those whose parents and grandparents had survived slaving voyages decades before? And what of those still enslaved throughout New Spain in 1669? How would they have reacted to the news coming from La Rinconada? With these questions in mind, the following pages offer a brief glimpse into key moments and longer processes in the history of freedom and slavery in colonial Mexico.

* * *

From the early sixteenth century to the mid-nineteenth century, Mexico was part of a vast territory and political unit known as the *virreinato de Nueva España*, or viceroyalty of New Spain. For three centuries, New Spain served as an essential element of the global Spanish empire. The viceroyalty was formally established in 1535 and expanded (at least in theory) to include a landmass that stretched from Costa Rica in the south to Louisiana and California in the north. To the west, New Spain was bounded by the Pacific-facing regions of Michoacán and Jalisco, but administratively, its viceroys claimed authority all the way to the Philippine Islands. To the east, there was the Gulf Coast of modern-day Veracruz, but several captaincies (Santo Domingo, Guatemala, Yucatán, etc.) also reported to the authorities of New Spain. In other words, there is immense flexibility in how we may think about "colonial Mexico." For the very same reasons, defining clear boundaries is one of the greatest challenges in writing the history of slaving and liberating practices in Mexico. This essay provides an overview of how several generations of scholars have studied slavery and freedom in this immense territory.

Most of the studies cited in the following pages focus on events that took place within the limits of the modern-day Mexican nation, comprised of thirty-one states and Mexico City as a federal entity. Whenever possible I have included cases that speak to slaving connections within a larger New Spain, but the book's focus remains on the spaces that today make up Mexico. There is an explicit intent behind this framework. There are currently no source collections focused on Mexican slavery in English. While scholars of the United States have produced dozens of documentary histories and primary source collections on slavery, the same cannot be said for Mexico. There is much to cover for the latter, from records on Asian enslavement to the generational freedoms won by people of African descent. The experiences of enslaved Indigenous people were central to the expansion, early abolishment, and continuation of various forms of bondage in New Spain.

This essay begins with a chronological and regional timeline of slavery and freedom. It offers an overview of Indigenous slaving systems before moving to early Iberian slaving practices and the origins of transatlantic slaving in the sixteenth century. The focus then shifts to the seventeenth century, when the trade in African captives peaked in Mexico due to the slaving networks of the Iberian Union. The next section addresses the transpacific trade in Asian and East African captives, before advancing a brief analysis of slaving practices in northern New Spain up to the mid-eighteenth century. The essay then shifts to an examination of practices of resistance, negotiation, and interaction among enslaved and nominally free people, followed by a section on the religious and political contexts that people of African, Asian, and Native descent navigated as they secured piecemeal freedoms. The essay concludes with a short examination of the Mexican War of Independence and the belated abolition of slavery in 1829.

Native Slaving Systems

The history of freedom and slavery in Mexico extends back well before the arrival of the conquistadors, in the late 1510s and 1520s. The Native peoples who inhabited the territories that we now consider Mexico held various concepts of communal belonging and foreignness. In Mesoamerica, a vast geographic and cultural area stretching from central Mexico through Honduras and Nicaragua, slavery was commonly practiced by Indigenous societies. Put simply, slavery was part of the fabric of Mesoamerican society, commerce, and ritual.[5] The Nahua populations of central Mexico were primarily organized around the concept of the *altepetl*, the indigenous city-state. These highly stratified populations were organized through various social levels: high nobles, lower nobles, artisans, merchants, commoners, and enslaved people. The latter, however, did not constitute a distinct racialized group. In the Nahua region, Nahua people could be enslaved, just as Maya individuals could be subject to enslavement in the Maya region to the south.

Enslaved people were often displaced, transported great distances from their natal societies and then sold in designated slave markets throughout Mesoamerica. For example, enslaved people were commonly bought and sold in Itzocan (modern-day Izúcar de Matamoros) and Azcapotzalco.[6] The Nahuatl language featured various terms that referred to slaving within the Mesoamerican region. Slave traders were known as *tlacanamacac*, while the term *tlacotli* could designate either an enslaved person or a servant. Finally, the verb *tlacocuepa* could be used to refer to enslaving another person or to reducing oneself to slavery.[7] An enslaved Nahua could be sold in different city-states and cultural regions.

---

5. Felipe Castro Gutiérrez, *Nobles, esclavos, laboríos y macehuales. Los nuevos súbditos indianos del rey* (Ciudad de México: Universidad Nacional Autónoma de México), 2021.

6. Carlos Paredes Martínez, *El impacto de la conquista y colonización española en la antigua Coatlalpan (Izúcar, Puebla) en el primer siglo colonial* (México: CIESAS/Cuadernos de la Casa Chata, 1991), 14–15.

7. For this distinction, see the entries for *tlacocuepa nino* (enslaving oneself) and *tlacocuepa nite* (enslaving someone else) in the 1571 edition of Alonso de Molina's *Vocabulario en lengua castellana y mexicana*, p. 178.

Camilla Townsend notes that "overlapping systems of slavery, concubinage and marriage" in the Nahua region of central Mexico produced societies in which enslaved people "were mostly women."[8] Townsend urges us to consider the fate of women who encountered enslavement as both *malli*, captives of war, and *tlacotli*, enslaved domestics.[9] The case of Malintzin, who would become a crucial interpreter for the conquistador Hernando Cortés, is perhaps the most studied case of the displacement of an enslaved Nahua.[10] Her case is remarkable because of the events that followed the arrival of the Spanish conquistadors, but her condition as an enslaved and displaced Indigenous woman would have been quite common in the Mesoamerican region before 1519.

Slavery in pre-Hispanic Mexico was not understood to be hereditary. The Roman legal concept of *partus sequitur ventrem*, by which a child inherited the mother's legal status, did not necessarily apply within the Mesoamerican region. Thus, because slavery was not transmitted generationally, slavery in pre-Hispanic Mexico was perhaps best understood as a situational condition. Mesoamerican slavery was therefore not a racialized phenomenon. Impoverished parents might sell themselves (or their children) into slavery in times of famine, or a drunkard might be legally enslaved for constantly bringing dishonor to a community. Likewise, the military defeat of one *altepetl* by another might produce male and female war captives. Enslavement in this Indigenous context consisted of a vast spectrum of experiences. Some of these would have aligned with European notions of slavery, while others retained distinctly Mesoamerican characteristics.

Indigenous slavery also operated on a ritual level, especially in relation to complex military cultures. A warrior from an enemy *altepetl* might enter a state of enslavement if captured on the battlefield. These ritual slaves were, however, honored, fed, and prepared for ritual sacrifice. In this regard, the cultural debasement that we perhaps associate with slavery was relatively absent from these forms of Native enslavement. In Tenochtitlan, enslaved people underwent a complex series of preparations and bathing rituals at the hands of their captors. These rituals were especially pronounced prior to the Panquetzaliztli ceremonies and sacrifices that took place between late November and mid-December.[11] In truth, far more research is needed on fifteenth- and early sixteenth-century Native slaveholding systems.[12]

---

8. Camilla Townsend, "'What in the World Have You Done to Me, My Lover?' Sex, Servitude, and Politics among the Pre-Conquest Nahuas as Seen in the *Cantares Mexicanos*," *The Americas* 62, no. 3 (January 2006): 354, 358.
9. Townsend, "What in the World," 358.
10. Camilla Townsend, *Malintzin's Choices: An Indian Woman in the Conquest of Mexico* (Albuquerque: University of New Mexico Press, 2006), 15–25.
11. John Schwaller, *The Fifteenth Month: Aztec History in the Rituals of Panquetzaliztli* (Norman: University of Oklahoma Press, 2019), 62–64, 70–74.
12. Outside of the Mesoamerican region, Native slaving persisted wherever Spanish control was weak. This was especially evident in Comanche raids against Ndé populations during the late seventeenth and early eighteenth centuries. See Paul Barba, *Country of the Cursed and the Driven: Slavery in the Texas Borderlands* (Lincoln: University of Nebraska Press, 2021), 99–101.

The Spaniards adopted many of these Indigenous slaving practices during the early colonial period, while discontinuing others. Slave markets and specialized slave merchants, for instance, continued to operate in the colonial period. Demand for women as enslaved domestics also remained central to slaving interactions in the region, especially in urban areas. However, the ritual elements of Mesoamerican slavery were suppressed by the Spanish conquistadors and colonizers, who were not constrained by Indigenous cultural practices and calendars. As we will see, this detachment from Native culture and ritual enabled Iberians to enslave on a vast geographic scale that extended well beyond the borders of the Mesoamerican region.[13] The Iberian brand of slavery operated from a more commercial and racialized perspective, drawing from extensive supply-and-demand networks that spanned oceans.

Early Iberian Slaving

During the 1520s and 1530s, Iberian expeditions scoured the Mesoamerican region. Accompanied by tens of thousands of Native allies, the conquistadors sought to subjugate other Indigenous city-states, extract tribute and precious resources, and establish the political vassalage of the city-states to European monarchs. The Iberian invaders gradually created a slaving system that initially targeted Indigenous populations but remained flexible enough to absorb enslaved people from other groups as well. In addition to the Mesoamerican influence, the slaving system established in early colonial Mexico was informed by three Atlantic and Caribbean processes. The first was the development of a Portuguese-led transatlantic slave trade from North and West Africa to Europe in the 1440s. The second was the final phase of the conquest and enslavement of the Guanche people, Native inhabitants of the Canary Islands, during the second half of the fifteenth century. The third was the exploitation and enslavement of the Arawak populations of the Caribbean. This last development began with the first Columbian voyage in 1492 and reached catastrophic proportions by the early 1520s.

The desolation of the Caribbean region between 1492 and 1542 is key to understanding the early slaving raids against the Native populations of the Mexican mainland. Iberian conquistadors rapidly expanded the geography of slavery in the Western Hemisphere by establishing just-war rationales that enabled massive slave raids against Indigenous populations. One cannot underestimate the sheer devastation of this violence. The Native people of the Lucayo Islands (modern-day Bahamas) bore the brunt of these slaving campaigns to such a degree that by 1520 their lands were depopulated. With the rapid decline in Indigenous Caribbean populations, Spanish officials in Cuba, Puerto Rico, and Hispaniola sent slaving expeditions to capture coastal mainland populations. During the late 1510s, the governor of Cuba,

---

13. Many thanks to Andrés Reséndez for his careful observations on this point.

Diego Velázquez, sponsored slaving expeditions against the people of coastal Florida and the Guanajas Islands (off the Honduran coastline). The campaigns against the Guanajas produced greater knowledge of the Yucatán peninsula and its populations.[14]

It is imperative, then, that we center this slaving context when thinking of the 1519–1521 military expedition and the Native allies that toppled the Mexica confederation. Beyond Hernando Cortés's crucial alliance with the powerful forces of Tlaxcala, an Iberian slaving logic demanded ever-greater numbers of Native captives for work in Caribbean pearl fisheries, cattle ranches, domestic settings, and the first sugar plantations. As Erin Woodruff Stone demonstrates, the years 1520–1524 were defined by indiscriminate slaving campaigns in Venezuela and Colombia.[15] The Native populations of Mesoamerica were not exempt from this violence and displacement. The military forces led by Cristóbal de Olid and Hernando Cortés infamously captured and branded thousands of women and children from Quecholac and Tepeaca during the summer of 1520, while Native men of fighting age were systematically killed.[16] Cortés would repeat this process in Cuernavaca and Huaxtepec (in modern-day Morelos). The conquistadors used the branding iron for war—shaped as a letter *G*—extensively on the bodies of Indigenous captives; additional brands spelling out an owner's name or initials were not uncommon.

During the 1520s, conquistadors exported thousands of Native captives from what is now the Mexican mainland to a rapidly depopulating Caribbean. The Pánuco region and port of Santiesteban (near modern-day Tampico, Tamaulipas) emerged as a site of slave exportation along the Gulf coastline. Conquistador-slavers, such as the notorious Nuño de Guzmán, enabled a stunning traffic in Native captives from the Gulf Coast to Cuban slave markets. In 1528 and 1529 alone, "sixteen or seventeen ships (though a witness, Lope de Savayedra, puts the number as high as twenty-one) sailed from Santiesteban filled with indigenous slaves. Of these numerous vessels, at least two carried one thousand or more slaves, including those belonging to merchants Miguel de Ibarra and Juan de Urrutia."[17] As a result, Iberian slaving projects were deeply tied to Caribbean conditions in the first decade of interaction between European and Mesoamerican populations.

Often, enslaved Native people were even displaced across the Atlantic for a life of enslavement in Iberia. Caroline Pennock has studied the case of three Mesoamerican children, Álvaro, Magdalena, and Andrés, who were enslaved in the 1520s by

---

14. Erin Woodruff Stone, *Captives of Conquest: Slavery in the Early Modern Spanish Caribbean* (Philadelphia: University of Pennsylvania Press, 2021), 49, 74–84.
15. Stone, *Captives of Conquest*, 74.
16. Matthew Restall, *When Montezuma Met Cortés: The True Story of the Meeting that Changed History* (New York: Ecco, 2018), 296.
17. Stone, *Captives of Conquest*, 108.

"Gerónimo de Trias, a Catalan living in Mexico City, for close to a decade when he decided to take them to Castile."[18] Their freedom would only be secured by a court case in 1543. Undoubtedly, these Indigenous children would have encountered many other groups of enslaved people on the Iberian peninsula, some of whom were bound for Mexico.

While the conquistadors were the leading forces in this new modality of slavery, they also advanced the introduction of the transatlantic trade in African captives. Black slavery was not foreign to conquistadors like Hernando Cortés, Bernal Díaz del Castillo, or Alonso Valiente. They were familiar with slave markets in Spain and Portugal. They were even more familiar with the slave markets they themselves had helped establish in Hispaniola, Cuba, and Puerto Rico during the first two decades of the sixteenth century. As the local populations of the Caribbean islands declined due to disease, abuse, displacement, and outright violence, the conquistadors and subsequent colonizers gradually turned to the transatlantic slave trade. At the time of his death in 1547, Cortés, for instance, left behind a vast estate in Cuernavaca that included 287 enslaved people, 193 of them Indigenous and 94 Black. Matthew Restall notes that the estate's inventory included "iron equipment for the disciplining of slaves . . . braces, collars, chains, and 'a cage [*prisión*] for slaves, with four iron chains,'" a clear example of the material culture of Iberian slaving introduced to early colonial Mexico.[19]

The captives on Cortés's estate embodied the vast reach of Iberian slaving networks in the first half of the sixteenth century. Native slaves from Ecatepec, Tlaxcala, Oaxaca, and Tepexi labored alongside displaced Africans and Taínos.[20] All of these enslaved people encountered a society painfully transitioning to colonial rule, yet their paths to bondage were quite varied. Enslaved Mesoamericans on the estate had most likely been victims of the war of conquest, even if a minority had been enslaved prior to the Iberians' arrival. By contrast, those first Black men and women to arrive in Mexico had survived a number of maritime voyages from the West African coastline or the Cape Verde Islands to cities in Iberia. After spending considerable time in Spain or Portugal, they had been transshipped from Seville or Lisbon to Caribbean ports and only then to Mexico.

The experiences of these Africans and their descendants placed them in an ambiguous position. Some had acquired extensive knowledge of European practices, weaponry, religion, and the Castilian or Portuguese language prior to arrival in Mexico. During the first half of the sixteenth century, some of these Black men participated as

---

18. Caroline Dodds Pennock, *On Savage Shores: How Indigenous Americans Discovered Europe* (New York: Alfred A. Knopf, 2023), 135.
19. Restall, *When Montezuma*, 296.
20. Restall, *When Montezuma*, 297, 303. Restall notes that prominent colonizers of the Caribbean also participated in military campaigns in Mesoamerica. As conquistadors, Pánfilo de Narváez, Vasco Porcallo de Figueroa, and Juan Bono de Quexo likely shipped indigenous Cubans to Mexico during the 1520s.

armed auxiliaries in the military phase of the Spanish conquest. Their participation in these early expeditions has led to scholarly interest in these "Black conquistadors." Among this grouping, Juan Garrido and Juan Valiente are the most studied individuals for the Mexican case.[21] Esteban of Azemour (Morocco), alias Estevanico, has also emerged as a fascinating figure of the early military conquest. But the disastrous failures of the 1527 Narvaéz expedition from Western Florida to New Mexico have tempered Esteban's association with the "conquistador" label.[22] Instead, he has been interpreted as a cultural mediator and polyglot in the service of Spanish men, up until his death or disappearance in a Zuni village circa 1539. In any case, the fluidity of the early military context allowed several of these men of African descent to establish themselves as members of colonial society by requesting privileges from the Crown, acquiring land, and (in the case of those who started out enslaved) negotiating for their freedom papers.

Women of African descent, however, did not participate in these military endeavors, so they do not fit neatly within the *conquistador negro* category. The archival record is largely silent on the experiences of free or enslaved Black women during the late 1510s and early 1520s. Still, archaeological research on a sacrificial site in Tecoaque (in modern-day Tlaxcala) has definitively established that women of African descent were present in Central Mexico during the summer of 1520.[23] Several of them were ritually sacrificed by Mexica priests after a raid, when they were taken along with other Spaniards and allied Native nobles. As a result, Black women also witnessed and experienced the terrible violence of the wars of 1519–1521, ferocious Indigenous resistance, and the gradual imposition of Iberian slaving practices in Mesoamerica.

Origins of Transatlantic Slaving in Mexico

During the first two decades of colonial rule in central Mexico, Mesoamericans and Africans labored simultaneously as enslaved people in both elite residences and mines. This development took place rapidly, just a few years after the fall of

---

21. Peter Gerhard, "A Black Conquistador in Mexico," *Hispanic American Historical Review* 58, no. 3 (August 1978): 454–457; Ricardo E. Alegría, *Juan Garrido: el conquistador negro en las Antillas, Florida, México, y California, c. 1503–1540* (San Juan: Centro de Estudios Avanzados de Puerto Rico y el Caribe, 1990); Matthew Restall, "Black Conquistadors: Armed Africans in Early Spanish America," *The Americas* 57, no. 2 (October 2000): 177–181. For an analysis of how Native people depicted these military auxiliaries, see Elena Fitzpatrick Sifford, "Mexican Manuscripts and First Images of Africans in the Americas," *Ethnohistory* 66, no. 2 (April 2019): 223–248.

22. Andrés Reséndez, *A Land So Strange: The Epic Voyage of Cabeza de Vaca* (New York: Basic Books, 2007), 54–56, 147–156.

23. Enrique Martínez Vargas and Ana María Jarquín Pacheco, "Sacrificios de negros al inicio de la conquista de México," in *¿Donde están? Investigaciones sobre Afromexicanos*, ed. Emiliano Gallaga Murrieta (México: Universidad de Ciencias y Artes de Chiapas, 2009), 111–113.

Tenochtitlan. As early as 1526, "a man named Jorge Díaz was given permission to import fifty Black captives (*negros esclavos*) for his 'personal service' (*para servicio personal*)."[24] These Black captives were evidently being used for more than domestic service. Viceroy Antonio de Mendoza stipulated that "the presence of 'slaves' was essential to maintaining possession of a mine" in the late 1530s. It is telling that the Crown's most powerful representative was encouraging widespread slave-ownership only three years before the abolishment of Native slavery in 1542. But despite Mendoza's endorsement, ideas about just who could be enslaved were changing. In her study of miners and prospectors in Taxco (1539) and Pachuca (1550), Dana Velasco Murillo reveals a gradual shift from Afro-Indigenous slave labor to that of nominally free, wage-earning Natives and enslaved Africans.[25] Spaniards increasingly equated enslavement with Black populations and intensified their investments in the transatlantic slave trade to Spanish America and Mexico.

The abolition of Indigenous slavery was a paradoxical process. By the early 1540s, the religious argument that Native populations were newcomers to Christianity and should therefore not be subject to enslavement had gradually gained hold. (The same religious rationale was not extended to the liberation of enslaved Africans.) Those who favored the abolition of Native slavery found further justification for their demands after the devastating smallpox, measles, influenza, and typhus epidemics that struck Native populations in 1520–1521, 1538, and 1545–1548. Massive depopulation continued with further outbreaks between 1576 and 1680. Where there had been fifteen to thirty million Indigenous residents of Central Mexico before Iberian contact, only two million remained by 1600.[26] The early phases of the demographic catastrophe, along with the considerable abuses by the Spanish colonizers, animated the work of Fray Bartolomé de las Casas on behalf of the Native population.[27]

With the passage of the New Laws of 1542, the enslavement of Native peoples was banned, in theory. Nancy van Deusen cautions us to consider how slow this process must have been. "Rather than a clean break with the past, the new law reflected a gradual transformation in legal reasoning that sought to move away from indigenous

---

24. Joseph M. H. Clark, *Veracruz and the Caribbean in the Seventeenth Century* (Cambridge: Cambridge University Press, 2023), 139.
25. Dana Velasco Murillo, "'To Search and Claim': Indigenous Prospectors, Silver Mining, and Legal Practices in Spanish America, 1530–1600," *Colonial Latin American Review* 30, no. 4 (2021): 510–513.
26. For a careful examination of cultural responses to these waves of epidemic disease, see Rebecca Dufendach, "Nahua and Spanish Concepts of Health and Disease in Colonial Mexico, 1519–1615" (PhD diss., UCLA, 2013), 5–8, 225, 257–259.
27. Las Casas was deeply troubled by the enslavement of Indigenous populations and by the practices of Spaniards who received *encomiendas*, grants of Native tribute and labor. For his denouncement of *encomenderos* in the Caribbean and Mexico, see Lawrence A. Clayton, *Bartolomé de las Casas: A Biography* (Cambridge: Cambridge University Press, 2012), 430–436.

slavery and servitude, but not to eradicate it," she explains.[28] In 1549, for instance, King Charles V referred to Native people as *naborías*, free but permanent servants in need of Spanish guidance.[29] Native servitude in colonial Mexico continued (in some cases, for centuries) under a variety of labels: *naborías, indios de servicio, indios de repartimiento, criados*, and *criadas*. Scholars of the north and northwest of New Spain (modern-day California, Arizona, New Mexico, and Texas) note that *criada* and *criado* were little more than euphemisms for enslaved Native children.[30]

Enforcing the abolition of Native slavery in Mexico was all the more difficult because Spaniards had enslaved thousands of Indigenous people in the aftermath of the Mixtón War (1540–1542). Nonetheless, an ideological transformation gradually took place in central Mexico. While Indigenous people were exploited through grants of labor and tribute (*encomienda*) or rotating allotments of Native workers (*repartimiento*), the ownership of their bodies was increasingly contested by political and religious authorities. Even Native captives taken under the pretext of just war (and labeled as *Chichimecas*) were not formally sold as enslaved people. Instead, they were "held in deposit" and "their service" sold or transferred to the colonizers for a determined number of years.[31] Indiscriminate slaving raids on Native communities continued in the northern regions of New Spain for centuries, but the Indigenous communities of central Mexico were gradually identified as protected, tribute-paying, and nominally free vassals of the Spanish Crown.

The opposite was true for people of African and, later, Asian descent who were explicitly purchased as human property. In the mid-sixteenth century, Spanish colonizers drafting early municipal codes increasingly defined Black individuals as the property of a given colonizer or family. Within thirty years of the conquistadors' arrival on the Mexican mainland, large enslaved Black populations were found in Veracruz, Antequera (Oaxaca City), Puebla de los Ángeles, and Mexico City. By the 1550s, the largest cities would produce registries, known as *cajas de negros*, to keep track of Black captives and their children (and to tax their owners) at the municipal level. During these years, the transatlantic slave trade to Mexico was inconsistent and irregular, but significant. Many of these enslaved Africans and their children had been transported to Mexico from Spain or Portugal, where they had been purchased. This was also the case when Crown officials requested permission to bring enslaved

---

28. Nancy E. van Deusen, *Global Indios: The Indigenous Struggle for Justice in Sixteenth-Century Spain* (Durham: Duke University Press, 2015), 101.
29. Van Deusen, *Global Indios*, 120.
30. In the context of late colonial New Mexico, "One out of every five slaves was listed as *criado* or servant (from the Spanish verb *criar*, "to rear")." See Ramón A. Gutiérrez, "The Genízaro Origins of the Hermanos Penitentes," in *Nación Genízara: Ethnogenesis, Place, and Identity in New Mexico*, ed. Moises Gonzales and Enrique R. Lamadrid (Albuquerque: University of New Mexico Press, 2019), 90–91.
31. Andrés Reséndez, *The Other Slavery: The Uncovered Story of Indian Enslavement in America* (Boston: Houghton Mifflin Harcourt, 2016), 90.

servants with them to Mexico. A similar process took place when Iberians instructed their relatives to join them in a given town or city, but made sure to also request the purchase of enslaved Black men and women as well.[32]

In subsequent decades, enslaved African people and their descendants became commonplace throughout the viceroyalty of New Spain. Enslaved men participated extensively in transportation, cattle ranching, and silver refining, while women were generally tasked with cooking and cleaning in elite households and convents, breast-feeding free children, and selling food and beverages in marketplaces or as itinerant vendors. Slaveholders with textile mills and sugarcane plantation owners invested heavily in the purchase of Black men, women, and children. With the rapid expansion of Atlantic slaving networks, forced African labor had become a ubiquitous feature of the colonial Mexican landscape by the late sixteenth century. Lolita Gutiérrez Brockington has perhaps summarized it best:

> Thus, African slavery spread swiftly throughout the entire colony. In Mexico alone a black slave population of 20,000 (conservative estimate) in 1553 had nearly doubled to at least 36,500 by 1595. Slaves were found in all colonial urban centers. The Central Valley, with its still highly visible Indian population, yielded the most dense black population, slave and free. Slavery spread to the farthest northern mines. It extended from Gulf coast to Pacific coast. And it found its way down to the southernmost reaches of the colony, including the Marquesado livestock haciendas in Tehuantepec.[33]

It is important to stress that enslaved Africans did not simply produce wealth for their owners. The purchase of a Black person was an expensive, conscious decision that colonists undertook in their quest for status. This was especially true in the urban context, where groups of elite Spaniards competed with each other for political, economic, and social power. Outfitting enslaved people in expensive clothes, for example, served as a reflection of a slaveholding family's financial might. In this sense, "African slavery offered a method of producing *and* performing wealth and status in society."[34] The performative dimension of slaveholding would increase considerably in New Spain by the 1550s.

With the gradual transition from the military phase of the conquest in Central Mexico and the expansion of colonial cities in the second half of the sixteenth century, greater numbers of Spanish women traveled to and established themselves in the viceroyalty. They too participated in the consolidation of a slaveholding culture

---

32. Enrique Otte and Guadalupe Albi Romero, eds., *Cartas privadas de emigrantes a Indias* (México: Fondo de Cultura Económica, 1993), 147–149.
33. Lolita Gutiérrez Brockington, *The Leverage of Labor: Managing the Cortés Haciendas in Tehuantepec, 1588–1688* (Durham: Duke University Press, 1989), 93.
34. Sherwin K. Bryant, *Rivers of Gold, Lives of Bondage: Governing through Slavery in Colonial Quito* (Chapel Hill: University of North Carolina Press, 2014), 19.

that demanded domestic servants in perpetuity. As Spanish families established generational roots in Mexico, they invested in the construction of female convents for their daughters. These urban religious communities concentrated large numbers of enslaved servants.[35] In sum, these urban dynamics signal a crucial dimension of slavery in colonial Mexico. Cities had a disproportionate impact on the culture, practices, expectations, and limitations of slaveholding in the Mexican setting. Unlike the plantation dynamic that traditionally informs hemispheric understandings of slavery (in Cuba, Brazil, Saint-Domingue, the United States, etc.), slavery in late-sixteenth-century Mexico was largely negotiated in cities.

In addition to the urban dynamic, Mexican slavery is perhaps most distinct for the early intensity of the transatlantic trade. As discussed previously, the first colonial slaving voyages took place in the 1520s and were led by conquistador-slavers who trafficked Indigenous captives. These voyages took eastward trajectories from the ports of Santiesteban (Tampico) and San Juan de Ulúa (Veracruz) to Cuban slave markets. Some of these enslaved Native people remained in the Caribbean or were forced to accompany their owners to Spain.[36] By the mid-1540s, however, the transatlantic trade in African captives was fully operational. Slave ship captains departed Seville for the Cape Verde islands and purchased Africans there with the intention of selling the survivors in Mexico or other Spanish-American slave markets. Although the documentary record is fragmented, the data available in *Slave Voyages: The Trans-Atlantic Slave Trade Database* indicates that at least twenty-seven slaving voyages were completed between 1545 and 1550 with New Spain as the "principal place of slave landing."[37] Such a large number of voyages in a short time span strongly suggests that other slaving expeditions had also been completed in the prior decade. Over the following thirty years, however, it seems that the trade in African captives slowed somewhat, as only twenty-six transatlantic slaving voyages are documented as having arrived in Mexico between 1551 and 1580. Future research on this topic should have considerable impact on our understanding of Mexican history in the mid-sixteenth century.

Mexico, Africa, and the Iberian Union

The most intensive period of the trade in African captives to Mexico took place during the Iberian Union (1581–1640). That period was defined by a catastrophic

---

35. Pablo Miguel Sierra Silva, *Urban Slavery in Colonial Mexico: Puebla de los Ángeles, 1531–1706* (Cambridge: Cambridge University Press, 2018), 107–143.
36. For the experiences of enslaved Mesoamericans sent to Spain, see van Deusen, *Global Indios*, especially chapters 1 and 2.
37. The SlaveVoyages Operational Committee, Trans-Atlantic slave trade database, https://www.slavevoyages.org/voyages/JzF3mIqM (accessed April 8, 2022).

decline in Native populations due to several waves of epidemic disease, an increasing demand for permanent Black laborers, and Philip II's unification of Spain and Portugal under a single dynasty. The latter event enabled Portuguese slave traders and ship captains to access Spanish-American markets and silver in exchange for enslaved Africans. During these years, older slave trading networks in Cacheu (Senegambia) and Cape Verde became enmeshed with newer ones on the island of São Tomé and the port of São Paulo de Luanda (Angola).[38] During the sixteenth century, most captives taken to Mexico hailed from Upper Guinea, while enslaved groups from West Central Africa became more prevalent by the early seventeenth century. Throughout these changes in Atlantic slaving, Veracruz remained the most important Mexican point of entry for enslaved Africans. San Francisco de Campeche (on the Yucatán peninsula) also emerged as an important port for slaving voyages during the Iberian Union, although it received smaller vessels that sailed from Santo Domingo (modern-day Dominican Republic) and other Caribbean ports. Acapulco, on the Pacific coast, also received enslaved Asians and Africans, but the volume of its trade in human captives was limited by the infrequent voyages of the Manila Galleon. Thus, Veracruz continued to be the primary port for slave trafficking to Mexico.

Between 1607 and 1639, then, Veracruz and Luanda were deeply tied by Portuguese slaving networks and the violence they produced. These two ports were inextricably bound by the African communities who survived and adapted to both Portuguese and Imbangala raids. The Black communities of both ports spoke Kimbundu, Kikongo, and a Portuguese-African hybrid language (*lengua de Angola*). The acquisition of Spanish (*castellano*) was a gradual process, only necessary after disembarking in Veracruz. Moreover, both communities demonstrated an increasing familiarity with Catholicism and, especially, with the Jesuit order.

These cultural, religious, and linguistic ties were largely explained by the slaving economy of West Central Africa. During the first half of the seventeenth century, Portuguese military, commercial, and religious incursions severely destabilized the kingdoms of Kongo, Ndongo, Matamba, and the other inland African states. At times, the Portuguese and their Lusophone descendants were able to consistently secure captives by negotiating with regional African elites. When those slave-trading networks broke down, however, the Portuguese and their Imbangala allies pursued military campaigns that also resulted in the capture of hundreds of men, women, and children at a time.[39]

---

38. For Spanish slaving transactions in the Cape Verde islands, see Malyn Newitt, *The Portuguese in West Africa, 1415–1670: A Documentary History* (Cambridge: Cambridge University Press, 2010), documents 37 and 38.
39. Linda Heywood and John K. Thornton, *Central Africans, Atlantic Creoles, and the Foundation of the Americas, 1585–1660* (Cambridge: Cambridge University Press, 2007), 110–117; David Wheat, *Atlantic Africa and the Spanish Caribbean, 1570–1640* (Chapel Hill: University of North Carolina Press/Omohundro Institute, 2016), 23, 70–71, 78–80.

The arrival of captive children was one of the defining, if often overlooked, dimensions of the slave trade to Mexico. Enslaved children under the age of fourteen were labeled *muleques* in Veracruz. *Bambos* was the term applied to breastfeeding infants, who were sold with their enslaved mothers. Ship captains and slave traders in Veracruz often emphasized that they should have to pay lower entry taxes on their slave coffles, precisely because so many of them were minors. In 1622, for instance, children and infants accounted for 23 percent of the 349 captives aboard the *San Francisco* slave ship upon its arrival in Veracruz.[40] These kinds of age and tax distinctions produced all sorts of fraudulent entries, which will forever distort what we actually know about transatlantic slave trade to Mexico. Despite these fragmented records, however, we do know that Portuguese independence in 1640 and the Dutch capture of the Lusophones' African bases (Elmina and Luanda) put an end to the mass arrival of West Central Africans in the ports of New Spain.[41]

The most recent information indicates that a total of approximately 150,000 African captives disembarked in Veracruz and Campeche during the colonial period. This is a tentative figure and should be used cautiously because it often relies on estimated averages for a given slaving voyage.[42] (It also does not account for the entries of enslaved Africans by way of Acapulco.) Nonetheless, the Veracruz and Campeche disembarkment records are useful and based on generations of scholarly research. They have been compiled into (and are constantly updated in) the Trans-Atlantic Slave Trade Database and a newer Intra-American Slave Trade Database. The first set of records, which provides evidence of slaving voyages from African ports, suggests that an estimated 145,700 captives survived the Atlantic crossing to Mexico.[43] The second set of records provides information on slaving voyages in which Africans were transferred from one American or Caribbean port to another. Approximately 7,400 captives entered Mexican ports on these intra-American slaving voyages, although that number will undoubtedly increase as further research is conducted on the port of Campeche.[44]

---

40. Wheat, *Atlantic Africa*, 97.
41. For a detailed discussion of the impact of Lusophone slaving networks in Mexico, see Pablo Miguel Sierra Silva, "Portuguese Encomenderos de Negros and the Slave Trade Within Mexico, 1600–1675," *Journal of Global Slavery* 2 (2017): 229–234.
42. Joseph Clark advances a state-of-the-field overview of slaving voyages to Mexico and the *SlaveVoyages* databases in *Veracruz and the Caribbean*, especially chapter 2, 106–113.
43. Trans-Atlantic Slave Trade Database (https://www.slavevoyages.org/voyages/JzF3mIqM), accessed October 18, 2022. Search for "sum of disembarked slaves" with New Spain, Campeche, and Veracruz as "principal place of slave landing." Approximately 107,000 captives disembarked between 1591 and 1640.
44. Intra-American Slave Trade Database (https://www.slavevoyages.org/american/database), accessed October 18, 2022. Search for "sum of disembarked slaves" with New Spain, Campeche, and Veracruz as "principal place of slave landing." These intra-American records indicate that 3,571 enslaved Africans were trafficked during the period from 1721 to 1740. This remains a very poorly studied period.

The traffic of enslaved Africans to Mexico did not end in the mid-seventeenth century; it continued irregularly and in diminished form well into the eighteenth century. For instance, we know that during the 1650s and 1660s, English slave traders based in Barbados and Jamaica introduced African captives to Veracruz. These captives hailed from Lower Guinea, a region that now comprises the nations of Ghana, Togo, Benin, Nigeria, and Cameroon. A similar process took place in the 1680s, as Dutch slave traders sent intermittent shipments of African captives to Veracruz from the Caribbean island of Curaçao. Because the survivors of these slaving voyages had been held in Caribbean depots prior to their arrival in Mexico, they were often sent in mixed groups. Captives labeled as *Mina*, *Arara*, *Caravalí*, *Congo*, and *Angola* reflected more heterogeneous groupings than in the past. It is necessary to acknowledge the arrival of these later groups if we are to make sense of the full complexity and regional variations in slaveholding throughout New Spain. For instance, between 1690 and 1720, purchases and sales of African-born people surged in the sugar plantations of Córdoba (in the modern-day state of Veracruz).[45] The temptation is to dismiss this regional reality, because no other locale in colonial Mexico experienced a similar slaving boom for this period. But this would require ignoring the experiences of the Africans who toiled in Córdoba and whose descendants would later come to define the region culturally.[46]

The archival record suggests that at the end of the 1730s, Atlantic and Caribbean slaving voyages to Mexico practically ended. Undoubtedly, Mexican slaveholders still bought and sold people of African descent at local slave markets, but by 1750, there was no transatlantic slave trade to speak of. Slaving voyages from Caribbean ports would continue sporadically into the late colonial period, but they were few and far between. The contrast with other Atlantic societies—Brazil, Cuba, Haiti, and the United States—is extreme. In the antebellum United States bans on the transatlantic slave trade during the early and mid-nineteenth century had serious consequences for the hardening of racial relations and the eventual abolition of Black slavery.[47] This was not the case in Mexico, where a large-scale trade in African-born captives ended before any ban on slaving took effect and well before abolition in 1829.

---

45. Adriana Naveda Chávez-Hita, *Esclavos negros en las haciendas azucareras de Córdoba, Veracruz, 1690–1830* (Xalapa: Universidad Veracruzana/Centro de Investigaciones Históricas, 1987), 35–37.

46. Far more detailed research is needed for the 1700–1720 period in order to make sense of the experiences of enslaved Africans and their descendants in Córdoba. In theory, Portugal's Companhia de Cabo Verde e Cacheu, France's Compagnie de Guinée, and England's South Sea Company would have all participated in slaving operations to Córdoba.

47. In the Southern states of the nineteenth-century United States, "Slave codes became Black codes, and Black people who had gained a free status were increasingly forced to endure the same treatment that White society had formerly reserved for Blacks." Viola Franziska Müller, *Escape to the City: Fugitive Slaves in the Antebellum Urban South* (Chapel Hill: University of North Carolina Press, 2022), 67.

Asians, East Africans, and the Pacific Slave Trade to Mexico

The history of Mexican slavery is distinct in that captives also entered the mainland through Pacific slaving networks. Between 1571 and 1814, the port of Acapulco (Guerrero) was deeply entwined with the Philippines by way of the Manila Galleon. A lucrative trade in silks, spices, hardwoods, porcelain, and other high-end items flourished in exchange for Mexican silver. Unfortunately, slaving was also an important component of the Pacific trade. According to the research of Tatiana Seijas, approximately 8,000 enslaved people entered the port of Acapulco aboard the Galleon trade between 1565 and 1710.[48] Voyages on the Manila Galleon or *nao de China* could last anywhere from six to nine months. The sheer distances covered by free and enslaved people alike should give us pause. Diego Luis calculates that following the Galleon route across the Pacific from the port of Cavite (Philippines), down the coast of California, to a final destination in Acapulco entailed 15,496 kilometers (or 9,629 miles) of navigation.[49] To this stunning estimate, we would also have to add the displacement of enslaved people to the Philippines in the first place.

It is extremely difficult to establish just who these Pacific-traversing captives were, however. The slave markets of Manila drew from Indian Ocean and East Asian commercial networks, meaning that enslaved and quasi-free people from Mozambique, Goa, the Deccan, Macau, China, and Japan endured these voyages eastward across the Pacific. Some of these enslaved people were permanent members of the Galleon crew. In other words, they served as sailors and *grumetes* and were expected to return to the Philippines aboard the Galleon vessels.[50] Those who were formally enslaved (and considered disposable) typically entered Mexico in small groups, as part of the retinue of a merchant or Crown official. At their disembarkment in Acapulco, the enslaved were labeled either *chinos*, an umbrella term that generalized all those of Asian descent, or *negros*, a general category reserved for people of African descent but used to signal East African origins in this context.

The Pacific slave trade was defined by a constant, if numerically small, flow of captives and an extreme gender imbalance. Based on the analysis of bills of slave purchase for Asians in Mexico, scholars estimate a 3:1 or 4:1 male-to-female ratio.[51] This relative absence of enslaved Asian women would limit the reproduction of Asian

---

48. Tatiana Seijas, *Asian Slaves in Colonial Mexico: From Chinos to Indians* (Cambridge: Cambridge University Press, 2014), 83–84.
49. Diego Javier Luis, *The First Asians in the Americas: A Transpacific History* (Cambridge: Harvard University Press, forthcoming 2024).
50. Grumetes were apprentice mariners or attendants. They were often skilled translators and cultural intermediaries.
51. Sierra Silva, *Urban Slavery*, 134; Déborah Oropeza, *La migración asiática en el virreinato de la Nueva España: Un proceso de globalización (1565–1700)* (Ciudad de México: El Colegio de México, 2020), 143–144.

communities in central Mexico, although future studies may show that they were more numerous in communities along the Pacific coast. Regionally based research on Colima, Zacatula, and Coyuca will likely reveal new dimensions to the experiences of free and enslaved people of Asian descent during the colonial period.[52] In central Mexico, enslaved Asians typically worked as skilled laborers in textile workshops, hatmaking shops, or barbershops. Evidently, many others were expected to perform domestic labor for elite families.

The most notable disruption to the Manila–Acapulco slave trade took place in the years after 1672, when Mariana, the Queen regent of Spain, decreed the abolition of *chino* slavery. With this, the Spanish Crown reaffirmed the eradication of Indigenous slavery in northern New Spain under the argument that "chinos were Indians, and Indians were free vassals of the Spanish crown."[53] The abolition decree meant that during the last quarter of the seventeenth century, slave owners entering Acapulco were careful to establish that their captives were of African descent. To do so, they employed categories such as "cafre," "negro de pasa," or "Mozambique."[54] Nonetheless, it is safe to assume that enslaved people of both African and Asian ancestry were taken involuntarily to Mexico through the Pacific throughout the colonial period, albeit in diminishing numbers.

Slaving Practices in Northern New Spain

The Queen's 1672 abolition decree was an aspirational statement. It eventually did reduce the number of Asian captives trafficked through the Pacific, but it was ineffective in stemming the enslavement of Native people in what is today northern Mexico and the southwestern United States. Establishing the various modes of unfreedom that these Native populations experienced is an ongoing challenge. Nonetheless, it is worth emphasizing that Native populations were continually enslaved whenever they resisted Spanish rule. Between 1590 and 1679, Spanish soldiers, captains, and governors openly engaged in slaving raids in order to expand the silver economy. The discovery of the silver mines of Parral (in the modern-day state of Chihuahua) in 1631 produced a massive slaving zone that drew African captives from central Mexico and Native captives from the northern fringes of the viceroyalty. To these enslaved populations, we would have to add the nominally free Native workers who were sent as *encomienda* or *repartimiento* laborers. Regardless, the degree of exploitation was

---

52. Seijas, *Asian Slaves*, 96. In particular, see figure 3.3, "Where Chino Slaves Lived."
53. Seijas, *Asian Slaves*, 214.
54. Norah Gharala, "'From Mozambique in Indies of Portugal': Locating East Africans in New Spain," *Journal of Global Slavery* 7, no. 3 (October 2022): 253–254.

such that the "colonial archives of Parral include no less than 225 files on 'seditions,' 'uprisings,' and full-scale 'rebellions' from 1633 to 1789."[55]

Indeed, slaving raids on Native communities in Sinaloa, Chihuahua, and New Mexico were so integral to the colonial economy of northern New Spain that they required complicity from Spanish governors. According to Andrés Reséndez, "Slavers engaged in this trade were so active and brazen that in the 1650s and 1660s, they had actually used the royal carriages, meant to keep New Mexico supplied with manufactured goods and foodstuffs—to transport their captives, in complete and even mocking disregard of the royal regulations."[56] To evade possible sanctions for enslaving Native people, Spaniards on the northern frontier trafficked Pueblo, Apache, and Tobosos captives as prisoners of war or labeled enslaved youth as *criadas* or *criados*. By the late 1670s, the trafficking of New Mexican Indians was so firmly established that enslavers traded Native youth (tax free) in exchange for horses or cows.[57] This pervasive slaving context partially explains why the 1680 Pueblo Revolt was so successful in expelling the Spanish colonial forces from New Mexico for twelve years.

Unfortunately, slaving raids against Native communities on the northern edge of New Spain continued well into the eighteenth century. Paul Barba has demonstrated how a 1707 punitive expedition against the Pelones people "marked the arrival of the Spanish slaving frontier in the Texas borderlands."[58] In Texas, the Spanish encountered another powerful entity that challenged European rule and also conducted its own slave raids: the Ndé or Apache nations. As expert horsemen, Ndé warriors skirmished against other Native nations and against the Spanish forces in central Texas during the mid-eighteenth century. The violence and displacement produced by Ndé raids ultimately led to the enslavement of 500 to 600 Native people between 1720 and 1760. In San Antonio, only established in 1718, at least 175 Native captives were held in a modest community of 560 Spaniards by 1749.[59] All of this is to say that New Spain's northern slaving frontier was in constant flux during the eighteenth century, although it was definitely limited and challenged by the power of the highly mobile Native nations.

Resistance, Negotiation, and Interaction

Whether scholars ever effectively establish the total number of African, Native, and Asian people enslaved in Mexico is, ultimately, not the end goal of these studies. The greater objective is to understand how enslaved people dealt with their bondage. How did they contest enslavers' claims over their cultures, bodies, and families? After

---

55. Reséndez, *The Other Slavery*, 114.
56. Reséndez, *The Other Slavery*, 140.
57. Reséndez, *The Other Slavery*, 123.
58. Barba, *Country of the Cursed*, 23–24.
59. Barba, *Country of the Cursed*, 79–80.

all, the people who experienced enslavement in colonial Mexico constantly devised numerous strategies and practices to resist, negotiate, and transcend their captivity.

The extensive resistance of Indigenous and African groups to Iberian forms of slavery is perhaps expected in the context of the early military phase of the conquest. One of the earliest examples of explicit African resistance to enslavement is found in a 1537 plot in which Black captives in Mexico City coordinated an insurrection with other enslaved Africans in the mines of Amatepec (near the border of modern-day Guerrero and Mexico State). Viceroy Antonio de Mendoza was sufficiently troubled by this plot that he requested a suspension in the trade in African captives for some time. Mendoza, however, did not suspend Native slaving during those same years. The enslaved "indios Jaliscos" who were sold in the cities of central Mexico during the 1540s were themselves captives from the Mixtón War (1540–1542), a rebellion against Spanish rule. These early challenges to colonial rule occurred in quick succession. As a result, the repressive measures that followed often led to overlapping waves of slaving activity.

Viceroy Mendoza's fears of a Black uprising in 1537 evidently did not prevent the expansion of the transatlantic slave trade. But as greater numbers of African captives were forced into Mexican lands, many escaped and formed maroon communities known as *palenques*. Scholars have classified these collective acts of resistance as examples of *grand marronage*, collective attempts to establish permanent and autonomous Black communities. The most celebrated of these *palenques* in Mexico was undoubtedly the community formed by Gaspar Yanga, of the Bran nation, and his followers in the 1570s. Yanga's *palenque*—strategically perched in the Sierra Madre Oriental—survived numerous punitive expeditions during the late sixteenth and early seventeenth centuries. These attempts to dislodge the maroon community largely failed. In time, the colonial authorities decided it was preferable to negotiate with the maroon leadership and to recognize the *palenque* as San Lorenzo de Cerralvo or San Lorenzo de los Negros, a free Black town. It is today known as Yanga, Veracruz, in honor of its legendary founder.

It is important to emphasize that while the highlands of Veracruz concentrated many *palenques*, dozens of other maroon communities also formed in diverse locations throughout the Mexican mainland: around the silver mines of Pachuca (Hidalgo), along the fishing villages of Mazatlán (Sinaloa), and beyond the sugarcane fields of Chietla (Puebla). The transformation of a maroon community into a formal settlement in 1769 speaks to a continuous process of resistance to slaveholders' power throughout the colonial period: as demonstrated by Adela Amaral's research, several of the founders of Nuestra Señora de Guadalupe de los Morenos de Amapa (in northern Oaxaca) were maroons who had earlier participated in a 1735 rebellion in the Córdoba region.[60]

---

60. Adela Amaral, "Social Geographies, the Practice of Marronage and the Archaeology of Absence in Colonial Mexico," *Archaeological Dialogues* 24, no. 2 (2017): 208.

Most acts of slave resistance in colonial Mexico were temporary events that took place on an individual or familial level and would never be recorded in an archive. These undocumented acts of *petit marronage* destabilized the structure of slavery, even if they did not immediately produce permanent runaway communities. In this light, it may be worth challenging the distinction between *petit marronage*, as a temporary, short-distance, everyday act of disobedience, and *grand marronage*, as a politically charged threat to colonial rule. After all, enslaved people who joined *palenques* often did so individually or in small groups. They often entered a barter economy with surrounding rural communities and retained contact with relatives and fictive kin from the towns, cities, and villages they had fled. Moreover, individuals performing small acts of resistance could gradually lead to substantial consequences at a local or regional level. All of this is to say that we would do well to be flexible in how we think of resistance to slavery.

Enslaved people in flight forced slaveholders to reconsider their own claims to the minds and bodies of their human property. Put differently, people subjected to the condition of slavery constantly defied their bondage by escaping to different neighborhoods, towns, or plantations. They often sought to subvert their particular circumstances by seeking assistance from free and enslaved individuals, Catholic brotherhoods, religious authorities, politicians, or even other enslavers who seemed to be able to offer better living conditions. The 1645 case of Francisco de la Cruz, an Asian slave of the Bengala caste, is emblematic of the agency that some captives were able to deploy. After escaping his bondage and relocating to a small village in Tlaxcala, Francisco de la Cruz created a new identity for himself as "Diego." His frustrated owner eventually awarded "Diego" freedom papers in exchange for some money offered by a third party. Twenty years later, Nicolasa, a wet nurse of African descent and mother to a one-year-old infant, also fled her enslaver. Because so many enslaved women were forced into the roles of wet nurse, cook, and caretaker, Nicolasa's case speaks to the Mexican elites' profound dependence on gendered labor.[61] Whether free or enslaved, wet nurses (*chichiguas* or *nodrizas*) were influential because children suffered high mortality rates in colonial Mexico. The intimacy of their labor was further amplified because affluent Spanish women were often unable or unwilling to breastfeed their infants.[62]

---

61. María Elena Martínez, *Genealogical Fictions: Limpieza de Sangre, Religion and Gender in Colonial Mexico* (Stanford: Stanford University Press, 2008), 138; Alison Krögel, "Mercenary Milk, Pernicious Nursemaids, Heedless Mothers: Anti-Wet Nurse Rhetoric in the Satirical Ordenanzas del baratillo de Mexico (1734)," *Dieciocho: Hispanic Enlightenment* 37, no. 2 (2014): 242–243.
62. For a deeply satirical take on the moral and cultural perils of hiring wet nurses and other eighteenth-century Mexican behaviors, see Guillermo Espinosa Estrada and Éric Ibarra Monterroso's annotated edition of Joseph Carlos de Colmenares, *Ordenanzas del Baratillo de México* (Monterrey: Universidad Autónoma de Nuevo León, 2022).

While Spaniards and their descendants claimed political and economic power early in the colonial period, they were demographically at parity with African-descended populations and always outnumbered by Native communities. This means that Afro–Indigenous interactions were not rare, exotic encounters. On the contrary, they were common, mundane affairs among people typically relegated to manual labor (in textile mills, sugar plantations, or elite residences) and the lowest rungs of the colonial caste system. Of course, extreme regional variation made for very different interactions. The heavily agricultural lifestyle of a Black-Mayan family in Yucatán, for instance, would differ considerably from the lifestyle of an Afro-Indigenous household specializing in mule transportation in Michoacán. Regrettably, an older scholarship analyzed Afro–Indigenous exchanges mostly through the lens of friction and hostility. Patrick Carroll, however, argues that "in the colonial Mexican setting, blacks and natives engaged in more harmonious than antagonistic association with one another."[63] Shifting away from a conflict-centered perspective, then, requires paying much greater attention to records that shed light on everyday interactions (a community's marriage book, the selection of godparents, slight changes in rural census data, confraternity membership lists, etc.). Archaeological insights on mundane, domestic objects also provide much-needed counterpoints to texts focused on violence.[64] A shared experience of legal and economic oppression, but also of residential proximity, certainly brought both Native and African-descended groups into close and constant interaction.

In the 1580s, for instance, New Spain's viceroy issued a decree targeting women of African descent who wore Indigenous garb, a clear indication that women of various racial backgrounds encountered similar material conditions. However, the very same decree had to make exceptions for "the *mestiza* women, mulatta women, or Black women who are married to Indian men."[65] Other significant examples of Afro–Indigenous interaction are found in the numerous references to men of African descent who were fluent in the Nahuatl language and held official positions in rural communities as interpreters for Spanish authorities.[66] In a comparative study of Asian and African experiences of enslavement, Diego Luis has further developed this concept of intense cultural proximity to suggest that "at the level of lived experience,

---

63. Patrick Carroll, "Black-Native Relations and the Historical Record in Colonial Mexico," in *Beyond Black and Red: African-Native Relations in Colonial Latin America*, ed. Matthew Restall (Albuquerque: University of New Mexico Press, 2005), 249.
64. For a compelling case on the material culture of chocolate and its diffusion and adaptation by different groups, see Margaret A. Graham and Russell K. Skowronek, "Chocolate on the Borderlands of New Spain," *International Journal of Historical Archaeology* 20 (2016).
65. See Chapter 5, Document 53 in this volume.
66. For examples of these Afro-Indigenous dynamics in the southern Veracruz region, see Alvaro Alcántara López, *Gobernar en familia: disidencia, poder familiar y vida social en la provincia de Acayucan, 1750–1802* (Ciudad de México: Bonilla Artigas Editores, 2019), 77–78, 86.

the dominant trend during the seventeenth century was convergence."[67] In other words, people of Asian, African, and Native descent frequently resorted to similar strategies of resistance because they were observing, experiencing, and adapting to similar material and spiritual challenges.

What these studies demonstrate is that colonial Mexican families of mixed descent were often the product of Native-Black, Spanish-Native, Black-Asian, Native-Asian, Spanish-Black, and innumerable other variations of unions, who gave profound complexity to superficial labels like *mulato, mestiza, chino,* or *morisca.* These ethno-racial labels theoretically gave significance to the colonial caste system, or *sistema de castas,* which was intended to privilege Spaniards and their ancestry, culture, language, phenotype, and religion above all others. In theory, the caste system operated from the late sixteenth to the early eighteenth century, with mixed-race people occupying intermediate positions above the Black and Native populations. Yet as Douglas Cope has demonstrated for Mexico City, "Elite attempts at racial or ethnic categorizations met with resistance as non-Spaniards pursued their own, often contradictory, ends: social mobility, group solidarity, self-definition."[68]

By the 1690s, if not before, key pillars of the caste system had eroded beyond repair. Slavery was on the decline, and people of African, Asian, and Native descent increasingly contested notions of Spanish honor. Moreover, there was too much competition among the Spaniards themselves, who relied extensively on African, Asian, and Native labor to achieve economic, social, and political control. In a society with a considerable proportion of interracial unions (formal ones, but especially informal ones), there was simply too much fluidity by the early 1700s to maintain a rigid caste system.[69] Prejudice along caste lines undoubtedly continued throughout the colonial period (and beyond), especially at the highest political, educational, and religious levels. However, policing the boundaries of who was and (was not) reputed to be a mixed-race person, became treacherous, especially among mixed-race families.

Navigating Religion and Politics

Enslaved and free people fluent in Mexican cultural practices were often able to navigate differing legal, social, and economic expectations by claiming religious privileges as practicing Catholics. In some slaveholding societies of the

---

67. Diego Javier Luis, "Diasporic Convergences: Tracing Knowledge Production and Transmission among Enslaved Chinos in New Spain," *Ethnohistory* 68, no. 2 (April 2021): 292.
68. Douglas R. Cope, *The Limits of Racial Domination: Plebeian Society in Colonial Mexico City, 1660–1720* (Madison: University of Wisconsin Press, 1994), 5.
69. Paradoxically, the infamous *casta* paintings of the eighteenth century were produced (and largely exported to Europe) when Mexico's caste system had already collapsed. See Ilona Katzew, *Casta Painting: Images of Race in Eighteenth-Century Mexico* (New Haven: Yale University Press, 2004), 155–160.

Americas, captive people were excluded from organized religion altogether. This was not the case in Mexico, however, because the expansion of Catholicism was a primary justification for the colonial project. As a result, enslaved people were expected to participate in everyday religious practice, whether or not they had the same opportunities or incentives as their free counterparts. Africans and Asians, despite their enslavement, could marry other survivors of the Atlantic and Pacific slave trade or, indeed, seek spouses of any background. Rarely did an Angolan man marry a Spanish woman, but there was no religious edict or royal decree to prevent such a union (until very late in the colonial period). Free people were allowed to marry the enslaved, and vice versa. In practical terms, this meant that individuals of similar socioeconomic status were mostly able to enter formal unions if they chose to do so. There were certainly contexts in which slaveholders might influence or even force a couple into marriage, but this was often restricted to overly coercive spaces, such as a textile mill (*obraje*). This is not to say that religion and violence did not overlap in colonial Mexican society. Innumerable cases of blasphemy can be found in the Inquisition archives, as overseers often brutalized the bodies of the enslaved. In those cases, captives publicly renounced God or the saints in order to bring an end to their physical punishment.

In truth, the Catholic church was expansive and pervasive in most aspects of everyday life in colonial Mexico. The enslaved learned to navigate the landscape of religion by interacting with other enslaved or freed people or through everyday interactions with their enslavers. Densely populated cities inevitably resulted in greater interaction with Church officials and other religiously affiliated actors. Nuns, friars, parish scribes, bishops, and inquisitors all had interactions with enslaved people. Only the most isolated individuals in remote rural outposts could evade interactions with official representatives of the Catholic church. Yet even freed and enslaved people in Chiapas or Chihuahua found themselves subject to the information networks that reached the Inquisition headquarters in Mexico City. Over time, the capital's inquisitors lost interest in prosecuting the blasphemy cases sent along by regional commissaries and informants, but accusations of bigamy were investigated throughout the entire colonial period.

Religion in Mexico was not, however, solely concerned with punishment and surveillance; many free and enslaved people found community in chapels, churches, and the religious brotherhoods that animated local religion. Known as *cofradías*, religious brotherhoods became an integral part of colonial Mexico's cultural landscape. These groups were often organized along caste lines within a neighborhood church, chapel, or hospital. The brotherhoods were especially active and visible during Easter, Christmas, the feast of Corpus Christi, and on specific saints' feast days. Black brotherhoods often celebrated Santa Efigenia and San Benito de Palermo, the Franciscan friar born to enslaved African parents in sixteenth-century Sicily. In fact, a Mexico City confraternity devoted to San Benito was established in 1599, only ten years after the friar's death.[70] San Benito's statues still adorn any number of colonial churches in twenty-first-century Mexico, an ongoing reflection of the devotion to the Black saint by colonial brotherhoods of African descent (*cofradías de pardos y morenos*). Colonial brotherhoods also operated as mutual aid societies, helping their members secure medical treatment, freedom papers, and last rites. In 1655, the members of an Asian religious brotherhood in Puebla could request proper burial spaces for members of their community because a Black brotherhood had successfully secured the same privileges years before.

Slavery peaked during the seventeenth century in Mexico and then followed a slow, constant decline throughout the eighteenth century. During those two centuries, important transformations took place among the enslaved and those who managed to secure their freedom. Fewer Africans entered the ports of Veracruz, Campeche, and Acapulco after 1640, and even smaller numbers were trafficked after 1700; consequently, the vast majority of the enslaved population was composed of Mexican-born Creoles. These were typically the children of women of African descent, whose enslavement justified the continued bondage of their progeny. Despite their profound understanding of Catholicism, Spanish law, and Indigenous practices, enslaved *criollas* and *criollos* were sold in tens of thousands of transactions throughout the viceroyalty.[71] In the city of Puebla, for instance, slave sales for *negros criollos, negras criollas, mulatas,* and *mulatos* surged in the 1680s.[72]

By the 1700s, important changes had taken place in the Mexican slaveholding context. For one, African ancestry was no longer synonymous with enslavement, and vice versa. While many Black men and women were still owned in perpetuity on plantations, convents, and textile mills, they were outnumbered by enslaved mulattos. Based on research in Mexico City's notarial archives, Dennis Nodín Valdés has demonstrated that people of partial African ancestry accounted for "about one third of the total slaves sold in the 1660s." That number had escalated "to almost 90 percent by the 1780s."[73] Of course, significant regional variations impede us from projecting these figures onto Oaxaca, Zacatecas, or other locations. Nonetheless, two

---

70. For the emergence of Mexican brotherhoods devoted to San Benito, see Rafael Castañeda García, "Santos negros, devotos de color. Las cofradías de San Benito de Palermo en Nueva España. Identidades étnicas y religiosas, siglos XVII–XVIII," in *Devoción, paisanaje e identidad. Las cofradías y congregaciones de naturales en España y en América (siglos XVI–XIX)*, ed. Óscar Álvarez Gila, Alberto Angulo Morales, and Jon Ander Ramos Martínez (Bilbao: Servicio Editorial de la Universidad de País Vasco, 2014), 147–153.

71. In 2022, a multi-institutional project was created to bring together notarial information on the transactions involving enslaved people throughout colonial Mexico. This massive digital project, "Rutas de esclavizamiento de la Nueva España," supported by the University of California system and the Archivo General de la Nación (México), will enable scholars, students, and the public to trace the lives of enslaved people across various archives.

72. Sierra Silva, *Urban Slavery*, 128, 140–143.

73. Dennis Nodín Valdés, "The Decline of Slavery in Mexico," *The Americas* 44, no. 2 (October 1987): 177.

clear trends emerge from the study of eighteenth-century Mexican slavery. First, most enslaved people were racially mixed and labeled as *mulatos* or *mulatas*. Second, slaveholders valued them much less than they had a century before. Mulattos were usually sold for 20 percent less than their Black counterparts. Moreover, according to Valdés, "by the 1750s, young Black adult slaves sold for an average of about 170 to 175 pesos, only half what they had cost sixty years earlier."[74] This indicates that slaveholders had gradually shifted toward free wage labor as Indigenous communities recovered demographically and the mixed-race population expanded. Norah Gharala offers a stunning assessment to make sense of this change: "For every enslaved person who lived in New Spain at the end of the eighteenth century, there were at least thirty free people of color."[75]

How did this come to be? In the absence of a mass insurrection or a general abolition decree, how had enslaved people secured such claims to freedom by 1800? There were simply not enough manumissions awarded to explain the stunning increase in the number of free people of African descent.[76] Moreover, even when enslavers granted such a document (*carta de libertad*), they often stipulated that they would only award freedom either at the time of their death, immediately if compensation was given, or "with the imposition of service beyond the lifetime of the owner."[77] Awarding freedom papers with no financial compensation was rare. Several documents in this documentary history, especially those in Chapter 9, speak to the fickle nature of these manumission documents. Thus, this still does not resolve the puzzle of the rapidly growing free population.

I have argued elsewhere that Afro-Mexicans slowly but steadily eroded the foundations of slavery through familial strategies of liberation during the seventeenth century. By this, I mean that enslaved people and their biological and fictive kin (godparents and confraternity brothers and sisters) made concerted efforts to secure piecemeal freedoms. This might mean, for example, that a community would gather funds to purchase freedom papers for an enslaved child, especially a girl, well before an enslaver could raise the price of this document.[78] On other occasions, enslaved

---

74. Valdés, "The Decline of Slavery," 173.
75. Norah Gharala, *Taxing Blackness: Free Afromexican Tribute in Bourbon New Spain* (Tuscaloosa: University of Alabama Press, 2019), 32; Herbert Klein and Ben Vinson III, *African Slavery in Latin America and the Caribbean* (Oxford: Oxford University Press, 2007), 196–197. Klein and Vinson estimate that in 1810 there were 300,000 free people of African descent in Mexico, while the enslaved population was 10,000.
76. In my sample of the Puebla notarial archives, there were 19.5 times as many enslaved people being sold as there were freed for the years 1600–1699. This calculation is based on the sample of 3,528 enslaved people and 181 freed people in Notarías 3 and 4 at the Archivo General de Notarías del Estado de Puebla (AGNEP).
77. Frank Proctor III, "Gender and the Manumission of Slaves in New Spain," *Hispanic American Historical Review* 86, no. 2 (2006): 327–328.
78. In Mexico City, this approach was quite common before 1650, when children represented over half of those freed by manumission. By the 1720s, however, children only accounted for one of every four manumitted people. See Proctor, "Gender," 330.

people fled their bondage and attempted to adopt new identities in other locations. Nevertheless, members of maroon communities were vastly outnumbered by the African-descended populations that lived in Mexican villages, towns, and cities. After all, there were other avenues for securing freedom. Enslaved men consistently sought out free women with the certainty that their children would be born free. In Puebla, for instance, "two of every three infants of African descent were born to free mothers" in the Sagrario parish during the late 1670s.[79] Over time, this meant that fewer and fewer children experienced enslavement in colonial Mexico, reducing the future transmission of slavery along maternal lines.

The cumulative effect of these efforts—in combination with a dwindling transatlantic slave trade, the modest acquisition of freedom papers for enslaved women and girls, and the rise of free wage labor—resulted in the steady growth of a free Afro-Mexican population from the late seventeenth century onward. Colonial authorities in Mexico did not necessarily see this as a negative development. A free population was also a tribute-paying population. This line of reasoning became especially evident once the Bourbon dynasty claimed the Spanish Crown in 1700. The Bourbon reformers introduced several initiatives to extract greater amounts of tribute from their free colonial subjects, especially during the second half of the eighteenth century.

As a result, families of African descent developed other strategies for removing themselves from associations with slavery and with discriminatory taxation. For instance, Afro-Mexican families were keen to note that their fathers and sons had served in the free-colored militias and were thus not obligated to pay tribute. Norah Gharala has demonstrated the steep fiscal burden that families of African descent confronted once they were no longer enslaved. In the late eighteenth century, "the Ordinance of Intendants established the rate of Indian tribute at sixteen reales and the tribute of free *negros* and *mulatos* at twenty-four reales."[80] As a result, a *mulata* wife might adopt the caste label of her *indio* husband in order to reduce their tribute payments.[81] The long-term implications of this racial discrimination through taxation produced a situation in which families of African descent tried to avoid being categorized as such for pragmatic financial reasons. This was especially true in Guadalajara, San Luis Potosí, and Mexico City, cities where Bourbon reformers expanded their rolls of African-descended tributaries in the 1760s and 1770s.[82]

---

79. Sierra Silva, *Urban Slavery*, 170. These birthright freedoms were quantitatively significant. Based on surviving baptismal records for 1677–1680 and 1685–1688, at least 1,338 free children of African descent were baptized in one parish—Puebla's Sagrario—during those years.
80. Gharala, *Taxing Blackness*, 119.
81. Gharala, *Taxing Blackness*, 74.
82. Gharala, *Taxing Blackness*, 105.

In the rural areas of the Pacific coast, Black communities had high levels of *pardo* and *moreno* military service, which exempted them, in theory, from paying tribute and sales tax (*alcabala*). However, during the second half of the eighteenth century, Bourbon reformers chipped away at these exemptions. Gharala notes, "That tribute was demanded of *mulatos* but not mestizos made blackness particularly damaging to reputation and social standing regardless of whether a *mulato* had less Spanish ancestry than a comparable mestizo."[83] This fraught relationship between taxation and African ancestry had considerable consequences in the years leading to the War of Mexican Independence. Somewhere between 187,000 and 370,000 free people of African descent lived in New Spain in 1793.[84] Moreover, as members of families with deep connections to the *pardo* and *moreno* militias, they were profoundly affected by the eleven-year insurrection that began in 1810.

In 1813, the insurgent leader and priest José María Morelos y Pavón presented twenty-three articles as "The Sentiments of the Nation" in Chilpancingo, Guerrero. The many emendations to the text indicate that there was much that Morelos and his closest associates needed to rethink and revise as the War of Independence raged along the southern Pacific regions of New Spain. Yet the fourteenth article was an elegant, simple affirmation: "That slavery be proscribed forever, as well as the distinction of castes, leaving all equal so that only vice and virtue will distinguish one American from another."[85] As a man of African descent, Morelos understood the profound implications of abolishing both slavery and the *casta* labels that reinforced racially based taxation and social, political, and economic exclusion. He did not survive to see his vision implemented in an independent Mexico. However, a larger ideological process was already firmly in motion. Jorge Delgadillo Núñez has demonstrated that in cities like Guadalajara, baptisms for Afro-Mexican children declined by 43 percent in 1810 and 1811, not because Black families suddenly disappeared but because they contested the discrimination imposed upon them when labeled as *pardos, morenas, mulatos,* or *negras*.[86] In rejecting these markers of African descent, these families established their belonging to a new nation by embracing the language of citizenship.

The abolition of slavery in September of 1829 arrived eight years after Mexicans achieved their independence from Spain. President Vicente Guerrero, another insurgent fighter of African descent, understood the symbolism of such a declaration in a country where few people remained enslaved. Still, there were compelling reasons to declare the immediate end of slavery on Mexican soil. Spain attempted an unsuccessful military invasion of Mexico in 1829. Yet the greater concern was that

---

83. Gharala, *Taxing Blackness*, 207.
84. Ben Vinson III, "The Racial Profile of a Mexican Rural Province in the 'Costa Chica': Igualapa in 1791," *The Americas* 57, no. 2 (October 2000).
85. See Chapter 9, Document 116 in this volume.
86. Jorge E. Delgadillo Núñez, "Becoming Citizens: Afro-Mexicans, Identity, and Historical Memory in Guadalajara, 17th to 19th Centuries" (PhD diss., Vanderbilt University, 2021), 228–229.

Anglo cotton planters were expanding their slaving operations in Tejas and Coahuila. The success of the settler faction led by Stephen Austin, in particular, was dependent on the mass enslavement of African-descended people for the booming cotton economy. In fact, the pressure to allow Texan slavery to continue was such that President Guerrero eventually capitulated to the cotton planters and their Mexican political allies. In late December of 1829, slavery was reinstated in the only Mexican region where it remained economically significant.[87] It would take until 1837, and the loss of Texas to the United States, for the total abolition of slavery to finally occur in Mexico.

Conclusion

Ultimately, the history of freedom and slavery in colonial and early national Mexico is still largely unwritten. Whether or not Mexican slavery died a slow, official death in the 1830s is not the point. (There are many arguments for considering slavery as having persisted well into the twentieth century and even beyond.) The larger point is that enslaved people and their enslavers were absolutely central to the creation of Mexico's many societies. African, Native, or Asian enslavement was not theoretical. It was not marginal. It was formative. Mexican slavery was political, economic, and deeply symbolic. The fact that it is largely forgotten today only demonstrates its violent silences and voids. As a result, the following chapters provide entry points to much larger, deeper histories of multiracial enslavement and freedom in a land not far removed from the United States, Cuba, or Haiti. That Mexican slavery differed so notably from those three cases is an open invitation to reassess how we think of slavery, religion, community, and freedom.

---

87. Andrew J. Torget, *Seeds of Empire: Cotton, Slavery, and the Transformation of the Texas Borderlands, 1800–1850* (Chapel Hill: University of North Carolina Press, 2015), 150.

CHAPTER 1
Conquest, Slavery, and Physical Dominion

The documents highlighted in this chapter speak to the parallel processes of conquest and enslavement in Mexico. They also address the violent physical acts that colonizers used to subjugate and mark Africans, Asians, and Natives as enslaved people. How to control, tax, and extract labor from these groups became fundamental elements of the colonial project. As a result, the documents in this chapter span the years 1520 to 1645 with an emphasis on the language, ideas, and practices that slavers implemented during the early to mid-colonial period.

Marking the bodies of enslaved people or of those considered to be in rebellion was an important component of early colonial rule. Spanish conquistadors used the branding iron, or *carimbo*, extensively in the early phases of the military conquest of central Mexico in order to physically mark the inhabitants of conquered polities as enslavable beings. The selections from 1520 and 1528 by Bernal Díaz del Castillo clearly demonstrate this mentality and practice although they were written decades after the events in question. The branding iron, shaped like a "G" for *guerra* (war), was used indiscriminately against Native populations during these initial decades of the colonial period. As enslaved Indigenous people were displaced throughout the Spanish empire, they bore these permanent marks of conquest wherever they were forced to travel.

Yet the practice of branding enslaved people on their face, chest, or shoulders did not end with the fall of Mexico-Tenochtitlan nor with the end of the Mixtón War in the 1540s. On the contrary, transatlantic slave traders and royal officials exacerbated these practices by branding African captives during the early and mid-colonial periods. Branding continued well into the seventeenth century, as seen in the 1610 inventory of Bishop Alonso de la Mota. Crown officials relied on *carimbo* marks to determine which enslaved Africans had entered New Spain through official ports of entry. As a result, many slave traders designed their own *carimbos* to prove that they had paid import taxes on their captives. The shoulders and arms of enslaved Africans were therefore marked with "DG," "AS," "CR," "ATp," and multiple other such acronyms. Sadly, mutilating the bodies of the enslaved, especially those suspected of potentially running away, became a feature of colonial life. When Viceroy Martín Enríquez decreed running away to be a crime punishable by castration in 1579, he also betrayed a deeply gendered fear of Black men and their bodies.

Other markers of dominion were enforced by controlling the spaces where enslaved and quasi-enslaved people could work or live. For instance, coercive practices involving confinement can be seen in the selections from 1587, 1600, and 1621.

Colonizers and slaveholders sought to maximize their control of Asian, Native, and African-descended populations by concentrating their labor in specific locations, such as the Lake Texcoco draining project. In cities, Indigenous workers were exploited in bakeries and textile mills, where they labored alongside confined people of Asian and African descent. As "locked-in people" (*encerrados* or *encerradas*), they often experienced similar levels of mistreatment and malnutrition.

Enslaved women in these locations (but also on plantations) confronted an additional peril in that their Spanish owners saw in them the possibility of future generations of enslaved laborers. The document from 1645 that closes this chapter highlights the dangers of these imagined slaveries through women's wombs. By this point in the seventeenth century, the principle of *partus sequitur ventrem* was firmly established in Mexico. It was widely understood that children would inherit the legal status of their mothers.

Document 1: 1520—The conquistadors and the branding iron[1]

. . . and as Cortés saw all this, he communicated with all our captains and soldiers. And it was agreed that a scribe would produce a writ, to certify all that had happened, and that all the allies of Mexico who had killed Spaniards would be given as slaves. Because after having sworn obedience to his Majesty, they rebelled and killed more than 860 of our men and 70 horses, and the [people of the] other settlements were to be considered highway robbers and killers of men. Once the order was finished, we had it sent and made known to [the people of Tepeaca], who were warned and required to make peace. In return, they said that if we did not leave, they would come out to kill us, and they prepared themselves and we did the same. Another day we had a good battle with the Mexicas and Tepeaqueños on a plain. . . . After the victory, many Indian women joined us, along with youths who had been taken on the field and from houses. Any men we did not keep, the Tlaxcalans took as slaves. So as the people of Tepeaca saw that they were being torn apart by the Mexicas' threats and by the garrison in their settlement, they [the former] decided to come to where we were without telling them [the latter] anything. We received them in peace, and they swore obedience to his Majesty, and they threw the Mexicas from their homes. We went to the town of Tepeaca, where a village was established, which was named the Villa Segura de la Frontera. . . . And it was there that they [the conquistadors] made the iron that would be used on those taken as slaves. It was a G. that means war [*guerra*]. And from the Villa de Segura de la Frontera, we traversed the surroundings, which

---

1. Bernal Díaz del Castillo, *Historia verdadera de la conquista de la Nueva España escrita por el capitan Bernal Diaz del Castillo, uno de sus conquistadores* (Madrid: En la Imprenta del Reyno, 1632), Capítulo CXXX, 111–112.

were Cachula, Tecamachalco, and Town of the Guayavas, and other towns, whose names I cannot remember. It was in Cachula where they killed fifteen Spaniards in the rooms, in this Cachula we had many slaves, so that over the course of forty days we had those towns pacified and punished. . . .

[Spanish transcription]

. . . y como aquello vio Cortes, comunicòlo con todos nuestros Capitanes, y soldados: y fue acordado, que se hiziesse vn auto por ante Escrivano, que diesse fe de todo lo passado, y que se diessen por esclauos a todos los aliados de Mexico, que huuiessen muerto Españoles: porque aviendo dado la obediencia a su Magestad, se levantaron, y mataron sobre ochocientos y sesenta de los nuestros, y sesenta cauallos, y a los demas pueblos, por salteadores de caminos, y matadores de hombres: hecho este auto, embioseles a hazer saber [a los de Tepeaca], amonestandolos, y requeiriendo con la paz: y ellos tornaron a dezir, que si luego no nos boluiamos, que saldrian a nos matar, y se apercibieron para ello, y nosotros lo mismo. Otro dia tuuimos en vn llano vna buena batalla con los Mexicanos, y Tepeaquenos. . . Pues seguida la vitoria, allegaronse muchas Indias, y muchachos que se tomaron por los campos, y casas, que hombres no curavamos dellos, que los Tlascaltecas los lleuaua[n] por esclauos. Pues como los de Tepeaca vieron, que con el brauear que hazian los Mexicanos que tenian en su pueblo, y guarnicion, eran desabaratados, y ellos juntamente con ellos, acordaron, que si dezilles cosa ninguna, viniessen adonde estauamos: y los recebimos de paz, y dieron la obediencia a su Magestad, y echaron los Mexicanos de sus casas, y nos fuimos nosotros al Pueblo de Tepeaca, adonde se fundò vna Villa, que se nombrò la Villa Segura de la Frontera. . . y alli hizieron hazer el hierro con que se auian de herrar los que se tomauan por esclavos, que era vna G. que quiere dezir guerra. Y desde la Villa de Segura de la Frontera, corrimos todos los rededores, que fue Cachula, y Tecemechalco [sic], y el Pueblo de las Guayauas, y otros pueblos, que no se me acuerda el nombre, y en lo de Cachula fue donde auian muerto en los aposentos quinze Españoles, y en este de Cachula huuimos muchos esclavos, de manera que en obra de quarenta dias tuuimos aquellos pueblos pacificos, y castigados. . . .

Document 2: 1528—Bernal Díaz del Castillo destroys the branding iron in Coatzacoalcos[2]

. . . and at that time there came from Spain and from the Islands many poor Spaniards, greatly covetous and insatiable and ravenous to acquire riches and slaves, who took such measures that they branded free [people].

So that this matter may be more closely understood, at the time that Cortés was governing, before we went with him to the Hibueras, there were judicial proceedings about the branding of slaves, for they were not branded without ascertaining quite clearly whether they were free [or not]. After we set out from Mexico and went with Cortés to Honduras (for so they call it in this country), we were delayed in going and returning to Mexico two years and three months while we were conquering those provinces and bringing them to peace. During the time we were absent there took place in New Spain so many injustices, and revolts, and scandals among those whom Cortés had left as his Lieutenant-Governors that they took no care whether Indians were branded with good or bad title, but only looked after their own parties and interests. . . .

In addition to this there were other evils among the Caciques, who, in paying tribute to their encomenderos,[3] took poor Indian boys and girls and orphans and gave them as slaves. So great was the disillusion that resulted from this that the first to break away from the branding for barter was the town of Coatzacoalcos, where at that time I was a settler. When this happened more than a year had elapsed since we had returned to that town from the journey we had made with Cortés.

As the Senior Regidor and a person of trust, they had handed over the branding iron to me, and to a Curate of that town named Benito López, so that I should have charge of it. When we saw how the [natives of] the province were decreasing and the cunning which the Caciques and some encomenderos were practicing to induce us to brand Indians as slaves (and they were not doing it very secretly), we broke the branding iron, without informing the Chief Magistrate or the Cabildo, and

---

2. Spanish version in Díaz del Castillo, *Historia verdadera*, Capítulo CCXIII, 600–601. English version in Bernal Díaz del Castillo, *The True History of the Conquest of New Spain* (London: Hakluyt Society, 1916), chapter CCXIII, 308–310.

3. *Encomenderos* were Spaniards who held grants of Native tribute and labor (not land itself). The Spanish Crown intially awarded these grants, or *encomiendas*, to former conquistadors and their descendants.

sent a messenger posthaste to the President Don Sebastian Ramírez, then Bishop of Santo Domingo, who was a good President and an upright man of cleanly life, and informed him how we had broken the branding iron, and implored him, as a matter of good counsel, at once to order distinctly that no more slaves should be branded in any part of New Spain.

[Spanish transcription]

... y como en aquel tiempo vinieron de Castilla y de las islas muchos españoles pobres y de gran codicia, y caninos y hambrientos por haber riquezas y esclavos, tenían tales maneras que herraban los libres; y que para mejor se entienda esta materia, en el tiempo que gobernaba Cortés, antes que fuésemos con él a las Hibueras, había rectitud sobre el herrar de los esclavos, porque no se herraban sin primero saber muy de cierto si eran libres, y después que salimos de México y fuimos con Cortés a Honduras, que así se llaman [sic] esta tierra, y tardamos en ir y volver a México dos años y tres meses, que estuvimos conquistando y trayendo de paz aquellas provincias, en aquel tiempo que estuvimos ausentes hubo en la Nueva España tantas injusticias y revueltas y escándalos entre los que dejó Cortés por sus tenientes de gobernadores, que no tenían cuidado si se herraban los indios con justo título o con mal sin entender de sus bandos e intereses ... y además de esto hubo otras maldades entre los caciques que daban tributo a sus encomenderos, que tomaban de sus pueblos indios e indias, muchachos pobres y huérfanos, y los daban por esclavos.

Y fue tanta la disolución que sobre esto hubo, que los primeros que en la Nueva España quebramos el hierro del rescate fue en la villa de Guazacualco [Coatzacoalco], donde en aquel tiempo era yo vecino, porque cuando esto pasó había más de un año que había vuelto a aquella villa de la jornada que hicimos con Cortés, y como regidor más antiguo y persona de confianza me entregaron el hierro para que le tuviese yo y un beneficiado de aquella villa, que se decía Benito López; y como vimos que la provincia de disminuía, y las cautelas que los caciques y algunos encomenderos traían para que les herrásemos los indios por esclavos, no lo siendo, muy secretamente quebramos al hierro sin dar parte de elllo al alcalde mayor ni al cabildo, y en posta hicimos mensajero a México al presidente don Sebastián Ramírez, obispo que entonces era de Santo Domingo, que fue muy buen presidente y recto y de buena vida, y le hicimos saber cómo le quebramos el hierro, y le suplicamos, que por vía de buen consejo, que luego expresamente mandase que no herrasen más esclavos en toda la Nueva España.

Document 3: 1530—Cortés and his extended family receive slave licenses[4]

By the present, I give license and authority to you, Don Hernando Cortés, Marques of the Valley, and to the marchioness, your wife, and Doña Catalina Pizarro, your mother, and to Doña Juana Altamirano and Cecilia Vazquez, and to María de Muergas. [With this license] each one of you, or whoever has your power of attorney, may pass two Black slaves from these our kingdoms to New Spain to [?] and populate there. Altogether, these are [to be] twelve slaves, two for each of you. And returning them from the said islands, you will not be asked to pay any taxes for them. Done in Madrid on ~~December~~ January 11, 1530. I, the Queen, countersigned by Samano, marked by the bishop of the city, R.o. and the bachiller ~~doctor~~ Juarez de Carvajal

the Queen

[Spanish transcription]

por la presente doy licencia A facultad a vos don Hernando Cortés, marques del valle e a la marquesa vuestra muger e a doña Catelina Piçarro vuestra madre, e a doña Juana Altamirano, e a Zecilia Bazquez, e a María de Muergas para que destos nuestros Reynos podays pasar y paseys cada vno de vos, o quyen vuestro poder obiere dos esclavos negros a la nueva españa por quanto y sorbibir [¿?] y poblar en ella que son por todos doze esclavos A cada vno de vos dos esclabos en las dichas yslas tornandolos a enbarcar no vos pidan derechos algunos fecha en Madrid a honze dias del mes de ~~dizienbre~~ henero de myll e quynyentos e treynta años. Yo la Reyna refrendada de Samano Señalada del obispo de çibdad R.o y ~~doctor~~ el liçençiado Juarez de Carvajal

la Reyna

---

4. Archivo General de Indias, México, 1088, L.1, f. 146v. http://pares.mcu.es/ParesBusquedas20/catalogo/description/371011?nm

Document 4: circa 1553—Puebla's slave registry, *La Caja de Negros*[5]

We, García de Aguilar and Gonzalo Díaz de Vargas, alderman and regent of the city of the Angels [Puebla], and Andrés de Herrera, municipal scribe, as judges in what is referred to as the Black registry, we beg the illustrious Sir Don Luis de Velasco, viceroy and governor of this New Spain, to concede, decree, and provide the following for the sustenance of said registry of the said Blacks so that it might have its effect and not fail to accomplish what Your Grace has stipulated:

I   First, Your illustrious Grace should know that up to today there are CCLXXXX-VIII [298] Blacks in the said registry of this city before us, in accordance with the order that you have given. The payment, at two pesos of mine gold for each one, amounts to DLXXVI [576] pesos of said gold, which has been entered in said registry in said entries and is in our possession.

II Your illustrious Grace should know that to date, said gold pesos have been spent on the expense of said registry with its three keys and lock, and the books and payments that have been made to the bounty hunters who have sought and brought the registered Blacks that have been located. These have been brought back from Mexico [City] and other parts. These bounty hunters have been given and been paid 35 common gold [pesos], according to what Your Grace has decreed they should be paid in such cases.

III Of the salaries for the first third of the year, for us the said judges, scribe, and two bounty hunters, which at fifty common gold pesos a year for each, as Your Grace orders, are and amount to five hundred and four mine pesos. These have been removed as the salary of the first third of the year and expensed from all the said expenses and payments that have been made to the registry to date.

IV Your Illustrious Grace should know that there are other said Blacks that are registered in said registry, who are escaped, and who are being sought, which is

---

5. Efraín Castro Morales, ed., *Suplemento de el Libro Número Primero de la Fundación y Establecimiento de la Muy Noble y Muy Leal Ciudad de los Ángeles* (Puebla: Ayuntamiento del Municipio de Puebla, 2009), Documento 135.

why the bounty hunters are needed. On this and every day, the Blacks escape and this makes the costs, expenses, and payments from said registry necessary. This is also necessary due to the judges', scribes', and bounty hunters' salaries, as Your Grace has decreed.

V Your Illustrious Grace should know that for the registry to have its proper effect, as a just and necessary thing, and so that the registry does not end, but continues, it is appropriate and necessary that the Blacks who are registered in the surroundings of this city, as on the Orizaba sugarcane plantation, in Tehuacan, and in other parts that are closer to this city than to Mexico [City], Oaxaca, or Veracruz, be registered in this city's registry according to Your Illustrious Grace's ordinances. And that in order to make such a registry one of us judges should go [to those places], which should be done before the scribe who should be designated for such a task. The dates of these registries should be brought and placed in this city's registry. With the money from these registries, it will be possible to accomplish what Your Grace has decreed on this matter in your ordinances and decrees.

VI We beg Your Illustrious Grace to order and decree that the Blacks who currently are not registered because they are not yet fifteen years of age, be registered as soon as they have turned fifteen. For this is to the benefit of the registry and its effectiveness, and aligns with what Your Grace has decreed on this matter, which is that all Blacks, mulattos, and *moriscos* fifteen years of age and older be registered.

VII We beg that Your illustrious Grace decree and order that the Blacks who are brought from Spain or Guinea or other parts of this New Spain be registered once again in the registries of the cities where they are to live. Or that their buyers register them within thirty days of their purchase so that they may be obligated to register the Blacks in these registries under the penalties outlined in Your Grace's ordinances and decrees.

All of which we beg Your Illustrious Grace to order and decree, as it is clear that it is necessary for the desired effect as Your Grace has established it regarding the Black listings and their registries, all of which is in the service of His Majesty and for the common good of the entire republic of this New Spain and of the Spaniards and Indians in it. This is done in the city of the Angels [Puebla] on the _____ [*date blank*].

[Spanish transcription]

Lo que nos García de Aguilar e Gonzalo Díaz de Vargas, alguacil mayor e regidor de la ciudad de los Ángeles, e Andrés de Herrera, escribano de cabildo, como jueces que somos en lo tocante a la manifestación de los negros, suplicamos al ilustrísimo señor don Luís de Velasco, visorrey y gobernador desta Nueva España, conceda y haga merced e provea para la sustentación de caxa de los dichos negros y para fin que haya cumplido efecto y que no se acabe lo que su señoría acerca dello tiene proveído, es lo siguiente:

I Primeramente, sepa vuestra señoría ilustrísima que hasta hoy hay manifestados en la dicha caxa desta ciudad ante nosotros, por la orden que vuestra señoría manda que se haga, CCLXXXXVIII negros y paga por cada uno dos pesos de oro de minas, como por vuestra señoría está mandado, son y se montan DLXXVI pesos del dicho oro, los que hasta hoy han entrado en la dicha caxa de las dichas manifestaciones, los cuales están en ella en nuestro poder.

II Iten, sepa vuestra señoría ilustrísima que los dichos pesos de oro se han gastado hasta hoy en lo que costó la dicha caxa con sus tres llaves e cerradura, y los libros y pagos que se han dado a los dos cuadrilleros que han buscado y traído los negros manifestados que se han hallado, los cuales se han traído de México y de otras partes y se les ha dado y pagado hasta hoy a los dichos cuadrilleros XXXV de oro común, conforme a lo que vuestra señoría tiene proveído que se les dé y pague en tal caso.

III Iten, de los tercios primeros del salario del año, de nos los dichos jueces, scribano e dos cuadrilleros que son a razón de a cincuenta pesos de oro común por año a cada uno, como vuestra señoría lo manda, son y se montan los pesos de oro común del dicho primero tercio del año, y sacados todos los dichos gastos y pagas que hasta hoy se han hecho y pagado de la dicha caxa, como dicho es, quedan e hay en ella quinentos e cuatro pesos de minas.

IIII Iten, sepa vuestra señoría ilustrísima que hay otros de los dichos negros que están manifestados en la dicha caxa, que andan huidos, los cuales se procuran haber y para ello se buscan por los cuadrilleros, en lo cual y en otros que de cada día se huyen se hacen y de necesario se han de hacer costas, gastos y pagas de la dicha caxa; y asimismo en los salarios de jueces, scribano e cuadrilleros, conforme a lo que cerca de ello vuestro señoría tiene proveído que haya, lo cual es necesario.

V Iten, sepa vuestra señoría ilustrísima que para que haya cumplido efecto lo que tiene proveído cerca de la manifestación de los dichos negros, por ser como es cosa justa y nescesaria, y para que la caxa y efecto della no se acabe y que se continúe conviene y es nescesario que los negros que hay por manifestar en la comarca desta ciudad, ansí en el ingenio de Oliçaba, y en Teguacan y en las otras partes que son más cercanas a esta ciudad que a la de México, Guaxaca, a la de Veracruz, se manifiesten en la caxa desta ciudad conforme a las ordenanzas de vuestra señoría ilustrísima, y que al hacer la tal manifestación vaya uno de nosotros los jueces, la cual se haga antel y antel [sic] escribano que para ello él nombrare, y que fechas las dichas manifestaciones se traigan y pongan en la caxa desta ciudad, y con los dinero dellos para que haya cumplido efecto lo que vuestra señoría tiene proveído cerca dello por sus ordenanças e mandamientos que cerca de ello disponen.

VI   Iten, suplicamos a vuestra señoría ilustrísima provea y mande que los negros que de presente no se manifestaren por no tener edad de quince años, que se manifiesten cada que tengan cumplida edad de los dichos quince años, porque es pro de la caxa y del efecto della, y conforme a lo que vuestra señoría tiene proveído cerca dello que es que se manifiesten todos los negros, mulatos e moriscos esclavos de edad de quince años para arriba.

VII Iten, suplicamos a vuestra señoría ilustrísima sea servido de proveer y mandar que los negros que se truxeren de España o de Guinea o de otras partes a esta Nueva España, nuevamente se manifiesten en las caxas de las ciudades donde han de residir los tales negros, o los compradores dellos dentro de treinta días de cómo los compraren, so las penas contenidas en las ordenanças y mandamientos de vuestra señoria ilustrísima, que pone para que sean obligados a manifestar los negros en las dichas caxas y los registrare.

Todo lo cual que dicho es suplicamos a vuestra señoría ilustrísima sea servido proveer y hacer merced, pues claro consta ser necesario que ansí se haga y provea, para que haya cumplido efecto, lo que cerca dello vuestra señoría tiene proveído que se haga y guarde en lo tocante a las manifestaciones de los negros y caxas dellos, lo cual es servicio de su Magestad y lo en pro común de toda la república desta Nueva España y de españoles e indios de ella, y que es fecho en esta cibdad de los Ángeles, a [en blanco].

Document 5: 1579—Viceroy Enrriquez calls for castrating Black runaways[6]

Don Martin Enrriquez, etcetera. Since the justices of this New Spain have not been as careful as necessary in the punishment of the Blacks who flee their masters' service and go to the hills, great inconveniences have taken place and continue to take place. The Blacks come out to the roads to rob and commit other excesses, which has mostly happened and happens in the city of Veracruz and its surroundings, between the city of Oaxaca and the port of Huatulco, in the province of Pánuco, and on the cattle

---

6. Archivo General de la Nación, Ordenanzas, Vol. 1, ff. 34r–34v.

ranches of the Chichimecas, Almería, Tlacotalpan and other [places]. To remedy this and until His Majesty or I decree or order something else in His Royal Name, I order and decree that from now on, any Black slave who is found to have fled his master's service and found in the hills shall be arrested and castrated without need for an investigation of another crime or excess. If the slave has committed other crimes, he shall be punished for them, in addition to the aforementioned [punishment] as the case might require. I order His Majesty's justices to have this proclaimed in this city and in Antequera [Oaxaca City], Veracruz, Tampico, and in all the other places where they perceive that those who have escaped are hiding. The slaves are to return to the service of their masters within twenty days, and past [this date] the punishments on those who have fled and flee are to be applied if they are found in the hills as has been said. The Justices will be especially careful [to follow this order] after this decree has been given in each district, in the surrounding places where they may be found, and in this city of Mexico, because they will be asked to account for this order in the public inquiries that will be made. Done in Mexico City on the sixth of November of 1579. By order of his excellency, Don Martin Enrriquez. Juan de Cueva.

[Spanish transcription]

Don Martin Enrriquez, etcetera. Por quanto no aver Tenido Las Justiçias desta nueva Spaña el cuidado que conviene en el castigo de los negros que se huyen del serviçio de sus amos, y se ban a los montes sean seguido, y siguen grandes ynconvenientes; asi porque salen a los caminos a saltear, como por otros Exsesos que Se hazen, lo qual principalmente se ha hecho y ase en la çiudad de la Veracruz y su comarca, y entre la çiudad de Guaxaca, y el puerto de Guatulco, y en la provincia de Panuco, y en las estançias de ganados mayores de Chichimecas, Almeria y Tlacotalpa[n], y otras e para remedio dello Por la presente, ordeno y mando que de aqui adelante hasta tanto que por su magestad o por mi En su Real nombre otra cosa Se provea, y manda, qualquier Sclavo negro que se averiguare averse huido del serviçio de Su amo y se hallare en los montes E Por el mismo caso, Sea preso y capado, sin que sea necesario averiguaçion de otro delito, ni exçeço y si otros delitos oviere hecho, sea castigado por ellos demas de lo susodicho como el caso requiere. Y mando a las Justiçias de Su magestad que hagan pregonar lo susodicho en esta çiudad y en la de Antequera, y en la de La Veracruz, y en la de Tanpico, y en las otras partes donde les pareçiere aperçiviendo a los que estuvieren huidos Se recoxan, e buelvan al serviçio de Sus amos dentro de Veynte dias y pasados se executen Las penas en los que se ubieren Vydo y huyeren, siendo hallados en los montes segun dicho es, cada uno, en su distrito, aviendose dado el dicho pregon, en las partes declaradas de la comarca donde se hallaren, y en esta çiudad de Mexico, en lo qual las dichas Justiçias tentan expeçial cuidado por que se les a de pedir quenta dello En la residençia que se les tomare. Fecho en Mexico a seis de noviembre de mill e quinientos y setenta y nueve años. Don Martin Enrriquez Por mandado de du excelencia. Juan de Cueva.

Document 6: 1587—Chichimec captives from Nuevo León displaced[7]

Don Alvaro Manrique, etcetera. I make known to you, the magistrate of the city [Puebla] of the Angels, that Alvaro de Chillas, this court's bailiff with our commission, went to that said city to produce an investigation, before its justice, of the Chichimec Indian men and women who are there and in the other parts where they may have been sold, [after] being taken from the government of the kingdom of Nuevo León since the past month of July 1586. [This report was to include] their names, titles, physical marks, and ages. After this, the [Chichimecs] would be deposited with the people in whose power they are registered and would be delivered to them whenever this was ordered. In compliance with this order, [de Chillas] made some investigations into the Indian men and women who had been deposited, whom he found being held by certain people, as is seen in the files that he brought before me. Since it is appropriate that the said Indians be brought to this court [in Mexico City], I order that within fifteen days from the day that this decree is seen, you will return to me, with a trustworthy person, the Indian men and women who are to be delivered to you with this, my order, and it will be verified that they are deposited with the citations and original papers regarding their service. With these [documents] further investigations will be made into whether the [Chichimecs] are free or subject to the said service, which you will do and carry out without delay and with a warning that if this is not done, [another] person will be appointed at your expense. Let this be done. In Mexico City on January 23, 1587. By order of His Excellency, the marquess. Juan de Cucua.

[in the left-hand margin, "So that the magistrate of the city of the Angels returns the Indians listed herein to Your Excellency."]

[Spanish transcription]

Don Alvaro Manrrique &.a Hago saber a vos El allcalde mayor de la ciudad de los anjeles que alvaro de chillas alguaçil de esta corte con comision nuestra fue a esa dicha çiudad Para que ante la Justiçia della hiçiese Ynformacion de los yndios e yndia

---

7. Archivo General de la Nación, General de Parte, Vol. 3, 946/19, Exp. 18, f. 11r.

chichimecas que en ella y en otras partes ovuiesse que o oviesen vendido y llevado de la governacion del nuevo Reyno de Leon desde el mes de Jullio pasado de myll quinientos y ochenta y seis años con declaraçion de sus dueños, de sus nombres, titulos, señal, y hedad y esto hecho los depossitasse en las personas en cuyo Poder estuvieren de manifiesto y entregar los cada y quando se les mandase, el qual en cumplimiento de lo que se les mando, hiço çiertas diligencias y depositos de Yndios e yndias que hallo en poder de çiertas personas como consto de los autos que ante mi trujo y porque conviene se trayr a esta corte los dichos yndios por la presente os mando que dentro de quinçe dias Primeros siguientes que corren desde el dia que Viere del este mandamyento ynoveis ante mi con persona de rrecaudo Los Yndios e Yndias que Por los dichos auctos y depositos orijinales que se os entregaran con este mi mandamiento constare estar depositados con los Citaciones y rrecaudos originales de su servycio Para que con ellos aca se hagan mas diligencias sobre si son libres o sujetos al dicho servycio lo qual hareis y cunpliereis sin rremsion algunaa con apercevimiento que no lo haciendo se proveera persona que a vuestra costa lo cumplasse en mexico a veinte y tres de henero de myll quinientos y ochenta y siete años. El Marques, por mandado de su excelencia. Juan de Cucua.

[al margen izquierdo, "Para que el alcalde maior de la ciudad de los angeles, dentro de 15 dias Ynove ante Vuestra excelencia los yndios aqui contenidos."]

Document 7: 1600—Indigenous people held as slaves in bakeries[8]

Don Gaspar, etc. To you, Antonio Negrete, inspecting judge and accountant of the textile mills in the city [Puebla] of the Angels, let it be known that I have heard that the Indians who serve in the bakeries are wronged and deceived by the bakers. The latter charge them with great sums of money on their account, alleging that the Indians do not return with the proceeds of the bread they give them to sell, cheat the baker, or argue that the bakers did not give them baked bread. With this, the bakery owners charge them one hundred fifty, two hundred, and more pesos, and hold the Indians as slaves, forcing them to serve for life. As it is appropriate that this be remedied, I order you to produce an account of the said Indian bakers in this said city, with the bakery owners, without forcing the Indians to indebt themselves more than the advanced wages, as stipulated by the ordinance, unless the Indians themselves want to serve [this amount]. To date, there is no ordinance in place for the Indians not to pay. And if from this account that you shall produce, a crime worthy

---

8. Archivo General de la Nación, Ordenanzas II, 93v–94. Published in Silvio Zavala, ed., *Ordenanzas del Trabajo, Siglos XVI y XVII* (México, D.F.: Editorial Elede, 1947), 218–219.

of punishment should emerge, you will lead the investigation and send it to Dr. Luis de Villanueva Zapata, warning that no Indians should be held using prisons, or be locked in, on account of these debts, even if the Indians desire to be there [in the bakery], because in all respects they are to be and remain free, and exempted from any such oppression. Made in Mexico, on July 11, 1600. The Count of Monterrey, by order of the viceroy, Martin de Pedrossa.

[Spanish transcription]

Don Gaspar, etc. A vos Antonio Negrete, juez veedor y contador de los obrajes de la ciudad de Los Angeles, sabed que yo he entendido que los indios que sirven en las panaderías son agraviados y defraudados de los panaderos, cargándoles mucha cantidad de dineros en sus cuentas, so color de que no acuden con lo procedido del pan que les dan a vender y que hacen barata de ello o que no le dieron cocido, y con esto les vienen a hacer cargo de ciento y cincuenta, doscientos y más pesos, y los tienen como esclavos, obligados de por vida a servirles, a que conviene proveer remedio, y así os mando que hagáis la cuenta de los dichos indios panaderos de la dicha ciudad, con los dueños del pan, sin obligarles a pagar más alcance de lo que por la ordenanza se dispone poderse dar de salario adelantado a cada indio, sino fuere en caso que los mismos indios lo quieran servir, por no estar hecha ordenanza para que no lo paguen hasta ahora que la he proveído para lo de adelante; y si de las cuentas que hiciéredes resultare algún delito digno de castigo, haréis la averiguación y la remitáis al doctor Luis de Villanueva Zapata, advirtiendo que por ninguno de los alcances que se hicieren a los indios han de tenerlos con prisiones ni encerrados, aunque de su voluntad quiera estar ahí, porque de todo punto han de quedar y estar libres y reservados de semejante opresión. Hecho en México, a once de julio de mil y seiscientos años. El Conde de Monterrey, por mando del virrey, Martin de Pedrossa.

Document 8: 1607—Forced labor for draining Lake Texcoco[9]

In Mexico City, on December 4, 1607, Don Luis de Velasco, etcetera, said that as His Excellency has ordered the draining of this city's lagoon, because the lagoon causes the city's flooding and to free the city from the ruin and damages that it has received and that threaten it, for this reason certain necessary things have been arranged, such as the help of the Indians from towns and different parts, so that the draining may be finished with all possible brevity and what is sought be accomplished. And because with more manpower this will be less delayed, and His Excellency having

---

9. Archivo General de la Nación, Ordenanzas, Vol. 1, 120v–121.

considered that the current arrangements are not sufficient, it will be of great effect to commute the sentences, depending on the charges against them, of some of the Blacks and mulattos, free and slave, that are arrested and punished by the justices in this city's public and court jails. These [Blacks and mulattos] are charged with breaking the ordinances for carrying knives and other prohibited weapons. As a result, His Excellency decrees and orders to the judges and justices of this court and city that henceforth, for the duration of the drainage work, said Blacks and mulattos, free and slave, who are charged and punished for bearing arms or breaking some ordinance, be sentenced to serve and work on draining [Lake Texcoco] for a determined time. The judges and justices will send the Blacks and mulattos to the work site for this purpose and will notify them not to miss or absent themselves from the place where they will work on the site, under the penalties that the former find suitable. These penalties will be imposed on the Blacks and mulattos without pardon, and a copy of this order will be given to the royal criminal court of the royal assembly and another to the ordinary assembly, so that it be known. And Don Luis de Velasco decreed and signed it, before me, Pedro de la Torre.

[In the left-hand margin, "That the judges and justices of this court commute the punishments given to free Blacks and mulattos who break the ordinances and that they instead serve for some time in the drainage work [of Lake Texcoco]."]

[Spanish transcription]

En la çiudad de Mexico a quatro dias del mes de diziembre de milly seisçientos y siete Años. Don Luis de Velasco etcetera, dixo que por quanto su Excelencia A mandado Poner en execucion el desague de la laguna de esta dicha çiudad que causa la ynundaçion della, Para Librarla de la ruina y daños que por esta caussa A Reçevido y la amenaçan y Para ello se an prevenido las cossas neçesarias y ayuda de yndios de los pueblos y partes que a pareçido Para que con la brevedad, posible Se acave y Consiga lo que pretende y por quanto Fuere mayor la fuerça de la gente tendra menos dilaçion y aviendo considerado, Su excelencia que no basta para esto la que esta prebenida y que sera de mucho efecto que algunos de los negros y mulatos libres y esclavos que se castigan y prenden Por las Justiçias en las carçeles de corte y publica desta dicha Ciudad por traer cuchillo y otras Armas que les estan prohividas, y en quebrantamiento de ordenanças se les Comuten las penas que mereçian en que por algun tiempo sirvan y travajen en la obra del dicho desague conforme a la Culpa que resultare contra ellos Por tanto su excelencia Ordena y manda a los Juezes y Justiçias desta corte y çiudad que de aquí adelante Por el Tiempo que durare la obra del dicho desague en las causas que hizieren y fulminasen contra los tales negros y mulatos esclavos y libres Por traer armas O aver quebrantado alguna ordenança los penen y condenen Por la que mereçian a que sirvan y travajen Por el Tiempo que les señalaren en la obra del dicho desague entregandolos Para el efecto a las personas a quien esta encargada Para que miren por ellos, y los ocupen en la dicha obra, aperceviendoles a los dichos negros y mulatos que no falten ni hagan ausençia de la parte donde se les señalare Para trabajar en la dicha obra So las penas que les pareçiere Conbenir las quales executen en ellos yremisiblemente y se lleve Vn tanto desta orden a la real sala del Crimen desta Real audiençia y otra a la audiençia ordinaria Para que se tenga notiçia della y asi lomando e firmo Su excelencia don Luis de belasco = ante mi Pedro de la Torre

[Al margen izquierdo, "Para que los Juezes, y Justiçias, desta corte en las condenaçiones que hizieren a negros y mulatos Libres en quebrantamientos de ordenanças les comuten las penas que mereçieren en que sirvan por algun tiempo en la obra del deSague."]

Document 9: 1610—Bishop Alonso de la Mota y Escobar's inventory[10]

Note: marginal annotations in the original are marked in italics here.

Memory of the Black and mulatto slaves with whom I find myself today, August 1, 1610.

<u>Black men</u>

	Francisco, Bran, old Black man, married	
freed	Francisco Carmona. Bran, old man, married	
	Gaspar. Bran, married to another [owner's] Black woman	*already bought her, Ana, Biafara*
died	Pedro, Bran, single—*died*	
died on Dec. 12	Francisco, Portuguese ladino, married to a free [woman].	*Died*
	Gaspar, Creole from Compostela, ladino, single	
	Francisco, Biafara, tailor, single, great thief and traitor	
died in March	Mateo, Bioho, *bozal*, single, died	
gave to Pereira, my almoner	Felipe, Chocho, *bozal*, single. given away.	
died on July 26	Melchor, Creole, ladino, branded on the face [with the words] "bishop Mota"	*died*

---

10. Biblioteca Nacional de España, MSS 6877, 267r–267v.

Document 9: 1610—Bishop Alonso de la Mota y Escobar's inventory

gave to Don Antonio de la Mota	Francisco Dionisio, branded on the face, [brand] says "Fran.co Madaleno," I gave him to Don Antonio
	Andres, ladino, whom I bought from Alonso de Isla in Atlixco. sold him.

mulatto slaves

gave to Don Antonio	Juan Pascual, White mulatto man, single / branded with my name
gave to Don Fernando Portugal	Juan de Guadiana, youth, single, [branded] with an "S and nail" [image of a nail]
	Juan, mulatto, branded, already married to a slave of mine
	Juan, mulatto, 12 years of age, his brother [?]
	Clemente, his brother, ten years old
	Diego, his brother, one year old
died	Jacinto, mulatto, seven years old, son of the Black ladina Juana Penda
	Geronimo, mulatto, his brother, four years old
	Catalina ~~Getabel~~, girl, daughter of the Black ladina Juana, she is a dark-skinned little Black girl
	a mulatto, Francisco, born in Utrera, twenty years old, a tall youth
	a mulatto named Nicolas, son of Maria Escobar
	another mulatto, little Juan, son of the same woman
	another mulatto, Juan Ximenez, branded with my name, 20 years old
	another mulatto, Juan, [branded] with an "s and nail," a 25-year-old farrier

Black women slaves

died	Maria, Bran, wife of Francisco, Bran, my slave
freed herself	Cathalina, Bran, wife of Francisco, Carmona, my slave
gave her to Doña Catalina	Juana, creole ladina, married to a free mulatto man
died	Cathalina, Conga, old single woman
	Catalina, girl, Juana's daughter, 3-year-old little Black girl
	Maria, Biafara, *bozal*, single

46   Chapter 1: Conquest, Slavery, and Physical Dominion

<u>Gave her to Doña Catalina</u>   Petronila, Black Creole, 7 years old, Juana's daughter

<u>Catalina, Conga, Francisca, Creole</u>   Ana, Biafara, married to Gaspar, Bran, my Black [slave], she has a daughter named Ysabel, and another son named Alonso, my slaves.

Catalina Jolofa, married to another person's Black [slave]

<u>mulatto and china women slaves</u>

Luzia, White *china*, branded, elderly, slave

Maria, her White daughter, without brand marks, 14 years old, single

Maria, mulatta, branded with my name, married to a slave of mine, the branded mulatto Juan

died   Dominga, mulatta, 7 years old, [Maria's] daughter
Pascuala, mulatta, her sister, 4 years old
Luzia, her sister, a White girl
Maria, mulatta, her sister

[Spanish transcription]

Memoria de los esclavos negros y mulatos con que me hallo hoy primero de Agosto deste año de 1610.

<u>negros</u>

francisco bran negro viejo casado

ahorrose   francisco carmona bran viejo cazado

Gaspar bran casado con negra agena   *ya la compre ana biafara*

murio   Pedro bran soltero—murio

murio en 12 de diziembre   francisco Portugues ladino casado con libre. murio

Gaspar criollo de Compostela ladino soltero

francisco biafara sastre, soltero, gran ladron y traidor

murio en marzo   Mateo bioho boçal soltero murio

dile a mi limosnero Pereira   felipe chocho boçal soltero. dado.

murio en 26 de julio   melchior criollo ladino herrado en la cara "obispo Mota"   *murio*

dile a don Antonio de la Mota	Francisco Dionisio herrado en la cara, dize Fran.co Madaleno, di le a don Antonio
	andres ladino que Conpre de Alonso de Isla en Atrisco [Atlixco], vendile.

<u>mulatos esclavos</u>

dile a don Antonio	Juan Pascual mulato blanco soltero / herrado con mi nombre
dile a don Fernando Portugal	Juan de Guadiana moço soltero con S. y [imagen de clavo]
	Juan mulato herrado ya hombre casado con esclava mia
	Juan mulato de edad de 12 años su entenado [?] de Juan
	Clemente su hermano de diez años
	Diego su hermano de un año
murio	Jacinto mulato de siete años hijo de la negra ladina Juana Penda
	Geronimo mulato su hermano de quatro años
	Catalina ~~Getabel~~ niña hija de la negra ladina Juana, es negrita atezada
	un mulato Francisco nacido en Utrera de veinte años moceton alto
	un mulato llamado Nicolas hijo de Maria escobar
	otro mulato Joanillo hijo de la misma
	otro mulato herrado de mi nombre Joan Ximenez de 20 años
	otro mulato con s [y clavo] Juan herrador de 25 años

<u>negras esclavas</u>

murio	Maria bran muger de francisco bran, mi esclavo
ahorrose	Cathalina bran muger de francisco carmona mi esclavo
dila a doña Catalina	Juana criolla ladina, casada con mulato libre
murio	Cathalina conga soltera vieja
	catalina niña hija de Juana negrita de 3 años
	Maria biafara boçal soltera
<u>*dila a doña Catalina*</u>	Petronila negra criolla hija de Juana de 7 años

Catalina conga, *Francisca criolla.*	Ana biafara casada con Gaspar bran mi negro tiene una hija llamada Ysabel, y otro hijo llamado Alonso, mis esclabos. Catalina Jolofa casada con negro ageno.
	<div align="center">mulatas y chinas esclavas</div>
	Luzia china blanca herrada ya de dias esclaba
	Maria su hija blanca sin letras de 14 años de edad soltera
	Maria mulata herrada de mi nombre casada con esclavo mio, mulato herrado Joan
murio	Dominga mulata de 7 años su hija
	Pascuala mulata su hermana de 4 años
	Luzia su hermana niña blanca
	Maria mulata niña su hermana

Document 10: 1616—Textile barons demand Native workers and reject Black workers[11]

This day the regent Gaspar Gomez Vasconcelos made a written proposal of the following tenor: Gaspar Gomez Vasconcelos, regent and legal representative of this city of the Angels in the municipal council. Today on June 28, 1610, I make the following proposal. Your Grace is aware and knows well that the main business and commerce of this city is the production of textiles large and small, serges, coarse frieze fabrics, and hats that are made and worked here. Contracts for wools, dyes, corn and wheat foodstuffs, cattle, and other infinite things and the sustenance of many people depend on this business as well as the provision of the entire land, because textiles are taken from here to all the provinces of New Spain and to Peru and China. It is also well-known that this is made and done by the hand of the Indians who are taught and raised in these occupations, because there are no Spaniards who will make them. The Blacks are not appropriate because they are clumsy and lack the ability and skill that is required. Not enough of the Blacks can be had as is necessary, because they are very expensive and many die. And in the total absence of the Indians, the textile mills will fail, business will cease, fewer cattle will be raised, less corn and wheat will be consumed, the royal taxes and the privileges of His Majesty will decrease, and this republic and its *vecinos* will suffer much need and labor.

---

11. Archivo Municipal de Puebla, Actas de Cabildo, Vol 15, f. 110v–111v.

Your Grace has seen how these days the judge of the textile mills, in enforcing the mandates of the most excellent lord viceroy of New Spain, has thrown out all the Indians—contracted, locked in, and of all types—who were working in the textile mills. This has been proclaimed with grave penalties so that the Indians may no longer stay or serve [in the textile mills], nor may they be received even if the Indians want to do so of their own volition. With this everything has declined, stalled, and stopped. Whereas the intention of His Royal Majesty and his most excellent viceroy is that there be no Indians locked in, this [intention] should not prevent nor remove the business, commerce, and production of said textiles that is so important to this kingdom, where so many people are sustained and the general population dressed by it. It is also surely not your intention that the Indians, who are especially raised in the textile mills and know no other occupation, should become drifters and lazy, as they ought to occupy themselves and work. In two other occasions this has been experienced, when they were thrown out [of the mills] and committed enormous crimes and extremely grave thefts, robberies, fires, deaths, and acts of force and other excesses took place. [This occurred] on one occasion, when Dr. Santiago del Riego came, and on the other when Dr. Luis de Villanueva Zapata came with ample commissions to throw them out. This happened because they [the Indians] are lazy, wasteful people, enemies of work. They sustain themselves with an ear of corn, a bit of chile pepper, and water; and if they are not compelled to work they think nothing of going about naked and barefoot.

Therefore, it seems to me that Your Grace, concerned for the good of the republic, has the obligation to plead with the most excellent lord marquess of Guadalcazar, viceroy of this New Spain, who with Christian zeal and will and with such prudence governs and rules these kingdoms, that he should decree a suitable remedy so that the said textile mills should not fail or perish totally, so that the Indians on estates who want to work for a daily or weekly wage, by renting themselves out, should be able to do so. It should be possible to find them, direct them, and contract them without penalty or fees, as all nations do. With this, much good and benefits will come to the Indians, because by serving and working they will earn their food and sustenance, the means to pay the royal tributes. They will remove themselves from vices and will shelter in the houses where they work and will not wander aimlessly as we see them do today. Business and commerce will not cease, the taxes and rights of His Majesty will not diminish, the cattle ranchers and farm owners will keep going, and the poor will wear clothes as they have until now. I ask and beg Your Grace in the name of this city, that you represent all these needs to the most excellent marquess of Guadalcazar, viceroy of this New Spain, so that he may repair and offer the most appropriate remedy and order for the general good of this city and that it may be done quickly, as necessity asks and requires / Gaspar Gomez Vasconcelos . . .

Before me, Nicolás Fernández de la Fuente, scribe of the town hall

[Spanish transcription]

Este dia el rregidor Gaspar Gomez Vaconçellos Hizo vna propossiçion por escripto del thenor siguiente = Gaspar Gomez Basconcellos Regidor y Procurador mayor desta çiu[da]d de los angeles en el cabildo que se haze oy beinte y ocho de junio de mill y seisçientos y diez y seis hago la proposiççion siguiente = Bien sabe Vuestra Señoría y le consta que el principal trato y comercio que ay en esta çiudad es la fabrica de los paños mayores y menores, jergas y sayales y sombreros que en ella se hazen y labran de la qual pende la contrataçion de las lanas, tintas, Bastimentos de mayz, y trigo, ganados y otras infinitas cosas y El sustento de muchas personas y la prouission de toda la tierra Porque de aquí se llevan paños para todas las prouincias desta nueva españa y para el Piru y China—y tambien es notorio que estos se haze y labra por mano de los yndios que estan enseñados y criados en estos ministerios porque no ay españoles que los hagan y los negros no son a proposito porque son torpes y no tiene la abilidad y felma que se requiere y no se pueden tener tantos como son menester porque valen muy caros y se mueren muchos y si faltan los yndios totalmente faltaran los obrajes, cessaran las contrataciones no se criara tanto ganado no se gastaran tanto mayz y trigo se diminuyran las alcavalas Reales y derechos de su magestad, Y esta Republica y vezinos della padeceran mucha necesidad y trabajo =

ya bisto Vuestra Señoria estos dias como el juez de obrajes cumpliendo los mandamientos del Excelentisimo señor virrey desta nueva españa a echado todos quantos yndios avia en los obrajes laborios y Encerrados y de todo genero a pregonando (sic) con graues penas que no esten ni siruan ni los Resciban avn que ellos quieran de sv voluntad con lo qual de todo punto an caydo, parado y cessado—y como quieraque la ynténçion de la Magestad Real y de su excelentisimo Virrey es que no aya yndias [sic] encerrados no estorua ni quita el trato y comerçio y la fabrica de los dichos paños que tan ymportante y necessaria es En el Reyno de donde tanta gente se sustenta y con que se biste todo el comun En general ni sera su yintencion que los Yndios especialmente estos criados en obraje que no saben otro officio anden bagamundos y ociosos y deben de ocuparse y trabajar porque la experiencia a mostrado otras dos vezes que los an echado la vna quando bino el señor doctor Santiago del Riego y la otra quando vino el señor doctor Luis de Villanueva Çapata con amplias comiss.es a echarlos que cometieron delitos enormes y grauissimos de hurtos y salteamientos, incendios, muertes, fuerças, y otros excessos porque es gente para gana baldia floxa enemiga del trabajo y que se sustentan con vna maçorca de mayz y un poco de chile y agua y sino les compelen a trabajar no se les da nada de andar desnudos y descalços –

Por lo qual me a paresçido que Vuestra Señoria mirando por el bien de su repubica tendra obligacion de suplicar al excelentisimo señor Marques de Guadalcaçar virrey desta nueva españa que con zelo y pecho tan christiano y con tanta prudençia govierna y rrije estos Reynos proueua de rremedio conuiniente para que los dichos obrajes no se acaben ni perezcan de todo punto dando permiso para que los yndios laborios que quisieren trabajar por dias e por semanas por jornal alquilandose lo puedan hazer y los puedan buscar, conduzir y alquilar sin pena ni grauamen como todas las naçiones hazen de que se les seguira a los yndios mucho bien y prouecho pues sirvuiendo y trabajando ganaran la comida y El sustento y con que pagarlos tributos rreales y se quitaran de vicios y tendran amparo en las casas donde trabajaren y no andaran descarriados como los bemos / oy—y la contrataçion y comercio no cessara—las alcaualas y derechos de su magestad no se menoscabaran—los criadores de ganado continuaran y los labradores lo mesmo—y los pobres se bestiran de paño como hasta aquí = Por que pido y sup.co a V.S.a en nombre desta çiudad Represente todas estas necessidades al excelentisimo señor Marquez de Guadalcaçar virrey desta nueva españa para que lo rrepare y de el Remedio y orden que mas conuiniere para el bien general desta çiudad y que sea con breuedad pues la necessidad lo pide y rrequierre / Gaspar Gomez Basconcelos. . .

ante my, Nicolas Fernandez de la Fuente scriuano de cabildo

Document 11: 1621—Inventory of Pedro Gomez's textile mill[12]

In the name of God almighty, amen. May all who see this letter know that I, Pedro Gomez, am the legitimate son of the regent Alonso Gomez, deceased, and Catalina de Pastrana, who lives. I am a *vecino* of this city [Puebla] and native of this place and am now sick in bed. In my full judgment and capacity . . . I award this letter by which I make and order my testament. . . .

Also, I declare as my goods a fulling mill on the edge of the Atoyac River and an orchard in this city, in front of my textile mill.

* * *

Also, the main houses of my dwelling, in which a textile mill has been built and established. And within it, there is a living room and a kitchen, which the said Catalina de Pastrana, my mother, uses and she will continue to make use of it for the rest of her days.

* * *

Also, I declare as my goods the Black, mulatto, and *chino* slaves and the debts of the Indians and the other people of service, present and absent, who belong to the textile mill, which Alonso Parra, who has been the textile mill's administrator, will give information about.

---

12. Archivo Histórico Judicial de Puebla, Exp. 1235. Excerpts from ff. 1r–5r, 22r–30v.

* * *

Inventory of the goods that were left by the end and death of Pedro Gomez that we, Lazaro Gomez and Doña Maria de Alcanadre y Orozco, his executors, have made and finished as follows.

First, some houses in which the said Doña Maria de Alcanadre, widow of the said Pedro Gomez, lives, and where the textile mill is located.

Then, an orchard in front of the said houses, with a few small houses where some Indians live.

Then, one hundred and twenty Indian men and women who live in the said textile mill and owe 4,105 pesos and 6 tomines.

1. a Black man named Diego Cortes, sixty years of age, burler

2. a mulatto named Juan, wool carder, fifty years old more or less

3. another *chino* slave named Anton, shearer, forty-five years old more or less

4. another *chino* named Gonzalo, twenty years old more or less, spinner

5. another *chino* named Raimundo, twenty years old more or less, spinner

6. another mulatto named Andres, fifty-five years old more or less, burler

7. another mulatto wool carder, twenty-five years old more or less, named Andres

8. another mulatto named Geronimo Mansilla, thirty-five years old more or less, second carder

9. another *chino* named Ventura, shearer, thirty years old more or less

10. another *chino* named Josephe, shearer, twenty-four years old more or less

11. another *chino* named Hernando, weaver, twenty-four years old more or less

12. another *chino* named Alexo, weaver, twenty years old more or less

13. another *chino* named Pedro, sixteen years of age more or less, spinner

14. another *chino* named Antoñuelo, spinner, sixteen years of age more or less

15. a Black man named Juan, with a maimed foot and hand, who serves by bringing water, twenty-eight years old

16. another Black man named Maçanbique [Mozambique], fifty years old, nurse

17. another *chino* named Nicolas, twenty-eight years old, more or less, wool carder

18. another Black man named Pedro Miguel, who has a wooden foot, sixty years old more or less, cook for the Indians

19. another Black man named Luis, second carder, thirty years old more or less

20. another *chino*, washer, named Anton, thirty years old more or less

21. a Black man named Pedro, shearer, twenty-five years old more or less

22. a *china* named Gracia, who serves in the living quarters upstairs

23. a Black woman named Ana, who serves in the bedroom

... Also, a bronze pot, used for cooking for the Indians and Blacks.

[Spanish transcription]

En el Nombre de dios todo poderosso amen. Sepan quantos esta carta vieren como yo pedro gomez hijo legitimo del regidor Alonso Gomez deffunto y de Catalina de Pastrana, que oy vive, vecino desta ciudad de donde soy natural estando enfermo en cama y en mi libre juicio y entendimiento... otorgo por esta carta que hago y ordeno mi testamento... Yten declaro por mis bienes vn batan En la orilla del rio de Atoyaque y una guerta en esta ciudad ffrente de mi obraje... Yten las cassas principales
    de mi morada en que esta hecho y fundado un obraje de hacer paños y le perteneçe vna sala y coçina de que se sirve la dicha Catalina de Pastrana mi madre y lo a de gozar hasta despues de sus dias...
    ...Yten declaro por mis bienes los esclavos Negros e mulatos chinos y deudas de Yndios y demas gente de Serviçio pressentes y aussentes que pertenece a El obraxe de que tiene y dara notiçia Alonso Parra mayordomo que a sido en el.

* * *

Ynventario de los bienes que quedaron Por fin y muerte de Pedro Gomez que nos Lazaro Gomes y doña Maria de Alcanadre y Orosco, sus Albaceas Testamentarios emos echo y acabado que son los siguientes.

Primeramente unas casas en que al pressente vive la dicha doña Maria de Alcanadre viuda del dicho Pedro Gomez en que esta el obraxe.

Yten una guerta que esta frontero de las dichas casas con unas casillas en donde viven algunos indios.

Yten çiento y beinte indios e yndias que trabaxan en el dicho obraxe que deben quatro mill y çiento y çinco pesos y seis tomines

1. Yten un negro llamado Diego Cortez de edad de sesenta años despinsador
2. Yten un mulato llamado Jhoan enprimador de edad de cinquenta años poco mas o menos
3. Yten otro chino esclabo llamado Anton Tundidor de edad de quarenta y cinco años poco mas o menos
4. Yten otro chino llamado Gonzalo de edad de beinte años poco mas o menos hilador
5. Yten otro chino llamado Raimundo de edad de beinte años poco mas o menos hilador
6. Yten otro mulato llamado Andres de çinquenta y çinco años poco mas o menos despinsador
7. Yten. otro mulato enprimador de edad de beinte y çinco años poco mas o menos llamado Andres
8. Yten. otro mulato llamado Geronimo Mansilla de edad de treinta y cinco años poco mas o menos enborrador
9. Yten otro chino llamado ventura Tundidor de edad de treinta años poco mas o menos
10. Yten otro chino llamado Josephe Tundidor de edad de beinte y quatro años poco mas o menos
11. Yten otro chino llamado hernando Texedor de edad de beinte y quatro años poco mas o menos
12. Yten otro chino llamado alexo Texedor de edad de beinte años poco mas o menos
13. Yten. Otro chino llamado Pedro de edad de dies y seis años poco mas o menos hilador
14. Yten. Otro chino llamado Antoñuelo hilador de edad de dies y seis años poco mas o menos
15. Yten un negro llamado Jhoan manco de pie y mano que sirve de traer agua de beinte y ocho años
16. Yten otro negro llamado Maçanbique de edad de cinquenta años enfermero
17. Yten. otro chino llamado Nicolas de edad de beinte y ocho años poco mas o menos enprimador
18. Yten otro negro llamado Pedro Miguel que tiene un pie de palo de edad de sesenta años poco mas o menos coçinero de los indios

19. Yten otro negro llamado Luis enborrador de edad de treinta años poco mas o menos
20. Yten otro chino labandero llamado Anton de edad de treinta años poco mas o menos
21. Yten un negro llamado Pedro Tundidor de edad de beinte y cinco años poco mas o menos
22. Yten una china llamada Graçia del servicio de arriba
23. Yten otra negra llamada Ana que sirve en la Recamara.

...Yten una olla de cobre donde se guisa de comer a los indios Y negros.

Document 12: 1645—Enslaved labor and reproduction in the Fresneda textile mill[13]

May all who see this letter know that I, Augustin de Sierra Vargas, *vecino* of the village of Carrión, in the valley of Atlixco, as the executor and holder of the goods of Doña Francisca Rubo Parames, my deceased wife . . . award this lease for the La Fresneda textile mill and a fulling mill to Luis de Mesquita y Castro, owner of a textile mill and *vecino* of this city [Puebla]. They are located in the jurisdiction of the said village of Carrión, in the valley of Atlixco, and abut with the lands of Cristobal de Burgos's heirs on one side and on the other with the Doña Geronima Ynfante's lands. The included utensils, instruments, equipment, and slaves are as follows:

- the house of the textile mill and residence, and the other houses, pens, shacks, galleries, and the orchard of the said textile mill and fulling mill
- a house located behind the textile mill with its store, trough, and other rooms
- twelve [sic] slaves named Bernardo, a *chino* man, presser, forty years old = Thomas Anton, a *chino* man, dyer, thirty years old = Anton Cholula, a Black Angola man, napper, forty years old = Diego Moreno, a Black Creole man, napper, thirty years old = Domingo, fuller, a Black Angola man, fifty years old = Antonio de Morales, a Black Creole man, napper, twenty years old = Pedro de Robles, a Black Massanbique [Mozambique] man, second carder, twenty-eight years old = Juan del Castillo, a mulatto man, shearer, thirty-five years old = Juan Clemente, a mulatto man, shearer, fifty years old = Manuel, a Black Angola man, shearer, fifty-five years old = Joseph, a Black Creole man, carpenter, who belonged to Juan Lopes de Açevedo

---

13. Archivo General de Notarías del Estado de Puebla, Notaría 4, Box 170, 1645 October, Diego Cortés de Brito, ff. 451r–458r.

- Seven looms, two of them for *veinticuatreno cloths* and five of them for *dieciocheno cloths*,[14] with their combs and utensils.

    And I award this lease for the textile mill and fulling mill and all that pertains to it, along with the water for the fulling mill, and the uses, customs, rights, servitude, licenses, and grants that have been made to me, for a nine-year term that will start and be counted from the first of November of this year. It will run until this term is complete and be extended for more time, if we both agree to this, at a price of 2,200 common gold pesos for each year. The said Luis de Mesquita y Castro has paid the 1,700 pesos in cash for the first year's rent . . . and in this lease the following conditions and qualities must be observed and followed.

    i. The first express condition is that the said Luis de Mesquita is to retain 500 pesos of the rent each year to be used and destined for the upkeep and maintenance of major repairs on the textile mill, its houses, and residences in the fulling mill. . . . If after having made these major repairs as needed in the textile mill and fulling mill, there is money left from the 500 pesos, the said Luis de Mesquita will purchase a male or female slave for the said textile mill. . . .

    ii. It is a condition that if the slaves who have been named and delivered, or those to be entered into the textile mill as described in the clause above, should die (may God not allow this to happen), then I [Agustin de Sierra Vargas] will assume this risk and will lose all its value. The said Luis de Mesquita will contribute nothing to this = Moreover, if those born—either of the said mulatta who is currently in the said textile mill or of the other women slaves who might enter it—they will be exclusively of his [Mesquita's] property and dominion and I will only enjoy their use and utility during the time of the said lease = And if the said slaves were to flee, the said Luis de Mesquita is to search for them with all possible diligence at his own cost. If they do not appear, then he has no obligation to turn them in, as long as he has made a declaration to this effect and sworn to pursue the proceedings. He will not have to pay anything regarding the price [of the slaves].

    * * *

    iv. It is a condition that should the number of said slaves diminish by their death or absence, or if it should increase by births and new purchases, I [Sierra Vargas] am not obligated to provide others in their place. Nor will

---

14. Cloths in the Spanish empire were valued according to their thread count. A *dieciocheno* cloth was composed of 1,800 strings, while a *veinticuatreno* cloth was made of of 2,400 strings. See *Diccionario enciclopédico hispanoamericano de literatura, ciencias y artes*, Vol. 14, (Barcelona: Montaner y Simón Editores, 1894), 774.

I raise or lower the said rent, because in any event [Mesquita] will pay the amount of 2,200 pesos entirely and not more or less.

... on October 17, 1645, I, the notary, attest that I know the granting parties ... and the said Luis de Mesquita said that he is content with the commitments that the said Augustin de Sierra de Vargas makes for the property of his wife in this writ ...

Agustín de Sierra Vargas   Luis da Mesquita Castro

[Spanish transcription]

Sepan quantos esta carta vieren como Yo Augustin de Sierra Vargas besino de la villa de Carrion balle de Attrisco [Atlixco] como alvacea testamentario y tenedor de bienes de dona Francisca Rubio Parames, mi muger diffunta... doy en arrendamiento a Luis de Mesquita y Castro, dueño de obraje vezino de esta ciudad [de Puebla], vn obraje y batan que llaman de la Fresneda en jurisdiccion de la dicha villa de Carrion, valle de Atrisco, linde con tierras de los herederos de Cristobal de Burgos por una parte y por otra con tierras de Doña Geronima Ynfante, en que ay el avio y apero a der.te y pertrechos y sclavos siguientes

v. la Cassa de obrage y bivienda y las demas Cassas Corrales xacales galerias y huerta del dicho obrage y batan

v. una cassa a las espaldas del dicho obrage con su tienda y troxe y ottros apossentos

v. dose [sic] esclavos nombrados Bernardo chino aprenssador de quarenta años = Thomas Anton chino tintorero de edad de treinta años = Anton Cholula negro angola perchero de quarenta años = Diego Moreno negro criollo perchero de edad de treinta años = Domingo batanero negro angola de edad de cinquenta años = Antonio de Morales negro criollo perchero de edad de veinte años = Pedro de Robles negro Massanbique [Mozambique] enprimador de veinte y ocho años = Juan del Castillo mulato tundidor de edad de treinta y cinco años = Juan Clemente mulato tundidor de cinquenta años = Manuel negro Angola tundidor de cinquenta y cinco años = Jossephe negro criollo carpintero de treinta y cinco años que fue de Juan Lopes de Açebedo

v. siete telares de ancho, los dos de veinte y quatrenos y los cinco de dies y ocheno abiador Con ssus peines y lizos

... y les arriendo el dicho obrage y batan con todo lo que le pertenece de fecho y de derecho y que le sea perteneçiente y con la agua del dicho batan hussos y costumbres derechos y serbidumbre lizencias y mercedes que se me an hecho tocantes a los dichos obraje y batan para diberssos effetos por tiempo de nueve años que an de empezar a correr y contarsse desde el primero de noviembre proximo que biene de este año hasta sser cumplidos y por el demas tiempo que pareciendonos a ambos se prorrogare y en precio cada vn año de dos mill y docientos pesos de oro comun que los vn mill y setecientos pesos de los de la Renta de el primer año me a dado y pagado el dicho Luis de Mesquita y Castro en reales de contado. . . y en este arrendamiento se an de obsservar y cumplir las condiciones y calidades ssiguientes

i. lo primero es condicion expressa que los quinientos pessos que como va Refferido a de retener en si el dicho Luis de Mesquita de la renta de cada año an de ser y se destinar para el gasto y costa de los reparos mayores que a de hacer en el dicho obrage ssus cassas y de mas bivienda en el batan. . . y si hechos los Reparos maiores que fueren necessarios en el dicho obrage y batan sobrase de los dichos quinientos pesos alguna cantidad con la que fuere, a de comprar El dicho luis de mesquita un sclavo baron o hembra para el dicho obrage. . .

ii. y es condicion que ssi los sclavos que assi entrego y ban nominados o algunos dellos o de los que sse metieren en el dicho obrage procedentes del effeto que refiera la clausula precedente lo que dios no permitasse muriesen, e de correr yo el rriesgo y e de perder en el todo ssu balor sin que el dicho luis de mesquita contribuia con cosa alguna del = y por el conssiguiente los quales nacieren assi de la dicha mulata que al pressente esta en el dicho obrage como de las demas sclavas que en el entraren por la Razon Referida a de ser su propiedad y dominio y a mi y ssolamente a de gozar el hutil [sic] y husso [sic] dellos el dicho Luis de Mesquita en el tiempo del dicho arrendamiento = y si se huyeren los dichos sclavos a de ser obligado el dicho Luis de Mesquita a hacer las diligencias possibles en su busca a su costa y no pareçiendo no a de tener obligacion de entregarlos sino que a de aber cumplido con declarar para effeto las dichas diligencias jurandolo simplemente ni pagar cosa ninguna de su precio. . .

iv. Es condicion que por caussa de minorarse el numero de los dichos sclavos por muerte o aussencia o acrecentarsse por nacimientos e nuevas compras no e de tener obligacion de dar otros en su lugar ni a de crecer ni bajar la dicha rrenta porque en todo acontezimiento la a de pagar enteramente la cantidad de los dichos dos mill y dozientos pesos y no mas ni menos

. . . a dies y siete dias de el mes de otubre de mil y seiscientos quarenta y cinco años e yo el notario doy fe que conozco a los otorgantes. . . . y el dicho luis de mesquita dijo que se contenta con la obligacion que hace el dicho Augustin de Sierra de los vienes de la dicha su muger en esta scriptura . . .

Agustin de Sierra Vargas   Luis da Mesquita Castro

CHAPTER 2

The Transatlantic and Caribbean Slave Trade

The documents in this chapter address the trade in African captives from various Atlantic and Caribbean ports to Veracruz and Campeche. The chapter begins with a petition from the archbishop of Mexico to the Crown demanding the end of the transatlantic slave trade on religious grounds. In this rare and unsuccessful petition, the archbishop advanced a religious argument to expose the illegitimacy and hypocrisy of slavery. These documents indicate that, although this has scarcely been studied, the early colonists invested significantly in the trade for enslaved Africans. Overall, the case studies in this chapter span the years 1560 to 1681, well before and after the peak years of slave trading during the Iberian Union (1581–1640).

Documents 15 through 23 pertain to the first four decades of the seventeenth century, an era dominated by the vast Portuguese slaving networks that connected the ports of Lisbon (Portugal), Luanda (Angola), Cartagena de Indias (Colombia), and Veracruz and Campeche (Mexico) with inland slave markets. The trade in African captives had significant effects on the local economies of colonial Mexico, as slave traders paid pharmacists, muleteers, food vendors, and landlords for facilities and services to support this inhuman commerce. The cases from 1602, 1620, and 1630 reveal various dimensions of locals' direct and indirect participation in the slaving economy. Corruption was a consistent element in these and other slaving voyages.

The selections from 1621 and 1675 demonstrate how and why slave traders engaged in fraud when trafficking African captives. For our purposes, these practices shed light on the fate of African children and youths who were labeled *bambos, muleques, mulecas, mulequinhos*, etc.

The 1630 document included in this chapter also sheds light on the material culture that African survivors encountered on a slaving voyage that took them from the Atlantic African island of São Tomé with a final destination in the highland cities of central Mexico. This detailed ledger is quite unusual because it was produced when a Portuguese slave trader, João Nunes Franco (alias Juan Nuñez Franco), died in Mexico City, leaving his business partners and heirs to settle his debts. More importantly, the 1630 ledger allows us to understand how the African captives he transported adapted to new climates, foods, and disease environments. Tragically, many captives perished in Mexico after months of arduous travel and inhumane treatment.

The final selections in this chapter speak to a post-1640 period, when fewer enslaved Africans were taken to Mexico. Nonetheless, it is important to consider their experiences, because the transatlantic and Caribbean slave trade continued until late into the colonial period. The 1664 and 1681 slaving voyages documented in these pages provide insight into a period when English and Dutch slavers trafficked Africans to Mexico by way of Barbados, Jamaica, and Curaçao. But much more work still remains to be done on the experiences of survivors of the slaving voyages of the late seventeenth and eighteenth centuries, especially those who entered the port of Campeche.

Most of these case studies make use of troubling language, because the slaving voyages depended on profoundly dehumanizing ideas. Because African captives were considered disposable units of labor to be transported, branded, taxed, and sold, the slave traders and ship captains referred to them as *piezas*, literally pieces or units of labor. The names assigned to African survivors in these records were not their names of birth, but those conveniently imposed by European enslavers and traffickers.

Without a doubt, these are very violent documents. They should be studied and cited with a sober understanding of the harm they caused.

Document 13: 1560—Mexico's archbishop on the illegitimacy of the slave trade[1]

Sacred Catholic Royal Highness . . . in this land [of Mexico] Your Majesty has provided in a very Christian manner, through your many royal decrees, that the natural Indians of this New World who have received holy baptism should enjoy the liberty that they currently have and use. And because Your Majesty has provided and fulfilled in all these parts that the Indians who were captives be given their liberty, they are now free. Because this is no small feat, it will have Your Majesty in glory, and your fathers and grandfathers in holy memory, because they ordered and decreed it so.

Something very contrary to such a just and Catholic decree now happens in these parts with the Blacks. For shiploads from all over Guinea and Portugal's conquests arrive here, and contracts are made to buy Blacks over there and bring them here to be sold, which is a lucrative business in these parts. We do not know what cause there may be for the Blacks to be any more captive than the Indians, for, according to what is said, the former receive the Holy Gospel with goodwill. They do not war with the Christians, nor can the holy and Catholic doctors find causes for which they should be made captives. It does not seem that the wars that some Blacks have with other [Blacks] is a valid excuse, because the considerable expenses incurred in fulfilling these [slaving] contracts by going to buy them in their homelands is the reason or cause for which these wars flare up even more among them. Even the spiritual

---

1. Francisco del Paso y Troncoso, *Epistolario de Nueva España, 1505–1818* (México: Antigua Librería Robledo de J. Porrúa e Hijos, 1939–1942), tomo IX, 53–55.

and corporal benefits, there being no cause more just, that said Blacks receive in their captivity under Christians do not appear to excuse the greedy interest of these slaving voyages.

Especially because in said captivity, their salvation is often greatly damaged, since those who marry here left their natural and legitimate wives and husbands in their homelands. By taking their husbands to one land, and their first wives to another land, where they are converted and married with other spouses, or living in concubinage as they often do, the prelates are unable to remedy their situation. Their masters are also unable to remedy this and so they have their slaves in such a grave and daring state, that in lands ruled by such Christian kings and princes, who rule and govern with such Catholic and jealous zeal, this should be sentenced and condemned as evil. . . .

Therefore, this letter does not intend to define such a grave cause, rather it intends to inform Your Majesty of what is taking place and of the uncertainties that are born of this situation. These are discussed by many people of education and conscience, therefore we beg Your Majesty to let us know if there are [just] causes for the captivity of the said Blacks so that we may settle the aforementioned discrepancies. And if from this, some uncertainty were engendered by those of your Royal Council, it will please Our Lord God that these contracts and captivity for their bodies having ceased, there will be more care in bringing to them the preaching of the Holy Gospel. So that in their homelands they will be free in body and more so in spirit, by bringing them to the true knowledge of Jesus Christ.

May Our Lord God guard Your Majesty's holy person and augment your kingdoms and dominions as Christianity needs and as we, Your Majesty's vassals, desire. From Mexico, on the last day of June, 1560. I, your very loyal vassal and humble chaplain, kiss the royal feet of Your Sacred Catholic Royal Majesty.

Friar Alonso [de Montúfar], Archbishop of Mexico

[Spanish transcription]

Sacra Católica Real Majestad . . . en esta tierra Vuestra Majestad ha proveído cristianísimamente por mucha sus reales cédulas como los indios naturales deste Nuevo Mundo gocen de la libertad que gozan y usan los que están debajo del santo bautismo, y así por Vuestra Majestad está proveído y cumplido en todas estas partes que los indios que eran cautivos fuesen puestos en libertad, y así lo están, de lo cual no pequeña corona Vuestra Majestad tendrá en la gloria y vuestros padres y abuelos de santa memoria, porqué así lo ordenaron y proveyeron;

Y muy contrario a tan justa y católica provisión pasa en estas partes con los negros, y es que vienen barcadas de todas partes de Guinea y conquistas de Portugal, y se tiene por contratación comprar negros allá para traerlos a vender acá, que no es la menor granjería de estas partes. No sabemos qué causa haya para que los negros sean cautivos mas que los indios, pues ellos, según dicen, de buena voluntad reciben el Santo Evangelio, y no hacen guerra a los cristianos, ni en ellos, a lo que comúnmente se dicen, concurren causas de los que los santos y católicos doctores ponen por donde deban ser cautivos, ni parece que basta por causa las guerras que unos negros traen con otros, porque la recuesta grande que hay de esta contratación, y de irlos a comprar a sus tierras, es ocasión o causa para que las guerras más aviven entre ellos, con codicia del interés de los rescates, ni parece que excusa, no habiendo otra causa más justa, los beneficios espirituales y corporales que los dichos negros reciben en el dicho cautiverio de los cristianos,

Especialmente en el dicho cautiverio les suceden muchas veces o comúnmente muy grandes daños para su salvación, casándose acá los que dejaron vivas sus naturales y legítimas mujeres y maridos en sus tierras, y llevando a una tierra los maridos, y a otras sus primeras mujeres, do se convierte y los casan con otros, o viviendo como comúnmente viven amancebados, sin poderles dar remedio los prelados, ni aún sus amos, y los tienen en sus casas en negocio tan grave y tan general y tan osado, y en tierras de reyes y príncipes tan cristianísimos y que en todo se rigen y gobiernan con consejos de tantas y tan católicas y celosas letras, dar sentencia y condenarlo por malo . . .

Y por lo tanto, la presente no es para definir causa tan grave, mas de para hacer saber a Vuestra Majestad lo que de hecho pasa, y el escrúpulo que de ello nace y se trata en muchas personas de letras y conciencia, suplicando a Vuestra Majestad, si hay causas que el dicho cautiverio de los dichos negros excusen y permitan, nos lo mande hacer saber, para que depongamos los escrúpulos que de lo susodicho han nacido y nacen, y de ello se engendrase algún escrúpulo en los de vuestro Real Consejo y placerá a Nuestro Señor que, cesando este cautiverio y contratación como hasta aquí han ido a rescatarles los cuerpos, habrá mas cuidado de llevarles la predicación del Santo Evangelio, con que en sus tierras sean libres en sus cuerpos y más en las animas, trayéndolos al conocimiento verdadero de Jesucristo.

Nuestro Señor Dios la sacra persona de Vuestra Majestad guarde y en mayor estado de reinos y señoríos acresciente, como la Cristiandad lo ha menester, y los vasallos de Vuestra Majestad deseamos. De México, último de junio de 1560. Sacra Católica Real Majestad, besa los reales pies de Vuestra Majestad su muy leal vasallo y humilde capellán.

Fray Alonso [de Montúfar] Archiepiscopus Mexicanus

Document 14: 1561—The Crown licenses trafficking 1,000 African captives to Mexico[2]

By the present, I award license and authority to you, Hernán Vásquez of México, or to whomever holds your power of attorney, so that from your [sic] kingdoms and fiefdoms, or those of the Kingdom of Portugal, or the islands of Cape Verde, or Guinea, from wherever you may want, so that you may and will pass, to our Indies, islands, and mainland, of the Ocean Sea, one thousand Black slaves. A third of them will be females, free of the two ducat [fee] for each license, and of the almoxarifazgo tax [customs tax on goods traded by sea], and of any other rights on them that belong to us in our said Indies. We grant you said license, as you have paid us ten thousand ducats in cash, that are now in the hands of our officers of the House of Trade in the city of Seville, and have committed to pay and given sufficient ~~bond~~ security to pay another twenty thousand to our officials within the next year, all of which amounts to thirty thousand ducats at a rate of thirty ducats per slave. . . . You are not to embark in Cape Verde, or in any other part, more slaves than those you have registered. If you do embark them, they will be considered lost and may be taken from those that survive. We order the said officials who reside in the city of Seville at the House of Trade of the Indies, to take this original decree and enter it into our books on slave licenses. . . . And with respect to the said Black slaves, you, or whoever has your power of attorney, will be allowed to sell them at the price or fair prices that you may want or see fit. We have revoked the rate that we had [previously] imposed with regards to the price at which slaves were to be sold in the Indies. We order Francisco de Erasso, our secretary, and Antonio de Villegas, official of the accounts of our Council of the Indies and our accountant of the said House of Trade of Seville, to record this, my decree. Done in Madrid on September 24, 1561. I, the King. Countersigned by Erasso and marked by the said [men].

[Spanish transcription]

Por la presente doy Liçençia y facultad a vos Hernan Vazquez de mexico, o a quien vuestro poder oviere para que de sus [sic] Reinos y senorios o del Reino de portugal o yslas de cabo verde o guinea de donde quisieredes y por bien tubieres podais pasar y paseis a las nuestras yndias yslas E tierra firme, de mar oceano mill esclavos negros, la tercera parte embras libres de los dos ducados de la liçençia, de cada Uno dello y de los derechos de almoxarifazgo y de otros qualesquier derechos que dellos nos pertenezcan en las dichas nuestras yndias por quanto Nos abeis pagado en poder de los nuestros offiçiales de la cassa de la contrataçion de la çiudad de Sevilla diez mill

---

2. Archivo General de Indias, Indiferente, 425, L.24, ff. 60v–62r. http://pares.mcu.es/ParesBusquedas20/catalogo/description/260744?nm

ducados luego de contado, y os abeis obligado y dado fiança seguridad vastante de pagar otros Veinte mill a los dichos nuestros officiales dentro de un año primero siguiente que todo ello monta treinta mill ducados A Razon de a treinta ducados cada sclavo, la qual dicha liçencia a vos damos . . . y que no cargueis En cavo Verde ny en otra parte mas sclavos de los que Registraredes y que si los cargaredes sean perdidos y que se os puedan tomar de los que quedaren vibos y mandamos a los dichos offiçiales que Residen en la çiudad de sevylla en la cassa de la contratacion de las yndias que tomen en su poder esta mi çedula original y la Asienten en los nuestros libros que ellos tienen tocantes a las liçenças desclavos . . . y que los dichos negros, os los dexen vender a vos o a quienes el dicho vuestro poder obiere al preçio o preçios Justos que quisieredes y por vien tobieredes, por quanto la tasa que por Nos estava puesta çerca del Valor a que se avian de vender los negros en las yndias esta por nos Revocada y mandamos que tome la Razon desta mi çedula Francisco de Erasso nuestro secretario y Antonio de Villegas offiçial de quentas en el nuestro consejo de las yndias y El nuestro contador de la dicha cassa de la contrataçion De sevilla fecha en Madrid a Veinte y quatro de setiembre de mill E quinyentos y sesenta E vn años yo el Rey. Refrendada de Erasso y señalada de los dichos.

Document 15: 1602—Pharmacists, slave traders, and debts[3]

In the city [Puebla] of the Angels on October 24, 1602, the licenciado Francisco Sanchez, apothecary, *vecino* of the city, appeared before Pedro de Anzures, municipal judge in this city. The former said: I gave the medicines contained in this document, that I present, for the slave ship of Black *bozales* that Juan Nuñez Bohorquez brought from Cartagena [de Indias]. Bohorquez left this city for Mexico City and sent instructions to Alonço de Ribilla, in whose house he had stayed and with whom he left the power of attorney for his debts, so that the latter would pay me for said medicines. In the interim, he [Nuñez Bohorquez] died and I have not received payment for the medicines.

I ask and beg Your Grace to order Alonço de Ribilla summoned, so that he may declare under oath if what I have stated in this petition is true. And if it is, I ask Your Grace to order that the said medicines be priced, so that by their value I may be authorized to receive payment for the medicines from any of Nuñez Bohorquez's goods held [by Rebilla].

Francisco Sanchez

---

3. Archivo Histórico Judicial de Puebla, Exp. 550, f. 1r–1v.

... [Alonso de Rebilla] said it is true. He knows and saw that by order of Juan Nuñez Bohorquez, the said Francisco Sanchez gave the medicines, from his drugstore, that were needed to cure the said Juan Nuñez and his Blacks, as they were ill in this deponent's house. Having left for Mexico [City] without paying for said medicines, Juan Nuñez wrote this deponent a letter that said Francisco Sanchez was to be paid from the first debts to be collected. Alonso de Ribilla did not pay Sanchez because he had nothing from which to pay him. In the meantime, the said Juan Nuñez Bohorquez died in Mexico [City]. Rebilla knows that he has not paid the said Francisco Sanchez for his medicines and this is the truth under oath.

Alonso Rebilla　　　　　　　　before me, Baltazar de Montoya, public scribe

[Spanish transcription]

En la ciudad de [Puebla] de los Angeles En veinte y quatro dias del mes de octubre de myll y seiscientos e dos años ante Pedro de Anzures alcalde hordinario en esta ciudad la presento El licenciado Francisco Sanchez, boticario vezino desta Çiudad, digo quee yo di las mediçinas contenidas en esta memoria que presento para la armazon de negros bosales que traxo de Cartajena [de Indias] Joan Nuñes Bohorquez el qual se fue desta çiudad a la de Mexico y enbio horden Alonço de Ribilla en cuya Casa pozava y aquien Dexo poder para sus cobransas para que me pagase las Dichas mediçinas y en este interin murio y no se me ha pagado las dichas mediçinas

A vuestra merced pido y suplico mande pareser ante si a dicho Alonço de Ribilla y que con juramento declare si es berdad lo contenido en esta mi petiçion y siendolo mande tasar las dichas mediçinas y por su balor me de mandamyento para que de qualesquier vienes que aya Del dicho Joan Nuñes Bohorquez se me paguen las dichas mediçinas y pido justiçia e Juro en forma de derecho que me son devidos y por pagar

　　　　　　　　　　　　　　　　　　　　　　　Francisco Sanchez

... [Alonso de Rebilla] dixo que es verdad y save y bio que por mandamiento de Juan Nuñez Boorquez El dicho Francisco Sanchez dio de su botica las medizinas que fueron menester para curarse el dicho Juan Nuñes y los negros que tubo Enfermos En casa deste declarante y aviendose hido a Mexico sin pagar las dichas medecinas escrivio una carta a este declarante En que le decia que pagase al dicho Fran.co Sanchez las dichas medeçinas de lo primero que cobrase y no se las pago por no tener de que y en esto se murio El dicho Juan Nuñes Boorquez En Mexico y save que no se le an pagado al dicho Francisco Sanchez las dichas medizinas y esta es la verdad so cargo del dicho Juramento

Alonso Rebylla　　　　　　　ante my Baltazar de Montoya scrivano publico

Document 16: 1615—Bill of purchase for twenty-one Arara captives[4]

May all who see this letter know that I, Manuel Gonzalez, *vecino* of this city [Puebla] of the Angels, state that I truly sell to Joseph Ortiz de Aviles, merchant of this city, twenty-one pieces of slaves, eighteen of them Black men and three of them Black women. They are named Antonio, captain, fifty years old; Francisco, forty years old; another Francisco of the same age; Felipe thirty years old; Juan of the same age; Antonio twenty-five years old; Juan forty years old; Gabriel, captain, thirty years old; Antonio of the same age; Francisco twenty-five years old; Lorenzo forty years old; Francisco of the same age; Antonio thirty-five years old; Francisco of the same age; Big Francisco forty years old; Bartolome of the same age; Diego twenty-eight years old; Antonio thirty years old; Ana twenty years old; Maria eighteen years old; Catalina twenty years old. [A]ll of them are from Arara land and are on the account of Captain Jusepe Urtado [Joseph Hurtado], as captive slaves, free of any lien, mortgage, or any other special or general claim. Two of them have a cloud in their eye. [I sell them] as *bozales* recently brought from their land, with no guarantees that they are [not] thieves, drunkards, or runaways, nor [do I guarantee that they are free of] other flaws, defects, or public or secret diseases. [I sell them] for the price and sum of 7,770 pesos of common gold, that amounts to 370 pesos for each. Of this sum, [Hurtado] has given and paid me 2,000 pesos in reales, in cash, which I declare I have received . . . in the city [Puebla] of the Angels on September 7, 1615. The awarding parties, whom I, the scribe, know, signed the letter, witnesses Alonso Ramiro and Alonso Corona and Sebastian Rodrigues, *vecinos* of this city. . . .

Manuel González   Joseph Ortiz Áviles   before me, Gabriel de Anzures, public scribe

[Spanish transcription]

Sepan quantos esta carta vieren como Yo, Manuel gonzales, becino desta ciudad de los angeles, otorgo que vendo rrealmente a Joseph Ortiz de Aviles mercader, beçino de ella, beynte y una Piesas Desclabos diez y ocho negros, Y tres negras llamados antonio capitan de hedad, de cinquenta años, Francisco de quarenta años, otro Francisco de la mesma hedad, Felipe treinta años, Juan de la misma hedad, Antonio de beynte y cinco años, Juan de quarenta años, Grabiel [sic] capitan de treynta años, Antonio de la misma hedad, Franiscco de beynte y cinco años, Lorenso de quarenta años, Franisco de la misma hedad, Antonio de treynta y cinco años, Francisco de la misma hedad, Francisco grande de quarenta años, Bartolome de La misma hedad, Diego de beynte y ocho años, Antonio de treynta años, ana de beynte años, Maria de diez y ocho

---

4. Archivo General de Notarías del Estado de Puebla, Notaría 4, Box 78, 1615 November, no folio.

años, Catalina de beynte años todos de tierra arara y de quenta del capitan Jusepe Urtado [Joseph Hurtado] por esclabos cautibos libres de [e]npeño ypoteca y otra enagenaçion espeçial ni general y sin asegurarlos de ladrones vorrachos ni huydores ni de otras tachas defectos ni enfermedades publicas ni secretas y por bosales rreçien traydos de su tierra y los dos dellos tienen una nube en vn ojo; y en preçio y contia de çiete mill y seteçientos y setenta pesos de oro comun que a treçientos y setenta pesos cada uno montan la cantidad de los quales me a dado y pagado los dos mill pesos de ellos en rreales de contado de los quales me doy por entregado . . . que es fecha la carta en la çiudad de los angeles en siete dias del mes de nobiembre de mill y seyscientos y quinze años y los otorgantes que yo el scrivano conosco Lo firmaron testigos Alonso Ramiro y Alonso Corona y Sebastian Rodrigues becinos de esta ciudad . . .

Manuel Gonçales   Joseph Ortiz Aviles   ante my, Gabriel de
                                                          Anzures, escrivano publico

Document 17: 1620—A slave trader's petition to the Puebla municipal council[5]

In the very noble and very loyal city [Puebla] of the Angels of New Spain, on August 1, 1620, the said city entered its municipal council and city hall as is customary. It is convenient to know [that the members of the council are] Don Felipe Ramírez de Arellano, president of the council in place of Don Alonso Tello de Guzmán, who serves [in this role] for the King Our Lord; Lope de la Carreta, royal standard-bearer; and Juan Antonio de Aguilar, Francisco Sánchez de Guevara, and Don Juan Gómez Vasconcelos, regents, in the presence of me, Nicolás Fernández de la Fuente, scribe of the King Our Lord and of said municipal council, in which the following things took place and were agreed upon. . . .

This day a petition was presented and read in the said council, it says as follows = Manuel González, *vecino* of this city and commissioned agent of the slave ships that come to this city. I say that as is well-known, from year to year I give Your Majesty a great amount of pesos from the sales tax and sales of the said slaves. During the rainy season, I take the Blacks out to the public plaza of this city to sell them. When it rains, they retreat to the [covered spaces under] the portals and the *vecinos* throw them out and mistreat them, inhumanely beating the slaves with sticks, because they don't want them to stay under the portals as is customary. To avoid this affront = I ask and beg Your Grace to remedy this by ordering that the said *vecinos* not bother or perturb the said Blacks with ill treatment when the latter retreat and seek shelter under the

---

5. Archivo Municipal de Puebla, Actas de Cabildo, Vol. 16, ff. 2–3.

said portals, because it is for the common good and particularly in His Majesty's interest, if I am privileged to receive this [request] and a large penalty is imposed so that this be observed. I ask for justice and for whatever is necessary.

Manuel González

And [this petition] being seen by the city, it was agreed that as long as they leave the streets and walkways clear, the Blacks may not be impeded from seeking shelter, nor may they be mistreated by anyone. And with this the council came to an end and the city signed [the proceedings].

Don Felipe Ramírez de Arellano	Lope de la Carreta
Juan Antonio de Aguilar	Francisco Sánchez de Guevara
Juan Gómez Vasconcelos	Nicolas Fernández de la Fuente, council scribe

[Spanish transcription]

En La Muy Noble Y Muy Leal Çiudad de los Angeles de la nueva españa a primero dia del mes de Agosto de mill y siesçientos y veinte años la dicha çiudad entro en su cabildo y ayuntamiento como lo tiene de costumbre, conviene a saber Don Phelipe Ramirez de Arellano theniente de alcalde mayor por el señor Don Alonso Tello de Guzman que lo es por el Rey nuestro señor. Lope de la Carreta alferez mayor, Juan Antonio de Aguilar, Franiscco Sanchez de Guevara y Don Juan Gomez Vasconçellos regidores por pressençia de mi Nicolas Fernandez de la Fuente, escrivano del Rey nuestro señor y del dicho cabildo en el qual passo y se acordo lo siguiente . . .

 Este dia se presento y leyo en el dicho cabildo una petiçion que dize assi = Manuel Gonçalez vezino desta çiudad y encomendero de las armazones de negros que vienen a esta çiudad. Digo que como es notorio Yo doy a su Mag[esta]d entre año mucha cantidad de pesos procedidos de las alcavalas y ventas de los dichos esclavos y es ansi que a causa de fazer el tiempo de lluvias los negros que saco a vender a la plaça publica desta çiudad, cuando llueve se recogen en los portales della y los vezinos los echan y maltratan dandoles de palos todo con ynhumanidad y no quieren dejarlos estar en los dichos portales siendo como es comun y general. Y para eviar (sic) este agravio = a Vuestra señoria pido y suplico provea de remedio Mandando que los dichos vezinos no ynquieten ni perturben con malos tratamientos a los dichos negros cuando se quieran recoger y alvergar en los dichos portales pues es bien comun y particularmente por el ynteres que se le sigue a su Magestad que en ello resçebire bien y merced y se les ponga una gran pena para que lo cumplan e pido justiçia y en lo necessario.

Manuel Gonçalez =

E por la çiudad vista acordo que con que dexen las calles y passajes libres no se les ympida la guarida por ninguna persona ni hagan maltratamiento a los negros y con esto se acabo del cabildo y la dicha çiudad lo firmo =

Don Phelipe Ramirez de Arellano	Lope de la Carreta
Juan Antonio de Aguilar	Francisco Sanchez de Guevara
Juan Gomez Basconselloz	Nicolas Fernandez de la Fuente escribano de cabildo

Document 18: 1621—Illicit arrival of slave ships on the Isla de Cabezas[6]

In the city of Nueva Veracruz, on February 22, 1621, the licenciado Pedro de Vergara Gaviria, of His Majesty's Council and civil court judge in the Royal Audience of New Spain, visiting judge of the royal officials of this city and other ministers. I say that in addition to the slave ship captains who have been admitted without any registry or clearance from Seville's House of Trade . . . it has been recognized that Julián de Santa Clara brought two slave coffles in two ships in two ships [sic], with which he entered this port. First, he disembarked a number of slaves on the Isla de Cabezas, as was made public in all this city, so that the royal officials could not overlook it. The city was placed on guard, because having seen the said ships putting people on the island, they [the residents of Veracruz] understood these to be enemies, until the said ships came in [to the port]. Instead of investigating and punishing such a public affair and one that caused such commotion, not only did [the royal officials] not do so, but they secured safe passage for the rest, as ninety slaves had been left on the said island, and concealed other slaves, who entered the port as *bambos* and *muleques*. Therefore, [Don Pedro de Vergara Gaviria] ordered and formally charged that if anyone has something specific to say, allege, or prove with regards to this matter, that they do so during the amount of time that has been conceded, otherwise this matter will be definitively closed. And thus it was decreed and signed by the attorney Pedro de Vergara Gavira, before me, Martin de Soria, scribe.

[Spanish transcription]

En la nueba çiudad de la Veracruz a Veinte y dos dias del mes de Hebrero De mill y seisçientos y Veinte y un años el señor licenciado Pedro de Vergara Gaviria del Consejo de su Majestad y su oydor de la Real audiençia desta nueba españa Juez

---

6. Archivo General de Indias, México, 74, R.2, N.30, "Sobre la visita de los oficiales Reales de la Veracruz y cosas tocantes a ella," no folio, IMG 48.

Visitador de los offiçiales Reales desta dicha çiudad y otros ministros della. Dixo que por quanto a demas de los Armadores de negros que an admitido sin registro ni despacho de la cassa de la contratacion de Sevilla . . . A constado despues aver Admitido Dos armazones que traxo Julian de Santa Clara Por El año pasado de Seisçientos y diez y nuebe en dos navios en dos navios [sic] con que entro en este puerto Haviendo desenbarcado primero cantidad de esclavos en la ysla de las cabeças [Isla de las Cabezas] Como fue Publico en toda esta ciudad de Manera que los dichos Offiçiales Reales no lo pudieron ignorar, la qual estubo puesta En Arma porque aviendo visto los dichos navios que estavan echando Gente en la dicha ysla, entendieron eran de enemigos Hasta que entraron los dichos navios, Y en lugar de aberiguar y castigar cossa que fue tan publica y que Causo tanto alboroto, no solo no lo Hiçieron Antes el buen pasaxe que a los demas Aviendo dexado noventa esclavos en la dicha Ysla Y disimulando con otros que pasaron a titulo de bambos y muleques, de lo qual le Haçia y Hizo cargo en forma y mando Dar traslado Para que si tienen alguna Cossa particular que dezir, alegar, o probar lo Hagan en El termino de prueba que les esta Conçedido con cargo que passado quede conclussa esta Caussa diffinitibamente, Y assi lo probeyó y firmo el licenciado Pedro de vegara Gaviria, Ante mi Martin de Soria, scribano.

Document 19: 1621—Fraudulent officials in the slave trade[7]

9. He [Iñigo López de Salcedo] is charged on account of having forced and compelled the slave ship captains who come to this port [Nueva Veracruz] to stay in the house of the slaving agents and their friends in order to benefit the latter in this city, as in Puebla and Mexico City. And because a careful investigation has been carried out into Francisco Gómez Texoso and Luis Fernández Tristán, not only in this city but also by writing to Angola, Brazil, and Jamaica, it is known that the said slave ship captains in those places are told to go to the house of the said Texoso in this city or to the house of the said Tristan in Mexico City if they want to do good business. He has done this to know what the said slave ship captains were supposed to give in return, because the said Luis Fernández Tristán has gifted [López de Salcedo] things from China and Mexico, and a gilded silver dish and ewer. Manuel González, *vecino* of Puebla, [has gifted him] two chains, one made of gold, that was worth four hundred pesos and another one of gold, and a pomander. [López de Salcedo] did this with such rigor and forcefulness that he did not allow the slave ship captains the freedom to take their Blacks wherever they wanted and were most comfortable, but [made them go] to the places he ordered.

---

7. Archivo General de Indias, México, 74, R.2, N.30, "Sobre la visita de los oficiales Reales de la Veracruz y cosas tocantes a ella," no folio, IMG 25–26.

* * *

11. In the city of Nueva Veracruz, on January 22, 1621, the licenciado Pedro de Vergara Gaviria of His Majesty's Council . . . said that aside from the sums of money that the accountant Yñigo Lopez de Salçedo has received from slave ship captains, he was not charged the 2,300 pesos that he received and was given by Francisco Cartagena de Fuentes, *vecino* of Jamaica, who came to this port the past year of 1612 with the slave ship of Captain Fernando de Vargas, his son-in-law. [López de Salcedo] received half of the rights to the slaves who were concealed and were not counted, but divided between him, his partner, and the said Francisco Cartagena. So that the accused may respond to this charge and the rest, [Vergara Gaviria] makes this official denunciation, and orders it decreed, so that it may be proved along with the other charges during the amount of time that has been conceded, otherwise this matter will be definitively closed. And thus it was decreed and signed by the attorney Pedro de Vergara Gavira, before me, Martín de Soria, scribe.

[Spanish transcription]

9. Yten se le Haçe cargo que a obligado y conpellido a los armadores de negros que an venido a este puerto que los lleben a posar Assi en esta çiudad como en la de la Puebla y Mexico, a las cassas de los encomenderos [de negros] y persona Amigos suyos por darles por darles aprovechamientos y Por El que se le a seguido a El y en particular a hecho apretada Diligençia por Francisco Gomez Texoso y Luis Fernandez Tristan, no contentandose con hazerla en esta ciudad, sino escriviendo a Angola Brasil y Jamaica. Para que desde alli viniesen encaminados los dichos armadores si querian negociar bien a casa del dicho Texosso en esta ciudad y a la del dicho Tristan en la de Mexico lo qual a hecho asimismo Porque corriese por su mano lo que avian de dar los dichos armadores, y Porque el dicho Luis Fernandez Tristan le a regalado con cosas de China y Mexico y con una fuente y aguamanil de plata dorada y Manuel Gonzalez vesino de la Puebla con dos cadenas una de oro que valia quatroçientos pesos y otra de oro y pomas de olor. Haziendo los susodichos con tanto inperio y rigor que no dexava libertad a los dichos armadores para llevar sus negros a donde querian y les hazian mayor comodidad sino a donde el le Hordenaba.

* * *

11. En la nueva ciudad de la Veracruz a veinte y dos dias del mes de Hen.o de mill y Seiscientos y veinte y un años el señor Licenciado Pedro de Vergara Gaviria del consejo de su Majestad . . . Dixo que ademas de las cantidades que El contador Yñigo Lopez de Salçedo a Reçevido de Armadores de negros, se le dexo de Hazer cargo de Dos mill y trezientos pesos que Reçivio y le dio Francisco Cartagena de Fuentes vesino de Xamaica que vino a este puerto Por el año passado de mill y seiscientos y

doze con Armazon de negros del capitan Fernando de Vargas, su yerno, Por lo que le cupo de la mitad de los derechos de los esclavos que se ocultaron y dexaron de contar que se partieron Entre el y su conpañero y El dicho francisco Cartagena y Para que Responda a este cargo con los demas, Se le Haçe en forma, Y manda dar treslado y que corra en el La prueba como con los demas con el mismo cargo de que pasado quede esta caussa conclussa diffinitibamente Y asi lo probeyo Y firmo el licenciado Pedro de Vergara Garviria, ante mi scrivano Martin de soria.

Document 20: 1621—The royal slaves of the San Juan de Ulúa fortress[8]

Account of the slaves that His Majesty holds on account of the *avería* tax [tax to cover armed protection for merchant shipping], in the fortress of the port of San de Ulúa, and their occupations

There are seven Black men on the ordinary rowboat	7
When another rowboat is assembled to bring stone, wood, and other things for the fortress and to relieve the sick, there are eight [slaves] who are called *extravagantes* [for various undefined jobs]	8
There are six slaves, three of them male, in service of the fortress commander, who is in charge of all of the slaves of the said fortress	6
in the receptor's service by title, one Black man and one Black woman	2
in the service of the lead sergeant of the said fortress, another two [slaves], by decree	2
in the service of the fortress's ensign, a 9-year-old boy, by no decree	1
in the service of the sergeant, another [slave], seven years old, by no decree	1
in the service of the vicar, a Black man, by no decree	1
in the service of the overseer, two [slaves] by decree	2
in the service of the master stonemason, a Black woman and two slaves that he is decreed to have by his title	1
four Black men assist in the carpentry	4

---

8. Archivo General de Indias, México, 74, R.2, N.30.

in the ironworks, one [slave]	1
in the butcher shop, one [slave]	1
in the ordinary construction there is another [slave] who works on whatever has to be done	1
To bring the guard in, there is a drummer and an assistant	2
Two Black women serve in the Royal Hospital, on account of several others, who are ordered to be there by decree	2
in the galley, where all the slaves live in said fortress, four Black women do the work of cooking for them and cleaning their clothes	4
there are four children in their mothers' charge, two males, one a year and a half old and the other five years old, and two females, one a year and a half old and the other four years old	4
Besides these, there are thirteen other slaves, nine males and four females, all old and not of any particular service, and among these, there is the overseer of them all, and two who often serve as skippers of the second rowboat and another who works the bellows in the ironworks	13
Thus there are, in all, sixty-three slaves, thirty-one of them male, thirteen females in [domestic] service, four Black boys and two Black girls of young age, and nine Black men and four Black women, all of them old and not of any particular service	63

I, Matheo de Salas, treasurer, judge, official of the Royal Treasury of this city, and as the consignee of the *avería* tax, give this account . . . that has been given to me by the administrator of the said fortress, according to what has been decreed and ordered, on December 5 of last year, 1620, by Lord Licenciado Pedro de Vergara Gaviria, of His Majesty's Council, civil court judge of the Royal Audience of this New Spain, visiting inspector of the royal official of this city and other ministries. I was notified of this account on the first of the present month. [Signed] on February 4, 1621. Mateo de Salas . . .

Corrected with the original to which I refer.

Martín de Soria

[Spanish transcription]

Relacion de los esclavos que Por quenta del haveria tiene su magestad en la fuerça del puerto de San Juan de Vlua y de lo que se ocupan

En la chalupa ordinaria del pasaje Andan siete negros	7
Para quando se arma otra chalupa que sirve de traer piedra, madera, y otras cosas para la fuerça y para rremudo de los enfermos Ay ocho que llaman estravagantes	8
en Serviçio del castellano como A cuya orden estan todos los esclavos de la dicha fuerça ay seis, los tres barones	6
en el del rreçeptor, un negro y una negra, por su titulo	2
en el del Sargento mayor de la dicha fuerça otros dos por mandamiento el vno baron	2
en el del alferez de la dicha fuerça un muchacho de 9 años, sin mandamiento	1
en el del Sargento otro de siete años sin mandamiento	1
en el del Vicario un negro sin mandamiento	1
en el del mayordomo dos por mandamiento	2
en el del maestro mayor de canteria, una negra y dos esclavos que por su titulo se le mandan dar	1
en la carpinteria asisten quatro negros	4
en la Herreria uno	1
en la carneçeria otro	1
en las obras ordinarias sirve otro en lo que se la manda	1
Para meter la Guarda ay un atambor y un ayudante	2
en el ospital Real asisten dos negras por quenta de mas numero que por mandamiento le esta mandadado dar	2
en la Galera donde estan todos los esclavos que ay en la dicha fuerça asisten quatro negras a guisarles la comida y labarles la rropa	4
en poder de sus madres ay quatro niños los dos varones, el uno de año y medio y el otro de çinco, y las dos hembras, una de año y medio y otra de quatro	4

Demas de los quales ay ottros treze esclavos, nueve varones y quatro
hembras, todos viejos de ningun Serviçio, y en ellos se yncluyen el
mandador de todos y dos que suelen servir el uno de arraez de la
segunda chalupa y el ottro de Sonar los fuelles en la Herreria   13

Por manera que son Todos sesenta y tres esclavos, Treynta y un barones,
y treze hembras de servizio, quattro negritos y dos negritas de poca hedad,
y nueve negros y quatro negras todos viejos y de ningun serviçio   63

La qual dicha Relacion doy yo Matheo de Salas, thessorero Juez, oficial de la Real Hazienda de esta çiudad como Reçeptor que soy de la Averia . . . que me a dado el mayordomo de la dicha fuerça en cumplimiento de lo proveydo y mandado por autto del Señor Licenciado Pedro de Vergara Gaviria del consejo de su majestad, oydor de la Real audiençia de esta nueva españa, Juez Vissitador de los offiçiales Reales de esta çiudad y otros ministros, de cinco de diziembre del Año passado de mill y seisçcientos y veinte que se me notifico en Primero deste presente mes a quatro de febrero de mill y seisçiento y Veynte y un años. Mateo de Salas . . .

Corregida con El original a que me Remito.

Martin de Soria

Document 21: 1624—The slave trade from Santo Domingo to Campeche[9]

May all who see this debt contract know that by this letter I, Captain Andrés Muñoz, *vecino* of the city of Seville and currently a resident of the city and port of San Francisco de Campeche in Yucatán, grant and recognize that I owe and will truly give and pay to Captain Juan Ortuño de Olano, His Majesty's regent and military major in this village, 6,825 common gold pesos, each worth eight reales of good coin. I owe these pesos, among other amounts, because, to favor and assist me, he has lent me reales in cash to pay the transportation costs that I owed from the slave coffle that I brought to this port from the city of Santo Domingo on the ship *San Antonio*, captained by Lorenzo de Noli. [I also received this money] to pay other debts that I owed to other people. As such, I recognize that I have willingly received the said 6,825 pesos. . . . I promise and commit to pay [this debt] in full during the month of February next, 1625, to be paid in reales in cash in this village or anywhere else . . .

---

9. Archivo General de Notarías del Estado de Puebla, Notaría 4, Box 124, Alonso Corona, 1625 Marzo, ff. 555r–557r.

and to secure this debt contract and avoid invalidating it, I especially and expressly pawn and mortgage twenty-five pieces of slaves, males and females from the land of Angola, that are as follows = Miguel = Pedro = Antonio = Manuel = Andrés = Pedro = Amado = Gonzalo = Manuel = Bastian = Pedro = Bartolome = Gregorio = Juan = Miguel = Francisco = Marcos = María = Magdalena = Francisca = Blanca = Antona = Mariana = Catalina = Mari. The said twenty-five pieces of slaves I gave and delivered to you before the public scribe, who is present. And I, the scribe, attest that the said Captain Andrés Muñoz did [turn them over] to the said Captain Juan Ortuño de Olano, in my presence and before the witnesses to this debt contract.

And I, Captain Andrés Muñoz, transfer my authority and possession of the said slaves for the amount of money I owe said captain Juan Ortuño de Olano, so that he may sell them to any people at the prices he might secure in cash or on credit . . . he may do this, of course, before the term of this debt contract [expires], and should the said slaves not be enough to satisfy this debt . . . I am obligated to pay [the remainder] with my personal property. . . . This letter was written in the village and port of Campeche in Yucatán on August 31, 1624. I, the scribe, attest that I know the awarding party, who signed his name, with Jerónimo Osorio, Francisco de Gama, and Diego Hidalgo, *vecinos* and residents of this village, as witnesses.

Andrés Muñoz passed before me, Juan Martín Blanco, public scribe, copied from the original debt contract and mortgage, to which I refer. I signed in testimony of the truth. Juan Blanco, public scribe.

[Spanish transcription]

Sepan quantos esta carta de obligacion enpeño e ypoteco especial bieren como yo el Capitan Andres Muños vecino de la ciudad de Sevilla y residente a el presente en esta ciudad y puerto de San Francisco de Campeche de Yucatan otorgo e conozco por esta presente carta que debo y me obligo de dar y pagar y que dare y pagare rrealmente y con efeto a el Capitan Juan Ortuño de Olano regidor y sargento mayor por su magestad en esta villa conviente a saver seys mill y ochocientos y beynte y cinco pesos de oro comun de a ocho rreales, cada un peso de buena moneda, los quales le debo por otros tantos que por me hacer placer y buena obra me presto en rreales de contado para pagarlos fletes que vine debiendo de la armaçon de negros que truxe a este puerto desde de la çiudad de Santo Domingo en la barca San Antonio, maestre Lorenço de Noli y para pagar otras deudas que asimismo bine deviendo a otras personas de los quales dichos seis mil y ochocientos y veinte y cinco pesos me doy por contento y entregado a toda mi voluntad . . . prometo y me obligo de pagar en todo el mes de febrero del año que vendra de mill y seiscientos y veinte y çinco años pagados en rreales de contado en esta dicha villa o en otra qualquiera parte . . . e para mas seguridad, no viciando a esta obligaçion, vos doy en empeño y prendas por expecial y expresa ypoteca deuda veinte y sinco pieças de esclabos varones y henbras de tierra angola que son los siguientes = Miguel = Pedro = Antonio = Manuel = Andres = Pedro = Amado = Gonçalo = Manuel = Bastian = Pedro = Bartolome = Gregorio = Juan = Miguel = Francisco = Marcos = Maria = Magdalena = Francisca = Blanca = Antona = Mariana = Catalina = Mari, las quales dichas veynte y çinco piecas de esclavos vos di y entregue en presencia del pressente escrivano publico de cuyo entrego doy fee y yo el presente escrivano lo hisso el dicho capitan Andres Muños a el dicho capitan Juan Ortuno de Olando y en mi presencia de los testigos de la carta

e yo el dicho capitan Andres Muños transfiero el señorio y posession que tengo a los dichos esclavos para en quanto a esta cantidad que debo a el dicho capitan Juan Ortuño de Olano desde luego los pueda yr vendiendo a qualesquier personas por los precios que pudiere de contado o de fiado . . . lo qual pueda haçcer desde luego antes de cumplirse el dicho plaço . . . y en caso que los dichos esclavos no alcancen pagar esta deuda . . . me obligo a pagar con mi persona y bienes . . . fecha la carta en la villa y puerto de Canpeche de Yucatan en treinta y un dias del mes de agosto de mill seiscientos y veinte y cuatro años y el otorgante que yo el escrivano doy fee que conosco lo firmo de su nombre siendo testigos Jeronimo Osorio, Francisco de Gama y Diego Hidalgo, veçinos y residentes en esta villa.

Andres Muños paso ante mi Juan Martin Blanco, escrivano publico, sacado de la obligacion ypoteco original que me remito y lo signe en testimonio de la verdad. Juan Blanco escrivano publico

Document 22: 1630—A Portuguese slave trader's ledger[10]

Finalized sales of the pieces belonging to Juan Martínez, who is to receive the liquidity of these transactions

a Black man for 360	360 p
another for 370	370 p
another for 350	350 p
another for 315	315 p
another for 210	210 p
	1 605 pesos

---

10. Archivo General de la Nación, Inquisición, Vol. 279, Exp. 17, ff. 381r–381v, 383r–383v, 491r–513r.

Expenses for said pieces

For the taxes of Castile at 62 pesos 3 tomines, amounts to	311 p 7 t
For provisions from São Tomé to Jamaica	
For transportation fees, the cost of maintaining the slaves, and registry at 12 120 [reis], amounts to 176 pesos 7 tomines	176 p 7 t
For the provisions eaten in Jamaica by sea and land at 1 080 reis	16 p 7 t
For the customs barque, the slaving agent's warehouse, visit, and medic, at 9 and a half reales each	6 p
For food, up until they left for Mexico [City]	10 p
For five dresses	15 p
For expenses on the road until arrival in Mexico [City] at four pesos and two tomines, amounts to	21 p 2 t
For expenses in Mexico [City], until they were sold	51 p 5 t
For mule transportation at 4 pesos per piece	20 p
For the entry and visit 4 pesos	4 p
For blankets and petate mats	8 p
For documents two and half pesos	2 p 4
For brokerage fees 8 pesos 2 tomines	8 p 2
For sales tax at 2 per cent	33 p
For encomienda fees at 2 and a half percent	41 p 2
For pharmacy and medic	30 p
In addition to these 756 pesos 4 tomines, there remain the amounts owed to Juan Martinez of the deceased's goods after adding the pieces on his account, according to other external pieces whose costs I found the deceased had registered in his book—848 pesos 4 tomines	756 p 4 848 p 4 1 605 p

* * *

1630

Expenses for the 80 pieces that on May 18
I sent to Joao Fernandez Vergara [Juan Fernández de Vergara] in the Pobla [Puebla]

what I gave to the muleteer to spend on the road	100 p
four biscuit loads with 7 quarts at 5 pesos 2 tomines per hundredweight	36 p 6 t
for transportation fees at 3 pesos 6 reales for each Black, as far as Puebla	200 p
for expenses when they were in Puebla until [departure] for Mexico	p [sic, blank]
for the pieces that were sent to Mexico on June 15 to Sebastiao Vas [Sebastián Vaz de Acevedo]	<u>70</u>
for the muleteer to spend on the road with said pieces	100 p
for twenty ____ *arrobas* of biscuit, at 5 pesos 2 tomines each hundredweight	31 p 4 4
for 10 *arrobas* of dried meat at 12 reales per *arroba*	15 p
what I gave Balthasar Lourenço that he also spent on the road	12 p
for the transportation fees of each Black at 4 reales 4 tomines	315 p
what was spent in Mexico [City] until they were sold	p [sic, blank]
of the 34 pieces that I sent on July 10 that went from Puebla to Mexico [City]	
what Joao Fernandez Vergara [Juan Fernández de Vergara] gave to spend on the road	20 p
for three hundredweights of biscuit at 4 pesos each hundredweight	12 p
for transportation fees for each Black at 12 reales and for the provision mule that brought the biscuits at 3 pesos each	53 p 4 t

* * *

Account of the expenses that I have had for the pieces that were left after the death of Captain João Nuñes [Franco] . . .

Item. On October 14, for the burial of the Black woman who died	7 pesos
Item. A blanket for a sick Black girl	1 peso
What was paid to find a little Black boy who escaped	4 pesos

What I gave to Mendoza, the surgeon, for the treatment of a Black man belonging to João Nuñes	10 pesos
Item. On November 6, I paid 7 pesos for the burial of a little Black boy, who was part of the company and is inventoried. He died of measles on the said day. João Bautista attested to this	7 pesos
Item. On the said 6th [of November], I gave 104 pesos to Bernardo who departed to become a friar in Guadalajara	104 pesos

[Spanish and Portuguese transcription]

Ventas que se hallan bendidas de las piezas de Juan Martinez a quien se ha de hazer bueno lo liquido de Ellas

un negro en 360	360 p
otro en 370	370 p
otro en 350	350 p
otro en 315	315 p
otro en 210	210 p
	<u>1 605 pesos</u>

Gastos de dichas piezas

Por derechos de Castilla a 62 pesos 3 tomines, montan	311 p 7 t
de bastimento de San Thome hasta Xamayca [Jamaica] de flete pipa y caldera y registro a 12 120 [Reis], monta 176 pesos 7 tomines	176 p 7 t
de bastimento que comieron en xamayca [Jamaica] por tierra y mar a 1 080 Reys son 16 pesos 7	16 p 7 t
barca de Contaduria, bodega de Encomendero, bisita y medico a 9 Reales y media cada una	6 p
De comida hasta que fueron a mexico 10 pesos	10 p
de sinco bestidos 15 pesos	15 p
de gasto en el camino hasta llegar a mexico a quatro pesos y dos tomines monta	21 p 2 t
De gasto en mexico hasta se bender 51 pesos 5 tomines	51 p 5 t

de flete de mulas a 4 pesos piesa	20 p
de Entrada y bisita 4 pesos	4 p
de manta y petates 8 pesos	8 p
de escrituras dos pesos y medio	2 p 4
de Corretage 8 pesos 2 tomines	8 p 2
de alcavala a 2 por ciento	33 p
de Encomienda a 2 por ciento y medio	41 p 2
de botica y medico 30 pesos	30 p
Abatidos estos 756 pesos 4 tomines Restan que se le	756 p 4
Hasen bueno al dicho Juan Martinez de lahazienda del difunto	<u>848 p 4</u>
Por se aber abonado las piesas en su quenta conforme lo que	1 605 p

halle Por el costo de otras piesas agenas que el difunto tenia sentado en su libro –
848 pesos 4 tomines de que se le hase deudor al difunto en la quenta corriente . . .

* * *

1630

Gastos de 80 peças que Em 18 de mayo
Emveiei a la pobla a Joao Fernandez Vergara [Juan Fernandez de Vergara]

que dy ao aRieyro Para Gasta no Caminho Sem Pesos	100 p
quatro batates de biscouto com 7 q.tas a 5 pesos 2 tomines quintal	36 p 6 t
de frete a 3 pesos 6 reales Cada Negro até la pobla [Puebla]	200 p
de gasto em quanto estiverao na pobla ate para mexico	p [sic]
dos peças que forao para mexico	
em 15 de junho a Sebastiao Vas [Sebastian Vaz de Acevedo]	<u>70</u>
ao aRieyro para gastar no caminho com ditas peças	100 p
de vinte ____ arrobas de biscouto a 5 pesos 2 tomines cada quintal	31 p 4 t
de 10 arrobas de carne sequa a 12 Reales arroba	15 p
que dy [a] Balthasar Lourenço que mais gastou no Caminho	12 p

de frete de Cada Negro a 4 reales 4 tomines	315 p
que se Gastou em mexico ate se venderem	p [sic]
das 34 peças que em 10 de jullio	
forao de la pobla para mexico	
que deu Joao Fernandez Vergara [Juan Fernandez de Vergara] para gastarem no Caminho	20 p
de tres quintais de biscouto a 4 pesos cada quintal	12 p
de frete de Cada Negro a 12 Reais y da mula de selayda que trouxe o biscouto 3 pesos cada hua	53 p 4 t

* * *

Memoria de gastos que vou fazendo com as pessas que ficarão depos que faleçio o Cappitan João Nuñes . . .

iten en 14 de outubro de entero [entierro] de la negra que se murio	7 pesos
iten huã manta para huã molequa enferma	1 peso
que se dio de alhasgo de hum molequinho que se huio	4 pesos
dei a mendonsa el sirugano a conta hum negro q[ue] esta curando de joaõ nunes	10 pesos
iten en 6 de nob[iembr]o 7 p[eso]s que dei para entero [entierro] de hum molequiunho da conpanhia que esta enventariado que moreu de biruelas en dito dia de quee Joao Bautista deu fe	7 pesos
iten en 6 do dito 104 pesos que di a Bernardo que se foi meter frade a gadalhachara [Guadalajara]	104 pesos

Document 23: 1635—Jesuit College of Puebla purchases four African youths[11]

May all who see this letter know that I, Juan Fernández de Vergara, *vecino* and slaving agent of this city [Puebla] of the Angels, state that I truly sell, by means of this letter, to the College of the Company of Jesus, Advocation of the Holy Spirit, of this

---

11. Archivo General de Notarías del Estado de Puebla, Notaría 3, Box 152, ff. 1720r–1723v.

said city, and to the Rector, Father Rodrigo de Vivero, four slaves named Antonio, another Antonio, Diego, and Miguel, Angolas between thirteen and sixteen years of age, who belong to the captains Pedro Jorge and Antonio Abreu and their slave ships. I sell them as captives subject to servitude. They are free of any lien, mortgage, or other debt, which they do not have on them. I offer no guarantee against weaknesses, defects, or sicknesses because I sell them with all the ills, public or secret, that they may have as *bozales*, recently brought from their land and as "soul in mouth, bones in a sack"[12] at a price of 1,660 common gold pesos, or 415 pesos each. This sum will be paid to me in the manner and in the installments that will be described below.

I renounce and transfer the rights, actions, property, and dominion over said slaves to the buyer(s) and to Father Antonio Cuello, their legal counsel, in whose name I have turned over said slaves as a sign of true possession and tradition.

. . . And I, Father Antonio Cuello, legal counsel for said College, in its voice and name and in virtue of the power of attorney in my possession . . . recognize that I accept this document and the four slaves thereby included, and I renounce the laws of delivery and their proof, whereby I and the property and rents of said College are obligated to pay Juan Fernández de Guevara, and whomever might hold his power of attorney, 1,660 pesos in reales, in accordance with the price of this sale.

This sum will be paid in this city or wherever payment is demanded. One-third will be paid on February 23, the next third will be due on June 23, and the final third will be due on October 23, all of these dates in the upcoming year 1636. In this manner, the entire sum will be paid within a year's time. In order to safeguard this purchase, I mortgage said slaves and will not sell or loan them out in any way, under pain that if they are estranged in any manner, this arrangement will be annulled and said slaves will be taken from any third party who might hold them and be sold in order to secure payment. And if said sum cannot be reached by liquidating said goods, then the property and rents of said College will be confiscated under a simple oath to be made by Juan Fernández [de Vergara].

. . . This letter was made in the City of the Angels (Puebla) on October 23, 1635. The awarding parties, whom I, the scribe, testify that I know, signed the letter. Pedro Leonardo y Sevilla, Melchor Fernández de la Fuente, Antonio Juárez de Vargas, neighbors and people presently in this said city, served as witnesses.

Juan Fernández de Vergara	Antonio Coello	Before me, Alonso Corona, public scribe

---

12. *alma en boca huesos en costal*: term used in bills of sale to describe African captives who had very recently survived a slaving voyage.

[Spanish transcription]

Sepan quantos esta carta Vieren como yo Juan fernandez de bergara vezino y encomendero desta ciudad de los angeles otorgo Por esta Carta que vendo Realmente a el colegio de la compañía de Jesus adbocacion del espiritu Santo desta dicha Ciudad y a el padre Rector Rodrigo de Vivero, quatro esclavos, nombrados, antonio, otro antonio, diego y miguel de quenta y armason de los capitanes Pedro Jorje y antonio abreo, angolas de hedad, de trece a dies y Seis años Por cautivos Sujetos a Serbidumbre libres de empeño hipoteca Y otra Enaxenacion especial ni general sin asegurarlos de ningua tacha vicio defecto ni enfermedad Publica ni secreta Porque con las que tubieren se los bendo Por bozales Resien traidos de Su tierra, almas em boca huessos En costal Em precio de vn mill y Seiscientos y Sesenta pesos de oro comun a cuatrocientos y quince pesos cada vno que me a de Pagar en la forma y a los Placos que iran declarados =

Y Renuncio y transfiero los derechos de action propiedad y Señorio de los dichos esclavos en el Comprador, a quien y al padre antonio Cuello procurador en su nombre los tengo Entregado en señal de posecion y tradicion verdadera, y me obligo a su evicion Seguro y Saneamiento En la mas bastante forma que por derecho devo zerlo Por mi persona y bienes que obligo

. . . Y estando Presente yo el dicho Padre antonio Cuello Procurador del dicho Colexio Em voz y en nombre del y en virtud del poder que tengo . . . açepto esta escriptura y de los dichos quatro esclavos me doi Por entregado En el dicho nombre, sobre que rrenuncio leyes de la Entrega y Su prueva Por cuia Rasson, obligo a los bienes y Rentas del dicho Colexio a que sse le pagaran a el dicho Juan fernandes de bergara y a quien su poder Uviere los dichos Vn mill Seiscientos y Sessenta Pesos del Precio desta Venta En Reales En esta ciudad o En la parte que se Pidan la tercia Parte, Para Veinte y tres dias del mes de febrero, y la otra tercia Parta Para veinte y tres del mes de Junio, Y la otra tercia Parte Restante Para veinte y tres dias del mes de octubre, todo del año que viene de mill y Seiscientos y treinta y Seis Vna Paga Subsesiva a otra de suerte que dentro de vn año a destar Pagada toda la dicha Cantidad, Para Cuia Seguridad En Su nombre hipoteco Por especial y expressa hipoteca no derogando la general ni por el Contrario los dichos esclavos Para no venderlos i enagenarlos En manera alguna Pena que en el trato Enagenatorio sea ninguno y se puedan sacar de ajeno Poder y vendersse y hasserse Pago y Por lo que no alcanssare executara los dichos bienes Para Cuia liquidacion a de sser bastante Prueva e Juramento simple del dicho Juan fernandes En que sin otra alguna lo difiero y a ello obligo los bienes y rrentas del dicho Colexio, y todas las partes damos Poder a las Justicias que desta caussa Conoscan cada vno a su fuero Para que a ello nos apremien y a los dicho bienes Como por Sentencia difinitiva Passada En Cosa Jusgada. Renunciamos leies de nuestro favor y la general que es fha la carta En la ciudad de los angeles En veinte y tres dias del mes de octubre de mill y Seiscientos y treinta y cinco años y los otorgantes que yo el Scrivano doi fee que Conosco lo firmaron siendo testigos Pedro Leonardo y

Sivilla, melchor ffernandes de la fuente, y antonio Juarez de Bargas, vezinos y estantes En esta dicha Ciudad, va testado

Juan Fernandez de Vergara   Antonio Coello   Ante my Alonso Corona,
                                                              scrivano publico

Document 24: 1664—The arrival of the San Juan Bautista slave ship[13]

. . . having entered the island of Barbados, an English settlement, he [Captain Santiago Daza Villalobos] made contracts to acquire Black slaves that he brought to this port of Nueva Veracruz. During the inspection that this city's royal judges and officials conducted on July 28 of the said year [1664], with the assistance of the overseeing judge of the said slaving monopoly, six hundred and sixty-five pieces of slaves, Black males and females, small and large, healthy and ill, were found and counted. They were measured following the regulation size of seven *cuartas* in accordance with the first stipulation of the said slaving monopoly, in which the size of each piece of Indias is stipulated, and 100 pesos would be paid for each piece.[14] In the proceedings that followed on the counting of said slaves, seventy-one pieces and three-fourths were reduced on account of the seventy-three pieces that died within thirty days after the ship's arrival in this port, according to the scribe's testimony. . . .

Likewise, after the visit and inspection, according to the first condition of the slaving monopoly, fifty-three large pieces were regulated to seventeen pieces of Indies, as they were declared one-eyed, crippled, maimed, injured, and demented. . . . [In all,] the number was adjusted to five hundred and nineteen pieces of slaves and two-and-half palms, who at an established entry fee of one hundred pesos each, amount to fifty-one thousand, nine hundred, thirty-five pesos and six tomines. Captain Santiago Daza Villalobos was not charged this amount, nor was he compelled to disburse this money, because he presented His Majesty's royal decree, signed in Aranjuez on May 5, 1663, and countersigned by the said Dr. Juan del Solar. It decrees that neither the holders of the slaving monopoly, nor the factors [of the slave trade] are to be

---

13. Archivo General de Indias, Contaduría, 893, N.1, R.2, f. 10r–11v.

14. A *cuarta* was a unit of measurement, approximately 20 cm (or 7.8 inches) long. In the 1662 slaving monopoly between the Spanish Crown, Lomelín, and Grillo, it was established that an enslaved person of seven *cuartas* measured 140 cm (or 55 inches) in height. See Manuel Lucena Samoral, *Regulación de la esclavitud negra en las colonias de América Española (1503–1886): documentos para su estudio* (Alcalá de Henares: Universidad de Alcalá / Universidad de Múrcia, 2005), 183; José Miguel Lecaros Sánchez, *El fenómeno de la esclavitud y del trabajo esclavo: perspectiva histórico jurídica e histórica* (Sevilla: Caligrama, 2019), n351.

compelled to pay the entry fees of the pieces of slaves introduced to the Indies. . . . on March 3, 1665 = Andres de Aramburu = Bernardo de Sumbil = Francisco de Amilivia

[Spanish transcription]

. . . y haviendo entrado en la isla del Barbado poblada de yngleses contrato esclabos negros que trujo en el dicho navio a este puerto de la nueva veracruz y en la visita que se le hiço por los Juezes officialez Reales desta ciudad en el dicho dia Veinte y ocho de Jullio del dicho año con su asistençia del Juez conserbador del dicho asiento se hallaron y contaron seisçientas y sesenta y cinco pieças de esclabos negros barones y hembras chicos y grandes sanos y enfermos que se fueron midiendo para la rregulaçion del tamaño de siete quartas que conforme a la capitulacion primera del dicho asiento esta señalado el tamaño de cada pieça de yndias para la paga de cien pesos por cada una y segun los autos que se hicieron sobre La rregulazion de dichos esclabos haciendole rrebajado setenta y una pieças y tres quartas de otra a que se rregularon setenta y tres pieças que por testimonio de escrivano consto haverse muerto dentro de treinta dias despues de la entrada en este Puerto el dicho navio . . .

Y asi mismo se rregularon cinquenta y tres pieças grandes que de la dicha Visita y rreconoçimiento que se hiço Consto tener los defecttos que por la condizion primera del asiento se declara de tuertos, coxos, mancos, quebrados, y dementtados se rregularon a numero de diez y siete pieças de yndias . . . se ajusto a numero de quinientos y diez y nueve pieças de yndias y dos palmos y medio de otra cuios derechos a rraçion de Cien pesos por cada uno ymportan Çinquenta y un mill noveçientos y treinta y çinco pesos y seis tomines, los quales no se cobraron del dicho Capitan Santiago Daça Villalobos ni se le conpelio al desembolso dellos por aver presentado Real çedula de Su Magestad, su fecha a Aranjuez a çinco de Maio de Mill y seisçientos y sesenta y tres, rreferendada del dicho Señor Don Juan del Solar en que se sirbe de mandar que a los dichos asentistas ni a sus fatores no se les conpela al desenbolso de los derechos que inportaren las pieças de esclabos que introdujeren en las yndias . . . en tres de Março de Mill y seisçientos y sesenta y çinco años = Andres de Aramburu = Bernardo de Sumbil = Francisco de Amilivia

Document 25: 1664—Condition of the survivors of the *San Juan Bautista* slave ship[15]

. . . by order of Lord General Don Diego Ortiz de Largacha, Duarte Crispi [Edward Crisp?] is allowed to leave and go to his residence to inspect the Black *bozales* that were found there the day before and who were left in deposit, under Domingo de

---

15. Archivo General de Indias, Contaduría, 893, N.1, R.2, 35v–38r.

Ostoloja. With the assistance of Captain Santiago Daza and Duarte Crispi, forty-six slaves were counted in the said house, thirty-six of them female. One of the females has a slaving brand or mark and a Black male has the same brand or mark above his right chest. Captain Santiago Daza recognized this as his mark, which I, the scribe, attest that I know . . . and two of the females were about to perish, [the slaves] were naked and lying on the floor over a few sack mats . . . and all the other Blacks were thin, mistreated, and a few of them, up to three of the males, were crippled and dragged themselves along the floor.

And I, the scribe, attest that the said Santiago Daza receives forty-six Blacks who are now in his charge by way of deposit, with the assistance of the said Lord General Don Diego de Largacha. The latter gives [Daza] these Blacks separately, not as part of those he received before from Don Jiliscot [Gil Liscott?]. . . . [Daza] will assist in this matter as a good administrator and faithful depositary and will also give account of the slaves that may die, along with those he is currently receiving . . . and he signed this with the Lord General = and [Daza] asks that the Lord General order that the scribe who came to the slave ship recognize the slaves that he receives, as to their poor state and quality, so that their condition and state in which he received them always be acknowledged. Duarte Crispi [Edward Crisp?] and the Lord General were present . . .

[Spanish transcription]

. . . [por] orden del Señor General Don Diego Ortiz de Largacha sale de la detencion en que esta Duarte Crispi [¿Edward Crisp?] para ir a la cassa de su morada reconoser los negros boçales [bozales] que se hallaron en ella y quedaron el dia antes y quedaron a cargo de Domingo de Ostoloja en forma de deposito, estando en la dicha casa asistiendo el Capitan Sanctiago Dasa y duarte Crispi se contaron quarenta y seis negros, dies barones, las treinta y seis hembras y entre ellas vna que tiene una señal de carinbo ô marca y un negro con el mesmo Carinbo ô marca sobre el pecho derecho que los Reconoçio el dicho Capitan Sanctiago Dasa de su marca que yo el Scrivano doy fee Conosco . . . y dos de las hembras cassi para espirar desnudos y tendidos en el suelo sobre unos petates . . . todos los demas de los negros flacos maltratados y algunos dellos asta tres de los barones tullidos y arrastrandose en los suelos

Y yo el escrivano doy fee que con la asistençia de dicho señor General Don Diego de Largacha Reçive el dicho Sanctiago Dasa y pasan a su poder los quarenta y seis negros por via de deposito quien le otorga en forma por quenta aparte y no como los que â rrecevido antes de aora y Reçivio de Don Jiliscot [Gil Liscott?] . . . y asistira como buen administrador y fiel depositario y la dara tambien de los esclavos que fallesieren asi de los que Reçive de pressente . . . y lo firmo con el Señor General = y pide al Señor General mande que el scrivano que vino en la nao Reconosca Los esclavos que Reçive quanto al mal estado y calidad que Tienen para que Siempre conste la forma y estado con que Los Reçive y se le hallan pressentes Duarte crispi y el señor General . . .

Document 26: 1675—The governor of Nueva Veracruz recalls the old slave trade[16]

. . . This witness [Governor Felipe de Estrada] said that as a *vecino* of this city [Nueva Veracruz] for close to fifty years . . . he knew of the manners and methods of this port's slaving agents from the year 1626 up to 1640, when they went missing due to the Portuguese uprising. He knows that these slave ships paid a rate of eight percent on sales and collection. Likewise, he knows that the Blacks brought in each ship were disembarked that same day and that a peso was paid to the slaving agent for each head on account of their lodging = Likewise, he knows that then the royal accountants awarded a bond to pay for the fleet's dispatch. To pay the royal duties owed by the slave ship, a person of great credit was chosen, due to the risk of the slaves' dying, which was quite common. The person that ended up paying this bond was gifted two Blacks, who were chosen from the slave ship, and more was given to this person from time to time in appreciation of obtaining the bond = The manager who took care of the slave ship also received other benefits, which this witness will not mention because he is not being asked about this.

He knows that no man of standing or authority wanted to take on these administrative responsibilities because of how difficult they were and the stench that they brought with them, and for this reason, poor men took charge of this task. In those times, these men were Juan Mendez = Manuel de Solís Ulloa = Francisco Gómez Tejosso = Gonzalo Rodrigues = and Captain Rodrigo Serrano, after he had become impoverished, and other Portuguese men = And Gaspar Esteves Pardo = and Juan Mathias de Biedma = and Juan Bermudez served as cashiers for these administrators. . . . This witness was raised in the house of Blas de Burgos Estrada, his uncle, a man of much credit who was often sought out to pay the bonds on the royal duties. This witness knows and saw how his uncle paid these bonds and how the reward of two Black slaves from each slave ship entered his house. Everything he has said is true . . . and he is sixty years of age and signed this deposition. Felipe de Estrada = before me, Juan Bautista de Barrios, public and royal scribe.

---

16. Archivo General de Indias, Escribanía 292A, ff. 5v–7v.

[Spanish transcription]

... Dixo este testigo [el gobernador Felipe de Estrada] que como Vezino que es desta çiudad de serca de cinquenta años a esta parte ... tubo yntelijencia de la forma y estilo en que los encomenderos [de negros] en este Puerto de las armasones de negros, Portugueses desde el año de veinte y seis hasta el de quarentta, que faltaron Por el lebantamiento de portugal y save que el corriente de las encomiendas de estas armazones se pagavan a ocho por ciento Por la venta y Cobranza: y assimesmo que la cantidad de negros que traya la armazon es mesmo dia que se echava en tierra debia y se pagava vn pesso de cada cavessa a el encomendero por rrazon del bodegaje = y asi mesmo luego que en la rreal contaduria se otorgava la fianza para pagar al despacho de flotta, los derechos Reales que debia dicha armason que para el efecto se exccojia Persona de mucho credito por el peligro y rriesgo de muertes de los esclavos, que era muy hordinario, se le dava al subjetto que hassia la fianza Doss Negros de rregalo, excojidos en la armazon y de mas a mas se le agradessia de Haver querido afianzar = Y tambien thenia el administrador que se hassia cargo de la armazon otros aprobechamientos que omite el desirloz porqque no se le pregunta =

y save que ningun Hombre de comodidades Ni de authoridad queria entrar en estas administraçiones por lo duro de ellas, y la Hediondes que trayan consigo y Por esta rrazon, se hassian cargo hombres pobres, y en aquellos tiempos lo fue = Joan mendez = Manuel de soliz Ulloa = francisco gomez tejosso = Gonzalo rodrigues = y el cappitan Rodrigo Serrano despues que enprobeçio [sic] y otros todos Portugueses = y que Gaspar esteves Pardo = y Juan mathias de biedma = y Juan bermudes, que serbian de cajeros a los tales administradores ... este testigo se crio en cassa de Blas de Burgos Estrada su tio subjeto de mucho credito y soliçitado Para las fianzas de los derechos Reales, Save y vio que entravan en su cassa el premio de Dos negros de cada armazon, de que su tio hasia la fianza y que esto que tiene dicho es la verdad ... y que es de hedad de sesenta años y lo firmo. = Phelipe destrada = ante mi Juan Bautista de Barrios escrivano publico y Real.

Document 27: 1681—Sale of six recently arrived Africans[17]

May all who see this letter know that I, Captain Diego Pamplona, resident in this city [Puebla] of the Angels, acknowledge that I truly sell to Antonio Marselis and Doña Inés Negreros y Vargas, his wife, *vecinos* of this city, six Black *bozales* from the slave coffle in my charge, which I brought to the port of San Juan de Ulúa in my ship, named *Carlos Segundo*. The ship belonged to Captain José de Castro, now

---

17. Archivo General de Notarías del Estado de Puebla, Notaría 4, Box 217, ff. 761r–763r.

deceased, one of the [captains] of the traffic and commerce of the city of Seville . . . in accordance with the Sevillian Consulate's new Instruction, competence, and chapters [of the slaving monopoly], signed in the city of Seville on April 15 of the past year of 1680, the ships of said slaving monopoly may make two slave-trading voyages without returning to the kingdoms of Castile . . . [therefore], I sell them [the captives] as "soul in mouth, bones in a sack," recently brought from their land. Of course, the buyer assumes the risk of illness, death, or flight. . . . This sale took place under this stipulation, and I make this sale at a price of 2,310 common gold pesos to be paid in the installments that will be declared . . . in one year's time from the date of this writ . . . signed in the city [Puebla] of the Angels on September 16, 1681.

Diego Pamplona   Antonio Marcelis
Juan de Alfaro   Witness, Felipe Gómez
                     Before me, Antonio Gómez de Escobar, royal and public scribe

[Spanish transcription]

Sepan quantos esta carta Vieren como Yo el Capitan Diego Panplona Reçidente en esta ciudad de los angeles [Puebla] otorgo que vendo Realmente a Anttonio Marselis y a Doña Ynes Negreros y Vargas, su muger, vezinos desta ciudad seis negros Vosales de la armaçon de mi Cargo que conduje al puerto de San Juan de Vlua en mi navio nombrado Carlos Segundo que fue del Capittan Joseph de Castro difunto vno de los del trafico y Comerçio de la ciudad de Sevilla . . . y en conformidad de la nueva facultad y Capitulos de la nueva Ynstruçion del dicho Consulado su fecha en dicha Çiudad de Çevilla de dicha Ynstruçion a quinçe de Abril del año Pasado de mill y seis sientos y ochenta Para que los navios del dicho asientto puedan haser dos viajes de la armaçon sin Bolver a los rreynos de Castilla saliendo de ellos en conformidad de dicho açientto . . . se los Vendo alma en Voca huesos en costal y por reçien traydos de su tierra y desde luego el rriesgo de enfermedad muerte o aussensia corre por quenta del comprador . . . devajo deste pacto tubo efecto esta Venta que les hago en precio de dos mill tresçiento y dies pesos de oro Comun que me han de pagar al plazo que yra declarado . . . para de la fecha desta escriptura en Vn año Cumplido . . . en la ciudad de los angeles a dies y seis dias del mes de Septiembre de mill y seissientos y ochenta y vn años . . .

Diego pamplona   Antonio marcelis
Juan de alfaro   Por testigo Phelipe gomes
                     ante my Antonio Gomez Descobar scrivano Real y Publico

CHAPTER 3
Transpacific Slave Trade

The documents in this chapter range from 1570 to 1714 and focus on the experiences of enslaved individuals who entered colonial Mexico by way of Pacific slaving networks. In order to make sense of these sources, we must engage the experiences of enslaved Asians and East Africans in the main ports and settlements of the Spanish Philippines (which were considered part of the viceroyalty of New Spain and were governed from Mexico City). The port of Cavite operated as the main site of embarkment for the merchants, sailors, captains, and slavers of the city of Manila (just across the bay). To reach the port of Acapulco required some 15,500 kilometers of navigation and approximately six months of travel.

The Manila Galleons were not specifically designed for the transportation of enslaved people. They were primarily merchant vessels (of enormous dimensions) that transported ceramics, silks, and luxury furniture but also colonial officials, missionaries, soldiers, and sailors, along with enslaved people. Although the latter often hailed from Goa, Mozambique, and the Philippines, they were often labeled as *chinos* upon arrival in the port of Acapulco. How or why such groups were enslaved was subject to debate. Just five years after the opening, in 1565, of the Manila Galleon route, the Spanish monarch issued a complicated statement on the emerging Pacific slave trade based on his understanding of Muslim resistance in the Philippines. By the end of the sixteenth century, the sale of enslaved people from the Manila Galleons was openly accepted and, therefore, taxed, in Mexico. Eventually, the merchants and financiers who operated transatlantic slaving networks came to resent the Pacific slavers, as can be seen from Manuel Carrillo's 1607 complaint.

Many enslaved Asians and East Africans remained in Acapulco, but others were transported into the interior regions of colonial Mexico. The slave markets and notarial archives of New Spain offer considerable proof of the sale of such individuals. Large Asian communities could be found in urban centers such as Guadalajara, Puebla, and Mexico City. Within these urban centers, they fulfilled roles traditionally associated with enslaved people, as domestic and textile workers. The document from 1650, for instance, suggests that the *chinos* Lázaro de la Cruz and Nicolás would join a much larger workforce in the textile mill owned by Diego de Andrada Peralta. Crucially, a Mozambican man, Juan, and a mulatto man, Antonio, were also included in the bill of sale.

The transpacific slave trade continued throughout the colonial period, although the abolition of Asian slavery in 1672 did somewhat alter Pacific slaving. The Spanish

Queen Regent's abolition decree indirectly led to a shift in the labels used to describe enslaved individuals entering the Mexican mainland. As *chinas* and *chinos* gradually claimed freedom in the late seventeenth century, slaving merchants resorted to *cafre* or *pasa* labels, as seen in the documents from 1685, 1708, and 1714. Further research on Indian Ocean slaving will determine whether this shift in the identification of enslavable categories of people actually led to different slaving routes to Cavite and Manila. In sum, these sources on transpacific survivors are essential to reconstructing much lengthier, global, slaving voyages. While the experiences of Asians and East Africans trafficked into the cities of the highlands have received some scholarly attention, there remains much work to be done on those who were sent to rural settlements along Mexico's Pacific coast. The communities and cultural practices of transpacific survivors in Colima, Michoacán, Jalisco, and Guerrero are yet to be fully researched.

Document 28: 1570—Arrival of enslaved Muslims from the Philippines[1]

Don Martín Enríquez, our viceroy, governor, and captain general in New Spain, president of our royal audience, who resides in Mexico City. I saw your letter [dated] January 20 of this year and you are in my service. I recognize that you have advised us in great detail on the things that you have learned about that land. I charge you to continue doing so and to look after things in the service of God and in our service, and in the good government of that land, and the conservation of its natives, as we trust in your prudence and goodness.

You say that fourteen or fifteen slaves were brought by the *San Juan* ship from the Philippine Islands, and that some of them had been seized from the Portuguese. You have understood, from learned people, that the other [slaves] were among those that were captured on the same islands and that although they were Moors they have been converted [to Islam] for a short amount of time, because they used to be Gentiles. Therefore, you are not to believe that these are slaves, nor is it our desire that they be. You are to return them to their land, so that we do not open this door to the people who are over there [in the Philippines]. You are to write the governor that it seems to you that these things should not take place until we order it so. You will do the same for an Indian woman who was brought, because we do not want the natives of that land to think that we consider wronging or mistreating them as a good thing.

---

1. Archivo General de Indias, México, 1090, L.6, ff. 69r–70r, 78r. http://pares.mcu.es/ParesBusquedas20/catalogo/description/7263258?nm

Rather, we would have anything to the contrary punished. What you have done is good and from here on you will observe what is decreed and ordered by us in a section of a letter that we sent to Miguel López de Legazpi, our governor in that land, which is as follows—

We have also heard from you [López de Legazpi], that in that land [the Philippines], there are islands of Moors, who come and trade and make deals, and impede the preaching of the holy ~~office~~ gospel and disturb you. You ask us to give you license to enslave these said Moors and take their goods. You will be advised that if the said Moors are Moors of a single nation and nature, and they come to dogmatize their Mohammedan sect, or to make war against you or the Indians who are subject to you and to our royal service, then you may make them slaves. However, with regard to those who are Indians and converted to the sect of Mohammed, you will not make them slaves for any reason, but will seek to convert them and persuade them to our holy Catholic faith by good and licit means.

. . . on July 4, 1570. I, the King. Countersigned behind or marked with [the following signatures] Básquez, Don Gómez, Molina, Salas, Botello, Otalora, Gasca.

The King

[Spanish transcription]

Don Martín Enriquez nuestro Visorrey y governador y capitan general de la nueva españa y presidente de la audiencia Real que rreside en la ciudad de mexico vi vuestra Letra de Veynte de henero deste año y tengo os en servicio, he cuidado que aveis tenido de nos avisar tan en particular del estado en que hallastes y estan las cosas dessa Tierra y Asi os cargo lo continueis adelante y mireis mucho por las cosas del servycio de dios y nuestro y buena governaçion desa tierra buen tratamyento y conservaçion de los naturales della Como de vuestra prudencia y bondad se Confia.

En lo que dezis que aviendose traydo en el navio Sant Juan de las yslas phelipinas catorze o quinze esclavos que algunos dellos heran de los que se tomaron a los Portugueses y otros aveis entendido que heran de los que se Captivavan en las mysmas yslas Los quales os han dicho personas doctas que aunque son muoros [sic, moros] son de poco Tiempo combertidos porque antes heran gentiles y assi no Creeis que estos sean esclavos ni que nuestra Voluntad es que lo sean. Y los hazeis bolver a su tierra por no abrir esta puerta a la gente que alla esta, y Scrivis al governador que os pareçe no debe dar Lugar a estas cosas hasta que nos mandemos Lo que somos servido se haga en ello y que lo mismo hareis de Vna yndia que se Truxo porque no es bien entiendan los naturales de aquella Tierra que nos Tenemos por bien se les haga algun agravio ni maltratamiento y que antes mandamos castigar lo contrario esta vien Lo que en esto aveis hecho y de aqui adelante guardareis Lo que por nos esta proveydo y mandado en un capitulo de una Carta que mandamos Scrivir a Miguel Lopez de Legazpi nuestro governador de aquella Tierra el qual es del tenor siguiente –

Tambien se nos ha pedido de vuestra parte que atento A que ay en esa Tierra [Filipinas] yslas de moros y ellos vienen a tratar y contratar los quales ympiden la Predicaçion del sancto officio evangelio y os ynquietan os demos liçençia para hazer a los Tales moros sclavos y Tomarles sus haziendas, estareis advertido que Si los Tales moros son de una nacion y naturaleza moros y vinieren a domactizar su seta [sic, secta] maometica o A hazer guerra a vos otros o a los yndios que estan a nos Subjetos y a nuestro Real Serviçio los podeis hazer esclavos mas a los que fueren yndios y ovieren Tomado la secta de mahomia no lo hareis Sclavos por ninguna via ni manera que Sea sino procurareis de Los combertir y persuadir por buenos y licitos medios a nuestra sancta fee catolica.

. . . a quatro de Julio de myll E quinientos y setenta años yo El Rey. Refrendada detras o señalada de Basquez, Don Gomez, Molina, Salas, Botello, Otalora, Gasca

El Rey

Document 29: 1598—Sales taxes on five enslaved people from the Philippines[2]

In Mexico City on August 18, 1598, the lord president and civil court judges of New Spain's royal audience have seen this process and orders between the parties, Don Fernando de Castro on one side, and on the other, the licenciado Diego Nuñez Morquecho, His Majesty's fiscal attorney in this royal audience, with regard to [de Castro] not paying taxes on the five pieces of slaves he brought from the Islands of the West [the Philippines]. In regard to the order pronounced by the royal audience on July 10 of this present year, the said Don Fernando de Castro requests that this question be declared as something previously consented and passed as a judged matter. In this regard, the fiscal attorney was notified and he did not appeal it. They said they declare and declared the said order as a matter previously judged, agreed, and past. They ordered that notice of this be given to the said Don Fernando de Castro's part, on what has been determined on the cause. They pronounced and ordered it so. [four signatures]

Before me, Diego Tarrique

On August 6, 1598, an order was sent covering what had been determined regarding Don Francisco de Castro's case. He paid twenty-four reales for the writs of everything, the case, orders, and notifications, since he had not paid. Seen [signature]

---

2. Archivo General de la Nación, Indiferente Virreinal, Caja 1812, Exp. 18, ff. 1r–1v.

[Spanish transcription]

En la çiudad de Mexico a diez y ocho dias de El mes de agosto de mill y quinientos y noventa y ocho años Los señores presidente E oydores de La audiencia rreal de la nueva españa aviendo visto este proçeso y autos que es entre partes de la Una don Fernando de Castro y de la otra El Licenciado Diego Nuñez Morquecho fiscal de su magestad en esta real audiencia sobre que se declare no dever Pagar derechos de çinco pieças de esclavos que truxo de las yslas del poniente En el articulo de lo pedido Por parte del dicho don Fernando de Castro çerca de que se declare por consentido y Pasado En cosa Juzgada El auto En esta Causa pronunciado por esta rreal audiencia En diez de Jullio de este presente año atento que se notifico al dicho fiscal y no suplico del. Dixeron que declaravan y declararon El dicho auto Por consentido y Pasado en cosa Juzgada y mandaron se le de a la parte de El dicho don Fernando de Castro Recaudo qual convenga de lo determinado en esta Caussa y assi lo Pronunçiaron y mandaron. [cuatro rúbricas]

Ante mi Diego Tarrique

En el vi de agosto de 1598 años se despacho mandamiento de lo determinado a la parte de Don Fernando de Castro y Pago veinte y quatro Reales de las escrituras de todo El provecho y autos y notificaciones por no aver pagado Bista [rúbrica]

Document 30: 1607—The slave trade through the port of Acapulco[3]

Captain Manuel Carillo, as agent for and in the name of Gonzalo Vaez Coutiño, your governor in the Kingdom of Angola and a member of your council, as a person with whom the slaving monopoly was entered for licensing the slaves who pass to these kingdoms, I say that I have asked that a judge be named, according to the royal decrees on the slaves that entered fraudulently through the port of Acapulco and other places. . . . In the said galleons from the Philippine Islands come many kinds of slaves, among them a very large number of Blacks from Portuguese India, Mançabique [Mozambique], Malacca [Melaka], and from the islands and rivers [belonging] to the Portuguese Crown and its conquests. In no manner should these [slaves] be allowed to pass without my patron's permission, in accordance with the monopoly that was made with a royal person. According to the tenth chapter of the slaving monopoly contract, it is prohibited that any person who is neither my patron nor who holds his power of attorney be allowed to pass the said slaves to these

---

3. Archivo General de la Nación, Indiferente Virreinal, Caja 5801, Exp. 51, f. 1r–1v.

parts, under penalty of being taken as fraudulent. As a result, all those that come from the said crown of Portugal and its conquests, should they come from the said islands, or from any other part, are to be taken and considered lost. Otherwise, Your Majesty's rights could be defrauded by a very large amount and with this my patron would be greatly aggrieved. . . . Manuel Carrillo, January 26, 1607.

Received February 1, 1607

[Spanish transcription]

El capitan Manuel Carrillo en nombre y como fator de Gonzalo Vaez Coutiño, vuestro governador del Reyno de Angola y del vuestro consejo, como persona con quien se tomo asiento para las licencias de los esclavos que pasan a estos Reynos digo que aviendo yo pedido se nombrase Juez en conformidad de las Reales çedulas para todos los sclavos que vbieren venido descaminados por el puerto de Acapulco . . . en las dichas naos de las islas filipinas vienen munchos generos de sclavos entre los quales se pasan muy gran numero de negros de la Yndia de Portugal, Mançabique (Mozambique,) Malaca y de las islas y rios de la corona de Portugal y su conquista los quales por ninguna via se pueden pasar sin licencia de mi parte conforme al asiento que con una Real persona hiço por que por particular capitulo del dicho asiento que es el deçimo esta prohivido que ninguna persona si no fuere mi parte y quien su poder tubiere pueda pasar los dichos sclavos a esta parte so pena de que se tomen por descaminados por manera que todos los que vinieren de la dicha corona de Portugal y sus conquistas ora vengan por las dichas islas ora por otra qualquier parte se an de tomar por Perdidos pues de otra manera se podria defraudar en muy gran numero los derechos de Vuestra Real persona y hazer en esto muy grande agrabio a mi parte . . . Manuel Carrillo en 26 de henero de 1607 años.

recibido en primero de febrero de 1607 años

Document 31: 1650—Lázaro de la Cruz and Nicolás sold to a textile mill[4]

May all who see this letter know that we, Tomas Dies de Córdoba and Juana Bautista de Vega, his legitimate wife, and I [Juana] was first married to the senior council member Antonio Gomez Leal, deceased *vecino* of the city of Cholula . . . both [of us] husband and wife jointly and in union, in each other's voice . . . we state that we truly sell four slaves named Lázaro de la Cruz, a *chino* man fifty years old,

---

4. Archivo General de Notarías del Estado de Puebla, Notaría 3, Año 1650, Box 101, 1650 Junio, ff. 19v–20r.

Juan Mozambique, a Black man also fifty years old, Antonio, a mulatto twenty years old, [and] Nicolás, a *chino* man sixty years old, all textile journeymen, to Diego de Andrada Peralta, owner of a textile mill and *vecino* of this city. [We sell them] as our own captive slaves and they are free of all lien, mortgage, or any other claim. . . . We do not insure them against any flaws, vices, defects, nor of any public or secret diseases, for the price and sum of 900 common gold pesos. He has given and paid us 500 pesos in reales, which we declare we have received . . . and we are to be paid the remaining 400 pesos, which complete the said sum, in four months from the date of this letter . . . done in the city [Puebla] of the Angels on June 18, 1650. I, the scribe, attest that I know the grantors. The said Tomás de Córdoba and Diego de Andrada Peralta signed; a witness signed for the said Doña Juana Bautista de Vega, who said she did not know how to. Witnesses, Juan Bautista Sanz, Diego Ruíz, and Francisco de Chavez and Juan García, *vecinos* of this city.

Tomás Dies de Córdoba   Diego de Andrada Peralta   as a witness, [rubric]
                                                      Chavez Galindo

    Before me, Melchor Fernández de la Fuente, public scribe

[Spanish transcription]

Sepan quantos esta carta vieren como nos Tomas Dies de Cordoba y Juana Bautista de Vega su lexitima muger que Primero lo fui del alferes Antonio Gomez Leal difunto vesino que fue de la ciudad de Cholula . . . usando anbos marido y muger juntamente y de mancomun a bos de uno y cada uno de vos . . . otorgamos que bendemos Realmente a Diego de Andrada Peralta dueño obraje vesino desta ciudad quatro esclabos nonbrados Lazaro de la Cruz chino de hedad de çinquenta años, Juan mosanbique negro de otros cinquenta años = Antonio mulato de veinte años, Nicolas chino de sesenta años todos ofisiales de obraje Por nuestros propios esclabos cautivos libres de enpeño hipoteca y enajenasion . . . sin asegurarlos de ninguna tacha bissio defecto ni enfermedades publica ni secreta en Pressio y quantia de nuevesientos Pesos de oro comun de los quales nos a dado y Pagado quinientos Pesos en Reales de los quales nos damos Por entregados . . . y los quatrosientos Pesos restantes Cunplimyento a la dicha cantidad que nos a de Pagar para de la fecha desta en quatro messes cunplidos . . . fecha en la çiudad de los Angeles a dies y ocho dias del mes de Junio de mil y Seissientos y sinquenta años e io el Scrivano doi fe que conosco a los otorgantes e lo firmaron los dichos Tomas de Cordoba y Diego de Andrada Peralta y Por la dicha doña Juana Bautista de Vega que dixo no saber Vn testigo a su rruego siento siendolo Juan Bautista Sans, Diego Ruiz y Fransisco de Chabes y Juan Garsia vesinos desta ciudad

Thomas dies De cordova   Diego de andrada peralta   por testigo [rúbrica]
                                                       Chabes Galindo

    Ante mi Melchor Fernandez de la Fuente Scrivano Publico

Document 32: 1672—The Queen of Spain abolishes Asian and Chichimec slavery[5]

The Queen Regent

Viceroy, president, and civil court judges of the royal audience of Mexico City of New Spain. In a letter written to me on April 7 of this year, the audience of the city of Guadalajara, in the province of Nueva Galicia, explained that their attorney had requested that the decrees prohibiting the perpetual and temporary slavery of the Chichimec Indians be enforced and that those on the frontiers of the province of Nueva Vizcaya, Nuevo Leon, Nuevo México, and the Province of Sinaloa be freed, along with the *chinos*. [The attorney] asked their owners to present the title by which they possessed them, and declared that women and children under the age of fourteen were to be set free, even if they had been apprehended in just ~~land~~ ʷᵃʳ. They were to be set free because this had been resolved in different decrees, and especially in those of the years fifteen ~~sixty~~ ᶠⁱᶠᵗʸ three ᵃⁿᵈ ¹⁵⁶³. [The attorney found] that in the district of that audience, there are many slaves of this kind and that it would be very convenient to the service of God, Our Lord, for this to be carried out. The Council of Indies having seen what this attorney has said and requested, I have decided that it is good. Thus, I order you to free all the Indians who are held as slaves, in compliance with what is stipulated in the mentioned decrees, and remain vigilant that they are observed, followed, and carried out precisely and punctually, in consideration of the troubles caused by the opposite. Written in Madrid, on December 23, 1672. I, the Queen. By order of Her Majesty. Don Francisco Fernandez del Madrigal. Marked by the Council.

[in the left-hand margin, "To the king and audience of Mexico on freeing the Indians that are held as slaves, as is ordered in different decrees."]

[Spanish transcription]

La Reyna Governadora

Virrey, Presidente y Oydores de la Audiencia Real de la Çiudad de Mejico, de la Nueva españa en carta que me escrivio la Audiençia de la Çiudad de Guadalajara, en la Provinçia de la Nueva Galiçia, en siete de Abril de este año, da quenta de que con ocassion de haver pedido el fiscal de ella se diese cumplimiento a las çedula que prohiven la esclavitud perpetua, y temporal de los Indios chichimecos se pusiesen en livertad a los de las fronteras de la Provinçia de la Nueva Vizcaya, Nuevo Reyno de Leon, Nuevo Mexico, Provinçia de Sinaloa, y a los chinos, y mando a los posehedores, presentasen el Titulo, con que los poseian, y declaro que las mujeres y niños de menor Edad de Catorçe años, aunque fuesen apresados en ~~Tierra~~ ᵍᵘᵉʳʳᵃ Justa, fuesen

---

5. Archivo General de Indias, Guadalajara, L.4, ff. 71r–72r.

libres por estar resuelto asi por diferentes Çedulas, y en particular por las de los años de mil quinientos y ~~sesenta~~ cinquenta y tres ʸ ¹⁵⁶³' y que en el distrito de esa Audiença, ay muchos esclavos de esta calidad y que sera mui conveniente al serviçio de Dios nuestro Señor se ejecute lo mismo = Y haviendose visto en el consejo de las Indias con lo que sobre esta materia, dijo, y pidio el fiscal del [sic], lo he tenido por bien, y asi os mando, hagais poner en livertad, a todos los Indios que ᵉˢtuvieren por esclavos, en conformidad de lo que se dispone por las çedulas referidas, estando con todo cuidado de que se observen, cunplan y executen, precisa, y puntualmente, por el escrupulo que causa lo contrario. Fecha en Madrid a Veinte y tres de Diziembre de mil Seiscientos y setenta y dos años. Yo la Reyna = Por mandamiento de su Magestad. Don Francisco Fernandez del Madrigal = señalada de el Consejo =

[al margen izquierdo, "Al virrey y Audiencia de Mexico sobre que pongan en livertad a los Indios que tubieren por Esclavos como esta mandado por diferentes çedulas."]

Document 33: 1685—A bill of sale for a Mozambican *cafre*[6] in Cavite[7]

In the port of Cavite [in the Philippines], on June 11, 1685, before me, the scribe and witnesses. The ensign Manuel Andrés de León, *vecino* of this said port, whom I attest that I know, truly sells [his] slave, a *cafre de pasa*, named Juan de la Cruz, native of Mozambique, twenty years old more or less. He sells him to Joseph de Bolívar, for the price and sum of one hundred and ten common gold pesos in reales, and acknowledges that he received this from the buyer. In this regard, he renounces the exemption, financial laws, and the receipt and proof thereof as contained in the laws. As a true seller, he commits to following through and making good on this sale in the best manner according to the law. He does not insure the said slave against any public or secret defect or illness, other than that the latter is a good slave, a subject of perpetual servitude, free of any general or special lien, mortgage, or any other debt. He renounces the right and claim he has to said slave and transfers them to the buyer, in light of this writ, and an authorized copy was given to the [buying] party in due form. With this, the buyer has acquired true dominion over the said slave. The [seller] committed his person and present and future goods, and gave power to His Majesty's justices and renounced the laws in due form, including the general law. He

---

6. A physical descriptor, derived from the term *kafir*, to identify people of African descent. It was often used to describe enslaved people with tightly coiled hair, especially in the transpacific slave trade of the late seventeenth century.
7. Archivo General de la Nación (México), Indiferente Virreinal, Caja 1877, Exp. 35, ff. 1r–1v.

has granted and signed this writ. Witnesses, Francisco de Tolentino, Manuel Álvarez, and Juan Leonardo, who were present and to which I attest. = Manuel Andreo de León = before me, Juan Trujillo, public scribe.

I made my sign in testimony of the truth   Juan Trujillo, public scribe

[Spanish transcription]

En el Puerto de Cavite [en Filipinas] en onze dias del mes de Junio de mill seisçientos ochenta y çinco años ante mi el escrivano y testigos El Alferes Manuel Andres de Leon, Vezino de este dicho puerto a quien doy fee que conosco otorgo que Vende Realmente y con efecto mi [sic] esclavo cafre de pasa llamado Juan de la Cruz natural de Masanbique [Mozambique] de hedad de Veintte años por mas o menos a Joseph de Bolivar por preçio y quantia de Ciento y Diez pesos de oro Comun en Reales que Confeso aver Reçivido del Comprador y aserca de ello Renunçio la esempçion y leyes de la pecunia = y entrego y su prueba como se contienen y como Real Vendedor se obligo a la eviçion y saneamiento de esta Venta en la mas Mas Vastante forma que por derecho mejor lugar hubiere sin asegurar dicho esclavo de tachas o enfermedad que tenga Publica o secreta mas de Ser esclavo le [sic] bueno y Justo titulo sujeto a perpetua servidumbre libre de empeño ypoteca y de otra enegenazion Espeçial y general y Renunçia el derecho y assion [sic] que [d]el dicho Esclavo tiene se de traspassa en el Comprador en Virtud de esta Escritura de la qual entrego a la parte Vn traslado Autorisado en forma y con el ser Visto haver adquirido Verdadero dominio al dicho Esclavo y a la firmeza y [v]alidassion desta Venta obligo su persona y Vienes avidos y por haver Con poderio a las Justiçias de su Magestad su mision y Renunçiazion de leyes en forma Con la General del derecho y asi lo otorgo y firmo siendo testigos Francisco de Tholentino, Manuel Alvarez y Juan Leonardo presentes de que Doy fee = Manuel Andreo de Leon = ante mi Juan Trujillo escribano Publico.

Fize mi signo en testimonio de Verdad   Juan Truxillo sscribano Publico

Document 34: 1685—Legal title to enslaved *cafres* from the East Indies[8]

In the town of Cavite, January 27, 1684. Captain Sebastián de la Oliva, inspector and accountant of the royal works of this port, whom I attest that I know, appeared before me, the scribe, and witnesses. He states that he truly and indeed sells three of his slaves, *cafres de pasa* from eastern India, Benito who is no more than 30 years old,

---

8. Archivo General de la Nación, Indiferente Virreinal, Caja 1567, Exp. 8, ff. 1r–2r.

Juan who is no more than 35, and José, who is up to 25. All three of them are natives of Mozambique in the said India [sic]. He sells them to the Lord Doctor Don Pedro Sebastián de Bolívar y Mena of His Majesty's council and his civil court judge in the royal audience and chancery of these [Philippine] Islands for the price of 375 pesos in common gold in reales, 125 of them for Benito, and 240 for the remaining Juan and José at 120 pesos for each. [De la Oliva] acknowledged that he has received and did receive [this sum] from the said lord civil court judge . . . and to this effect, he gave [de Bolívar y Mena] an authorized copy of this writ in proper form and declared that he received and bought the said three *cafre* slaves from Mateo de Rocha, a Portuguese man in this said port and for the same price for which he now sells them, as can be seen in the bills of sale that he presented before me on September 14, 15, and 16 of the past year of 1683 . . . and he signed. Witnesses, the naval assistant Juan de Trujillo, Francisco de Solentino, and Nicolas Manzano, who were present. Sebastián de la Oliva = before me, Miguel Gutiérrez Hermosilla, public scribe . . .

I, Felipe Ferrer, quartermaster of the galleon *Santo Niño de Zebu*, flagship of the Philippine Islands, anchored in this port of Acapulco and soon to return to the said islands, declare that I hold two Blacks named Juan and José, *cafres de pasa* from eastern India, who are slaves of Doctor Don Pedro Sebastián de Bolívar y Mena, of His Majesty's council. As seen in the writ entered before Diego Gutíerrez Hermosilla, public scribe in the port of Cavite of said islands, the said Doctor Don Pedro Sebastian de Bolívar y Mena gave me the said slaves for me to sell in this port of Acapulco. I am to return the proceeds in goods that he has asked from me in a note. So that putting this sale into effect, I state that I sell and deliver the two Black slaves named Juan and José to the ensign Domingo de Anguiarro, grant-holder of this port [of Acapulco] and *vecino* of Mexico City, for the price of 625 common gold pesos that he has given me in cash for the said two slaves. I sell them without insuring them against any flaw, defect, or any other vice, other than to note that they are slaves in good title . . . in this said port of Acapulco on March 20, 1685. Witnesses, Don Tomás de Urquiola, the ensign Felipe del Bosaue, and Juan Osuna, who were present.

Felipe Ferrer

[Spanish transcription]

En el pueblo de cavite en Veinte y siette Dias del mes de henero de mill seisçientos ochenta y quatro años ante mi el escrivano y testigos el captian Sebastian de la Oliva, veedor y apuntado de las obras Reales deste puerto que doy fee conosco, otorgo que Vende Realmente y con efecto tres esclavos suios cafres de pasa de la Yndia oriental nombrados, Benito de hasta treinta años de hedad = Juan de hasta treinta y çinco: y Joseph de hasta Veinte y çinco todos tres naturales de mosambeque en dicha Yndia [sic], al señor Doctor Don Pedro Sebastian de Bolivar y Mena del consejo de Su magestad y su oidor en la audiencia Y chansilleria Real destas Yslas por preçio y quantia de treçientos y Sesenta y çinco pesos de oro comun en Reales, los çiento y beinte y çinco de ellos por el dicho Benito, y los dosçientos y quarenta Restantes por los dichos Juan y Josephe a çiento y Veinte por cada uno que confesso aver Resevido y Resivio de dicho señor . . . y para ello entrego copia de esta escriptura authoriçada en forma y declaro que ubo y compro dichos tres esclavos cafres de Matheo de Rocha portugues en este dicho puerto y por el mesmo preçio que al presente los vende como constara por las escripturas de Venta que dixo aberle otorgado ante mi en catorçe, quinçe y dies y seis de septiembre del año proximo pasado de seisçientos ochenta y tres . . . y lo firmo siendo testigos el ayudante Juan de Truxillo, Françisco de Solentino, y Nicolas Mansano presentes Sebastian de la Oliva = ante mi Miguel Gutierres Hermosilla escrivano publico . . .

Digo Yo Phelipe Ferrer contramaestre del Galeon Santo Niño de Zibu capitana de las Yslas Phelipinas surto en este puerto [de Acapulco] y proximo a hazer tornaViaje a dichas Yslas, que por quanto tengo en mi Poder dos negros nombrados Juan y Joseph cafres de passa de la Yndia oriental esclavos del Doctor Don Pedro Sebastian de Volivar y Mena del consejo de su magestad como consta de su escriptura ante Diego Gutierres Hermosilla escrivano publico en el puerto de cavite de dichas Yslas los quales dichos esclavos me entrego dicho Doctor Don Pedro Sebastian de Bolivar Y Mena para que en este dicho Puerto de acapulco los Venda y su prosedido se lo Retorne en los generos que por Memoria me tiene pedidos; Y poniendo en efecto su Ventta Digo que se los vendo y entrego dichos dos negros esclavos nombrados Juan y Joseph a el alferes Domingo de Anguiarro encomendero deste puerto y vezino de la ciudad de mexico por preçio de seisçientos y veinte y çinco pesos de oro comun que me ha dado y entregado en dicha Moneda de contado por dichos dos esclavos y se los Vendo sin asegurarselo de tacha o enfermedad ni otro Viscio alguno sino que son esclavos de buen titulo . . . en este dicho puerto de acapulco, en Veinte de março de mill seisçientos y ochenta y çinco años siendo testigos Don Thomas de Vrquiola, el alferes Phelipe del Bosque, y Juan de Osuna, presentes =

Phelipe Ferrer.

Document 35: 1708—Arrival of the Black *esclavos de pasa* from Manila[9]

In the city of the Kings, Port of Acapulco, on February 11, 1709, His Grace, Lord Don Juan José de Veitia Linage, knight of the Order of Santiago, head accountant of

---

9. Archivo General de Indias, Filipinas, 205, N.1, ff. 229v–230v, IMG 478–480. http://pares.mcu.es/ParesBusquedas20/catalogo/show/1931209?nm

the tribunal and royal audience of this New Spain, superintendent judge of the galleons from the Philippines that dock in the bay of this Port. I say that, with respect to the third clause in the instruction that is being observed and practiced in this kingdom according to His Majesty's orders, which are being cited, on the introduction of Black slaves from the Philippine Islands, with respect to the inspection done on the flagship galleon [that is named] *Nuestra Señora del Rosario, San Francisco Javier, and Santa Rosa*, on January 13 past, different Black *pasa*[10] slaves were found. According to the declaration made by Captain Don Juan Francisco de Yrrisarri y Ursua, master of the said galleon, they come in service and assistance of their masters in order to return them to the Philippines. Antonio, Bartolomé, and Gaspar belong to General Don Juan Ignacio de Vertis, and one of them is a clarinet player. Another, named Juan, belongs to Captain Don Domingo de Lexarsar. Bartolomé belongs to Juan Antonio Romero, the guard. Miguel belongs to Captain Don Manuel de San Juan Santa Cruz, a passenger. José belongs to Don Francisco de Tagle. Another José belongs to Don Antonio Sánchez Serdán. Antonio belongs to Pedro Blanquin, assistant pilot. Salvador Justo belongs to Miguel de Medina, the quartermaster. Cristóbal belongs to José Melendes, naval ensign. His Grace [Veitia Linage] ordered all the owners of the said slaves that have been listed to secure [their slaves] with secular, honest, and creditworthy people, who are *vecinos* of this kingdom, so that they will take said slaves to the Philippine Islands, without disposing of them, selling, or alienating them, and thus he decreed and signed.

Don Juan José de Veitia Linage, before me,
Antonio Jiménez de Guzmán, royal scribe

[Spanish transcription]

En la Ciudad de los Reyes, Puerto de Acapulco, â ônze dias del mes de febrero de mill Setesientos y nueve años, su merced, el Señor Don Juan Joseph de Veitia Linage, Cavallero del orden de Santiago, contador mayor del tribunal y Real Audiensia de quentas de esta Nueva Spaña, Juez Superintendente de los Galeones de Philipinas Surtos en la bahia de estte Puerto = Dijo que por quanto, por la Clausula tercera de la Ynstrucçion que se esta observando y practicando en que se sitan las Ordenes de Su Magestad, que tiene dados sobre la Yntrodusion de Negros Esclavos de las Yslas Philipinas, en estte reyno, y respectto a que en la Visitta fha, en el Galeon Capitana Nuestra Señora del Rosario, San Francisco Xavier, y Santta Rosa, el dia treze de Henero proximo passado, se hallaron diferenttes Esclavos negros de passa, que segun la Declarasion, fecha, por el Capitan Don Juan Francisco de Yrrisarri y Ursua, maestre de dicha Capitana, vienen en servisio y assistensia de sus amos para bolberlos

---

10. *Pasa* was a shortened version of the *cafre de pasa* label; see Glossary at the beginning of this book.

â Philipinas, Y que Antonio, Bartholome, y Gaspar = pertenesen al General Don Juan Ignacio de Vertis y el uno de ellos es Clarinero = Otro nombrado Juan es del Capitan Don Domingo de Lexarsar = Bartholome = toca y pertenese â Juan Antonio Romero, Guardian = Miguel al Capitan Don Manuel de San Juan Santa Cruz, passajero = Joseph â Don Francisco de Tagle = Otro Joseph a Don Antonio Sanchez Serdan = Antonio â Pedro Blanquin, ayudante piloto = Salvador Juzto â Miguel de Medina, contramaestre = Xptoval â Joseph Melendes, Alferez de mar y guerra = Mandava su merced [Veitia Linage] y mando se notifique â todos los Dueños de dichos Esclavos que ban expresados afianzen con personal legas, llanas y abonadas, vezinos de este reyno de que bolveran dichos Esclavos â dichas Yslas Philipinas sin disponer de ellos, venderlso ni Enajenarlos, y assi lo proveyo Y firmo =

Don Juan Joseph de Veitia Linage antte my Anttonio Ximenez de Guzman, scrivano Real =

Document 36: 1714—Investigation into enslaved Blacks arriving in Acapulco[11]

In the city of the Kings, port of Acapulco, on March 1, 1714, Lord Don Alejo López de Cotilla, gentleman of the Order of Santiago, royal accountant of the royal treasury of Mexico City, superintendent judge for the intendancy, dependency, and affairs of the Philippines galleon *Nuestra Señora de Begoña*, which is anchored in this port's bay and under the charge of General Don Francisco Medrano until its departure. He said that it is [his] responsibility and obligation to investigate the entry of Black slaves from the Philippine Islands to this kingdom, which is against His Majesty's orders. In this respect, different slaves were found during the inspection that His Grace carried out on said galleon on January 27 of this year. These were Juan, Alejandro, Cayetano, and Manuel, who according to the quartermaster, Captain Don Antonio de Chávez, belong to him and two of them belong to the most excellent lord viceroy of New Spain. Another Manuel is the slave of Sergeant Major Don Juan Pablo de Orduña. Lorenzo is the slave of Don Antonio de Savalegui, captain of sea and war. Vicente is the slave of Constable Don Nicolás de Rivera. Cosme Damián belongs to Ensign José Martínez Guardián, and Javier Agustín. Luis and Joseph who belong to the said General. Their [owners] say that they bring the said slaves to assist and serve them, and not to sell them. Therefore, His Grace ordered that the said masters be notified that they must provide full, honest, and thorough surety that they will not sell or

---

11. Archivo General de Indias, Filipinas, 206, N.1, ff. 220r–221r, 223r–223v, IMG 467–469. http://pares.mcu.es/ParesBusquedas20/catalogo/show/1931210?nm

transfer the abovementioned [slaves] in any way. The said General was required to explicitly commit to keeping those who belong to him since he intends to remain in this kingdom. Should he not comply with this order, the said slaves will be seized. The [judge] decreed and signed in this manner. Don Alejo Lopes de Cotilla, before me, Antonio Jiménez de Guzmán, royal scribe.

[in the left-hand margin, "Notice"]

In the city of the Kings, port of Acapulco, on the said day, I notified Captain Don Antonio de Chavez, quartermaster of the Philippine galleon, of the preceding order. He said that he was bringing two of the four slaves to the most excellent Lord Viceroy of this New Spain. The other [slave] is extremely sick and unable to embark, so he leaves him in this city's hospital as alms. If he heals, he is to serve the poor sick for his entire life. Cayetano, who is the fourth, will return in his service to the Philippine Islands. [Chávez] responded that he is ready to provide surety, to which I attest. He signed. Antonio de Chávez, before me, Antonio Jiménez de Guzmán, royal scribe. . . .

* * *

[in the left-hand margin, "Notice"]

In the city of the Kings, port of Acapulco, on March 3 . . . General Don Francisco Medrano y Asiain, whom I [the scribe] attest that I know, of the Philippine galleon *Nuestra Señora de Begoña*, anchored in the bay of said port. He said that he owns and has brought four Black men from said islands as his slaves. They are Agustín, Luis, Javier, and José. Agustín is a trumpet player by trade and will return to this same occupation to assist the person who will succeed him as general. Since he [Medrano] will remain in this kingdom and must have [people] to serve and assist him, he commits to keeping Javier, Luis, and José in his possession and will not transfer them for any pretext, and they will be registered as such, for whatever the lord judge orders . . . and he signed it. Witnesses, Don Juan de Umaña, Don Matías de Sadava, Francisco Zurita, present. Francisco de Medrano y Asiain, before me, Antonio Jiménez de Guzmán, royal scribe. . . .

[Spanish transcription]

En la ciudad de los Reyes Puerto de Acapulco a primero de Marzo de mill setecientos y catorse años el señor Don Alejo Lopez de Cotilla, cavallero del order de Santiago, Contador oficial Real de la Real hacienda y caja de la ciudad de Mexico, Jues Superintendente Pribatibo para la Yntendencia dependencias e Yncidencias del Galeon de Philipinas Nuestra señora de Begoña del cargo del General Don Francisco Medrano surta en la Vahia deste Puerto hasta su partida: Dijo que por quanto es descargo y obligacion imbestigar la Yntroduccion de Negros esclavos de las Yslas Philipinas â este Reyno contra las ordenes de su Magestad, Y respecto a que en la Visita que su Merced ejecuto luego que dio fondo el dicho Galeon el dia Veinte y siete de henero passado deste año se hallaron diferentes esclavos, como fueron Juan = Alexandro = Cayetano = Manuel = que estos dijo el Capitan Don Antonio de Chaves contramaestre perteneserle y ser dos de ellos del Excelentísimo Señor Virrey de esta Nueva España = otro nombrado Manuel esclavo del Sarxento Maior Don Juan Pablo de Orduña = Lorenzo esclavo de Don Antonio de Savalegui capitan de mar y Guerra = Vizente esclavo de Don Nicolas de Rivera condestable = Cosme Damian del Alferez Joseph Martinez Guardian, y Xavier Augustin = Luiz y Joseph que lo son de dicho General, todos los quales dizen traer los referidos Esclavos para su asistençia y serviçio, y no para su Venta, por lo qual mandaba y Mando su Merced se Notifique â dichos sus amos den fiansas legas, llanas, y Abonadas de que no venderan ni enageraran a los Susodichos, en ninguna manera, y a dicho General se le requirio haga obligaçion de tener los que le pertenesen, de manifiesto, para lo que pudiere resultar respecto a estar el susodicho en pretençion de quedarse en este reino, y no lo cumpliendo los susodichos se aseguren dichos Esclavos, y assi proveio, y firmo = Don Alejo Lopes de Cotilla = Ante mi Antonio Ximenes de Gusman Escribano Real.

[al margen izquierdo, "Notificacion"]

En la Ciudad de los Reies, Puerto de Acapulco en el dicho dia, notifique el auto presedente a el Cappitan Don Antonio de Chaves Contra Maestre del Galeon de Philipinas, a quien dijo que los dos de los quatro Esclavos que trae el Excelentísimo señor Virrey de esta Nueva España, el otro que por sumamente enfermo ê ympoçibilitado para embarasarse [sic, ¿embarcarse?], lo deja en el hospital de esta Ciudad de Limosna para que si sanare sirva a los Pobres enfermos toda su Vida, y el quarto que es Caietano le buelve en su serviçio a las Yslas Philipinas, y que esta presto â afianzar, y esto respondio de que doi fee, y lo firmo = Antonio de Chaves = Ante mi = Antonio Ximenes de Gusman Escribano Real. . . .

* * *

[al margen izquierdo, "Notificacion"]

En la Ciudad de los Reies Puerto de Acapulco en dicho dia tres de Marzo . . . el General Don Françisco Medrano y Asiain que lo es del Galeon de Philipinas *Nuestra Señora de Begoña* surta en la Bahia de este dicho Puerto a quien doi fee conosco y Dixo que tiene por sus esclavos y trajo de dichas Yslas quatro Negros, que son Augustin = Luis, Xavier y Joseph, y que Augustin es de ofiçio clarinero el qual ha de bolver en la mesma ocupaçion en asistençia de la persona que le subsede en dicho Puesto de General, y que respecto â quedarse en este Reino y aver de tener quien le sirva y asista, por lo que toca a Xavier, Luiz y Joseph obliga â que los tendra en su poder, y no los enagenara con ningun pretesto, y estaran de manfiesto para lo que se le mandare por el Señor Juez . . . y lo firmo siendo testigos Don Juan de Umaña = Don Mathias de Sadava = y Francisco Surita, presentes = Francisco de Medrano y Asiain = Ante mi Antonio Ximenes de Gusman Escribano Real. . . .

CHAPTER 4

Rebellion and Marronage

The documents included in this chapter span the years 1537 to 1804 and are focused on resistance to enslavement and colonial rule. There is immense regional and chronological variation in the documents included here because exploited and enslaved people fled, rebelled, and contested their subjugation throughout New Spain. The first two documents speak to the violence of the early colonial period, but also to Spaniards' fears and anxieties in a land where they were vastly outnumbered by Native populations. Rumors loomed large in the alleged 1537 conspiracy in Mexico City and the mines of Amatepec. During those years, two slaving dynamics operated in parallel: the enslavement of Native war captives in northwestern regions (such as Culiacán) and the trafficking of enslaved Africans through early transatlantic routes. The New Laws of 1542, which abolished Indigenous slavery (in theory), were implemented very slowly in New Spain. During the late 1540s, the Caxcan noble Francisco Tenamaztle led a ferocious military effort—apparently aided by Black fighters—against the colonizing forces in Nochistlán (located in the modern-day state of Zacatecas).

By the early seventeenth century, the actions of the *cimarrones*, or maroons, had captured the attention of the colonial authorities. The 1619 and 1622 documents in this chapter focus on the maroon communities (*palenques*) of the Río Blanco-Acultzingo region, where escaped Africans formed autonomous settlements and repeatedly resisted punitive expeditions. Above all, Spaniards feared the maroon leader Gaspar Yanga, whose supposed death was described in a 1619 pamphlet published in Málaga, Spain and is translated into English here for the first time. Resistance continued throughout the colonial period, as seen in the selections from Chietla and Córdoba, in 1659 and 1760, respectively. Maroon communities, however, were not monoliths, and significant differences often divided their leaders. The depositions of María Josefa and Gertrudis Simona about the *palenque* of Mandinga reveal the extreme consequences that could follow such internal disagreements. This chapter also includes eyewitness accounts of the uprising led by Crax Bomba and 300 survivors of the *San Vicente* slave ship in late 1669.

Most acts of rebellion, however, took place on an individual scale or in groups of two or three and were never recorded before a notary, ecclesiastical judge, or any other official. Therefore, they are poorly documented. The cases included here provide some sense of the personal motivations that led an enslaved person to flee her or his owners. The 1665 case of Nicolasa, a wet nurse, and her infant daughter,

María, demonstrates how enslaved domestics could actively seek better living conditions. Similarly, Francisco de la Cruz's flight from Mexico City to Tlaxcala reveals how the enslaved developed a profound understanding of legal systems, to the point that they could productively adopt false identities to their benefit. This chapter ends with three documents that reveal how diverse populations resisted the colonial state in the northern reaches of New Spain (including Spanish Louisiana) during the last decades of colonial rule. These years were marked by the westward expansion of the United States and the transferral of the Louisiana territory from France to Spain in 1763 and back to France in 1801 before finally being sold to the United States in 1803. Enslaved people did not stand idle as shifting legal and property codes were imposed on them. To the contrary, the documents from 1790 and 1804 indicate that escaped people forced Mexican colonial authorities in Chihuahua and Nacogdoches to reassess long-standing policies regarding asylum and freedom.

Document 37: 1537—Black rebellion in Mexico City and the mines of Amatepec[1]

Sacred Imperial Catholic Majesty,

I have received two letters, the first from September 9 past and the other from February 3, that Your Majesty sent in response to other letters of mine. I will respond to what is needed from both of them in this letter. . . . Your Majesty orders that an inspecting judge be sent to Nueva Galicia. I have ordered a copy of the investigation that Nuño de Guzmán led against those who exceeded themselves in branding the slaves. As soon as that copy arrives, I will send it to Your Majesty. . . .

I also wrote Your Majesty about how I decreed that no slaves be made in Nueva Galicia, unless by Your Majesty's order. Those who have settled there have come to complain that they cannot sustain themselves unless they do so. Still, I have replied to them that they cannot do this, and I delay them with kind words. Now Melchor Díaz has come here, representing the town of San Miguel de Culiacán, and has told me that the *vecinos*[2] there have nothing with which to sustain themselves if the profit of slaving is taken from them, because they have no other business and have nothing else to do there except for this. Since this has been prohibited, they want to abandon said town. They gave me notice of this so that I might decree whatever might be most convenient to Your Majesty's service. In light of this and because sustaining that

---

1. Archivo General de Indias, Patronato, 184, R.27, no folio, IMG 1–31. http://pares.mcu.es/ParesBusquedas20/catalogo/show/125239

2. *vecinos*: Although the plural use of this term includes women, in this early colonial frontier, *vecino* referred almost exclusively to a Spanish male head of a household.

town is very important, given its location and because it is so far forward [north], I decided it would be fine, at least while consulting with Your Majesty, to help them in some way. I sent them up to a thousand *tepuzque*[3] pesos in ironwork and other necessary things, with which they may occupy themselves until Your Majesty orders what should be done. . . .

On September 27 past I received word that some Blacks had chosen a king, and had agreed among themselves to kill all the Spaniards and take over the land. The Indians were also a part of this. But because the person who came to tell me was one of those Blacks, I did not entirely believe him, though I secretly endeavored to find out whether this was true. While this was being done, I sent some [people] from my house to go out at night and stay hidden among the Indians without being detected. They were to see if there was some news and, if there was, to come report it, because I knew that I did not want to be unprepared, although I had not believed it. But if by chance it were true, I did not want them to come upon us if they felt that I knew [about the plot]. With things in this manner, I was able to find a lead through the investigations I carried out. And then I arrested the one who had been chosen as king, along with the rest of the leaders that we were able to arrest. I sent an order about this to the mines and to the Spanish towns, so that they should be prepared and on the lookout for the Blacks that might be in those parts. And, thus, it was done. The Blacks who were arrested confessed that it was true that they had made an agreement to take over the land. Up to two dozen of them were quartered[4] in this city [Mexico City] and in the mines of Amatepec, where I sent Francisco Vázquez de Coronado for this purpose. [Another] four Black men and a Black woman were captured; the Indians killed them and brought them back to me [preserved] in salt. These were those who had gone missing, and I had ordered that they be apprehended or killed. With this, it came to an end. Efforts were made to find out how much blame the natives had in this, but they seem not to have been involved other than knowing about it, and that if the Blacks started [the uprising] and things went poorly for us, they would finish it.

It is thought that the Blacks were encouraged to make this uprising, first by the wars and needs that Your Majesty has. Because everything that happens over there [in Europe] is written about with more detail than is necessary and is learned by the Blacks and Indians, with nothing left out. Second, the delay in ships arriving, as is now the case, was an important part of this, because a friar said that no ship from Spain would come in ten years, although he denies saying this. I am not astonished by what the Blacks tried to do, because even the Spaniards want to show and convey the need they have of them, although everything is now accounted for. Your Majesty should order that ships come frequently, so that things from over there [Spain] might

---

3. A gold-copper alloy coin that circulated extensively in early colonial Mexico.
4. Their bodies violently dismembered.

often be known here. This will contribute so that all will be happy and the land in greater contentment and calm.

Having seen all this, and how even though there were not many Blacks in this land, they wanted to attempt [an uprising] with such impudence, it seemed that I would write Your Majesty so that for now you would order to cease sending the number of Blacks that I had asked to be sent. Because if there were a greater [number of them] and another thing like this were to take place, they could put us in great difficulty and we would be at risk of losing the land.

Due to this uprising of the Blacks, I determined to make a review of our forces in order to alert the people and know the state of the weapons and horses that each person had. We found up to six hundred and twenty men on horseback, of whom four hundred and fifty would be able to serve in good order, with another such number well-prepared on foot. Many others were unable to go out because they were indisposed or because of other understandable impediments.

In past days I wrote Your Majesty about the necessity of bringing weapons to this land, and I sent a report on which ones should be sent. Your Majesty replied that you had charged the officials of Seville to look into this, but nothing has come of this up to now. There are very few weapons here. Were it not for the ones that I wrote Your Majesty about, that I purchased in Veracruz to send to Peru but did not send because the profit being made by those going there and by some others was considerable, there would almost be none here. If the uprising of the Blacks had gone forward, I would have found myself the most vexed man by the absence of weapons with which to resist them. I beg Your Majesty to send them with all haste, because the need of them is so great. I ask that the quantity be double what I requested in my report. Likewise, I ask that you send saltpeter for gunpowder, two or three hundred hundred-weights, because what is produced here is very little and is made at great expense.

... In light of what has happened with the Blacks and some things that move this person, it seems to me that it would be convenient to Your Majesty's service to build a stronghold on the Tacuba causeway. There would be rooms for the president and judges [of the royal *audiencia*], for the foundry, for officials, and for the mint. At the very end, there should be an even stronger room for the magistrate, where munitions, artillery, and some amount of wheat and maize foodstuffs should be kept. ... From Mexico City, December 10, 1537.

Holy Imperial Catholic Majesty, your humble servant kisses your royal feet and hands.

Don Antonio de Mendoza.

[Spanish transcription]

Sacra Cesárea Católica Majestad

    Doss cartas, que Vuestra magestad me mando screvir en rrespuesta de otras mias Recebi, la una, de ix de Settiembre del pasado, y la otra, de tress de hebrero del presente, y lo que á entream[b]as ay que rresponder, lo hare en esta. . . . El treslado del proceso que Nuño de Guzman hizo contra los que heçedieron en el herrar de los esclavos, que vuestra majestad manda que se enbie al Juez de rresidençia de la Nueva Galicia, [he] ˢᶜʳⁱᵗᵒ que lo haga sacar, como sea venido, Se enbiará a vuestra magestad. . . .

    Tanbien escrevi a vuestra majestad como proveý que en la Nueva Galizia, no se hiciezen sclavos, sino fuese por la horden que vuestra majestad tiene mandada dar, y aunque los que allí an poblado, se me an venido a quexar que no se pueden sostener sino es haciendose, todavia les he respondido que no se puede hacer, y los entretengo con buenas palabras. Agora ha venido aqui Melchior Díaz, de parte de la villa de San Miguel de Culuacan [Culiacán], y me a dicho como aquellos vezinos, quitadoles El ynterese que tenian del hazer los Sclavos, no avia con que se poder sustentar porque no tenian otra granjeria, ni les hazia estar allí otra cosa sino esta, y que pues se la avia proybido quellos querian desmamparar [sic] aquel pueblo que me daban notiçia para que proveyese en ello lo que mas Conbinisese al servyçio de vuestra majestad. Visto esto y que El sostener aquella villa ymporta mucho, por estar tan adelante y en la parte questá, me pareçio que hera bien hasta tanto que se consultaba con vuestra majestad, de hazelles alguna ayuda y fue enballes en herraje y otras cosas nesçesarias hasta mill pesos de tipuzquen [tepuzque] con que se entretengan, hasta tanto que vuestra majestad enbiava a mandar lo que fuese servido. . . .

    A xxvij del mes de Settiembre pasado Tuve aviso de como Los negros Tenian elegido un rrey, y conçertado entrellos de matar a todos los españoles, y alçarse con la tierra y que los yndios heran tambien En ello y por ser El que me lo avia venido A dezir un negro dellos no le di mucho crédito mas de procurar secrettamente de saber si hera verdad y mientras esto se hazia, mande a algunos de mi casa que se fuesen de noche, y estuviesen entre Los yndios escondidos, sin que dellos fuesen sentidos y mirasen si avia alguna novedad, y aviendola, viniesen a dar mandado Dello porque como yo lo sabia aunque no lo avia creydo, no quise estar desaperçebido, para si por Ventura fuese verdad, y sintiesen ellos que lo sabia, y quisiesen venir sobre nosotros, y estando la cosa assi, con las dilegençias que hize, vine a hallar Alguno Rastro y luego a la hora hize prehender al que estaba helegido por rrey y a los más prinçipales que se pudieron aver y di mandado Dello a las minas y a los pueblos que aquí ay de españoles, para que estuviesen sobre avyso y tuviesen a buen Recabdo [sic, recaudo] los negros que en Cada parte destas huviese; y así se hizo, los negros, que se prendieron, confesaron ser verdad de estar entrellos hecho este conçierto de alçarse con la tierra; y se hizieron quartos en esta çiudad y en las minas de Amatepeque [Amatepec], donde enbie a ello a Francisco Vazquez de Coronado, hasta dos docenas dellos, con quatro negros y una negra, que los indios mataron y me trujeron salados de los que se habian ausentado, porque yo les mande que los prendiesen, o los matasen, y con esto se atajo. Procurose de saber, todo lo que fue posible la culpa que en esto tenian los naturales y hasta agora, no se a podido averiguar quellos fuesen en ello mas de creer que lo sabian, y que si los negros lo Començaran y nos fuera mal quellos acabaran la cosa.

Tienese por çierto que dio atrevimiento a estos negros para querer hazer este levantamiento, lo vno las guerras y nesçesidades que vuestra majestad tiene porque de alla todo se escrive más particularmente de lo que seria nesçesario y viene A notiçia de los negros y de yndios, sin que se les encubra nada, y lo otro El tardar en esta coyuntura Tanto los navíos como agora que no dejo de ser harta parte para ello a causa que vn frayle dixo que en diez años no avia de venir navio dEspaña, avnque el dize que se lo levantaron y no me maravillo de lo que querian hazer los negros porque aun los españoles quieren mostrar y dar á entender la nesçessidad que dellos se tiene, aunque todo esta muy saneado. Vuestra magestad deve mandar que hordinariamente vengan navios, por manera que a menudo se sepa de alla, porque sera mucha parte para que todos esten alegres y la tierra en mas Contentamiento y sosiego.

Visto esto, y que con no aver muchos negros en esta tierra querian intentar Tan gran liviandad me paresçió de escrevir á vuestra magestad que por agora çesase de mandar enbiar aca la cantidad de negros que tengo scritto que se enbien; porque aviendo mucha, y subçediendo otra cosa como esta, podrian nos poner en mucho trabajo y la tierra en terminos de perderse.

Deste levantamiento de negros Resulto que hize hacer alarde, para más despertar la gente y saber El adereço de armas y Cavallos que cada uno tenia, y hallaronse hasta seysçientos y veinte de Cavallo. Destos serian vtiles para poder servir los quatroçientos y cincuenta dellos bien en horden y otros tantos de pie bien Aderesçados sin otros muchos que por yndisposiçion y otros impedimentos Justos Dexaron de salir.

Los días pasados Screvi a vuestra magestad la nesçessidad que avia de traerse armas a esta tierra y enbie vn memorial de las que me paresçia que devian ser y vuestra magestad me mando Responder que lo avia Cometido a los ofiçiales de Sevylla, para quellos lo cumpliese / hasta agora no ha venido nada, y aqui ay muy pocas, y sino fuera por las que screvi a vuestra magestad, que avia hecho comprar en la Veracruz para enbiar Al Peru, que las dexe de enbiar por Ver que la saca dellas de los que alla yban y de otros que las llevaban por Su interese hera grande no hubiera casi ningunas y si este levantamiento de los negros fuera adelante, yo me hallara El mas Confuso del mundo por la falta que avia de armas para resitirlos. A vuestra majestad suplico mande que con Toda brevedad se me enbien, pues la nesçessidad Dellas es tan grande y que la cantidad se al doble de lo que por el memorial tengo pedido y que asimismo se me mande enbiar dozientos o trezientos quintales de Salitre para polvora porque lo que aca se saca es muy poco, y hazese a mucha costa.

. . . Y visto lo que ha subçedido de los negros y algunas Cosas que la persona siente, me paresçe que lo que Conviene al serviçio de vuestra magestad, es que en la calçada de Tacuba se haga Vna casa fuerte en que haya aposentos para El presidente y oidores y para la fundiçion y ofiçiales y para casa de moneda y al cabo vn apartamiento que sea más fuerte para El alcayde donde se tengan muniçiones y artillería y alguna Copia de bastimentos de trigo y máiz. . . . De Mexico X de dizienbre de MDXXXVIJ [1537] años.

Sacra Cesárea Católica Majestad, humilde criado de Vuestra Majestad, sus reales pies y manos besa.

Don Antonio de Mendoza.

Document 38: 1549—The ruler of Nochistlán allies with Black fugitives[5]

Your Imperial Catholic Majesty,

Bachiller Hernando Martínez de la Marcha, Bachiller Lebrón de Quiñones, Bachiller Miguel de Contreras, your civil court judges and local magistrates, we kiss Your Majesty's royal hands and let you know that beginning on July 24, 1549 . . . we went together to this city of Compostela,[6] where your audience is located in your new kingdom of Galicia, as Your Majesty ordered. . . .

- Some of the mine owners, especially those of Zacatecas, were removing and looking to remove the metal [silver] from the said mines to refine and cast it outside of this kingdom . . . and this would be cause for the land to be depopulated and this kingdom would return to its past poverty. This would also ruin the royal [settlement] which by divine permission, we presume, was established in the place by the mines, where the past uprising took place. This would also lead to greater risks in controlling and frightening the Cazcan, Zacatecas, and Chichimeca Indians who live over there. It is the case, as certified in a summary investigation, they have still raided, burned, and killed, and continue to do so in this area, as is evident. Due to this and other notorious inconveniences that could take place to said [royal] chamber, we ask Your Majesty not to permit the said metal to be taken out of this, your new kingdom.

- And since the Indians' previous daring attempts have been mentioned, we inform Your Majesty that since the raids [against them] have been prohibited, they have

---

5. Archivo General de Indias, Guadalajara, 51, L.1, N.2, f. 1r, 8r–8v. http://pares.mcu.es/ParesBusquedas20/catalogo/show/12728500?nm

6. Compostela, also known as Compostela de las Indias, is located in the modern-day state of Nayarit, Mexico.

decided to take it upon themselves and have made entries along the Tepeque river, as they call that part, and have entered fourteen leagues into peaceful lands. The Cazcanes have done so and in such a fashion that sometimes they have killed and taken for sacrifice about a hundred people, in addition to burning a ranch house or town and killing whomever they could. These are the people of Chapoli, the Indian, who is at war. And according to what is said, they have gathered with the ruler, Captain Tetenamaztle [Francisco Tenamaztle], who escaped as a prisoner from the Peñol de Nochistlán, where he was a ruler. Many slaves and Black fugitives join and settle with them abundantly. . . .

- Likewise, farther north, almost halfway between Guadalajara and Compostela, there are some Indians called Chichimecas and among them there are some called the Tecoles. These have led raids against the peaceful Indians and have killed, taken, and sacrificed as many as they have been able to, and they eat them. Father north are the Chichimeca Indians of Guaxacatlan, who used to come to the Christian doctrine at Aguacatlán, but no longer do so. In this province there were nine churches, but they have become more warlike than peaceful. The Chichimecas live next to peaceful people, who see that the former are idle, avoid tribute, and do not want to subject themselves.

. . . your officials, from Compostela, November 28, 1549.

[Spanish transcription]

Su Cesárea Católica magestad

El Licenciado Hernando Martinez de la Marcha, el Licenciado Lebron de Quiñones, El Licenciado Miguel de Contreras vuestros oydores alcaldes mayores besamos las reales manos de vuestra magestad y hazemos saber como dende 24 de Jullio de [1]549 . . . fuimos Juntos En esta Cibdad de Compostela adonde Como por Vuestra magestad fue mandado Esta asentada Esta Vuestra Audiencia deste vuestro nuevo reino de Galizia. . . .

v. y Porque algunos dueños de minas En especial En los Çacathecas [Zacatecas] sacavan y procuravan sacar el metal De las dichas minas para lo beneficiar y fundir fuera deste reino . . . y seria Cavssa de despoblarse la tierra y tornarse Este reino a su passada pobreza, y el real que por permission divina se presume a sido asentada a la parte de las dichas mynas por donde El alçamyento passado tubo origen y mayor peligro para guardar y atemorizar los yndios Cazcanes y Çacathecas y Chichimecas que por alli Confinan que aun Con Ser assi como a Vuestra magestad por vna sumaria ynformaçion constara de porque aca an hecho y hazen Entradas y las quemas y muertes que por ello consta: porque a vuestra magestad suplicamos asi por Estos como por otros notorios yncombenientes de que de la tal Sala podrian suçeder. Vuestra magestad no permita al tal metal sea fuera deste vuestro nuevo reino sacado.

v. Y Pues Se a tocado En los atrevimientos que los yndios de sussonombrados an tenido y tienen, significamos y hazemos saber a Vuestra merced que como tan prohibidas Sean las entradas ya su noticia aya Venido an acordado de tomar Ellos la mano y por la parte que dizen Del rio de tepeque an Entrado y hecho saltos al pie de qatorze leguas dentro En tierra de paz los Cazcanes y de tal arte que algunas Vezes an muerto y llebado a Sacrificar ciento y tantas perssonas sobre averse atrebido a quemar un Estancia o pueblo y muerto los que pudieron aver Esta jente es la del yndio Chapoli que Esta de guerra y conforme se dize an se Juntado el Cacique Capitan Tetenamaztle [Francisco Tenamaztle] que se Escapo de preso de la del peñol de Nochistlan en donde era Cacique. Acojense a ellos muchos Esclabos y negros fugitibos y pueblan gran Copia Cada dia . . .

v. Asimesmo mas arriba Casi en el medio de Guadalajara y Compostela ay los indios llamados Chichimecas y entre Ellos ay Vnos que dizen los Tecoles Estos an hecho en las yndios que Con ellos conforman de paz Entradas y an muerto llebado y sacrificado los que an podido y pueden y los comen / Mas arriba Estan los yndios chichimecas de Guaxacatlan que venian a la doctrina cristiana a Aguacatlan y ya no vienen. Avia dentro de la provinçia nueve yglesias an se puesto mas de guerra que de paz. Confinan junto a la Jente de paz que los Ven holgar y no tributar ni querer se Subjetar.

. . . vuestros officiales de Compostela 28 de noviembre de [15]49 Años. . . .

Document 39: 1609—Two accounts of the maroons of Amatlan[7]

Most excellent sir, December 12, 1609 . . .

Don Juan López Mellado, *vecino* of the city of [Puebla of] the Angels, says that as Your Excellency is aware, he owns haciendas with cattle [ranches] in the Tierra Caliente [region]. These haciendas abut with the Black maroons' quarters, where three servants have died and where they have taken the wives of others. Were it not for the aid rendered by Baltazar Rodríguez, his overseer and ranch people, who killed the Blacks, greater damages and deaths would have fallen on the towns and their natives. According to two investigations carried out by the ordinary justice, the place where the Blacks enter and leave their quarters is a strategic pass. He [López Mellado] is aware that while Captain Pedro González de Herrera is organizing people and an expedition [against the maroons], the said Blacks may descend on [his] haciendas, burn the land and the towns, and cause other greater damages, as it is a necessary pass for them.

---

7. Archivo General de la Nación, Indiferente, Virreinal, Caja 4156, Exp. 38, ff. 1r–2r.

He asks Your Excellency to order that the said Baltazar Rodríguez, his overseer, and cowboys guard the said pass, which is called Coapa, with their people, horses, and weapons. With respect to [López Mellado's] people and horses, he is willing to sustain them at his own expense, as this is in His Majesty's service and for the common good. With this prevention, the said pass and the town will be safe and the said Blacks will have no place to shelter.

* * *

In the town of Amatla, on October 31, 1619, before Gaspar Ruíz de Balboa, regent in this jurisdiction, the following petition was presented.

Baltazar Rodríguez, overseer of the haciendas of Don Juan López Mellado, *vecino* of the city of Puebla of the Angels. I declare that I am required to provide information on the state of my weapons, horse, and people in my charge, with spears, horsemen's blades, and rifles, after the death of the fifteen Black maroons, while in His Majesty's service. Gaspar Ruíz de Balboa, the representative of the Crown[8] for this jurisdiction, was also present. The first people [in my service] who died and were killed, I helped them kill [the maroons] and was the first to attack them. When the people arrived where I was alone, I had already run through two [maroons] with my lance, one of them being their field marshal. The maroons killed my horse with arrow strikes, along with one of my young servants and his horse. . . . On the feast of Saint Lucas, this past year, the [maroons] came to attack me in revenge for the said deaths. They searched for me in the said Don Juan's haciendas with twenty Blacks armed with their bows and arrows. They asked where I was and since they could not find me, they entered the [main] house of the said hacienda and killed Cristóbal Fernández, a man from the hacienda, and they took the wife of Pedro Dávila. When I heard the news of what had happened I was three long leagues away. I left immediately with twelve armed men and their horses and spears. I followed [the maroons] until we arrived at the entrance of their quarters, but I did not attempt to attack because the land is arid and I had no provisions. So, I ask to remain in the haciendas that are on the pass where the said Blacks enter and leave. [I ask] not to be compelled to leave the [haciendas] by Captain Pedro González de Herrera, so that the said Blacks do not cause greater damages if they feel there is no [armed] force in this [place]. I ask for justice.

Baltazar Rodríguez

---

8. *corregidor*: a representative of the Crown with wide-ranging judicial, political, and fiscal power.

[Spanish transcription]

Excelentísimo señor   en 12 de diziembre 1609 años . . .

    Don Juan Lopez Mellado vezino de la çiudad [de Puebla] de los Angeles dize que como a Vuestra excelencia consta el tiene sus açiendas de bacas en Tierra Caliente y alinde de la rrancheria de los negros Çimarrones adonde Se an muerto Tres Criados y llevado Las mugeres de ottros y sino fuese El socorro de Baltasar Rodrigues su mayordomo y gente de su baqueria que se an allado en la muerte de los negros que mataron uvieran Echo mayores Daños y muertes en los pueblos y naturales dellos por ser aquel passo forzosso Por donde los dichos negros entran y salen en su Rancheria como consta y pareze destas dos ynformaçiones que la Justiçia hordinaria a Echo y atento que podria ser que en el ynterin que el Capitan Pedro gonzalez de herrera açe La gente y enttrada los dichos negros Con la libertad Con que andan al presente se desgalgassen Por sus açiendas a quemar la Tierra y pueblos y ottros Daños mayores Por ser El passo forzosso Dellos.

    Pide a Vuestra excelencia Mandamiento Para quel dicho Baltasar Rodrigues su mayordomo y su gente vaqueros Guarden el dicho Passo que dizen de Coapa con sus personas y Caballos y armas que en lo que toca a su gente y Caballos por ser cosa del serviçio de su magestad y bien del comun La quiere sustentar a su costa Porque Con esta prebençion estara El dicho passo y pueblos Seguros y los dichos negros Por aquella parte no tendran donde se guarezer.

                               *   *   *

en el pueblo de Amatla en ttreinta y un dias del mes de octubre de mil y seisçientos e nueve años ante Gaspar Ruiz de Balboa theniente De rregidor en este partido se presento esta peticion

    Baltasar Rodrigues mayordomo de las açiendas de don Joan Lopez Mellado vezino de la ciudad de la Puebla de los Angeles Digo que yo tengo nezesidad De açer Ynformaçion De como en serviçio de su magestad me allo con mys armas Cavallo y ocho personas myas y de mi cargo Con Lanzas Dales [lanzaderas?] e jarretaderas y escopetas en la muerte De los quinze negros cimarrones en que se allo asi mysmo gaspar Ruiz de balboa theniente De corregidor Deste partido y de los primeros que murieron y se mataron yo los ayude a matar y el primero que les acometio y quando La gente llego donde Yo estaba solo ya yo tenia con my Lanza attravesados dos Dellos quel uno ffue el mahese (maestre) De canpo que ellos trayan y me mataron mi Caballo a fflechaços y uno De los myos mozos y su caballo . . . el dia de señor San Lucas passado deste año vinyeron conttra mi en Venganza De las dichas muertes a buscarme a las açiendas Del dicho don Juan veinte negros armados con sus arcos e flechas preguntaban a Donde yo estaba y de que no me allaron enttraron en la Cassa De la dicha hazienda e mataron a flechaços a un honbre de la açienda llamado Xpoval Fernandez e llebaron la muger de un Pedro Davila y de como luego que me fue dado el aviso De alli ttres Leguas grandes parti De carrera con doze honbres armados con caballo y lanzas y dales e les ffui siguiendo asta la boca de la rrancheria Donde estan sitiados e por la poca gente que llebaba e la tierra ser aspera e no llevar bastimentos ninguno no acometi La enttrada para que para que [sic] atento estas açiendas estan en el passo Donde entran y salen los dichos negros yo no salga Dellas ni me obligue dello el capitan Pedro Gonzalez de Herrera por que no sentir ffuerza en este para Zelo dichos negros pueden açer Mayores daños pido Justicia

Baltassar Rodrigues

Document 40: 1619—Yanga, King of the Black Maroons[9]

The Uprisings and Beginnings of Yanga, King of the Black Maroons of New Spain.

An account of how he distributed and disposed of his republic's offices, choosing priests, governors, field marshals, and all the other offices, both of peace and war. The deaths, robberies, and cruelties that he committed on the royal roads of Veracruz and Mexico are also told, whereupon he took the title of king of the hills of Río Blanco.

Published under license by Juan René in Málaga. Year 1619.

Many years ago, some of the Blacks of New Spain became maroons, which is the same as saying ferocious, because they are not domesticated, nor do they trade in or enter into cities. Instead, they sustain themselves and live off the robberies they commit in the countryside, in the style of the thieves of Spain, or the *Bandolers* of Catalonia. Well, these [maroons] chose for their king and natural lord a Black man named Yanga, who was a native of Spain and had been born and raised in Seville. He passed to the Indies with the Marquess del Valle, Don Fernando Cortés, in whose service he remained a few years. He was constantly pursued by the law for the deaths, wounds, and mischief [he caused], and undoubtedly would have been hanged if the marquess had not intervened. . . . Eventually, after the death of a man and escaping the law, he sought refuge in a given church. Upon hearing this, the marquess was so upset with these acts and so tired of interceding for him that he swore he would let Yanga be punished so that his life and crimes would end once and for all. Finding himself exposed without this support, Yanga decided to make his way to the maroons. They greatly esteemed him for his bravery, especially their king at the time, a Black man of the Cazanga nation, whom Yanga later on stabbed to death. He explained to the others that their [former] king had been trying to turn them over to the viceroy of New Spain, and had promised this betrayal in exchange for his own freedom and

---

9. Biblioteca Nacional de España, Fondo Antiguo, Sala Cervantes, VE/1461/13, 1r–2v.

privileges. This was also a lie and falsehood, yet Yanga was able to persuade them such that they not only let him live, but elected him as their king. With this he began to more fully extend his cruelties, entering ranch houses, robbing, and killing their owners. He titled himself king of the hills of Río Blanco, which are those on either side of the royal roads leading to Veracruz and Mexico. This was the site where they usually were, and where they became strong, and defended themselves against the Spaniards' companies, who sometimes were sent out to capture [the maroons], but mostly returned with more damage than gain.

After taking possession of his kingdom, Yanga then dealt with the government of his republic, distributing all its offices and removing those who had held them before, in order to give them to those he trusted most. He passed the most notable orders and acts, naming himself, as we have said, king of Río Blanco. He elected as priest a ceremonious Black man, named Sun of August. The latter baptized and carried out marriages with a few ceremonies that resembled those of our Holy Mother Church, although mixed with many barbarous rites, which they themselves made up. He established a few laws and civility, both in the government of his vassals and in the service of his person, desiring to imitate like a monkey what he had seen in Spain and in the house of his lord the Marquess del Valle. He named an old Black man of advanced age and experience as governor of the peaceful settlers, who were the women, the elderly, and those who on account of some impediment did not bear arms. The governor was tasked with the things of the law and with settling the disputes that emerged among them. For the militia, he chose as field marshal another Black man, a brave, hardy, and above all, extremely cruel youth of the Behagó nation [Bijago]. He had been born in the deserts of Guinea and was just as used to making a good meal of the flesh of turkey as of a man. This man had such a frightful aspect that just looking at him put fear in the others. He had a scarred face, with a large mustache and reddish eyes. His whole head was full of white locks of hair, not due to his age, as we said he was young, but due to nature, who wanted to make note of him so that he might be more easily known even by those who were unaware of his deeds. Due to his cruelty, this Black man was always quite esteemed and favored by his king, Yanga, so that both resembled each other a great deal, and were just as loathed by the same vassals for their tyranny.

Yanga organized all his people into troops, reserving the most clear-headed for the protection of his own person, and arranged the positions they were to hold. This was done in such a manner that, not separating themselves too much one from another, they could help each other with one signal if they found themselves under duress. After these preparations, they had gathered some amount of weapons, although just a few muskets, but with many ranged weapons, such as lances, darts, half-pikes, swords, and other weapons of this kind.

With this, the new King Yanga began to commit robberies, all along the road, as in the ranch houses and other places, causing considerable damage to passengers and residents, taking the lives of some and stealing the goods of others. He endeavored in all manners to bring all the women [he could find] back to his ranch house and army, because his vassals asked for them. So that with the children they would have with these women, his people and power would extend and propagate. This led some to be persuaded that in time, Yanga would become lord of all or of a great part of New Spain; and that even if this did not happen in his days, it would at least take place in the time of his sons, as long as he left it in a good state. The complaints of the poor offended people reached the ears of the viceroy. He heard a wife cry for her dead husband, the father for the son, the kinsman for the relative, and the friend for the friend. The viceroy, as a pious and Christian man, desired to prevent these damages before the strength of the maroons made the remedy even more difficult. Although he attempted this with all sorts of approaches, at times by sending spies or soldier companies, the roughness of the land kept the maroons so safe that it seemed impossible that they could be conquered by human power. And he was not mistaken, because it was only the industry of the man who captured him, an innkeeper named Lobillo, and the betrayal (if it can be called that) of Yanga's very vassals that brought him to the hands of death. As this is a case that deserves more pages, it is left for other [accounts] that will follow this one, where his imprisonment, the harshness of the site, the manner of his fortifications, and the justice that was visited upon him will be told. PRAISE BE TO GOD.

[Spanish transcription]

LEVANTAMIENTOS Y PRINCIPIOS DE YANGVA REY DE LOS NEGROS
Cimarrones de la Nueva España
   Dase cuenta de como despuso y destribuyò los oficios de su Republica, eligiendo Sacerdotes, Gouernadores, Maesses de campo, y todos los demas oficios, assi de paz, como de guerra. Y assi mismo se dizen las muertes, robos, y crueldades que hizo en los caminos reales de la Veracruz y Mexico, intitulandose rey de los montes de Rioblanco
   Con licencia impresso en Malaga por Iuan René. Año 1619.

Muchos años avia, que aviendose algunos negros de la nueva España hecho Cimarones, que es lo mismo que dezir bravios, porque no se domestican, ni tratan o entran en las ciudades, sino que solo se sustentan y passan de los robos que hazen en el campo, al modo de los salteadores en España, o Bandolers de Cataluña. Estos pues eligieron por su Rey, y natural Señor á un negro llamado Yangua [sic, Yanga], el qual era natural de España, y se avia criado y nacido en Sevilla. Passo a las Indias con el Marques del valle Don Fernando Cortez, en cuyo servicio estuvo algunos años, siempre tan perseguido de la justicia por sus muertes heridas, y travesuras que sin duda le uvieran ahorcado, si el mismo Marques no le uviera valido . . . Vltimamente auiendo por la muerte de vn hombre librado de la justicia acogiendose a sierta Iglesia, en ella tuvo noticia que el Marques estava tan enfadado de sus cosas, y tan cansado de ser su valedor, que avia jurado de dexarle castigar, para que de vna vez acabassen justamente su vida, y sus delitos, y assi viendose desamparado deste arrimo, detirminó passarse a los Cimarrones, como lo hizo, siendo por su valentia muy estimado dellos, y particularmente del que entonces tenia por Rey, que era vn negro de nacion cazanga, a quien despues mató a puñaladas, haziendo entender a los demas, que aquel tratava de entregarlos al ViRey de la nueva España, por solo el interes de la libertad, y mercedes, que por esta traicion le prometia, y aunque esto era mentira y falsedad, el se lo supo persuadir de suerte, que no solo le dexaron con vida, sino tambien le eligieron por su Rey, con lo qual empessó a usar mas ampliamente de sus crueldades, entrando en estancias, robando, y matando a los dueños de ellas. Intitulandose Rey de los montes de Rio blanco, que son los que Quedan de vna y otra parte de los caminos reales de la Veracruz, y Mexico, y este era el sitio donde mas de ordinario assistian, y adonde se hazian fuertes, y defendian de las compañias de Españoles, que algunas vezes salian a buscarlos para prenderles, boluiendo casi siempre con mas daño que prouecho.

Auiendo tomado possesion de su Reyno, trató luego del gouierno de su Republica, repartiendo todos los officios della y quitandoles de los que primeros los tenian, por darlos a otros de quien se fiava hazia mas confiança. Passó provisiones y despachos destacadisimos, nombrandose, como emos dicho, Rey de Rio blanco. Eligio por Sacerdote a un negro ceremonioso, llamado Sol de Agosto: este bautizaua, y hazia los casamientos con algunas ceremonias, que re[semb]lavan a las de nuestra Santa Madre Iglesia, aunque mescladas con muchos ritos barbaros, inventados por ellos mismos. Establecio algunas leyes y vrbanidad, assi en el gouierno de sus vasallos, como en el servicio de su persona, queriendo como mono, imitar a lo que en España, y en casa de su Señor el Marques del Valle auia visto. Nombró por gouernador de los moradores pacificos, como eran las mugeres, los viejos y que por impedimento no tomauan armas, a vn negro viejo de mutha edad y esperiencia, y de los primeros Cimarrones; a quien encargó las cosas de la justicia, y el componer las discordias que entre ellos se levantassen. Y para la milicia eligio por Maesse de campo a otro negro mosso robusto, valiente y sobre todo cruelissimo, de nacion Behagó [Bijago], nacido en los desiertos de Guinea, y costumbrado a hazer tan buen estomago a la carne de vn hombre, como a la de vn pauo. Era este hombre de tan temeroso aspecto, que solo mirarle ponia miedo a los demas, tenia rayado el rostro, grandes los bigotes, bermejos los ojos, y llena toda la cabeza de vnas blancas guedejas, no por la edad, que como diximos era mosso, sino por naturaleza, que lo quiso señalar, para que mas facilmente le conociessen aun los que no tuviessen noticia de sus obras. Fue siempre este negro tan estimado y fauorecido de su Rey Yangua, por solo su crueldad, en que anbos se parecian mucho, como aborrecido de los mismos vassallos por su tirania.

Repartio por esquadras toda su gente, reservando la mas lucida para la guarda de su persona, y repartiendoles los puestos que auian de tomar, de suerte que no apartandose mucho unos de otros, se pudiessen socorrer si a caso se viessen apretados, con sola vna señal que se diessen. Tras estas preuenciones, auian juntado alguna cantidad de armas, aunque pocos arcabuzes, pero muchas de arremesso, como lanças, dardos, chuços, espadas, y otras deste genero.

Con esta gente empezó el nuevo Rey Yangua a robar, assi por todo el camino, como por las estancias y lugares, con notable daño, assi de los passageros, como de los moradores, a vnos quitandoles las vidas, y a otros robandoles las haziendas, y procurando en todas maneras traer a su estancia y exercito todas las mugeres que pudiesse assi por que sus vasallos se las pedian, como porque mediante los hijos que en ellas uviessen, su gente y poder se fuesse estendiendo y propagando, aviendose como algunos dizen persuadido, a que por tiempo podria venirse a hazer señor de toda o de gran parte de la nueva España: y quando esto no tuviesse efeto en su dias, a lo menos lo tendria en lo de sus hijos, dexandoselo el en buen estado. Sonauan las quexas de los pobres ofendidos en las orejas del VisoRey, oya llorar la muger al marido muerto, el padre al hijo, el deudo al pariente, y el amigo al amigo: desseava como piadoso y Cristiano, que estos daños se atajassen, antes que la fuerça de estos Cimarrones hiziesse el remedio mas dificultoso, y aunque lo procuraua por todos medios, ya echan[do]les espias, ya embiando compañias de soldados, la aspereza del lugar los tenia tan seguros, que casi parecia imposible que todo el poder humano los pudiesse conquistar, y no se engañava, pues solo pudiera la industria del que lo prendio, que fue un ventero llamado Lobillo, mediante la traicion (si asi se puede llamar) de sus mismos vasallos traerlo a manos de la muerte, que por ser caso que pide mas papel, se dexa para otros que saldra tras este, en que se dará cuenta del progresso de su prission, de la aspereza del citio, modo de sus fortificaciones, y justicia que del se hizo LAVS DEO.

Document 41: 1622—A bounty hunter and the maroons of Río Blanco[10]

In complying with and executing what was ordered in His Majesty's royal decree and orders, which were proclaimed in this city, that all the specified people should manifest and produce an inventory of all the goods they hold or had acquired from the year of 1592 to the present, as explained in the decrees, I, Captain Antonio Rodríguez Lovillo, *vecino* of the plains of Perote, make an inventory of the goods that I presently hold, which are as follows.

The first office I held was that of the *hermandad* (civil armed force) under the marquess of Salinas, viceroy of this New Spain. His grace appointed me on December 10, 1610 and I served His Majesty for three years at my own expense and distinction, without receiving any reward from His Majesty.

---

10. Archivo General de Indias, México 261, N.195, ff. 504r–505r.

Likewise, the same marquess, in acknowledgment of my punctuality, gave me a commission on June 7, 1611 to capture those guilty of the death of Captain Gonzalo de Hoces, captain of the flagship, which took place in the port of San Juan de Ulúa. I spent three years on this, traveling to remote lands at the expense of the guilty parties. I captured all of those who were guilty in this cause. And I also captured thirty Black maroons. In recompense for my good services, Don Francisco García Guerra, archbishop of Mexico and viceroy of this New Spain, gave me the title of captain for the imprisonment of these criminals. The royal criminal court owes me four thousand pesos since that time.

I had at the time, as is public and well-known, seven thousand pesos worth of rent in my haciendas, but because the [above] cases were serious and I had funds to spend, I was tasked with what happened in His Majesty's name.

In the time of the marquess of Guadalcázar, viceroy of this New Spain, a Black man named Hernando Brañianga [Bran Yanga], who called himself king of Río Blanco, rose up. It had been fifty-four years since he and five hundred other Blacks led an uprising all over that land, killing many Spaniards, stealing from many haciendas, and kidnapping many married and single Indian women. Many other captains had tried to conquer that Black man years before, but he had always escaped victorious. He was so haughty that the marquess of Guadalcázar, viceroy of this New Spain, summoned me from my house and hacienda so that I would conquer and destroy this Black man and the rest. I was named by the said viceroy as captain of the said maroons and went [on this campaign] on March 14, 1618. I was on the said campaign for two years. I captured the said Hernando Brañianga and killed and hanged all the others, and I brought many Black women, and little Black boys, and their leaders alive to this court, where justice was done unto them. At this same time, I held the title of corporal of the companies who came to assist me. I spent over forty thousand pesos in His Majesty's service, up until today when I am detained in this court for not having finished my accounts, as they are pending in the tribunal. I did not have a salary, nor did my son, who served as an ensign for His Majesty, in the said accounts despite what I contributed from my own funds to relieve my soldiers. I make a claim of ten thousand pesos to the royal treasury, as I am currently detained in this court for the said account. I was tasked with the capture of Chamisso, the bandit, and as I was bringing him to this court, other bandits came out to take him away from me in the town of Tlapa. Many gunshots and deaths took place there. [But] they did not take him from me and he was hanged in this court.

When the royal audience was governing, I was given commission for many things that were taking place in Mexico City, so that I would be on guard and custody. I defended and kept watch over the city with twelve harquebusiers at my expense and appointment, without receiving any salary from His Majesty for me or the said twelve harquebusiers. . . .

Likewise, I have had many commissions that I do not list in order to avoid becoming tedious, all of them at my expense, without ever having received a salary from His Majesty, or help for any expense, though I have spent what is referred to above. I have during this time sold a sheep hacienda and another hacienda for [breeding] goats to serve His Majesty, spending their rents in addition to everything else that I have today, which is as follows.

First, a bread mill that yields me a thousand pesos each year	1000 pesos
Then, an hacienda for wheat, maize, and other seeds, another hacienda for raising cows and mares, another site for raising pigs, all of which yields a thousand pesos, without the mill	1000 pesos
In the plains of Perote I own an inn that yields three hundred pesos a year	300 pesos
In addition to this, I have my own hacienda and houses where I live; these yield two thousand, three hundred pesos each year	2300 pesos
All these haciendas and those that I have sold were acquired and gained on my own and were transferred before I held any office for His Majesty	
Likewise, I have a Black man who is worth four hundred pesos	400 pesos
I have in my possession four Black women from the conquest of the maroons. The fifth [of their value] belongs to His Majesty. They have not been sold because they are old.	
I declare that I have five hundred pesos in wrought silver, [although] it is pawned for two hundred pesos, after paying this three hundred pesos are left	300 pesos
Likewise, I have the weapons, chain mail, leather jerkin, harquebuses, and lances with which I serve His Majesty in the things that I am ordered	1000 pesos
Likewise, I have two hundred pesos worth of irons, fetters, shackles, and chains with which to serve His Majesty	200 pesos

I do not include the furniture for the house and residence in Perote because I have been serving His Majesty for three years since my wife passed away, and I do not know what furniture there is since I have been in this court and the time is very short. It has been five years since I was last at my hacienda, waiting for my accounts to be settled, in order to see His Majesty's face, may God keep him for many years.

Antonio González

[Spanish transcription]

En execucion y cumplimiento de lo mandado por su magestad en su rreal çedula, y decretos que se pregonaron en esta ciudad serca de que todas las personas contenidas Manifestasen, e ymbentariasen todos los bienes que tuviesen e hubiesen adquirido por la forma que rrefieren Los dichos Reales decretos desde el año de [15]92 a esta parte = yo el capitan antonio rrodriguez lovillo vezino de los llanos de Perote hago ymbentario de los bienes que al presente tengo que son los siguientes.

Primero oficio que tuve fue de la hermandad por el marques de Salinas Virrey que fue desta nueva españa cuya merced me hizo a dies dias del mes de diziembre de mil y seiscientos y dies años, en que servi a su magestad por tres años a mi costa y minçion sin llevar gaxes de Su magestad.

Ytem el mismo marques atendiendo a mi puntualidad me dio comission en siete dias del mes de Junio de mil y seisçientos y honce años para prender a los culpados de la muerte del capitan Don Gonzalo de Hoces, capitan de la nao capitana que suçedio en el puerto de San Juan de Ulua, y me ocupe en ella tres años a costa de culpados en este tiempo andando por tierras rremotas, prendi a todos los culpados desta caussa, y treinta negros cimarrones de que rresulto por mis buenos serviçios darme titulo de capitan de ellos Don Francisco Garcia Guerra, arçobispo de Mexico Virrey desta nueva españa, desta prission destos diliquentes [sic]. Me deve esta Real sala del crimen desde aquel tiempo quatro mil Pesos.

Tenia En este tiempo, como es publico y notorio, siete mil pesos de rrenta de mis haziendas y por ser casos graves y tener hazienda que gastar, me encomendavan lo que assi suçedia en nombre de su magestad.

En tiempo del Marques de Guadalcaçar, Virrey que fue desta nueva españa, suçedio quererse alçar Vn negro llamado hernando brañianga, que se yntitulaba Rey de Rio blanco, que avia cinquenta y quatro años que el y otros quinientos negros que estavan en su compañia se avian alçado con toda aquella tierra, matando muchos españoles y rrovando muchas haziendas y rrovando muchas yndias cassadas y solteras y aviendo muchos capitanes ydo en años atras a conquistar a este negro havia salido siempre con vitoria, y estava tan soberbio que el Marques de Guadalcaçar Virrey que fue de esta nueva españa, me enbbio a llamar a mi cassa y hazienda para que fuera a conquistar y asolar a este negro y a los demas y fui nombrado por el dicho virrey por capitan de los dichos çimarrones a donde fui a catorçe dias del mes de março de mil y seisçientos y dies y ocho años, estuve en la dicha conquista dos años, prendi al dicho hernando brañianga y matte y haorque [a] todos los demas, y truxe muchas negras y negrillos y las caveças Vivos a esta corte de los que governavan entre ellos donde se hizo Justicia de ellos y en este mismo tiempo tuve titulo de cabo de las compañias que acudieron a darme socorro gaste en serviçio de Su magestad mas de quarenta mil pesos asta Oy que estoy en esta corte detenido por no aver acabado mis quentas, que estan pendientes en el tribunal de ellas, no tuve salario yo, ni un hijo mio que fue por alferes de Su magestad en las dichas quentas de lo que pusse de mis haziendas para socorrer mis soldados, hago alcançe de dies mil pesos a la rreal hazienda estando detenido en esta corte por las dichas quentas se me encomendo la prission de chamisso, el bandelero y trayendole a esta Corte salieron otros bandoleros a quitarmelo en el pueblo de Tlapa, donde hubo muchos balaços y muertes. No me lo quitaron, haorcaronle en esta corte.

Governado la Real audiençia se me dio comission por muchas cosas que suçedian en esta ciudad de Mexico para que tuviera en guarda y custodia esta dicha ciudad guardandola y velandola con doçe arcabuçeros a mi costa y minçion sin llevar salario de su magestad Yo ni los dichos doze arcabuçeros . . .

Assimismo e tenido muchas commissiones que no las pongo por no ser prolixo todas a mi costa sin aver tirado Jamas sueldo de Su magestad ni ayuda de costa ninguna donde e gastado lo que arriva esta rreferido e Vendido en este tiempo para servir a su magestad Vna hazienda de ovejas y otra de cabras gastando las rrentas de las de mas que tengo oy, que son como se sigue.

Primeramente Vn molino de Pan que me rrenta mil pesos en cada Vn año	1000 pesos
Yten Vna hazienda de labor de trigo y maiz Y otras çemillas, otra hazienda de ganado mayor de bacas yeguas, otro citio de ganado de çerda que todo ello rrenta sin el molino mil pesos	1000 pesos
Yten tengo en los llanos de Perote Vna Ventta que rrenta Treçientos Pesos en cada vn año	300 pesos
Juntamente Con esto esta en la Propria hazienda las casas de mi morada Son de rrenta en cada Vn año dos mil y treçientos pesos	2300 pesos
Todas estas haziendas y las que E bendido son adquiridas y ganadas por mi persona y mercadas antes que tuviera ofiçio por Su magestad	
Assimismo tengo Vn negro que vale quatroçientos Pesos	400 pesos
Yten tengo en mi Poder quatro negras de la conquista de los çimarrones que Perteneçe el quinto de ellas a su magestad que por ser viejas no se an bendido	
yten declaro que tengo quinientos pesos de Platta labrada que esta empeñada en duçientos Pesos, pagando quedan treçientos pesos	300 pesos
assimismo tengo de armas cotas y cueras y arcabuçes y lanças con que sirvo a su magestad en las cosas que se me mandan	1000 pesos
Assimismo tengo ducientos pesos de prissiones grillos y esposas Y cadenas para Servir a su Magestad	200 pesos

No pongo los muebles de la cassa y morada de Perote Por quanto ando sirviendo a su magestad a tres años que murio mi muger, y no puedo saber los muebles que ay por estar en estar corte y el tiempo es tan breve. Y haver çinco años que no boy a mi hazienda aguardando se concluyan mis quentas Para yr a ver la cara a su Magestad que Dios guarde muchos años . . .

Antonio Gonsales

Document 42: 1645—Francisco de la Cruz, enslaved *chino*, escapes[11]

In the name of God, amen. May all who see this letter know that I, Luis González, *vecino* of the town of Cuautitlán, say that I have Francisco de la Cruz, a *chino* of the Bengala caste, thirty-four to thirty-five years old, as my slave. I received and bought him from Florisso M.e [Martínez ?], a baker and *vecino* of Mexico City. The said [Francisco de la Cruz] fled and absented himself from my service four months ago, more or less, and, in order to hide, changed his name from Francisco to Diego. Having looked for him, I found him in the town of San Juan Ixtenco, in the jurisdiction of Tlaxcala. As I tried to subject him to my service, we came to an agreement. I offered to give him freedom since the said Franciso de la Cruz is required to pay Juan Diego, a *mestizo* mule pack driver and *vecino* of Celaya, 257 pesos for a writ that passed before the public scribe, Diego Cortes de Brito, in this city on February 28 of this year. This writ belongs to me and is mine . . . and for other reasons that I have considered, I therefore acknowledge that in the best form and manner before the law, I free and release the said Francisco de la Cruz, *chino*, my slave, from the subjection and captivity in which he has been so that from this day forward, he may use his freedom by virtue of this writ. May it serve him as a title that he or his attorneys may use to be and appear in court, make deals, contracts, and his will and dispose of his goods as a free person is allowed to do. . . .

Being present, I, the said Francisco de la Cruz, accept this writ and the grace and grant that the said Luis Gonzalez, my master, makes me in awarding this [letter of] freedom. I state that I will use it as I can and should. I am aware I acquired the 257 pesos ^{of the debt contract} while I was a slave of the said Luis Gonzalez. I declare that the said Juan Diego, *mestizo* mule pack owner and *vecino* of Celaya, awarded said writ and loan in my favor and these [pesos] belong to him and are his to have and charge as his own. To this effect, I have given him the said debt contract and, if necessary, award him power of attorney and transfer my rights on this matter to him . . . the

---

11. Archivo General de Notarías del Estado de Puebla, Notaría 3, Juan Guerra, 1645 Abril, ff. 390r–390v.

said writ was made in favor of Diego de la Cruz, [but] the truth is that it was done on my initiative as I changed my name from Francisco to Diego as I intended to hide. I am the same [person] who secured this loan by which the debt contract was issued. I state this so that there may be no further doubts on the matter. This letter was done in the city [Puebla] of the Angels on April 15, 1645. The grantors signed it and Luis González presented Bachiller Salvador de Cabrera, attorney of the royal audience, and Nicolás de Avalos, *vecino* of Guatitlán, as his known witnesses. The said Francisco de la Cruz presented the said Nicolás de Avalos and Francisco Ramírez, a *chino* man who said this was his name, as his witness. [The witnesses] swore to God and on the cross that they knew [the grantors] and that they are named as stated in this acknowledgment. Juan Francisco Valverde, Nicolas Álvarez, Juan de Vargas, *vecinos* of this city.

Luis González	Francisco de la Cruz	Before me, Juan Guerra, public scribe

[Spanish transcription]

En el nombre dios amen Sepan quantos Esta Carta vieren Como yo Luis Gonçalez vesino del pueblo de Guatitlan [Cuautitlán] digo que tengo por mi sclavo a Francisco de la Cruz chino de Casta bengala de edad de treinta y quatro a treinta y Cinco años poco mas o menos que Vbe y Compre de Florisso M.e [¿Martínez?] panadero vesino de la ciudad de Mexico el qual se huyo y ausento de mi servicio abra quatro messes Poco mas o menos y Se mudo el nombre de francisco En diego Por ocultarse y aviendo venido en Su busca le halle en el pueblo de San Juan Istengo [San Juan Ixtenco] Jurisdiccion de Tlaxcala y tratando de reduzirle a mi servicio nos Combenimos y ofresi darle livertad declarando el dicho Francisco de la Cruz en Una Dita de Ducientos y Cinquenta y siete pesos que esta obligado a pagarle Juan Diego mestiço dueño de requa vesino de calaya (Celaya) Por scriptura fecha en esta ciudad a veinte y ocho de febrero Passado deste año ante Diego Cortes de Brito escrivano Publico me pertenece y es mia Por haverla adquirido Siendo mi Sclavo . . . y otras Caussas que a ello me mueben otorgo que en aquella via y forma que mejor lugar tenga en derecho ahorro y liverto al dicho Francisco de la Cruz chino mi Sclavo de la sujecion y Captiverio en que a estado Para que de oy en adelante Ussando de su Livertad en Virtud desta scriptura que le sirva De titulo pueda por ssi o Sus procuradores estar y Parecer en Juicio hacer tratos y Contratos y Su testamento y disponer de sus Vienes y lo demas que a perssona libre es permitido . . .

= y estando pressente yo el dicho Francisco de la Cruz acepto esta Scriptura y la gracia y merced que el dicho Luis Goncalez mi amo y señor me hace en Concederme Livertad de la qual Protesto Ussar Segun puedo y devo y atento que los ducientos y Cinquenta y siete pesos ^{de la obligacion} que en mi favor otorgo el dicho Juan Diego mestiço dueño de requa vezino de Calaya [Celaya] por la scriptura zitada y Prestamo que les hice fueron adquiridos siendo sclavo del dicho Luis Goncales declaro Le pertenecen y los a de aver y Cobrar Como suyos Proprios Para Cuio efecto le tengo entregada dicha Scriptura De obligacion y siendo necessario Le doy Poder y traspasso en Caussa propria concession de mis derechos . . . Como se refiere en dicha Scriptura fue en favor de Diego de la Cruz la verdad es que fue a mi ynstanzia Con animo de ocultarme y que mude el nombre de Francisco en Diego y soy el mismo que le hiso prestamo y en Cuio favor otorgo la obligacion y asi lo advirtio que no se sigan dudas fecha la carta En la ciudad de los angeles a quince dias del mes de abrill de mill y seiscientos quarenta y cinco años y los otorgantes lo firmaron y dieron por testigos de Conocimento el dicho luis gonçales a el Lizenciado Salvador de Cabrera abogado de la Real audiencia vezino desta ciudad y a Nicolas de Avalos vezino de Guatitlan y el dicho Francisco de la Cruz al dicho Nicolas de Avalos y a Francisco Ramirez chino que asi dixo llamarse los quales Juraron a dios y a la Cruz conocerlos y Ser los Contenidos y llamarse Como se an nonbrado del otorgamiento. Juan Francisco Balverde, Nicolas Alvarez y Juan de Vargas vezinos desta ciudad

Luis Gonzalez	Francisco de la Cruz	Ante my Joan Guerra
		scrivano publico

Document 43: 1659—Precautions against the Black maroons of Chietla[12]

Your Grace, [this is the] report of Lord Licenciado Don Juan Manuel de Sotomayor, who grants permission to Domingo Hernández, a noble and native of the town of San Nicolás, to carry a sword and dagger, and to possess a lance in his house for the defense of his person when leaving [town].

Don Francisco Fernández de la Cueva, duke of Alburquerque, etc., for as Fernando Olivares de Carmona has made a petition for Domingo Hernández, a noble and native of the town of San Nicolás Tenescalco, in the jurisdiction of Chietla . . . on account of the great troubles and harassment they have received from the Black maroons that had gathered and congregated on a bluff that is very close to the said town. The maroons, coming down from the bluff, entered the houses and ranches of the natives and took all the provisions the latter had for their sustenance, which they lived off. The natives live in dire distress due to the great troubles that they receive from the maroons. The former are today in an even worse state because all the Blacks that escape the sugar plantations in the vicinity of that area [Chietla] have

---

12. Archivo General de la Nación, Indios, Cont. 13, Vol. 23, Exp. 312, ff. 278v–279r.

gathered on those hills and from there they leave and commit great thefts of the natives' livestock and seeds [maize] . . . these thefts are apparently increasing each day because, as was well-known, the said Blacks and other people of bad inclinations were there in the hills. And they were not content with what they took from the natives, but also came out to the roads to rob the passengers that pass by those places. For all of which and so that the natives of said town may have defense and protection from such injustices . . . I allow said Don Domingo Hernández to have in his house a harquebus, lance, cattle prods, and other defensive weapons for the occasions on which he might need them in defense and protection of the natives and to free them of the troubles and harassment that they receive from the said Black maroons and the people of bad inclinations. . . .

[Spanish transcription]

Vuestra excelencia, compareser del señor Lissensiado Don Juan Manuel de Sotomayor, consede lissensia a Domingo Hernandez, prinsipal y natural del pueblo de San Nicolas para traer espada y daga y para defensa de su perssona saliendo fuera una lansa para cuio efecto la pueda tener en su casa

    Don Francisco Fernandez de la Cueva, duque de Alburquerque et cetera por quanto Fernando Olivares de Carmona por Domingo Hernandez, prinsipal y natural del pueblo de San Nicolas Tenescalco de la jurisdicion de Chietla como mas le conbenga, me hisso Relacion de como . . . por las grandes molestias y bejaciones que reçivian de los negros simarrones que se havian juntado y congregado en una peña agajada que esta muy cerca del dicho pueblo los quales vajando della se entravan en las cassas y ranchos de los naturales que della les llevavan todo el bastimiento que tenian para su subsento con que vivian y viven muy desconsolados por las grandes molestias que dellos reçiven por estar oy de mucho peor calidad por que todos los negros que se huyen de los yngenios que estan çircunvezinos aquel partido se havian agregado en dicha serrania y que de halli (sic) salen y hazen de los natturales grandes hurtos de sus ganados y semillas que tienen . . . los qual havia de yr cada dia en creçimiento porque como hera notoria en dichas serranias estavan los dichos negros y otra gente de mal vivir que no tan solamente se contentavan en lo que llevavan a los natturales pero salian a los caminos a saltear a los pasageros que pasan para aquellos parajes por todo lo qual y para que los natturales del dicho su Pueblo tengan el amparo y defensa que requieren semejantes agravio . . . [se concede al dicho Don Domingo Hernandez] que pudiese tener en su cassa un arcabus, lanza, garrochas y otras armas defensivas para que en las ocasiones de que necesitare della en defensa y amparo de dichos natturales y librarles de los agravios y molestias que reciben de dichos negros simarrones y gente de mal vivir . . .

Document 44: 1665—A wet nurse and her daughter escape[13]

In the city [Puebla] of the Angels on March 17, 1665, Captain Juan Valera, *vecino* of this said city, presented himself before me, the scribe, and witnesses. I attest that I know him. He said that Antonio García Bueno, *vecino* of this city, presented a petition in the name of Captain Don Andrés de Carvajal y Tapia, *encomienda* holder of the town of Zacatlán, on the 16th of this present month and year. The petition was made before Captain Don Diego de Alvarado, His Majesty's court justice in this city. It said that a Black slave woman named Nicolasa and her infant, named María, a one-year-old mulatta, absented themselves from the house and sugar plantation of the said Don Andrés de Carvajal y Tapia, which is in the jurisdiction of the town of Teutitlán. Mother and daughter were born in the sugar mill of the said Don Andrés de Carvajal and it had come to his attention that María had come to this city where she was hiding. . . .

. . . Today Captain Don Antonio Guerrero de Ávila, His Majesty's magistrate in the province of Teutitlán del Camino, handed over a written message stating that he had heard of Antonio García Bueno's request, in representation of the said Don Andrés de Carvajal y Tapia. By order of His Grace, the magistrate, it was ordered that Nicolasa, the Black woman, and María, her little mulatta daughter, one year and two months old, be taken from his [Antonio Guerrero's] power, because it was said that she had fled her owner's sugar mill. And, in effect, she was brought to the presence of His Grace the said magistrate. It was explained that the said Nicolasa, Black woman, was raising Don Joseph Guerrero, his legitimate son who was fourteen months old, and if the said Black woman's breast was taken from him, he would die, because he did not accept the breast of any other person. Thus, it was required and necessary that the said Black woman continue raising his said son for the customary amount of time. In this, he [Antonio Guerrero] was supported by natural law, piety, and charity, and offered to pay her master what he justly deserved for the service of the said Black woman for each month that it took to raise his said son. After this, he would return and deliver her with her infant to their master and, otherwise, he would pay her value in reales and would offer surety under insurance. He asked and begged that the said Black woman, Nicolasa, and her daughter, María, be delivered to him for this purpose and asked to be given testimony of this to protect his rights and ask for justice. Considering the person and dignity of the said Captain Don Antonio Guerrero de Ávila and the causes that he represented, the said magistrate ordered that the said Nicolasa, Black woman, with the said María, her little mulatta daughter, be delivered to [Antonio Guerrero] so that she might continue to raise the said child, Don Joseph

---

13. Archivo General de Notarías del Estado de Puebla, Notaría 3, Nicolás López Gallegos, Caja 116, ff. 137v–139v.

Guerrero, for the customary time. He would give surety that the said slave and her daughter would be returned and delivered to the said Don Andrés de Carvajal y Tapia or in his name, to the said Antonio García Bueno, and that he would pay her value in reales for the said amount of time at three pesos each month, starting today. . . .

. . . In addition, the said Antonio García Bueno asked the said Captain Juan Valera to commit himself to favoring the said Don Andrés de Carvajal y Tapia and himself, so that in two months' time, starting from today's date, he would give and deliver the said Nicolasa, Black woman, and María, her mulatta daughter, in this city with no argument for further extensions. The said Captain Juan Valera assented to this. . . . He commits his person and his present and future goods, and gave power to His Majesty's justices to fulfill this writ wherever he may be asked. So that he might be compelled to what has been said as in a matter of a past sentence in a judged matter, he renounced the laws in his favor and the general law, stated so and signed. Witnesses, Lorenzo Rodríguez Santiso, Joseph Ruíz de Mesa, Tomás de Ortega, His Majesty's scribe, *vecino* of this City.

Juan Valera   before me, Nicolás López Gallegos, public scribe

[Spanish transcription]

En la Ciudad de los angeles a dies y siete dias del mes de marzo de mill y seissientos y sesenta y sinco años ante mi el scrivano y testigos Paressio el Capitan Joan balera vezino desta Ciudad a quien doi fee que conosco y dijo que antonio Garsia bueno vezino Desta ciudad en nonbre del Capitan Don andres de Caravajal y tapia encomendero del pueblo de Sacatlan a los Diez y seis deste presente mes y año de la data presento Petision ante el Cappitan Don Diego de Alvarado alcalde ordinario desta Ciudad Por su magestad en que dijo que de casa e Yngenio del dicho don Andres de Carvajal y Tapia que es en Juridision del pueblo de Teutitlan se le abia ausentado vna sclava negra nonbrada nicolassa con vna cria nonbrada maria mulata de vn año que madre e hija abian nasido en el trapiche de haser asucar del dicho Don Andres de Carvajal y que abia llegado a Su noticia que se abia benido a esta ciudad Donde estaba oculta . . .

. . . y oi dicho dia El Capitan Don Antonio Guerrero de Abila alcalde mayor Por Su magestad de la provinsia de teutitlan del camino Por escripto que parese entrego a Su mersed de dicho alcalde Dijo que a Su notissia abia benido que a pedimiento del dicho antonio Garsia bueno en nonbre del dicho Don andres de Carvajal y Tapia y por mandado de Su mersed de dicho alcalde estaba mandado Se sacase de su poder a Nicolasa negra y a Maria mulatilla Su hija de edad de vn año y dos meses por desir se habia huido del trapiche de su amo y que con efecto se abia traido a la Presenssia de Su mersed de dicho alcalde y que porque la dicha Nicolasa negra estaba criando a Don Joseph Guerrero su hijo lexitimo de edad de catorse messes y que si se le quitaba el Pecho de la dicha negra se abia de morir por no querer admitir el Pecho de otra ninguna persona y que era presiso y necesario que la dicha negra Continuase en la Crianssa del dicho su hijo el tiempo acostunbrado Pues le asistia de derecho natural y claro de piedad y charidad y que ofressia pagar a Su amo Lo que Justamente meresiese el servisio de la dicha negra cada mes Durante el tiempo que acabase de Criar al dicho su hijo y a que por fin del La bolberia y entregaria con Su cria al dicho su amo y que por su defecto Le pagaria su balor en Reales de que ofressia fianssa debajo de cuyo seguro pidio y suplicose Le mandase entregar la dicha negra Nicolasa y su hija Maria para dicho efeto y que se le Diese testimonio Pare en guarda de su derecho sobre que pidio Justisia a que se proveyo Por dicho alcalde que atendiendo a la persona y dignidad del dicho Capitan Don Antonio Guerrero de Abila y a las Causas que rrePresentaba mando se le entregase a la dicha nicolassa negra Con la dicha Maria mulatilla su hija Para Que Continuase la Criansa del dicho Don Joseph Guerrero niño Dando fiansa de que cunplido que fuese Bolberia y entregaria al dicho Don andres de Carvajal y Tapia y en su nonbre al dicho Antonio Garsia Bueno la dicha sclava y su hija Y por su defecto Les pagaria Su balor en Reales y Durante el dicho tiempo a rrazon de a tres Pessos Cada mes de los que corriesen desde oi dicho dia . . .

. . . de mas de lo qual el dicho Antonio Garsia Bueno Pidio al dicho Capitan Joan Balera se obligase en fabor del dicho Don Andres de Carvajal y Tapia y suyo a que dentro de dos messes contado desde oi dia de La fha desta les dara y entregara en esta Ciudad a las dichas Nicolasa negra y Maria mulata su hija sin mas Plaso Por Cuyo defecto se le pudiese conpeler a ello en lo qual asintio el dicho Capitan Joan Balera . . . obligo su persona y vienes abidos y Por aber dio poder a las Justissias de Su magestad de la parte donde se pidiere cunplimiento desta escriptura Para que le conpelan a lo dicho como por Sentensia pasada en cosa Jusgada Renunssio Leyes de su fabor y la general del derecho y asi lo otorgo y firmo testigos Lorenzo Rodriguez Santiso, Joseph Ruiz de Mesa y Thomas de Ortega scrivano de Su magestad, vezinos desta Ciudad =

Juan Balera   ante mi Nicolas Lopez Gallegos sscrivano Publico

Document 45: 1669—Two eyewitness accounts of Crax Bomba's rebellion[14]

In the city of Nueva Veracruz on November 10, 1669, the Lord Doctor Don Frutos Delgado of His Majesty's council . . . summoned Miguel de Herrera, as he called himself, the overseer of the mule train belonging to Don Francisco de la Higuera, owner of the *Ingenio Grande* [sugarcane plantation], which is in the jurisdiction of

---

14. Archivo General de Indias, México, 45, N.57, ff. 16r–19v, 35v–37v.

Xalapa. Before me, the present scribe, and his grace, he swore to God Our Lord and on the sign of the cross, according to law, that he promised to tell the truth. . . .

He says that what he knows and what happened is that on Tuesday, October 1 of this present year, this witness left the *Ingenio Grande* of his master, Don Francisco de la Higuera. The sugar plantation is in the jurisdiction of Xalapa. He left with fifteen mules loaded with sugar, another two loaded with *melado* [a syrup of molasses and sugar], another two with bottles of *melado* and other things, and with ten bottles of spirits. Around noon on the following Wednesday, this witness arrived at the Rinconada inn and stayed at the inn with his mule train. Two or three hours later, he saw a great number of Blacks arrive at the inn on horseback and, then, the other half [of the Blacks] arrived on foot. After the said Blacks and mule trains had arrived with the young men who went along with them, a litter arrived. Within the litter was the owner, or the factor, of the said Blacks. They then put all of the said Blacks in a long room inside the inn, where they remained that entire afternoon and night, until daybreak.

In order to clear some space at the inn, this witness moved all his loads to the horse stables and took them with two young men that went with him. And as he has declared, at daybreak, a servant of the owner of the Blacks came to the place where he was and bought a bottle of spirits from him. [The servant] returned to the place where the Blacks were and then this witness heard one of them say two or three times, "*Aguardente, Aguardente.*"[15] Then he heard the enormous sound of blows with sticks and yelling, an enormous noise, and it felt like everything was sinking, and this witness understands that this took place when they were killing their owner and one of his servants. The Blacks then spread out [and attacked] all the muleteers who were camped out around the inn and attacked the place where this witness was, trying to kill them with sticks and rocks. And indeed, they hit him with two rocks in the left arm, and having seen this, this witness tried to escape. He yelled to the others and they went fleeing to the town of La Rinconada, which is about two leagues from this place. . . .

On the morning of the day of San Francisco [October 4], the said Blacks sent Diego Hernández, a young servant from the said inn, to call this witness and the other muleteers and people. He was sent to tell them that they should send them the mules, because they wanted to return to Veracruz and did not want to go any farther [inland]. So this witness and the others returned to the inn, which was entirely in the possession of the said Blacks. All together there were three hundred, two hundred and fifty Black men and fifty Black women. He also saw how they held and named one of the said Blacks as king, and he was wearing the outfit of his master. This witness saw the master dead on the road behind the inn, along with a servant of his, according

---

15. *Aguardiente* is an alcoholic beverage produced through a mixture of sugarcane, fruits, spices, and other ingredients. The "*aguardente*" pronunciation presented in the document suggests that the speaker was familiar with the Portuguese or a creolized form of the language.

to the said muleteers. He [also] saw a dead young man who had been part of the mule train belonging to the magistrate of Perote. There were two other dead people whom this witness did not know. He only heard that they were muleteers and that one of them had married in Atrisco [Atlixco].

And when the said Blacks saw this witness and the others, they became disorderly. The king, who was called Crax, was in a separate room and ordered them to enter with a Black man. Having done so and entered, this witness saw that the said Black man Crax was eating. A Black woman, his wife, whom they called Queen, and another old Black man were at his side. The remaining Blacks served at the table, on which there was a plate with cooked chicken and a very large dish of *bobo* fish, also cooked. Once this witness entered, the said petty king gave him the chicken dish to eat. As it was Friday, he took it and gave it to a young man who had gone along with this witness. The said petty king indicated that he should sit and eat from the *bobo* dish. Finally, he told them that he had called them so that they would bring the mules that had been taken away. He told them that they should not be afraid, because what they [the Blacks] wanted was to return to this city [Nueva Veracruz]. To this, they answered that they would take them. Then, as they were leaving, this witness and the others saw that the Blacks had started to pursue them in order to kill them. This witness spoke to the captain who was eating with the said Crax and told him to speak with them [the Blacks outside the inn]. Crax then ordered the said captain to walk out with this witness and another young man, and take them to the road that leads to the [town of] La Rinconada. On this occasion, this witness saw that all the loads of sugar and everything else had been undone and wasted. The [mule pack] rigging and the blankets were broken and everything was destroyed. They [the Blacks] had made small sacks and short garments from the blankets.

They then returned to the town of La Rinconada, where they remained until Sunday, when the people of Xalapa arrived with Don José de la Higuera, their magistrate. They had been called by the person acting as magistrate of the said town, which is in the Marquesado del Valle.[16] They remained there all that day and night, until Monday at daybreak when they and this witness left the said town. They gathered with the people of Old Veracruz at the site called Las Cruces, where they arrived before daybreak but did not find the said people, who had said they would wait for them. So that Don José de la Higuera and his people, along with this witness, went back around to the inn to look for them. At daybreak, as they ascended the side of the hill to reach the said inn, they heard the noise and shouting of the said Blacks and a harquebus shot. Afterward, he learned that the Blacks had fired the shot. He immediately heard the noise of harquebus shots and climbing up this witness saw

---

16. A vast estate granted by the Spanish Crown to Hernando Cortés and his heirs. The Marquesado del Valle consisted of thousands of acres of non-contiguous lands and their Native subjects in the modern-day Oaxaca, Morelos, Mexico State, Mexico City, Veracruz, and Michoacán.

that the people of Old Veracruz had charged against the said Blacks and killed some of them, among them the said petty king. Then, when they [the Blacks] saw so many people, many of them started to flee and others to hide, climbing on the beams of the inn's rooms. This witness entered with others to catch them, when one of the Blacks had a stick with a half sword tied to it, like a half-pike, and was defending the entrance to the room. This man struck this witness with a blow to the chest so that the others who were there carried this witness out, thinking him dead. . . . and he certified that he is thirty-two years old and he did not sign because he does not know how to write. . . .

* * *

In the town of Xalapa on March 15, 1670. The said magistrate summoned Felipe Arias, *zambaigo*,[17] a resident of Captain Don Francisco de la Higuera Matamoros's sugar plantation. He swore to God Our Lord and on the sign of the cross, according to law, that he promised to tell the truth. . . .

He said that this witness was traveling from the said plantation to Veracruz with the said captain's mule train. He was transporting a load of small bottles of spirits, six pitchers of preserves, and twelve pesos in reales, twenty-five pounds of sugar, three Rouen shirts of his own, British linen sleeves, a pair of new silk tights, his saddle and sumpter horse, and a mule equipped with its saddle blanket. . . . He was sleeping in the unloading area of the said inn with Miguel de Herrera, the overseer of the said captain Don Francisco's mule train, who was transporting twelve loads of sugar with the said captain, and with another mulatto named Bartolome Rodríguez, who resides in the said sugar plantation and who was also taking honey and other things to sell in Veracruz. At the break of dawn on the Thursday, they heard great shouting and yelling from the housing area of the said inn, where the passengers lodge, and they realized that these were caused by the Black *bozales* who had arrived with their master and other people to sleep at the said inn that evening. Suddenly, many of them were throwing rocks toward the unloading area, where this witness and the others were located, and as all of them were naked they started to flee the said Blacks, so that they might not be killed by the rocks they were throwing at them. They went into the brush, where they could see what would come of all this. After sunrise, they saw that they had gathered everything that this witness had, along with the other loads, riggings, and blankets, and the said Blacks took these things to the said inn. Seeing that the Blacks had rebelled and that this witness and the others had lost what they were transporting, they left, as naked as they had started out, for the town of La Rinconada, which is a league from the said inn. They stayed in the town until he left with the people of the said magistrate and with the [people] brought by the magistrate of Antigua Veracruz and was with them after they pacified [the Blacks] with

---

17. A label used to describe a person of Afro-Indigenous descent.

said people. This witness came [to the town of La Rinconada] because he had been injured in one leg and because he had found his horse and pack mule that he had brought from the plantation in town, but nothing else. The said Blacks had broken and destroyed all the blankets, riggings, small leather trunks, and everything else. . . .

To defend themselves, they had named one of their own as king, and his wife as queen. They called him Bomba Grande in their language. Then, as he was in the said town on the day of San Francisco, he [the king] summoned them to the inn with a safe passage assured by Diego Hernández, a mulatto, who lives in the said town of La Rinconada. So this witness went with Miguel de Herrera and other muleteers from Orizaba, whose names he does not know, to learn why they had been called and to see what had been taken from them. Once they arrived at the said inn, the said Bomba Grande was eating in a room with great majesty, with much wrought silver, and with the woman by his side. All the Blacks were standing by him making great reverences, so that this witness understood that what had been said was true, that they had made him their king. Then, this witness and the others made three reverences, because they had been advised to do so by Juan de León, the innkeeper, who was being held prisoner by the said Blacks. As soon as he saw them, the said Bomba invited them to eat and sat them at his table. They were given fish, milk caramel [*cajeta*], and bread to eat. Once they had risen from the table, the said Bomba walked out with them to the patio. He told the said Blacks to take them behind the house and not to do them any harm; then he entered his ~~room~~ quarters. As soon as he did this, the said Blacks charged after this witness and the others with their swords and guns drawn. Seeing this, they all fled, because there is no doubt that they would have been killed. With all of this, after finding his horse and mule, and nothing else, he came to the said plantation and to his house, where he has been sick since the said event. This is what he knows and what is public and well-known and the truth, under the oath that he has made. He certified it after it was read to him. He declared that he is not covered by any of the general laws and that he is twenty years old. He did not know how to sign. The said magistrate signed it.

Don José de la Higuera Matamoros = before me, Alonso de Neira Chávez, public and royal scribe

[Spanish transcription]

En la Ciudad de la Nueva Veracruz a diez dias de el mes de noviembre de mill seiscientos y sesentta y nueve años el señor Doctor Don Frutos Delgado de el Consejo de su Magestad y su alcalde del crimen mas antiguo . . . mando parezer ante su merced a Miguel de Herrera que asi se nombro y ser mayordomo de la Requa de don Francisco de la Yguera, dueño de El yngenio grande de Asucar que es en la jurisdicción de Xalapa de El qual por ante mi el pressente esscribano su merced Recivio

Juramento por Dios nuestro señor y la señal de la Cruz segun forma de derecho so cargo de el qual prometio dezir Verdad . . .

Dixo que lo que save i pasa es, que martes primero de otubre proxsimo pasado deste presente año, salio este testigo del Yngenio grande de asucar de Don Francsico de la Yguera su Amo que esta en la Jurisdiccion de Xalapa Con quinçe mulas las doçe Cargadas de Asucar y otras dos de melado y otras dos de votixas de melado [sic] y otras Cosas, y diez Votijuelas de Agua ardiente y el miercoles siguiente a medio dia llego este Testigo a la venta de la Rinconada y este testigo se quedo en la dicha venta, con la dicha su Requa y pasadas dos o tres horas vido como fueron llegando a la dicha Venta vna Cantidad de negros a cavallo, y despues entro la otra mitad a pie y asi mismo llego despues de haver llegado los dichos Negros y las Requas, y moços que Venian Con ellos vna litera y en ella el dueño o factor de los dichos negros y los metieron a dichos negros en vn aposento Largo de la Venta donde estubieron toda aquella tarde, y aquella noche, hastal [sic] amaneçer

y este Testigo habia mudado sus cargas y se habia ydo con ellas y con dos moços que llebaba, a la Cavalleriza por dejar desocupada La Venta, y al amanecer como dicho lleva fue al rancho de este Testigo vn criado de el dicho Dueño de los Negros y le compro vna votijuela de Agua ardiente y se Volvio con ella a donde estaban los negros y oyo este Testigo que vno de ellos dijo dos o tres Vezes. Aguardente. Aguardente. Y luego oyo grandissimo Ruido de golpes como Con palos y grandissimo Ruido, y algazara, que pareçia se hundia aquello y tiene entendido este Testigo que fue quando estaban matando al Dueño de ellos y a un Criado suyo, y Luego se desparramaron sobre todos los arrieros que estaban Rancheados alrededor de la dicha Venta, y sobre el Rancho de este Testigo con palos y piedras a matarlos como con efecto le dieron dos pedradas en el Braço ysquierdo y visto esto tiro a huir este testigo dandoles vozes a los demas y se fueron huyendo al Pueblo de la Rinconada, que esta de alli çerca de dos leguas . . . = Y el dia San Francisco por la mañana los dichos negros embiaron a un moço de la dicha Venta llamado Diego hernandez a llamar a este Testigo y a los demas arrieros y personas imbiandoles a dezir que llevasen las mulas, porque se querian Volver a la Veracruz y no pasar de alli, y con esto este Testigo y los demas se Volvieron a la Venta donde estaban apoderados de ella todos Los dichos negros, que serian hasta tresçientos por todos, Los duçientos y Çinquenta negros, y las Çinquenta negras, y vido asi mismo como tenian a vno de los dichos negros nombrado por Rey y este tenia puesto el Vestido de su Amo a quien vio este testigo muerto detras de la Venta azia el camino, y otro que los dichos arrieros dixeron era paje suyo, y vn moço de la Requa de El alguaçil mayor de Perote, y otros dos que no conoçio este testigo solo que oyo dezir este testigo a los arrieros que el vno de los dos era casado en Atrisco [Atlixco]

y Luego que los dichos Negros Los vieron a este testigo y a los demas se alvorotaron, y el Reyesuelo que estaba en el aposento aparte llamado Crax les mando que entrasen con Vn negro que lo dio a entender asi y haviendo entrado Vido que el dicho negro

Crax estaba comiendo y una negra que llamaban Reyna mujer de el, y otro negro viejo a su lado, y los demas negros sirviendole a la mesa, y en ella vn plato con gallina guisada, y un plato mui Grande de pescado Vobo [pescado bobo], asimismo guisado y luego que entro este Testigo el dicho Reyesuelo Le dio el plato de gallina para que comiese, y por ser Viernes lo tomo, y se lo dio a un moço que Yba con este testigo y el dicho Reyesuelo le hiço que se sentase y comiese, de el plato de el Vobo y por ultimo les dijo que el llamarlos era para que trujesen las mulas los que las habian llevado que no tubiesen miedo porque se querian volvera a esta Ciudad [Nueva Veracruz] a que les Respondieron que los llevarian, y con esto vido este testigo y los demas que haviendo salido, la mitad de los que Yban dieron tras de ellos Los negros para matarlos y este testigo le hablo al capitan que estaba comiendo con el dicho Crax para que le[s] hablase, el qual mando saliese el dicho Capitan con este testigo, y otro moço, y los llevo hasta ponerlos en el camino que ba a la Rinconada,

y en esta ocaçion vido este Testigo como todas las Cargas de Asucar y las demas las tenian desechas y desperdiçiadas por alli y los aparejos Rotos y que de las mantas habian hecho talegas y Capisayos y todo destroçado Con que se volvieron a la Rinconada, donde estubieron hasta el Domingo que llego la gente de Xalapa con Don Joseph de la Yguera, su alcalde mayor que los habia Ymbiado a llamar el theniente alcalde mayor de el dicho pueblo que es de el marquesado de el Valle, donde estubieron todo aquel dia, y aquella noche hasta el Lunes al amanecer que salieron de el dicho pueblo y con ellos este Testigo a yncorporarse con la gentte de la VeraCruz Vieja al sitio que llaman de Las Cruzes donde haviendo llegado antes del amaneçer no hallaron alli la dicha gente habiendo ymbiado a deçir Los aguardarian Con que el dicho Don Joseph de la Yguera y su jente y Con ellos este testigo se fueron la buelta de la Venta en su Vusca y al amanezer yendo subiendo el Repecho para subir a la dicha Venta oyeron el Ruido y algazara de los dichos negros y un arcabuzaso, que despues de dijo que lo abian tirado los negros, y inmediatamente Ruido de arcabuzasos, y aviendo subido arriva vido este Testigo que la gente de la Veracruz Vieja Les habia dado vna Carga a los dichos negros y muerto a algunos y entre ellos al dicho Reyesuelo, y luego comença ron a huyr muchos de ellos Como vieron tanta gentes y otros a esconderse, y subiendose arriva en las tirantes de los aposentos de la Venta, y este testigo se entro dentro con otros a cogerlos en occasion q.e vno de los Negros tenia en Vn palo atada Vna media espada hecha como chuso defendiendo la entrada de el aposento el qual le tiro a este testigo Vn hurgunazo que le paso el pecho que lo sacaron por muerto otros que se hallaron alli, y todos los daños que causaron, y hisieron los dichos negros no save este testigo se ayan pagado . . . y Ratifico y que es de hedad de treinta y dos años y no firmo porque dijo no saver escrevir . . .

* * *

En el Pueblo de Xalapa a quince dias del mes de Março de mill y seiscientos y setenta años para la dicha averiguacion el dicho alcalde [Don Joseph de la Higuera

Matamoros] hiço parezer ante si a Phelipe Arias Sambaygo Residente en el Yngenio del Capitan Don Francisco de la Yguera Matamoros del qual se Recivio juramento por Dios y la Señal de la Cruz en forma de derecho y lo hiço y prometio deçir Verdad . . .

Dijo que este testigo yba con la Requa del dicho Capitan, y llevaba del dicho yngenio para la Veracruz Vna Carga de Votijuleas de Agua ardiente, y seis cantaros de Conserva, y doçe pesos en Reales, y vna arrova de Asucar, y tres Camisas de su Vestir de Ruan y mangas de bretaña, vn par de medias de Seda nuevas, su silla y cavalgadura y vna mula aparejada con su manta de jerga . . . estando durmiendo en el descargadero de dicha venta con Miguel de Herrera mayordomo de la Requa del dicho Capitan Don francisco que llebaba doçe Cargas de Asucar de dicho Capitan con otro Mulato llamado Bartolome Rodriguez que Reside, en dicho yngenio y llebaba tambien a la Veracruz miel, y otras cosas para Vender, al Romper el dia Juebes oyeron grandes gritos, y algazara açia la parte de la Vivienda de la dicha Venta, y donde se aloxan los pasajeros, y Reconoçieron lo Causaban los negros vosales que con su amo y otras personas que benian con ellos habian llegado a dormir a la dicha venta antes que por muchos de ellos venian tirando piedras açia la parte, de dicho descargadero donde estaba este testigo y los demas que a dicho, y que teniendolos todos desnudos, arrancaron a huir de los dichos Negros porque no los matasen con las piedras que tiraban, y se metieron en el monte, desde donde se pusieron a ber en lo que paraba aquello. haviendo amaneçido y salido el sol, vieron que juntaron todo lo que tenian este testigo y las demas Cargas, aparejos, y mantas, y se lo llevaron, para la dicha Venta, Los dichos negros y viendo que estaban alçados y que ya tenian perdido lo que llevaban este testigo y los otros se fueron desnudos como habian salido para el Pueblo de la Rinconada que estar vna legua de dicha Venta, y se estubieron en el hasta que fue con Gente dicho alcalde mayor, y en su Compañia despues de pacificados con la dicha gente y La que trajo el alcalde mayor de la antigua Veracruz, Vino este testigo [¿a Xalapa?] porque se habia quedado malo de Vna pierna en el dicho Pueblo y hallo su Cavallo, y mula de carga, que habia llevado del dicho Yngenio sin otra Cosa alguna, porque mantas y aparejos, petacas y lo demas Rompieron y destruyeron los dichos Negros . . .

y que para defenderse abian nombrado por Rey vno de ellos, y Por Reyna a su Muger, y le llamaban en su lengua Vomba grande, y que estando en el dicho Pueblo el dia de San Francisco embio a llamarlos a la dicha venta con seguro de paz, que les dio de su parte Diego Hernandez, mulato, que Vive en dicho Pueblo de la Rinconada, y que assi por ver lo que habian llevado, como por saver la Caussa de llamarlos fue este Testigo, y Miguel de herrera y otros Arrieros de Orizaba, que no save como se llaman, y que haviendo llegado a la dicha Venta estaba comiendo en vn aposento que tenia el dicho Bomba grande, Con mucha Magestad, con mucha plata labrada y la mujer a su lado, y todos los negros em pie haçiendole mucho acatamiento, de que Reconoçio este testigo ser çierto lo que habian dicho de que lo habian hecho su Rey, y que le hiçieron este testigo y los demas tres Reverençias porque asi se lo advirtio Juan de Leon, el ventero de dicha Venta, a quien tenian Como presso los dichos negros, y que El dicho Bomba asi que los vio los Convido a comer, y sento a su messa y les dieron pescado Cageta y pan a comer, y que estando Levantados de la dicha messa, el dicho Bomba salio con ellos al patio y les mando a los dichos negros Los llevasen detras de la Cassa y que no les hisiesen mal ninguno y que se entro en su ~~quarto~~ aposento y apenas lo hiço quando arrancaron dichos Negros tras este Testigo y los demas, Con espadas desnudas, y escopetas y visto, partieron a huir dellos, que a no valerles los pies no es dudable, de que tambien los mataran, y que Con lo Referido despues de haver hallado su Cavallo y mula sin otra Cosa como lleva dicho se Vino al dicho yngenio y a su Cassa, donde a estado siempre enfermo despues del dicho suçeso y que esto es lo que save y es publico y notorio y la verdad so cargo del Juramento que fecho tiene, en que se Ratifico siendole Leydo. Declaro no tocarle ningunas generales y ser de hedad de Veinte años no supo firmar firmolo dicho alcalde mayor =

Don Joseph de la Higuera Matamoros = ante mi Alonso de Neyra Chavez, sscrivano Publico y Real

Document 46: 1760—María Manuela escapes from the Hacienda Santiago[18]

In the city [Puebla] of the Angels, on February 16, 1760, this petition was presented before Captain Don Cándido González Maldonado . . . deputy for the royal sales tax of this city, municipal court justice for the second vote for the city.

Don Felipe Caloca, *vecino* of this city, farmer in its jurisdiction, owner of the Hacienda Santiago, in the religious jurisdiction of Cuautinchan, by the best recourse to law with all the useful, legal, and competent statements in my interest, I appear before Your Grace and declare: That, I have a mulatta, my slave, named María Manuela, in my possession and servitude with my family on my hacienda. She has fled, because a person and *vecino* from the city of Tepeaca has unsettled her with counsel, favor, and help. He has associated with her and taken her to said city. Disregarding for now the presumption of malice that this case provokes, [I state that] it is within my best interest to recover her so that once she is sold, I may receive the sum of money from her sale. I do not intend to keep her in my service, but I also cannot allow this sale to be made to the person who truly removed her or [to someone] in that entire province, since this would not be convenient to the service of God Our Lord, or to the peace of my house and family. Because although people subjected to

---

18. Archivo Histórico Judicial de Puebla, Exp. 3739, ff. 1r–2r.

servitude have the right to ask for a change of owner or lord at their pleasure, to avoid inconveniences and troubles, because this is their natural right. The same right assists the Lord so that the servant does not cause them [inconveniences and troubles]. . . .

In compliance with this, I appeal to Your Grace's justification, to order a letter of justice be given to me, in the form of a warrant, so that His Majesty's justices of the city of Tepeaca remove her from the house where she might be and have her transported to this city and placed in deposit with the General Depository of this city. So that from this place, one of the brokers may search for a [new] master during the amount of time Your Grace considers appropriate. Having found this person, I will be returned the cost that I spent on her, as I am ready to award the writ of her sale and hand over the titles of her possession in the manner that is required. Two of her sons, whom I purchased with her, and whom I have with me, were also part of those titles, by which it will be certified that I had her for the amount of one hundred pesos. As all of this is so, according to law, so that following these terms,

I beg Your Grace to take heed of and order as is requested, that this is just. I swear in form, expenses, and in what is necessary, etcetera.

Felipe de Caloca   Bachiller Antonio Martínez

[Spanish transcription]

En la Ciudad de los Angeles a diez y seis de Febrero de mill setecientos y sesenta ante el Cappitan Don Candido Gonzales Maldonado . . . Deputado de las Reales Alcabalas de esta Ciudad y Alcalde Ordinario de Segundo Voto en ella por Su Majestad se presento esta Petision

Don Phelipe Caloca, Vecino de esta ciudad, Labrador en su Jurisdiccion y Dueño de la hacienda nombrada Santiago, en la Doctrina de Guatinchan [Cuautinchan] por el mejor recurso de derecho, con las protextas utiles, legales, y competentes que me ymporten paresco ante vuestra merced. y Digo: que, teniendo en Dominio, y servidumbre, una mulata mi esclava, nombrada Maria Manuela, con mi familia en dicha mi hacienda, hà echo fuga, por haverla inquietado un sujeto vecino de la ciudad de tepeaca, con concilios, favor, y ayuda, associandola, y llebandola consigo à dicha ciudad, y prescindiendo por aora de la presuncion de malicia, que induce este echo, en exercicio de la acción que me compete, à recuperarla, para que efectuada su Venta, se me entregue su monto, porque mi animo no es conservarla en mi servicio, no pudiendo tampoco permitir que esta se haga â el sujeto que verdaderamente la extràjo, y en toda aquella Provincia, por no convenir ni al servicio de Dios nuestro señor, ni à la quietud de mi casa, y familia, y que aunque las persònas sujetas â servidumbre, tienen derechô â pedir amo, ô Señor â su placito, para evadirse de molestias, y Vejaciones, por ser esto de derechô natural, el mismo assite â el Señor para que el siervo no se las cause . . .

En cuya conformidad, ocurro â la Justificiacion a Vuestra merced: y se hà de servir mandar se me libre carta de Justicia, requisitorio en forma, para las de Su Magestad de dichâ ciudad de tepeaca, por quien en su virtud se extraiga de la casa, en que se hallare, y se reduzga â esta ciudad, y en ella se ponga en deposito de en el Depositario general de esta ciudad para que desde alli, encargada â uno de los correedores (sic), le solicite amo dentro de el termino que Vuestra merced estimare competente, y hallada se me debuelba el precio, que por ella di, estando como estoy prompto â otorgar la escriptura de su venta, y entregar los titulos de su dominio, en el modo que corresponde, porqué comprehenden â dos hijos suyos, que con ella comprè, y tengo conmigo, por donde constarà, que la huve en cantidad de cien pesos por ser todo assi, conforme â derecho en cuios terminos

A Vuestra merced: suplico, se sirva de proveèr, y mandàr como và pedido, que es de Justicia, Juro en forma, costas, y en lo necèsario etcetera.

Phelipe de Caloca   Bachiller Antonio Martinez

Document 47: 1760—María Josefa, Gertrudis Simona, and Captain Matute's politics[19]

In the town of Córdoba, on May 5, 1660. I, the said magistrate, and general captain of this town and its jurisdiction, by the king, Our Lord. As judge of this investigation that I am leading with assisting witnesses, due to the impediment of the public scribe and the absence of another scribe, for this effect I summoned before me an imprisoned woman to take her testimony. She is one of those who have been brought to this village on my order, according to the initial decree. I received an oath from her, which she made in the name of God Our Lord and on the sign of the holy cross in due form, by which she offered to say the truth in everything she knew or was asked, according to the said investigation. She said that her name is María Josefa, she is a Black woman from Guinea, and a slave of the San Antonio hacienda which belongs to the said Don Diego de Bringas in this jurisdiction. She is married to José Ignacio, who is also a Black slave of the said hacienda.

About five months ago, a Black relative of hers (whose name she does not remember) passed from the Cacahuatal hacienda to the deponent's house and disturbed her by encouraging her to escape. She indeed did so with her relative, leaving behind her husband in their residence at the hacienda. This deponent walked with her runaway relative for four days in the brush, after which they arrived at a place named

---

19. Archivo General de la Nación, Indiferente Virreinal, Caja 2506, Exp. 2, ff. 95r–97v. Courtesy of Professor Adela Amaral.

Mandinga, which is settled by the Black fugitives. In this place they found other companions, with whom they stopped and stayed for the said five months. She is aware that <u>all her companions were led by Diego Matute, whom they recognized as captain;</u> before this [event] he had been captain of the old maroons. <u>This deponent knows that the said Matute had had a disagreement with his old companions. This took place because several slaves were fleeing the haciendas and seeking refuge in the *palenque*</u> [maroon community], but the old maroons decided to round them up and hand them over to the dominion of their owners. The said Matute was opposed to this, so he formed a company with the [new] residents and some of the old party.

She says that she cannot account for the war that took place between the two bands, because at the time they had taken this deponent to the lowland. <u>The maroons only arrived the following day with their said Captain Diego Matute,</u> who had been <u>wounded by two gunshots</u> he received in the war. From other companions, she learned that five of them had died in the skirmish. After they were led to Estanzuela [an hacienda], they were turned over to free people who would take them to their owners, which was done. This is what she has to say and the truth of everything she knows, under the oath she has made. Her [deposition] being read to her, she affirmed and ratified it. She was unable to state her age, which seems to be over thirty years. She did not sign because she does not know how to. I signed, with my witnesses, as is stated.

Matías de Mojorena
With the assistance of Mariano José Almería
With the assistance of Francisco José de Mendieta

Immediately, the said day, month, and year, I the said magistrate, acting as receiving judge with assisting witnesses, due to the impediment of the public scribe and the absence of another scribe, for this effect I summoned before me an imprisoned woman to take her testimony. I received an oath from her, which she made in the name of God Our Lord and on the sign of the holy cross in due form, by which she offered to say the truth in everything she knew or was asked, according to the tenor of the order at the start of this investigation. She said that her name is Gertrudis Simona, *parda* slave of the De la Punta hacienda that belongs to Don Joseph Mesa in this jurisdiction. She is the widow of Rafael Cobos, a Black slave who belonged to the said hacienda.

A little under a year ago, the deponent fled the mentioned hacienda in the company of her husband and for two months she supported herself by serving on a ranch. Then she moved on with her husband to the *palenque* [maroon community] named Mandinga, where they stayed <u>and were governed by Diego Matute, their captain</u>. During the time the deponent was there, she did not see or hear anything about their companions going out to the road or committing thefts, nor did their companions wrong any of the few travelers that transit along the road. Instead, they lived off what they sowed from their corn, rice, peanut, and banana fields. She knows <u>that Diego Matute had been captain</u> of the old maroons and that he had had a disagreement with them. Because, <u>as several fugitive slaves had sought refuge in the big palenque, the old [maroons] did not want to consent to this</u> and decided to round them up and send them back to their owners. The said Matute opposed this by defending those newly arrived.

Because of this, <u>Matute distanced himself from the old maroons and formed a troop,</u> leading the recent arrivals. The old Blacks came to his *palenque*, calling for the said Matute and for his followers in order to turn them in at La Estanzuela. As they attempted to carry this out, the said <u>Matute resisted, along with his troop, one band and the other making war</u> on each other. <u>Rafael Cobos, husband of this deponent,</u> and <u>four of her other companions</u> perished in this war. Captain Matute was wounded with two gunshots, leading his troop to declare defeat. As a result, this deponent and the rest of her companions, along with the captain, were brought to La Estanzuela. They were handed over to free people and taken to their owners, which was carried out. This that she has declared is the truth, based on the oath she has taken. Her [deposition] being read to her, she affirmed and ratified it. She stated that she is thirty years old. She did not sign because she does not know how to. I signed, with my witnesses, as is stated.

Matías de Mojorena
With the assistance of Mariano José Almería
With the assistance of Francisco José de Mendieta

[Spanish transcription]

En la Villa de Cordova â cinco de Mayo de mil setecientos y sesenta años: Yo el referido Alcalde mayor Teniente de Capitan generâl en ella y Su Jurisdizion por el Rey nuestro señor; Juez de estos Autos que autuo [sic] por ante mi con testigos de Asistencia por impedimiento del esscribano publico y falta de otro, hize comparazer ante mi para efecto de tomarla Su declarazion a una muger presa y de las que se an conducido por mi orden a esta [villa] conforme a el Auto cabeza de proceso; à la qual le recibi Juramento que hizo por Dios nuestro señor y la señal de la santta Cruz; en toda forma de derecho, por el qual ofreció decir verdad en lo que Supiese y fese [sic] preguntada, y Siendolo al tenor de dicho auto = Dijo, llamarse Maria Josepha, ser negra de Guinea, y esclaba de la hazienda de san Antonio perteneziente â don Diego de Bringas en esta Jurisdizion, casada con Joseph Ygnacio, igual negro Esclavo de la dicha hazienda;

y que hà tiempo de cinco meses que haviendo pasado de la hazienda del Cacahuatal, un negro su pariente (de cuyo nombre no se acuerda) a la Casa de la que declara la inquietò para que hiciese fuga, lo que con efecto executò en Su compañía dejando à Su marido en la dicha hazienda de Su residencia, y que haviendo caminado la declarante, en compañía de Su desertor pariente por el monte quatro dias, llegaron al parage nombrado Mandinga, y uno de los que ocupan los negros fugitibos, y en el hallaron otros compañeros con los que hicieron Mancion [se detuvieron] y se mantubieron el tiempo que lleba referido de cinco meses, y todos estos Sus compañeros le consta <u>los acaudillaba Diego Matute, al que reconozian por capitan, y que</u> este antes lo havia Sido de los cimarrones antiguos; y que <u>sabe la que declara que el motibo de haverse disgustado dicho Matute con Sus compañeros Viegos</u> fuè, <u>porque yendo à ampararse varios Esclabos que hacian</u> fuga de las haziendas al Palenque, determinaron los cimarrones antiguos dar recogida de ellos, y venir à entregar al dominio de Sus dueños, à lo qual se opuso el espresado Matute formando Compañía con los residentes y algunos que se extrajo de los viejos;

y que no puede dar razon de la guerra que entre los dos Vandos hubo, porque al tiempo de ella havian sacado à la que declara à la Sabana, hasta que al otro dia llegaron <u>los cimarrones con Su dicho Capitan Diego Matute,</u> el qual <u>venia erido de dos</u> valazos que le dieron en la Guerra, y Supo por Sus otros compañeros que havian muerto en la refriega cinco de Sus compañeros; y haviendolos conducido à la Estanzuela, los entregaron à Gente libre, para que los condugezen â sus Dueños, lo qual se executò Y que esto que lleba dicho es la verdad de todo lo que sabe so cargo del Juramento que fecho tiene en que se afirmò, y ratificò siendole leyda, no supo declarar su edad que serà al parezer de mas de treinta años, no firmò por no saber, hizelo yo con mis testigos como và dicho =

Matías de Mojorena
De Assistencia, Marianno Joseph Almeria
de assistencia, Francisco Joseph de Mendieta

Yncontinenti dicho dia mes, y año yo el expresado Alcalde mayor autuando por ante mi como Juez receptor con testigos de Asistencia por impedimento del esscribano publico, y falta de otro, hize parezer a una muger presa por esta causa para efecto de tomarle su declarazion à la qual le recibo Juramento que hizo por Dios nuestro señor y la señal de la santta cruz en toda forma de derecho, por el qual ofrecio decir verdad de lo que supiere y fuere preguntada y siendolo al tenor del auto cabeza de prozeso = Dijo, llamarse Gertrudiz Simona, Parda esclaba de la Hazienda de la Punta que perteneze à don Joseph de Meza en esta Juridizion viuda de Rafael Cobos, negro esclabo que era de la dicha hacienda,

y que habrà poco menos de una año en compañía del dicho Su marido se huió de la referida hacienda, y que se mantubo dos meses sirbiendo en un Rancho del qual se passò con Su marido para el Palenque nombrado Mandinga en donde se mantubieron <u>governandolos Diego Matute su Capitan Sin que en el tiempo</u> que alli estubo la que declara ubiese visto ni oydo decir que Sus compañeros saliesen al Camino à executar algunos latrocinios, ni que perjudicasen à ninguno de los pocos caminantes que por alli trancitan, sino que se mantenian de las Siembras que hacian de Maiz, Arroz, Cacahuate, y Platanos; y que sabe que Diego Matute havia sido capitan de los cimarrones antiguos, y se hallaba discordado con ellos, porque, yendo ampararse distintos Esclavos fugitibos à el Palenque grande, no los querian consentir los viejos determinando hacer reculta [sic], y mandarlos entregar à Sus dueños, à lo qual se opuso el relacionado Matute defendiendo à los nuebamente introducidos,

y por esto formo Su quadrilla apartandose de los cimarrones antiguos y acaudillando à los recientes; y que los negros antiguos vinieron a Su Palenque solicitando à el rememorado Matute y los que le seguian para entregarlos en la Estanzuela, y haviendo llegado à quererlo executar, hizo resistencia el referido Matute con los de su Cuadrilla, formando Guerra uno, y otro vando, en la que perecio Rafael Cobos, marido de la que Declara, y otros quatro de sus compañeros; y que haviendole dado dos valasos a su Capitan Matute se dio por vencida Su quadrilla; por lo que à la declarante, y Sus demas compañeros con el Capitan, los trageron à la Estanzuela, y los entregaron a gente libre, para que los condugesen â Sus dueños, lo qual se executò, Y que esto que lleba dicho es la verdad de lo que sabe so cargo del Juramento que tiene fecho en que se afirmò, y ratificò siendole leyda, declarò ser de edad de treinta años, no firmò por no saber, hicelo yo con mis testigos como dicho es =

Mathias de Mojorena
De Assistencia, Marianno Joseph Almeria
de assistencia, Francisco Joseph de Mendieta

Document 48: 1790—Freedom for Black fugitives in Chihuahua[20]

Most excellent lord

I will order that Your Excellency's proclamation of May 2θ last be published, in the provinces under my command. I will also insert the Royal Decree of April 14, 1789, by which His Majesty orders that the Black fugitives of the foreign colonies acquire their freedom just by the act of seeking refuge in his domains. With this, I reply to Your Excellency's letter of May 31 past, with which I received 20 copies of the said proclamation.

May God keep Your Excellency many years, Chihuahua, June 25, 1790.
Most excellent sir, Jacobo Ugarte y Loyola

---

20. Archivo General de la Nación, Provincias Internas, Vol. 84, Exp. 1, f. 237r.

[left-hand margin, "The general commander of the Internal Provinces confirms he received 20 copies of the proclamation on slaves that recover their freedom."]

[Spanish transcription]

Excelentísimo señor

Dispondré se publique en las Provincias de mi mando el Vando de Vuestra Excelencia de 2θ de Mayo ultimo, insertando la Real Cedula de 14 de Abril de 1789; por la qual manda Su Majestad que los Negros fugitivos de las colonias extrangeras adquieran su livertad solo por el hecho de acogerse à los dominios de Su Magestad: con lo que contexto [sic] à la orden de Vuestra Excelencia de 31 de Mayo anterior, acompañatoria de 20 Exemplares del expressado Vando.

Dios guarde à Vuestra Excelencia muchos años Chihuagua 25 de Junio de 1790.
Excelentísmo señor, Jacobo Ugarte y Loyola

[al margen izquierdo, "El comandante General de Provincias Ynternas. Acusa recibo de 20 exemplares del Vando; sobre esclavos que recobran su libertad."]

Document 49: 1799—Apache women fight and escape from La Rinconada[21]

Mexico City, July 27, 1799

Viceroy Azanza refers to the investigation launched against Don Juan de Dios Cos, the lieutenant of the dragoons of that capital [city], for the escape of fifty-one Apache Indian woman, prisoners of war, and a male youth of the same nation. Cos was transporting them to the Veracruz garrison with a coffle of convicts and a greater number of prisoners.

The investigation reveals that said officer was on the convoy on the night before, February 5, at the Rinconada inn, near the said garrison. He was guarding the coffle with all possible precautions given the number of troops he had with him and the little security that the rooms in the inn could offer. The prisoners were separated into [different] rooms, when loud shouting was heard from the Indian women, to which the Indian men responded, and the men and women charged the sentinels in their respective rooms. At that instant, the officer called his troop to contain the Indian men, during which time the Indian women overcame the sentinels in their rooms

---

21. Archivo General de Simancas, SGU, Leg. 6980, 13, ff. 210r-210v. http://pares.mcu.es/Pares Busquedas20/catalogo/show/1297847?nm

and escaped, though it cost the life of one of the women. The officer could not attend to this, since he was busy with the primary objective of securing the men by force and with blows.

The Generals' Council, who tried this officer, has found that he has committed no crime. It decreed that he be freed and that the imprisonment he has suffered should not appear on his records, nor should it affect his promotions.

Approved.

[in the left-hand margin, "Dated February 5, 1800. R."]

[Spanish transcription]

Mexico 27 de Julio de 1799

El Virrey Azanza Remite el Proceso formado contra el Teniente del Regimiento de Dragones de aquella Capital, don Juan de Dios Cos, por haversele escapado cincuenta y una Yndias Apaches prisioneras de Guerra, y un muchao [sic] de menor edad y de la misma nacion, que conducia à la Plaza de Veracruz con un[a] cuerda de Presidiarios y mayor numero de Prisioneros.

De todo resulta que hallandose el expresado oficial con la escolta la noche del 5 de Febrero anterior en la Venta de la Rinconada cerca de dicha Plaza, custodiando la cuerda con la[s] precauciones posibles, respecto al numero de Tropa que tenia, y à la poca seguridad de los quartos de la venta en donde estavan con separacion los presos, se oyó un fuerte alharido de las Yndias al que correspondieron los Yndios, hechandose unas y otros sobre las centinelas de sus respectivos quartos, en cuyo instante llamando el Oficial à su Tropa acudieron todos à contener los Yndios, en cuyo tiempo forzando las Yndias las centinelas de sus quartos, se escaparon à costa de la vida de una de ellas a que no pudo atender el Oficial, ocupado en el principal objeto de asegurar á los hombres à la fuerza y á palos.

El Consejo de Generales por el qual fue juzgado este oficial, no hallando delito en èl, sentenció que se le pusiese en libertad, y que la prision que ha sufrido no le sirva de nota, ni perjudique para sus ascensos.

Aprobada

[al margen izquierdo, "Fecho á 5 de Febrero de 1800. R."]

Document 50: 1804—Escaping territorial Louisiana for Spanish Texas[22]

Desiring to remove any motive for complaint from the United States that may be presented with some semblance of justice in an affair that could have unfortunate consequences, unless we proceed with care and prudence, it seemed to me proper to turn to Your Lordship, despite having immediately given an account of this incident to the Superior Court.

Last August, the territorial governor of this province, William C. C. Claiborne, complained to me about the insubordination of the Black slaves of Natchitoches, which he understood was produced by the Nacogdoches commander's offer of freedom and all protection to deserting slaves who sought refuge in those dominions of His Majesty. Reflecting on this, I took the initiative of writing to the Superiority that this offer should be suspended, since the cession and successive sale of the Louisiana Province [to the United States] would require some modification or a new declaration from the [Spanish] Sovereign. With things in this state, I received a response from the commander of Nacogdoches and I find myself with new complaints from the said American governor. He describes the details of the Natchitoches slaves' insubordination. He says that nine have found refuge in the Pilar garrison. Six were arrested along the way. The militia and the troops had to take up arms to contain the insurrection, which presented symptoms of becoming a general [uprising]. In addition to this notice dated October 30, he sent another the 9th of the present month [November], informing me that the insubordination of the Blacks was taking over the Port of Punta Cortada [Pointe Coupée], one of the most important ports of lower Louisiana.

A simple understanding of this news will give Your Lordship foresight into the consequences of this evil if it is not stopped in its beginnings, along with the grave reciprocal effects that will take place if the Royal Decree of April 14, 1789, published in this kingdom in 1790, is not suspended. Thus, I beg Your Lordship to issue the most efficient orders to this effect by ordering, at the same time, that no Black or mulatto slave fleeing Louisiana be given asylum and that those found in Nacogdoches or in other frontier locations be returned [to their owners] in Natchitoches or Atakapas, so as not to offend them. May God keep Your Lordship many years. New Orleans, November 10, 1804. The marquis of Casa Calvo.

This is a copy. Chihuahua, January 22, 1805.

Bernardo Villamil

---

22. Archivo General de la Nación, Provincias Internas, Vol. 200, Exp. 3, ff. 311r–311v.

[Spanish transcription]

Deseando remover qualquier motivo de quexa de parte de los Estados Unidos, que pueda presentarse con alguna àpariencia de Justicia, sin embargo de haber inmediatamente dado cuenta a la Superioridad de este incidente, me parece propio ocurrir à Vuestra Señoría en un asunto que puede tener consequencias desagradables, sino se precede con el tino y prudencia que exigen los de esta naturaleza.

El Gobernador Territorial de esta Provincia Guillerm C.C. Claibone [William Claiborne], ya en el mes de Agosto proximo se me quexò de la insubordinacion de los Negros Esclavos de Natchitoches, producida según significó de haber ofrecido el Comandante de Nacogdoches la livertad, y toda proteccion à los Esclavos desertores, que se refugiasen à aquellos Dominios de S.M. Reflexionando yo, que qualquiera Real orden sobre el particular huviera, en la circunstancias de retrocesion y sucesiva venta de la Provinicia de la Luisiana, exigía alguna modificacion ó nueva declaracion del Soverano; tomé sobre mi el medio de representar á la Superioridad, escribiendo mientras para que se suspendiese la execucion: En este estado de cosas, haviendo recivido Respuesta del Comandante de Nacogdoches, me hallo con nuevas quexas de dicho Gobernador Americano, manifiestando los efectos de la insubordinacion de los Esclavos de Natchitoches, de los que nueve se hàn refugiado, dice en el Presidio del Pilar, se arrestaron seis en el camino, y la Milicia y la Tropa hà havido de tomar las Armas para contener la insurrecion, que presentaba sintomas de ser general: À este aviso que me pasò con fecha de 30 de Octubre añadió otro con la de 9 del corriente, participandome que la insubordinacion de los Negros ganaba ya el Puerto de Punta Cortada [Pointe Coupée] uno de los mas poderosos de la baxa Luisiana.

La simple lectura de esta noticia harà preveér á Vuestra Señoría las consequencias del mal sino se ataja en los principios, y los graves reciprocos perjuicios, que ha de producir si hasta la resolucion de Su Majestad no se suspende el cumplimiento de la Real Cedula de 14 de Abril de 1789, publicada en estos Reynos en 1790. Asi se lo suplico á Vuestra Señoría para que se sirva dar las mas eficaces disposiciones al efecto; mandando al mismo tiempo no se dé asilo, à ningun Negro ó Mulato esclavo que se presente fugitivo de la Luisiana, y que los que se hallaren en Nacogdoches, ù otros Establecimentos fronterizos se devuelvan à [sus dueños en] Natchitoches, ò Atakapas, vajo la caucion de no ofenderlos. = Dios guarde à Vuestra Señoría muchos años Nueva Orleans 10 de Noviembre de 1804 = El Marques de Casa Calvo.

Es copia Chihuagua 22 de Enero de 1805.

Bernardo Villamil

CHAPTER 5
Afro–Indigenous Interactions

This chapter offers passing glimpses into the everyday interactions between people of African and Indigenous descent in Mexico. These Afro–Indigenous exchanges and their liberating potential were a source of anxiety for colonial officials, especially during the early and mid-colonial period. The 1538 royal decree included here demonstrates that marriages between Black men and Native women were considered problematic, not for religious reasons but because of the association between freedom and Catholic matrimony. For colonial authorities, it was necessary to police Afro–Indigenous interactions in order to maintain a fragile, untenable caste system. The viceroy's 1582 decree targeting women of African descent who wore Indigenous clothing demonstrates just how difficult (and ridiculous) it was to prevent interactions between the two groups.

Evidently, Indigenous people and those of African descent spoke, worked, fought, celebrated, and generally lived with one another despite the existence of ordinances meant to separate them. They worshipped in the same churches, participated together in local festivities, and drank in the same taverns. The selections in this chapter have been chosen in order to move past an archive of colonial conflict, overly focused on interracial violence and tension. Instead, the documents that follow gesture toward much more common dealings among working people who encountered similar material conditions. From an archival perspective, the problem is that most of these interactions were never recorded. A leisurely game of cards between Black and Native friends would not produce a judicial record; a homicide undoubtedly would. The challenge, then, is to determine how people of African and Indigenous descent—to say nothing of their children—interacted with each other. What languages did they speak? What foods did they prefer during the colonial period? What kinds of spiritual and medicinal remedies did they share with one another?

Examples of linguistic and cultural proximity may be found in the 1590 and 1662 documents in which men of African descent operated as interpreters of Nahuatl, the indigenous lingua franca of colonial Mexico, and Castilian Spanish. A more complex case of such interactions, one with considerable political implications for residents of Huaquechula, is found in the document dated 1693. The cases included in this chapter foreground the importance of space in determining the nature of Afro–Indigenous interactions in colonial Mexico. The 1639 selection on religious syncretism in Tehuantepec speaks to a cultural openness between rural communities of Indigenous and of African descent. A similar rural dynamic, marked

153

by the absence of religious and political authorities in the Pánuco region, is also evident in the 1624 document on Lucas Olola.

In the urban setting, Afro–Indigenous exchanges were often conditioned by labor expectations. The textile mill (or *obraje*), for instance, was a notoriously exploitative work setting in which Native, African, and Asian-descended people labored throughout the colonial period. The 1590 and 1603 selections give some sense of the coercion that led enslaved and nominally free people to the work in the textile mills. Other urban cases, however, speak to relationships of trust and community formation. The 1682 case of Domingo de la Cruz reveals how Afro-Indigenous families mobilized all types of resources to ensure a better life for their children. Such cases were common, even if the archival record has left few detailed traces of these interactions.

Document 51: 1538—On Black-Indigenous unions and claims to freedom[1]

Bartolomé de Zárate, *vecino* and regent of Mexico City, has written an account of how the Black slaves who pass into that land cohabit[2] with the native Indian women and with Black women, both in their masters' house and elsewhere. The owners of such slaves marry them [to each other], in order to remove them from sin. And once married, the said slaves, without any other cause, say that they are free and procure their freedom. Despite the fact that people who own Black or Indian slaves marry them in said land, Zárate begged me to order that the slaves should not be free because of this, nor should they ask for their freedom. This being seen by our Council of the Indies, it was agreed that this, my royal decree, should be sent, by which [we state the following]. We order that although the Black and Indian slaves marry in New Spain with their masters' blessing, from here on they should not be free because of this, nor may they ask for freedom. We order Don Antonio Mendoza, our viceroy and governor in the said New Spain, and any other of our justices there to observe and comply with this, my decree, and that they not go against, pass, or consent against its form and tenor in any manner. We order that this decree be proclaimed by a town crier and

---

1. Archivo General de Indias, México, 1088, L.3, ff. 128r–128v. http://pares.mcu.es/ParesBusquedas20/catalogo/description/371994?nm

2. The original *amancebar* does not have a ready equivalent in either sixteenth-century or twenty-first-century English. The spirit of Zárate's complaint is that enslaved Black men and Native women were living in informal unions, out of wedlock. Baretti's Spanish-English dictionaries define *amancebar* as "to live in a state of fornication." Robert Cawdrey's *A Table Alphabeticall of Hard Usual English Words* (1604), in turn, defines fornication as "uncleannes between single persons." Neither of these definitions represents the dynamic presented in this document, so I have opted for the anachronistic concept of "cohabitation."

before a public scribe in the said Mexico City and in other cities, towns, and places in New Spain so that the aforementioned may be made public and well-known. Done in the town of Valladolid, July 20, 1538. I, the Queen. Countersigned by Samano, and marked by del Conde, Beltrán, Carvajal, Bernal, and Velázquez.

[in the left-hand margin, "Bartolome de Çarate, on the slaves' marriages"]

[Spanish transcription]

Por quanto Bartolome de Çarate vezino y Regidor de la çibdad de Mexico ha hecho relaçion que los esclavos negros que pasar a aquella tierra luego que llegan a ella se amançeban y estan amançebados con yndias naturales E ella [sic] y con negras ansy en casa de sus amos como fuera dellas / e que los dueños de los tales esclavos por los quitar de pecado los casan e ansy casados los dichos esclavos sin otra causa alguna dizen ser libres e procuran libertad e me suplico mandase que no enbargante que las personas que tuviesen esclavos, negros o yndios, en la dicha tierra los casasen no pudiessen por Ello ser libres ny pedir libertad o como la my[s]mo fuese lo qual visto por los del nuestro consejo de las yndias fue acordado que debia mandar dar esta my çedula vos por la qual mandamos que agora ny de aquy adelante aunque en la dicha nueba españa se casen los esclavos negros e yndios que en ella hoviere con voluntad de sus amos no sean por ello libres ny puedan pedir libertad e mandamos a don Antonyo de Mendoça nuestro virrey E governador de la dicha nueva españa E a otros qualesquier nuestros Justicias della que guarden y cunplan esta my çedula y lo En ella quando e contra el tenor y forma della / no vayan ny pasen ny Consientan ir ny pasar en manera alguna e para que lo susodicho sea publico e notorio a todos mandamos que sea apregonada en la dicha Cibdad de mexico y en las otras Cibdades villas y lugares de la dicha nueva españa por pregonero e ante scrivano publico fecho en la villa de Valladolid a XX dias del mes de Jullio de myll e quinientos e treynta y ocho años yo la Reyna Refrendada de Samano y señalada del Conde y Beltran y Carvajal y Bernal y Velazquez.

[al margen izquierdo, "bartolome de çarate, sobre los casamientos de los esclavos"]

Document 52: 1563—Complaint regarding Black and Indigenous laundresses[3]

In the city [Puebla] of the Angels, on April 26, 1563. The lords, justices, and regents of this city entered their council and town hall as is customary . . . in the presence of me, Alonso de Olivar, His Royal Majesty's scribe due to the absence of Juan de Cueva, scribe of the said town hall. The said lords ordered and decreed what follows. . . .

Item. This day the said council heard an appeal, presented by Juan Ruíz, who asked that the Black and native women not be allowed to wash in the sewer that is in front of the houses of Diego Cortés, as this is harmful. And the said lords ordered that it be proclaimed on the corner where the said sewer is located that no Black or Indian woman wash in it, not even their *misallera*.[4] A punishment of fifty lashes will be given to any Black or Indian woman or to any Indian or Black man who does so. The said lord magistrate . . . ordered that it be obeyed and followed thus.

[Spanish transcription]

En la çiudad de los angeles en veinte e seis dias del mes De abril de myll e quinientos E sesenta e tres años. Entraron En su cabildo e ayuntamyento segun lo an de costumbre Los muy mags. Señores Justicias e rregidores de esta dicha ciudad . . . Por presençia de mi Alonso dOlivar el escribano de su magestad rreal e por ausençia de Juan de Cueva escrivano del Dicho cabildo los dichos señores mandaron e proveyeron lo susodicho . . .

Item. Este dia aviendose visto otra apelacione en el dicho cabildo una apelacioon de Juan Rruiz por la qual pedia Que negras ni yndias no laben en la alcantarilla que esta frontero de las casas de Diego Cortes por ser perjudicial y los dichos señores mandaron que se pregone En la esquina donde esta la dicha alcantarilla que ninguna negra ni yndia no labe en ella ni su *misallera* so pena de çinquenta azotes a cada negra o india o indio o negro que lo assi hiziere el dicho señor alcalde mayor . . . mando (mando) que se guarde e cumpla ansi.

Document 53: 1582—Black women and mulattas dressed as Indigenous women[5]

Don Lorenzo Suárez de Mendoza, etcetera. In this New Spain there are many *mestiza* women, mulatta women, and Black women dressed in the habits of Indian women,

---

3. Archivo Municipal de Puebla, Actas de Cabildo, Vol. 9, ff. 5/4.
4. An archaic word for a clothing item, possibly used by women in church settings.
5. Archivo General de la Nación, Ordenanzas, Vol. 1, ff. 75r–75v.

which results in inconveniences that should be addressed. So that by this ordinance, I decree that from here on, no *mestiza* woman, mulatta woman, or Black woman may wear the habit of Indian women, but only the habit of Spanish women. Any of the said persons who are found dressing in the habit of Indian women will be arrested and taken to jail and given one hundred lashes publicly on the public streets of this city. They must also pay a fee of four reales to the alderman who arrests them, but this [ordinance] does not apply to the *mestiza* women, mulatta women, or Black women who are married to Indian men, because these women are allowed to wear the habit of Indians, since this is the habit of their husbands. So that [these women] may not be made prisoners, pay any fees, nor should they be bothered, I order this ordinance to be decreed publicly in the plaza and markets of this city and the rest of this New Spain. Having been decreed, I order the justices to carefully follow this decree and its execution. Done in Mexico [City], July 31, 1582. By order of his excellency, the Count of Coruña. Juan de Cueva.

[Spanish transcription]

Don Lorenzo Suarez de Mendoza, etcetera Por quanto de andar en esta Nueva Spaña muchas mestizas, mulatas, y negras Vestidas en avito de yndias se siguen inconvenientes que conviene Se reparen. Por la presente mando que de aqui adelante ninguna mestiza, mulata ni negra ande Vestida en avito de yndia, sino en avito de española so pena que cualquiera de las dichas personas que Se hallaren vestidas en el dicho avito de indias, sea presa y llevada a la Carzel y le sean dados çien açotes públicamente y en forma Por las calles publicas de esta ciudad y pague cuatro Reales de pena para el alguacil que la prendiere, con que esto no se Entienda con las mestizas, mulatas y negras que fueren casadas con yndios, porque a estas Se les permite que anden en el avito de yndias, que es el de Sus maridos, Sin que por ello yncurra En pena alguna ni sean presas ni se les haga molestia, y mando Se pregone publicamente en la plaça y tiangues de esta çiudad y en las demas de esta Nueva Spaña y pregonado las Justiçias Tengan Cuidado del cumplimiento y execucion dello. Fecho en México, vltimo de Julio de mill e quinientos y ochenta y dos años. El conde de Coruña, Por mandado de su excelencia. Juan de Cueva.

Document 54: 1590—A mulatto interpreter of Spanish and Nahuatl in Coatepec[6]

In the town of Coatepec, on February 1, 1590. The lord Juan de Villegas, Crown representative of this said town and its jurisdiction, declared that in order to examine

---

6. John Carter Brown Library, Codex SP 97 TEMP, "Testimonio de los titulos antiguos de la hazienda de labor nombrada el Barco," ff. 15v–16v.

the business deals that take place among Indians in his jurisdiction, it was necessary to name a Spanish interpreter of the Castilian and Mexican language. By the present [document] and in His Majesty's name, he named Joseph Lopez, of mulatto color, a resident of this said town of Coatepec, who was present. And he received his oath according to the law . . . and the said Joseph Lopez did not sign because he said he did not know how to write. Juan de Villegas. Before me, Cristóbal de Santa Clara, the named scribe.

[Spanish transcription]

En el pueblo de Quatepeque en primero dia del mes de Febrero de mil y quinientos y noventa años el señor Juan de Villegas Tiniente [sic] de Corregidor en este dicho Pueblo y su Partido Dijo: que por quanto para la esaminasiones de los negocios que se ofrecen entre Indios en su juridicion avia necessidad de nombrar Ynterprete Español de lengua Castellana, ê Mexicana por la presente en nombre de su Magestad nombraba, è nombrò por interpete [sic] â Jusepe Lopez de color mulato estante en este dicho Pueblo de Quatepeque que presente estava è del tomò ê recivio juramento en forma de derecho . . . y no firmò el dicho Jusepe Lopez porque dijo no sabia escrebir = Juan de Villegas = Passò ante mi Christoval de Santa Clara Escribano nombrado.

Document 55: 1590—Labor, value, and death by *cocoliztli*[7]

May all who see this letter know that I, Alonso Gómez, am a *vecino* of this city [Puebla] of the Angels of New Spain. I grant and acknowledge by this letter that I lease and rent to Marcos de la Cueva, *vecino* of this said city, a textile mill for making cloths with its wool, Indians, looms, and everything attached and belonging to it as will be declared. I lease him the textile mill for four years' time that will run and count from today, the date of this letter, on account of three thousand common gold pesos, at eight reales per peso, that the said Marcos de la Cueva is to pay me each year for the lease of the textile mill and all the other things. These are to be paid in thirds, every four months.

I also lease him a fulling mill that I own on the bank of the river that runs by Totomehuacan with four troughs for fulling and scouring cloths, three of them in good order. For the said four years he is to pay me eight hundred pesos of rent each year, to be paid in thirds, every four months. The things that are in the textile mill that I gave to the said Marcos de la Cueva and the conditions of this lease are as follows.

---

7. Archivo General de Notarías del Estado de Puebla, Notaría 4, Rodrigo Alonso de León, Box 36, ff. 600r–600v, 602r.

First, one hundred and thirty-four Indian men and women, who owe four thousand pesos of common gold.

Six Black shearers named Hernando, Gaspar, Baltazar, Bartolomé, Antón, and Diego.

Antón, a Black man, fuller

Bartolomé, a Black man, dyer

Dieguillo, the Black man of Espinosa

Juan, a Black man, shearer

María, a Black woman, cook

Also. It is a condition [of this lease] that if during the said time an Indian were to die or flee, then the said Marcos de la Cueva is obligated to give another in his place. However, should a notable *cocoliztli* epidemic cause the death of many Indians, in that case he has no obligation to replace them. Likewise, if the justices [of the city] were to remove a few Indians wrongly held in the textile mill, Marcos de la Cueva has no obligation to return them.

Also. It is a condition that should any of the aforementioned Black men or the Black woman die, then I, the said Alonso Gómez, am responsible for this charge and risk.

Also. It is a condition that any and every time that the said Alonso Gómez wants to take one or two of the said Blacks from the textile mill, he will be able to do so.

... done and awarded in the city [Puebla] of the Angels on December 8, 1590. I, the scribe, attest that I know the grantors, who signed their names. Witnesses present, Bartolomé Rodríguez, Rodrigo del Castillo, and Francisco Zamorano, tax-paying residents and inhabitants of this city.

Marco de la Cueva	Alonso Gómez	Before me, Rodrigo Alonso de León, His Majesty's scribe

[Spanish transcription]

Sepan quantos esta carta Vieren como Yo Alonso Gomez vezino que soy en esta ciudad de los angeles de la Nueva España otorgo y conozco por esta presente carta que arriendo y doy a rrenta a Marcos de la Cueva vezino desta dicha ciudad questa presente un obraxe myo que tengo de hacer paños con la lana yndios y telares y lo demas a el anexo y perteneçiente de la manera que de yuso yra declarado el qual le ariendo por tiempo de quatro años que corren y se quentan desde oy dia de la fecha desta carta en adelante por Raçon que el dicho Marcos de la Cueva me a de dar e pagar de arrendamyento por cada año de obraxe y todas las demas cosas que yran declaradas para el abio del tres myll pesos de oro comun a ocho rreales cada peso que se me an de pagar por sus tercios de quatro en quatro meses

Y asimismo le arriendo un batan de quatro pilas que las tres dellas con molientes y corrientes que yo tengo en la Ribera del rrio que pasa junto a Totomehuacan por los dichos quatro años y me a de pagar de rrenta cada año ochoçientos pesos de oro comun por los tercios del año de quatro en quatro meses y las cosas que ay en el dicho obraje que entrego al dicho Marcos de la Cueva y condiçion es deste arrendamyento son las siguientes

Primeramente ciento y treynta yndios e yndias que deben quatro myll pesos de oro comun.

Seis negros tundidores llamados Hernando, Gaspar, Baltazar, Bartolome, Anton, Diego.

Anton negro batanero

Bartolome negro tintorero

Dieguillo negro de Espinosa

Juan negro cardador

Maria negra coçinera

Yten es condiçion que si durante el dicho tiempo se muriere o huyere alguno de los dichos yndios el dicho Marcos de la Cueva a de ser obligado a dar otro por el Eçeto si ubiere cocolistle notable que dello se mueran muchos yndios que en tal caso no tiene obligaçion a dar ninguno de los que se muriereren del dicho cocolistle y asimismo si por la Justicia fueren sacados algunos yndios por mal abidos del dicho obraje no tiene obligaçion el dicho Marcos de la Cueva a bolberlos tales yndios.

Yten es condiçion que los negros que se murieren de los que ban declarados o la dicha negra es a cargo e Riesgo de my el dicho Alonso Gomez.

Yten es condiçion que cada y quando el dicho Alonso Gomez quisiere sacar del dicho obraje uno o dos negros de los susodichos los e de sacar del.

. . . ques fecha y otorgada en la çiudad de los angeles en ocho dias del mes de diçiembre de myll e quinientos e nobenta años e yo el scrivano doy fee que conozco a los dichos otorgantes los quales lo firmaron de sus nonbres siendo presentes por testigos Bartolome Rodriguez y Rodrigo del Castrillo y Francisco Zamorano vezinos y estantes en esta ciudad.

Marco De La Cueva   Alonso Gomez   Paso ante mi, Rodrigo Alonso de
                                                 Leon, escribano de su magestad

Document 56: 1603—Native men kidnapped on textile mill owner's orders[8]

In the city [Puebla] of the Angels, on July 14, 1573, before Fernando de Castro, gentleman of the Order of Santiago, magistrate of this city.

Jerónimo López de Saavadra, chief constable of this jurisdiction, I appear before Your Grace and criminally denounce Sebastián Tomelín, textile mill owner, and Miguel García, his overseer, and Antón and Francisco, mulatto men, and Francisco ladino and Juan Gabriel, Indian men, and all the other people who appear guilty in the prosecution of this cause. As I explain in my denunciation, I say that the aforementioned, each of them, have favored the said textile mill owner by stealing and tricking many Indians and taking them to the said textile mill, where they have sold them. The said textile mill owner has given them fifteen to twenty pesos for each Indian. He has made [the Indians] accept money by force, so that they will enter into a contract [with him], while locking them into the said textile mill. They did this to Diego, an Indian youth from Tepeaca, Melchor from Tecamachalco, Juan Martín and Juan Fernández from Amozoc, Baltazar from Calco, another Baltazar from Texcoco, with Juan and Agustín from Pachuca, and with Luis Mochatlo from Mexico [City]. Each of the aforementioned [accused men] stole, brought, and sold them to the said textile mill, where the said Tomelín has held them and has them locked in. The accused have committed grave crimes worthy of punishment.

I ask and beg Your Grace to address my account as true or the part that is sufficient. I ask that you order the aforementioned men to be arrested and punished according to the laws and ordinances related to this. I ask for justice and swear according to the law that this denunciation is not done with malice. I affirm that I will accuse them further once they are imprisoned.

Jerónimo López

[Spanish transcription]

En la çiudad de [Puebla de] los angeles A catorse dias del mes de Julio de myll y seisçientos y tres años ante don Fernando de Castro caballero del abito de Santiago allcalde mayor desta ciudad la pressente

Geronimo Lopez de Saavedra Alguaçil mayor de esta rresidencia parezco ante vuestra merced y denunçio Criminalmente de Sevastian Tomellin obrajero y de Miguel Garcia su mayordomo y de Anton y Francisco mulatos y de Francisco Ladino y Juan Gabriel yndios y de las demas Personas que la prosecuçion de la Causa paresçieren Culpadas y contando el caso de esta mi denunciacion digo que los susodichos y a cada uno de ellos favoresçiendo las del dicho obrajero an urtado y engañado a

---

8. Archivo Histórico Judicial de Puebla (AHJP), Exp. 643, f. 2r–2v.

muchos yndios y llevandolos al dicho obraje y vendiendolos ellos e dandoles el dicho obraxero a quinze y veinte pesos por cada yndio haziendoles tomar dineros por fuerza y que hagan asientos Teniendolos ençerrado en el dicho obraje como lo hizieron con Diego Yndio de Tepeaca muchacho y Melchor de Tecamachalco y con Juan Martin y Juan Fernandes de Amoçoque [Amozoc] y con Baltasar de Calco y otro Baltasar de Tezcuco [Texcoco] y con Juan y Agustin de Pachuca y Luis Mochatlo de Mexico que los susodichos los hurtaron y truxeron y vendieron en el dicho obraxe donde el dicho tomellin los a tenido y tiene ençerrados en lo qual los susodichos y cada uno dellos an cometido grabes delitos dignos de castigo

A vuestra merced Pido y supplico que acuda mi Relacion por verdadera o la parte que vaste mande prender y castigar los susodichos conforme a las leyes y hordenanzas que sobre ello disponen y pido Justicia y Juro en forma de derecho que esta denunciacion no es de maliçia y protesto estando pressos acusar los mas en forma.

Geronimo Lopez

Document 57: circa 1624—Lucas Olola and the religious beliefs of the Huasteca[9]

Throughout the province of Pánuco, the Huasteco Indians had a small pitcher made of various colored feathers. Among their gods, they held this to be their greatest [god], from whose mouth flowers come out. Carrying it, the lightest among the Indians dance to the sound of a stick instrument that is called *teponastle* in Mexican [the Nahuatl language] and of a drum in their style. They hold wooden rattles in their hands and wear a long hairstyle on their head. In general, this dance has continued until today throughout the province, in some towns with the superstition and Gentile rite that was customary before. The said PAYA[10] is celebrated with branches and a gathering of commoner Indians who eat and drink what was offered to the small pitcher, and other sins and abominations take place, in which not even the nefarious [sin] is pardoned. In other villages, the natives only dance to make merry. In any case, most of them ask the said small pitcher [for aid] in their diseases and health and make offerings for this.

Although this dance and superstition is only of the Indians, it is so that some Blacks, mulattos, and *mestizos* also dance to it, in particular one named Lucas Olola, a Black slave of Hernán Pérez. Dressing himself in the garb of the said Indians used for said dance, he feigns as if he were elevating himself, showing himself weakened,

---

9. Archivo General de la Nación, Inquisición, Vol. 303, Exp. 39, fs. 255 y 256. Spanish version in Boletín del Archivo General de la Nación, 3rd Series, Tome X, Vol. 1, No. 31 (1986), pp. 83–84.
10. An indigenous deity of the Huasteca region represented in the form of a ceremonial vessel.

and as such he lets himself fall. And he remains senseless for a long time, foaming at the mouth, and then he raises himself with notable fury and says that his spirit has arrived. He penetrates the walls, and enters and leaves through the walls of the [local] houses. All of this is done so that he will be held as divine and powerful, and so that the fathers, brothers, relatives, and husbands will give him the Indian woman he wants so that he can take advantage of her, without any resistance from her or anyone. Thus, after having heard his whole speech, they flee and leave the Indian woman he selects alone. And it is so, that by selling the Indians [the notion] that he is divine, he heals their infirmities, by lighting a stick and sucking it, a specific ceremony they use when pretending to heal, or truly healing, through a pact with the devil. He makes them believe that he sees and knows the person who did evil to them, causing that disease, because this is true and a lamentable thing, and can be affirmed without any doubt, that there is no Huasteco Indian, adult in age, nor young, whose disease and death is not related to some Indian sorcerer. And the said Black man says that he knows them and sees who it is. These are called healers and knowers, and in Huasteco are known as *chutones*. They hold them to be more powerful sorcerers than those who only cause harm. All of them and the said Black man as one of them, end up taking the miserable Indians' goods. They summon the women, who, out of fear that they will be killed, allow the sorcerers to enjoy themselves. They make the sick die with others' hate, and with such grave fault as believing in such power and attributing it to the devil. For in leaving God, they turn to such tricksters. By blows and torments, the said Black man has killed many Indian men and Indian women who were held to be sorcerers, showing himself to be a divine and powerful lord and someone within his right to punish. A mulatto named Quintero has been found guilty of this kind of healing and knowing about who caused a disease. The Black man often makes great speeches against him to the Indians, so that they might be persuaded that he [Olola] is the most powerful, along with seven gods. In effect, in the entire Huasteca region, among the friars and clerics, there is but one minister of doctrine who preaches, and the mulattos, Blacks, and *mestizos* are interpreters because they were born there. As a result, the Indians are indoctrinated by them and convinced in all the opinions he [sic] has. All of these opinions [are based] on his freedom to sin, and mainly on his carnalities, in such a way and to such a degree that it is well-known among the Huastecos and the said Black and mulatto people and all the rest, that there is no life, suffering, or glory after death. Thus, they say which of the dead came from the other life [?], and another said that, so that those living may say that only the bestial life is what matters. The royal justices do not surveil the continuous and close communication between the said Blacks and mulattos and the Indians, nor do they [prevent] their living amongst each other as is prohibited by His Majesty. And so, this leads to very severe harm, which would cease if only the truth were investigated and the guilty were punished, and if it was ordered with rigor by the Holy Tribunal of the

Inquisition as is ordered by the King Our Lord, that the Indians and such types of people should not live and communicate with each other.

And for further investigation of what has been said, and other things that are just, it is necessary that the said Holy Tribunal give commission to a minister who knows the said language, and to his notary or scribe, a Spanish person of his satisfaction, and, if at that moment it were necessary, as executor.

[Spanish transcription]

Los indios guastecos en toda la provincia de Pánuco, tuvieron entre los dioses, por el mayor, a un cantarillo hecho de diversas plumas de colores, de cuya boca salen flores de lo mismo; y cargándole los indios más ligeros, bailan al son de un instrumento de palo que llaman en mexicano teponastle, y un atambor a su usanza, llevando sonajas de madera en las manos y una cabellera larga en la cabeza. Este baile dura hasta hoy en general por toda la provincia, en unos pueblos con la superstición y rito de gentilidad que antes, celebrando al tal PAYA con ramos y junta de indios maceguales a comer y beber lo que se ofrenda al dicho cantarillo, y a otros pecados y abominaciones en que ni aun se perdona al nefando, y en otros pueblos sólo se baila para alegrarse los naturales; pero al fin, todos los más piden al tal cantarillo, en sus enfermedades, la salud, y le ofrendan para ello.

Y siendo este baile y superstición de solamente indios, es ansí que algunos negros, mulatos y mestizos le bailan, y en particular uno llamada Lucas Olola, negro esclavo de Hernán Pérez; y revistiéndose del traje de los dichos indios, usado para el dicho baile, finge que se eleva mostrándose amortecido, y como tal se deja caer, y está sin sentido por mucho tiempo, echando espumarajos por la boca, y luego se levanta con notable furia y dice le vino ya su espíritu, y penetra la paredes y entra y sale por ellas en las casas, y todo viene a parar en que le tengan por divino y poderoso, y en que los padres, hermanos, parientes y maridos, le dejan a la india que quiere para que se aproveche de ella, sin que ella ni nadie lo resista; y ansí después de haberle oído todo su parlamento se salen huyendo y dejan sola a la india que él señala. Y justamente esto, vendiéndoseles a los dichos indios por divino, les cura de sus enfermedades encendiendo ocote y chupándoles, cerimonia cierta de que ellos usan cuando fingen tener, o verdaderamente tienen en sus curas, pacto con el demonio, y les hace cree que ve y conoce a la persona que les hizo mal, causándoles la tal enfermedad, porque esto es cierto y cosa lastimosa, y que se puede afirmar por sin duda, que no muere indio guasteco adulto, en edad ni pequeño, cuya enfermedad y muerte no se aplique a algún indio hechicero; y el dicho negro dice que los conoce y ve lo que es; y a estos que llaman curanderos y conocedores, que en guasteco se dicen chutones, los tienen por hechiceros más poderosos que los que solamente son dañadores; y todos y el dicho negro como todos, les sacan a los miserables indios sus haciendas; y a las mujeres, de miedo que no las maten, las atraen a que se dejen gozar, y a los enfermos los hacen morir con odio de otros, y con tan grave culpa como es creer semejante poder y atribuirle al demonio, y que dejando a Dios acuden para su salid a semejantes ambaydores [sic]. El dicho negro ha muerto indos e indias que se tenía por hechiceros, a puros azotes y tormentos, mostrándose señor divino y poderoso, y que como a cuanto pertenece a esto les castiga.

En este modo de curar y conocer al que causó la enfermedad está culpado un mulato llamado Quintero, contra quien el dicho negro suele hacer grandes pláticas a los indios para que se persuadan es él el más poderoso y siete dioses. Y en efecto, como en toda la Guasteca no hay ministro de doctrina que predique, entre frailes y clérigos, sino solo uno, y los mulatos, negros y mestizos son lenguas de su misma naturaleza por haber nacido allí, los indios son doctrinados de ellos y convencidos de las opiniones que quieren, todas en orden de su libertad en pecar, y principalmente en sus carnalidades, de manera y en tanto grado, que es cosa muy asentada entre los guastecas y la dicha gente de negros y mulatos y los demás, que no hay más vida, pena ni gloria después de la muerte; y ansí dicen que cuál de los muertos vino de la otra vida, y dijo tal, para que los vivos solamente lo digan, y que ansí sola la vida bestial es lo que importa. Las justicias reales no celan la comunicación tan continua y estrecha de los dichos negros y mulatos con los indios, ni el vivir entre ellos con estar prohibido por su Majestad; y ansí es el daño muy grande, que cesaría si averiguada la verdad y castigados los culpados se mandase con rigor por el Santo Tribunal de la Inquisición lo que está mandado por el Rey nuestro señor, que ni vivan ni se comuniquen entre indios los susodichos géneros de gente.

Y para la averiguación de lo dicho y lo más que con ello anda justo, es necesario se dé comisión en forma por el dicho Santo Tribunal, a ministro que sepa la dicha lengua, y para su notario o escribano, a persona española de su satisfacción y de momento, y si fuere necesario, de ejecutor.

Document 58: 1628—Juana and Diego Pablo charged with trespassing[11]

Juana de Zumaya, an Indian woman, native of this city [Puebla], in the San Francisco neighborhood, says that when Isabel Francisca, my legitimate mother and also an Indian native to the said neighborhood, died, she left a few houses. These residences are on the street that goes from the houses of Don Felipe de Arellano to the countryside. On one side they abut the houses of Isabel Morales, a *mestiza* woman, and on the other they abut the houses of Juan Andres, an Indian man, native of the said

---

11. Archivo Histórico Judicial de Puebla, Exp. 1480, f. 1r–1v.

barrio. Juana, a Black woman, and Diego Pablo, an Indian man, have entered these houses with no cause, title, or reason. Without being theirs, they have divided and partitioned the houses among themselves. According to the law of Soria [which established who could and could not inherit property], I must be granted possession of the said houses, indivisibly, as the heir that I am of the said Isabel Francisca, who had me and gave birth to me by the legitimate marriage she entered *in facie ecclesia*[12] with Francisco Santos, my father, an Indian man, who was a native of this city.

Therefore, I ask and beg Your Grace to take this information and order to the tenor of this request . . . and I swear as is accustomed that this [statement] is not made out of malice.

Bachiller Mendiola

[Spanish transcription]

Juana de Çumaya, india natural de esta ciudad [Puebla] al barrio de San Francisco, digo que abiendo fallecido Ysabel Francisca mi madre ligitima, yndia ansimismo, natural del dicho barrio, dejo en el unas cassas de bibienda que estan en la calle que sale de las cassas de Don Felipe de Arellano y ba a dar al campo y lindan por una parte con cassas de Ysabel Morales mestiça y por otra con las de Juan Andres, indio natural del dicho barrio en las quales sin causa titulo ni rraçon se an entrado Juana negra y Diego Pablo indio porque sin ser suyas las dibidieron y partieron entre si y conforme a la lei de Soria se me deve dar posesion *pro indiviso* de las dichas cassas como a eredera que soi de la dicha Ysabel Francisca habida y nacida de lejitimo matrimonio que contrajo yn facie eclesie con Francisco Santos mi padre yndio natural que fue desta ciudad a tento a lo qual

A vuestra merced pido y suplico mande se me reçiba informaçion al tenor deste pedimiento . . . y Juro en forma que no es de malicia

Bachiller Mendiola

Document 59: 1631—Marriage license for Juan Francisco and Juliana de la Torre[13]

Juan Francisco, Black slave of Antonio de Anis, goldbeater, *vecino* of this city. I say that I intend to marry Juliana de la Torre, Indian widow of Mateo de la Cruz, the Black slave who belonged to Doctor Herrera. So that this marriage takes place, I ask and beg Your Grace to accept the following information that we are single and free of

---

12. A marriage celebrated according to the instructions of the church, literally "before the church."
13. Archivo General de la Nación, Indiferente Virreinal, Caja 1841, Exp. 25, ff. 20r, 21v.

marriage, so that we may receive the license and the priests of this city's cathedral may post our wedding banns. So that if there is no impediment, the priests may espouse and marry us. I ask for justice.

In Mexico City, on April 19, 1631, this petition was read before and seen by the Lord Doctor Luis Sifuentes, the provisor and general vicar of this city and archbishopric. He ordered that the information contained in the petition be referred to any receiving notary and once given, it should be brought [back] to see what is convenient.

Before me, Alonso de Carvajal, public notary

* * *

[Juliana de la Torre's statement]

... Asked if she is a widow and free of marriage, and if so does she want to contract marriage with Juan Francisco, Black slave of Antonio de Anis, the goldbeater. And asked if she knows that the aforementioned man is a slave and that he is required to go wherever they may take him or sell him, to make a married life with the said man, even if it is out of this city and kingdom. And if she wants to contract a marriage with the said man with this condition. She said that she is the widow of Mateo de la Cruz, the Black man, and as such wants to contract a marriage with Juan Francisco, slave of Antonio de Anis. She knows that he is a slave and wherever his master sells him, she will go with the aforementioned man to make a married life. She swore under oath that this is the truth. Done, and she did not sign because she says she does not know how to. She said that she is more than twenty-seven years old.

Before me, Pedro de Rueda, public notary

[Spanish transcription]

Juan fransisco negro esclabo de Antonio de Anis tirador de oro vezino desta Ciudad Digo que tengo tratado de Casarme con Juliana de la Torre india viuda de Matheo de La Crus negro esclabo que fue del Dotor herrera y para que tenga efecto A Vuestra merced Pido y Suplico que se me reçiba informasion de como somos solteros y libres de matrimonio y dandonos Licencia para que los Curas de la Catredal desta Ciudad nos amonesten y no resultando inpedimento nos desposen y Casen y pido Justicia

En la ciudad de Mexico A diez y nuebe dias del mes de abrill de mill y seiscientos y treinta y un años ante el señor dotor Luis Zifuentes probisor y bicario general desta ciudad y arçobispado se leyo esta peticion e vista por su merced mando De ynformacion de lo contenido en la peticion y la cometio a qualquier notario Recetor y dada se le trayga para hara haver lo que conbenga

Ante mi Alonso de Carvajal Notario Publico

* * *

[respuesta de Juliana de la Torre]

... Preguntada si es biuda y libre de matrimonio y como tal Lo quiere contraher con Juan Francisco negro esclabo de antonio de añiz tirador y si sabe que el susodicho es esclabo y que tiene obligacçion de ir donde lo llebaren o bendieren açer bida maridable con el suso dicho aunque sea fuera desta çiudad y Reino y si con la dicha calidad quiere contraher matrimonio con el susodicho = digo que es viuda de mateo de la cruz negro y como tal quiere contraher matrimonio con Juan Francisco esclabo de Antonio de Aniz tirador y que sabe que hes esclabo y que donde quiera que lo bendiere su amo yra con el susodicho aser bida maridable juro es la berdad so cargo del Juramento fecho y no lo firmo porque dijo no saber dijo ser de mas de veinte y siete años

ante mi Pedro de Rueda, notario Publico

Document 60: 1639—Religious syncretism and *nahuales* in Tehuantepec[14]

Most Illustrious Sir,

With Your Lordship's order, I read the edicts of the Holy Tribunal in the Villa Alta de San Ildefonso and preached a sermon about each of the edicts with the greatest ostentation possible in all that was required. I give an account of this to Your Lordship in a letter that accompanies this one.

After I read the edicts, some accusations and causes came to me, which I remit to Your Lordship so that you may see to what is best. In visiting this land of Tehuantepec, I have found that it is commonly known that in this land there are many mulatto men and women, Black men and women, and *mestizo* men and women who have a pact with the devil by having *nahuales*.[15] This, they say, originates from the great communication that they have with the Indians, because they are the sons and daughters of Indians and Blacks, and are therefore involved in this evil without any fear of the Holy Office [of the Inquisition]. I understand that they have not heard the edicts, because they live around the ranch houses and never congregate where the

---

14. Archivo General de la Nación, Inquisición, Caja 1131, 2 pages, no folio.
15. A person with the ability to invoke and take on the physical form of an animal. Present throughout the Mesoamerican region, *nahuales* were closely associated with witchcraft and sorcery during the colonial period.

edicts are read. I give notice of this to Your Lordship so that you may see to what is best. May Our Lord keep Your Lordship. Tehuantepec. June 26, 1639.

[Friar] Juan de Noval

[in another hand, "received on August 5, 1639"]

[Spanish transcription]

Yllustrisimo señor,

Con orden de Vuestra Señoría, Leý los edictos de esse sancto tribunal en la villa alta de San Ylefonso [sic, San Ildefonso] con la mayor ostentaçion que se pudo haçer en todo lo Requissito aviendo sermon en cada uno de los Edictos. De todo lo qual se da Relaçion a Vuestra Señoría que ba con esta.

Algunas delaçiones y causas Vinieron ante mi Despues de haberlos leydo lo qual Remitto a Vuestra Señoría Para que provea lo que mas convenga. Visitando esta tierra de Tehuantepeque, he allado que corre comunmente una boz y fama de que en toda esta tierra muchos mulatos y mulatas negros y negras mestiços y mestiças Tienen pacto con el Demonio Teniendo naguales, lo qual diçen Dimana De la mucha communicaçion que tienen con Los indios y ser hijos e hijas de indios y negros, y estar en aqueste mal metidos sin temor del santo officio. Entiendo ques el no haber oydo Los Edictos por que estan Por estas estancias y nunca se congregan adonde se leen Los Edictos aviso desto a Vuestra Señoría Para que provea lo que fuere mejor. Nuestro señor guarde a Vuestra Señoria Tehuanteque. Junio 26 de 1639 años.

[Fray] Jhoan de Noval

[en otra mano, "recivida el 5 de agosto 1639"]

Document 61: 1662—Criminal charges against Gregorio for attacking Diego de la Cruz[16]

In the city of Puebla [of the Angels] on November 21, 1662, before Don Nicolás Bañuelos Cabeza de Vaca, court justice in this city by His Majesty. An Indian man, fluent in the Castilian language, appeared along with Diego Martín, a mulatto man, as an interpreter who speaks and understands the Mexican language [Nahuatl], who swore to use his office well and truly as he must and is obligated to do. The latter swore to God and on the cross, according to the law. The plaintiff said his name is Diego de la Cruz and that he is a native of this city and a baker. He works in the house of Captain Ignacio de Saldaña. Taking the necessary requirements and

---

16. Archivo Histórico Judicial de Puebla (AHJP), Exp. 2216/1689, f. 1r.

solemnities of the law, he presents a complaint against Gregorio, a mulatto man and slave of Licenciado Antonio Suarez, presbyter. Diego de la Cruz accuses the said mulatto, who with no fear of God Our Lord and in contempt of the royal justice, approached and hit him many times with a rock this afternoon, at three o'clock more or less. He was quietly and peacefully standing on the street that goes from the door of the Augustinian convent to the old church of Las Mercedes, giving [the accused] no cause or occasion for this. He sustained an injury on the left side of his head, another on his nose, and another over one of his lips. He [Gregorio] would have undoubtedly killed him [Diego de la Cruz], if a Spanish man named Francisco and, later, the regent Don Gabriel Hidalgo had not defended him and pacified the said mulatto. In all of this, [the accused] has committed a grave and atrocious crime worthy of punishment. So that the accused may be held and condemned to the greatest and most grave punishments, the plaintiff asks and begs His Grace to admit this complaint and the information he offers and gives. He asks this to be sufficient to order a warrant for the imprisonment of the said mulatto Gregorio and once he is apprehended, he will accuse him further in proper form. I ask for justice and expenses. I swear to God and on the cross in proper form for this complaint. He did not sign, nor did the interpreter, because they said they do not know how to do so.

His Grace having seen this complaint, ordered that the information presented by Diego de la Cruz, Indian man, be given and admitted. He will decree to it and sign. And that the injuries that [the plaintiff] be attested.

Don Nicolás de Bañuelos   Before me, Nicolás Alvarez, royal and public scribe

[Spanish transcription]

En la Ciudad de [Puebla] de los angeles a beinte y Vn dias del mes de nobiembre de mill y seisscientos y sesenta y dos años ante don Nicolas Bañuelos Cabesa de Baca alcalde hordinario en esta Ciudad Por su magestad Paresio Vn yndio que demas de ser Ladino en lengua castellana mediante Diego Martin mulato que habla y entiende La lengua mexicana que hiso ofisio de ynterprete y Juro a dios y a la Cruz en forma de derecho de Vsarlo bien y fielmente como deve y es obligado, dixo llamarse Diego de la Cruz y ser natural desta ciudad y Panadero que trabaja en casa del Capitan Ignacio de Saldaña y premisos los requisitos y solemnidades del derecho querello criminalmente de Gregorio, mulato esclavo del Lizenciado Antonio Suares presbitero en Rason de que el dicho mulato sin temor de dios nuestro señor y menospresio de la Real Justisia esta tarde serian las tres della poco mas o menos estando el dicho Diego de la Cruz quieto y pasifico parado en la Calle que ba de la puerta Reglar del conbento del señor San augustin a la yglessia Vieja de las Mercedes sin darle Causa ni ocasion alguna llego a el el dicho mulato y Le enpeso a dar muchos golpes con Vna piedra de que le dio Vna herida en la cabesa al Lado ysquierdo, otra en la naris y otra ensima de Vn Labio y sin duda lo matara si no llegara, a defenderlo y a apasiguar al dicho mulato Vn hombre español nombrado francisco y despues El Regidor Don Gabriel Hidalgo en todo lo qual a cometido grabes y atros delicto Digno de Castigo y Para que le tenga y sea condenado en las mayores y mas grabes penas en que a yncurrido Pidio y Suplico a su merced admita esta querella y a su tenor ynformasion que ofrese y dada en la parte que baste mandese le libre mandamiento de prision contra el dicho gregorio mulato que estando preso Protesta acusarlo mas en forma pidio Justisia y Costas y Juro a dios y a la Cruz en forma esta querella y no firmo ni dicho ynterprete Porque dixeron no saber escrebir.

y Por su merced Vista admitio esta querella y mando se le Resiva al dicho Diego de la Cruz Yndio la ynformasion que ofrese y dada la bera y probeera y lo firmo = y se de fee de las heridas que tubiere

Don Nicolas de Bañuelos   Ante my Nicolas Alvarez scrivano Real y publico

Document 62: 1682—Domingo de la Cruz establishes his son's free status[17]

In the city [Puebla] of the Angels on February 4, 1682. Lord General Don Estacio Coronel Benavides, gentleman of the Order of Santiago, magistrate and captain general in this city for His Majesty, said that a Black man appeared before His Grace. He said that his name is Domingo de la Cruz and that he is the slave of the widow of Juan Bautista Saenz, the textile mill owner, a *vecina* of this city. He informed His Grace that a little mulatto named Simón de los Santos is in the care of Josefa María, who had raised the child since he was born. [Simón de los Santos] was the son of Sebastiana, an Indian woman, and of the said Black man, Domingo de la Cruz. With this information, His Grace summoned the said little mulatto Simón de los Santos, who came with the said Indian woman Josefa María. His Grace was told about all of the above. So that at all times it be certain that the said little mulatto Simón de los Santos is a free person, not subject to slavery, and so that he can enjoy his said liberty, he ordered that he be placed in the charge of Juan de Anzures, the free mulatto overseer of Jose García Cortéz's slaughterhouses, who acknowledged this in proper form. His Grace ordered that the said Indian woman be given four pesos in reales, a white blouse, a petticoat with lion [designs?], and a Chinese Rouen blanket, as payment for raising the said little mulatto. He decreed it in this manner and signed.

Estacio Coronel y Benavides   before me, Antonio Gomez de Escobar, royal and public scribe

---

17. Archivo General de Notarías del Estado de Puebla, Notaría 4, Antonio Gómez de Escobar, Box 218, ff. 123r–123v.

[Spanish transcription]

En la ciudad de [Puebla de] los Angeles a quatro dias del mes de febrero de mil seisscientos Y ochenta i dos años el Señor General don Estacio Coronel Benabides Cavallero del orden de Santiago Alcalde maior i teniente de Capitan General en esta Ciudad por su magestad dijo que ante Su mersed a paresido un negro que dijo llamarse Domingo de la Cruz i Ser Sclavo de la biuda de Juan Bautista Saenz dueño de obraje vesina de esta Ciudad el qual informo a su mersed que en poder de Jusepa Maria paraba un mulatillo nombrado Simon de los Santoz la qual lo havia Criado desde que nasio el qual era hijo de Sebastiana Yndia i del dicho Domingo de la Cruz negro Con Cuia notisia Su mersed hiso pareser Ante si al dicho Simon de los Santos mulatillo el qual trujo a su presensia La dicha Josepha Maria yndia que le Ynformo todo lo Referido y para que en todo tiempo Conste que el dicho Simon de los Santoz mulatillo es Persona Libre no sujeta a esclavitud i que pueda gosar de dicha Libertad mandaba i mando que se ponga en deposito de poder de Juan de Ansurez mulato libre maiordomo de los Rastros de Jose Garsía Cortez, el qual lo otorge en forma i a la dicha yndia en pago de la Crianza del dicho mulatillo se le den quatro pesos en Reales vn guipil blanco unas naguas de Leones [sic, ¿?] i una cobija de Ruan de china assi lo proveio i firmo

Estacio Coronel y Venavides   ante my Antonio Gomez Descobar scrivano Real y Publico

Document 63: 1693—Charges against Juan de Medina, governor of Huaquechula[18]

Don Gaspar de Sandoval Cerda Silva y Mendoza, count of Galvez, etcetera. Whereas the following report was presented to me: Most excellent sir, Juan Eligio de Arissa, representing the nobles, magistrates, officials of the republic, electors, and the remaining commoners and natives of the town of Huaquechula, in the jurisdiction of the town of Atlixco, in the best form before the law . . . I say that in contravention of the royal decrees and ordinances that prohibit the election of Spaniards, mulattos, and other categories of people who are not legitimate and noble natives as governors, this present year Juan de Medina, mulatto, has been elected as governor of the said town. However, as an inept and incapable person, he does not embody the qualities necessary by law for the use and exercise of said office. He has occupied himself in the mechanical occupations of butcher houses and has intruded in this way with the natives, which has led to extortions and mistreatments. Therefore, I contradict

---

18. Archivo General de la Nación, Indios, Contenedor 18, Vol. 32, Exp. 88, ff. 92v–93v.

and protest once, twice, and more times the election made in favor of said Juan de Medina, mulatto, in the best manner before the law, so that he may not continue to pursue the said office for the reason expressed above. Thus, I ask and beg Your Excellency, that by contradicting the said election for the aforementioned governor, you order it annulled and conducted anew if necessary. I ask to be allowed to pursue justice for my clients by suspending the [governor's] confirmation, and that notice be given in the other proceeding, so that it might not be dispatched. I ask for justice and swear to God and on the cross, and in what is necessary, etcetera.

Juan Eligio de Arissa

. . . By the present writ, [the viceroy] ordered the magistrate of this jurisdiction and his lieutenant to pursue this investigation, which he refers to the lord prosecutor's answer, in relation to its content and giving me an account of the orders given, so that I may see them and decree what is most convenient. Mexico City, January 19, 1693. The Count of Galve. As ordered by His Excellency.

Don Pedro Velázquez de Cadena

[Spanish transcription]

Don Gaspar de Sandoval Zerda Sylva y Mendoza conde de Galvez etcetera = Por quanto ante mi se presento el memorial siguiente = Excelentísimo señor: Juan Elixio de Arissa por los Principales Alcaldes Officiales de Republica electores y demas comun y Naturales del Pueblo de Guacachula [Huaquechula] de la Jurissdiccion de la Villa de Atrisco, como mejor aya lugar . . . = Digo, que en contravencion de las Reales Cedulas y ordenanzas, que prohiben, el que no se elixan en officios de Governadores, mulatos, españoles, y otros Generos de gentes, que no sean naturales legitimos y Prinicipales; han electo por Governador de dicho Pueblo para este pressente año a Juan de Medina Mulato, sin concurrir en el las calidades dispuestas por Derecho y ser (como es) persona inepta e yncapaz para el usso y exercicio de dicho officio, y averse ocupado en officios mecanicos de carnicerias, yntroduciendose con los Naturales, siguiendose de dicha Yntroduccion extorciones y vexaciones. Por lo qual y lo demas, que protesto alegar en la mexor forma, qual lugar aya en Derecho contradigo una, dos o mas vezes la eleccion hecha en dicho Juan de Medina, mulato, para que no prosiga en la prosecusion de dicho Officio por la razon expressada. Por lo qual = A Vuestra Excelencia pido y supplico que (haviendo contradicha la eleccion hecha en el sussodicho de tal Governador) se sirva, de mandarla anular, y que se haga nuebamente y en casso necessario que se presente; se me entregue para alegar de la Justicia de mis partes, suspendiendo su confirmacion, y que se de noticia en el otro officio, para que no se despache. Pido Justizia y Juro a Dios y a la Cruz, y en lo necessario etcetera =

Juan Elixio de Arissa

. . . Por el Pressente mando al Alcalde mayor de este partido o su theniente proceda a la aberiguacion, que refiere el sseñor fiscal en su respuesta, arreglandose a su contenido, y dandome quenta con Autos; para que por mis vistos, mande lo que mas convenga. Mexico diez y nueve de henero de mill seissientos y noventa y tres años = El Conde de Galve = Por mandado de su Excelencia =

Don Pedro Velasquez de la Cadena

CHAPTER 6

Navigating Religion and Politics

The documents in this chapter address the complex negotiations that enslaved and freed people entered into with religious authorities and political institutions in Mexico between 1587 and 1787. Viceroys and archbishops and their respective political structures constantly competed for influence and power in colonial times. Free and enslaved people also participated in these tense interactions, often pitting secular authorities against their religious counterparts. Telling examples of these dynamics may be found in the opening case of the Toluca textile mill workers and the friars who interceded on their behalf. A very different scenario emerges in the case of the priest of Huazolotitlán and his diminishing influence over a dispersed, rural community of African descent at the end of the eighteenth century. The examples from 1596 and 1625 selected for inclusion here offer a window into the lives of those who had renounced God, as well as the settings, conditions, and witnesses that enabled such cases to reach the inquisitors. The Inquisition sought to enforce religious orthodoxy, yet in order to do so, it had to understand the backgrounds and motivations of those who were accused (or who accused themselves). The 1725 and 1731 documents on bigamy reveal how the enforcement of monogamy was policed and resisted in the late colonial period.

Catholicism was a dominant force in everyday life in colonial Mexico, and one that affected enslaved people, especially those newly arrived. The 1606 cases of Pedro and Lucía, who were recent survivors of the transatlantic slave trade, shed light on the religious technicalities they were expected to observe even as they were still adapting to a new cultural and religious landscape. The 1642 life narrative of an enslaved African man, Sebastián Domingo de Munguía, offers a highly detailed account of his lengthy experiences with clergymen, but also with slaveholders and politicians who were truly indifferent to the tenets of the Catholic faith.

In many ways, then, the 1640 "Dance Performed by the Black Creole Women" in honor of the arriving viceroy represents a fascinating foil to Munguía's testimony. The published account of the festivities is a deeply allegorical text, composed in verse and prose, which explains the complex choreography and costumes for the dancers performing for Viceroy Diego López Pacheco y Portugal (1640–1642), the marquess of Villena. Translated here into English for the first time, courtesy of Professor Miguel Valerio, the description of the feast immerses the reader in the symbols, materials, and tropes often associated with women of African descent.

Many freed people also found opportunity in the organized religion and local politics of *cofradías*, or brotherhoods. The document on the *chino* brotherhood of Our Lady of Guadalupe speaks to the ways in which freedmen of Asian descent negotiated and created a space for their community in 1655. Another remarkable case about religious confraternities may be found in the constitutions drafted by a community of African descent in Toluca at the end of the seventeenth century. This confraternity was dedicated to Santa Efigenia, an Ethiopian saint whose devotional communities could be found in Mexico, Portugal, and Brazil. Another Black saint who was widely revered throughout Mexico (and other parts of the African diaspora) was San Benito de Palermo. The 1710 printed *octava*, a set of instructions for eight days of prayer, reveals how, why, and when priests, friars, and common people turned to this Franciscan saint. While the author of San Benito's *octava* recommended starting the days of prayer on April 4, in modern-day Venezuela, his feast is widely celebrated on December 27 and 28.

Document 64: 1587—Toluca friars warned to not intercede for textile mill workers[1]

Don Alvaro Manrrique, etcetera. I make it known to you, the Crown representative of the village of Toluca, that certain Spanish *vecinos*, who own textile mills in the said village, have written an account of how they hold a number of Indians, Blacks, and mulattos as slaves and as people condemned by justice to serve in the said textile mills for crimes they have committed. They are paying the condemnations for which they were sentenced. In order to secure them, they have some of them shackled during mass in church. The guardian and religious men of the monastery of the said village, [however] have held some of them in the monastery to help them escape and go to wherever they want. In this, the *vecinos* are affected and they have asked me to remedy it. So that having seen this, I order by the present letter that it will not be tolerated or allowed that the Indians, Blacks, or mulattos who have been given to the service of the textile mills with just title be released by the said friars. The latter will also not involve themselves [with the former] in the church or monastery. I order that the said textile owners not be aggravated by this. Done in Mexico City on June 19, 1587. By order of His Excellency, the Marquess. Juan de Cueva.

[in the left-hand margin, "That the Crown representative of the village of Toluca may not allow the friars to take out the Indians, Blacks, and mulattos from the textile mills"]

---

1. Archivo General de la Nación, General de Parte, Vol. 3, Exp. 248, f. 110v.

[Spanish transcription]

Don Alvaro Manrrique etcetera, hago saber a vos El corregidor de la villa de Toluca que por parte de ciertos vecinos españoles que Tienen obraxes en la dicha billa me han hecho rrelacion quellos tienen cantidad de Indios negros y mulatos assi esclavos como condenados por la Justicia a servir en los dichos obraxes por delitos que an Cometido por los quales tiene Pagadas Las condenaciones en que fueron sentenciados y para los tener seguros y ____ [¿?] algunos de ellos Con prisiones a misa a La yglesia y El guardian y rreligiosos del monesteryo de la dicha villa detienen en el monasteryo a los quales los hechan para que se huyan y ban donde quisieren en lo qual se les hasse Agravio y me pidieron mandasse rremediarlo y por my bisto por la Presente es mandado que no consentare ni deje lugar que los yndios negros o mulatos que estuvieren dados a Servicio a los dichos obraxes con Justo titulo los suelten los dichos frailes ni se entrometan adentro en la yglesia ni monesterio dando Orden que en esto no se agavie a los dichos dueños de obraxes fecho En mexico a diez y nueve dias del mess de Junio de myll e quinientos y cohenta y siete años. El marques por mandado de su excelencia, Juan de Cueva.

[al margen izquierdo, "Para que el corregidor De la villa de Toluca no consienta que Los frailes saquen los los [sic] yndios negros y mulatos que estan en obraxes"]

Document 65: 1596—Juan Carrasco and the Inquisition[2]

In Mexico City, on Friday, November 29, 1596. During the morning audience, the lord inquisitor Doctor Lobo Guerrero summoned a Black man, who was brought imprisoned from the city [Puebla] of the Angels and is being held in one of the secret jails of this Holy Office. He was present and after taking the oath in due form, he promised to tell the truth in this audience, and in any others to be held with him.

He was asked what his name is, where he is native to, and how long it has been since he was brought imprisoned to this Holy Office. He said his name is Juan Carrasco, slave of Juan Banegas, *vecino* of the city of the Angels. He is a Creole, born in the house of Diego Arias Atalaya, *vecino* of the said city. He said that he is twenty years old more or less and that they just brought him from the city of the Angels by order of the commissary of the Holy Office who resides there.

---

2. Archivo General de la Nación, Inquisición, Vol. 145, Exp. 12, ff. 240r–241r.

Parents

Hernando, a Black man, and María, a Black woman from Guinea. He said that his mother is alive and his father is deceased. He is not married and does not have children.

Asked if he is a Christian, baptized and confirmed. He said that he is and that he was confirmed in the city of the Angels by a bishop, who he believes was a Franciscan friar.

Asked if he has confessed, taken communion, and heard mass on the occasions ordered by the Holy Mother Church. He says, yes. This Lenten season he confessed with a cleric, whose name he does not remember. He has never taken communion because his master said he was not old enough. He made the sign of the cross and blessed himself and said the four prayers of the church well. He does not know the commandments.

[in the left-hand margin, "life narrative"]

He said he was born and raised in the said city of the Angels in the house of the said Diego Arias Atalaya and that he has always resided in Puebla without leaving it. He is tasked with gathering firewood and grass fodder for his master's house. He has not traveled to foreign kingdoms, nor has he left the Indies. He does not know how to read or write.

Asked if he knows or presumes why he was brought to be imprisoned in the jails of this Holy Office. He says that he knows and presumes that it is because about six months ago he was in a textile mill by order of his master, the said Juan Banegas. He [Carrasco] had been ordered to be whipped, and while he was being whipped, with the pain of the lashes, <u>he said that he denied God, which he only said once, and that he asked for mercy.</u>

[in the left-hand margin, "First admonishment"]

He was told that in the Holy Office of the Inquisition, no person is arrested without sufficient information of having done, been seen, or heard saying to others something that is or seems to be against our Holy Catholic faith and evangelic law. . . . He is admonished and charged with telling the truth and discharging his conscience, because if he does so, he will receive the mercy that the Holy Office uses with good [people]. . . . He said that he has told the truth, that he denied God as he has declared. He has nothing else to say, other than to ask and beg that mercy be used on him because he is very remorseful for having offended God, such a Great Lord, and denied him. He was read what he has said, and he approved it. He does not know how to write. The lord inquisitor signed on his behalf.

And admonished to recall his memories and keep the secret, he was sent back to his jail.

Doctor Lobo Guerrero   Before me, Pedro de Vega

[Spanish transcription]

En la ciudad de Mexico viernes veinte y nueve dias del mes de noviembre de mil y quinientos e noventa y seis años ante el señor ynquisidor Doctor Lobo Guerrero en su audiençia de la mañana mando traer a ella a un negro que traxeron preso de la çiudad de los angeles y lo esta en una de carceles secretas deste sancto officio y estando presente e aviendo jurado en forma de derecho prometio de deçir verdad asi en esta audiencia como en todas las demas que con el se tuviesen.

Fue preguntado como se llama y donde es natural y hace quanto a que vino preso a este santo officio

Dixo llamarse Juan Carrasco esclavo de Juan Banegas vezino de la ciudad de los Angeles, criollo, que naçio en casa de Diego Arias Atalaya, vezino de la dicha ciudad, e dixo ser de hedad de veinte años poco mas o menos y que le acaban de traer preso de la dicha ciudad de los angeles por mandado del comisario del santo officio que alli reside

Padres

Hernando negro e Maria negra de Guinea, e que su madre es biva y el padre difunto y que no es casado ni tiene hijos

Preguntado si es xpistiano bautiçado e confirmado. Dixo que si que se confirmo en la dicha çiudad de los angeles un obispo que le pareçe hera fraile de San Francisco.

Preguntado si a confesado, comulgado, e oydo misa los tiempos que manda la santa madre yglesia. Dixo que si e que esta quaresma que paso confeso con un clerigo cuyo nombre no sabe e que nunca a comulgado porque deçia su amo que no tenia edad. Signose e santiguose e dixo las quatro oraçiones de la yglesia bien dichas e que no sabia los mandamientos.

[al margen izquierdo, "Discurso de vida"]

Dixo aver naçido y criadose en la dicha çiudad de los angeles en casa del dicho Diego Arias Atalaya y que siempre se a ocupado en la puebla sin salir della, ocupado en traer leña y çacate [zacate] en casa de su amo e que no a pasado a rreinos estraños ni salido de las Yndias ni sabe leer ni scrivir.

Preguntado si sabe o presume la causa por que a sido traido preso a las carçeles deste sancto officio

Dixo que si sabe e presume y es porque abra como seis meses que teniendo el dicho su amo Juan Vanegas a este en un obraxe e abiendole mandado açotar y estandole açotando con el dolor de los açotes <u>dixo que rrenegava de Dios lo qual dixo una vez sola de que pedia misericordia.</u>

[al margen, "Moniçion primera"]

Fue le dicho que en el santo officio de la ynquisiçion no se prende a persona ninguna sin bastante ynformaçion de aver hecho dicho, visto haçer o deçir a otros alguna cosa que sea, o parezca ser contra nuestra santa ffee catholica y lei evangelica . . . se le amonesta y encarga diga la verdad y descargue su conçiençia porque Haziendolo asi se usara con el la misericordia que El sancto officio usa con los buenos . . . Dixo que el a dicho la verdad que rrenego de Dios como tiene declarado y no tiene que deçir mas de pedir y suplicar se use con el de misericordia porque el esta mui arrepentido de aver ofendido a dios tan gran señor y rrenegado del y siendole leido lo que tiene dicho lo aprobo e por no saber scrivir firmo por el El señor ynquisidor.

Y amonestado que recorra su memoria y guarde secreto fue mandado bolver a su carçel.

El Doctor Lobo Guerrero   Ante mi Pedro de Vega

Document 66: 1606—Pedro takes communion[3]

In the city [Puebla] of the Angels, on January 16, 1606, before Canon Alonso Fernández de Santiago, commissary of the Holy Office of the Inquisition, in my presence, Pedro de Irala, notary of the said Holy Office. A Spanish man, who said his name was Alonso de Peralta, native and *vecino* of this city, silk weaver, 31 years of age more or less, presented himself willingly and without being summoned. He took the oath in proper form, under which he promised to tell the truth in anything he knew and would be asked, I mean, in what he comes to declare and announce.

He said that the day of Our Lady of Conception, which was December 8 past [1605], a Black man who is said to be Pedro, who is *bozal* and was bought and recently arrived from the land of Angola a year ago, went to mass at the monastery of San Agustín. As some people were taking communion, the said Black man arrived and received the holy sacrament. That afternoon, the wife of Cifuentes, the muleteer, whose name he does not know, went to the house of this deponent's mother, Ana de Peralta. . . . And the said wife of the muleteer Cifuentes told this deponent's mother

---

3. Archivo General de la Nación, Inquisición, Vol. 471, Exp. 66, ff. 249r–250r.

that she had seen their Black Pedro take communion that morning. That night, his mother called the said Black Pedro and asked if he had taken communion that day in San Agustín. He responded that he had. Then the said mother asked him, "Well, did you confess before?" He responded that he had not. And his mother replied, "Well how did you arrive at communion if you had not confessed before?" The said Black Pedro replied that he had already confessed on the [feast] day of San Juan and that he arrived to take communion as others did. Then this deponent's mother called him [Peralta] and told him, "Look at what this Black Pedro says, that he took communion today in San Agustín." This deponent then asked the said Black man if it was true that he had taken communion in San Agustín without confessing, and he said that it was. [Pedro] then referred to the same words that he had told [Peralta's] mother. It seemed to [Peralta] that he was obligated to denounce this case to discharge his conscience. Everything that he has said is the truth, according to the oath he has made. [His statement] was read to him as written, which he approved and ratified. He signed it and was charged with keeping the secret, which he promised to do.

Asked how long ago they baptized the said Black Pedro.

He said that he was baptized two or three months after he was purchased, because [Alonso de Peralta's mother] was very careful in teaching the doctrine to the said Black man. He learned it quickly and prays well, although he has proven to be very ignorant in his actions. This deponent's brother, Alonso Rodríguez, says that the said Pedro knows [the Catholic doctrine] well, because the former was present when this deponent asked the said Pedro if he had taken communion. And everything that he has said is the truth.

Canon Santiago	Alonso de Peralta	passed in my presence,
		Pedro de Irala

[Spanish transcription]

En la çiudad de los Angeles A diez y seis de henero de mill y Seisçientos y Seis Años Ante El Canonigo Alonso Fernandez de Sanctiago, Comisario del santo oficio de la ynquisicion en presencia de mi Pedro de Yrala notario del dicho santo officio Pareçio sin ser llamado y de su Propia Voluntad vn hombre español que dixo llamarse Alonso de Peralta natural y vezino desta çiudad tejedor de sedas que dixo ser de hedad de treynta E un años poco mas o menos del qual fue Rezibido Juramento en forma de derecho so cargo del qual prometio de dezir berdad en lo que supiere y le fuere Preguntado digo en lo que biene a declarar y dar notiçia

Y dixo que El dia de la fiesta de nuestra Señora de la conçebçion que fue A ocho de diziembre Pasado Un negro que se dize Pedro ques boçal que Abra un Año Le conpraron Rezien benido de tierra de Angola que fue Al monasterio de

Sant Augustin A missa y estando comulgando alguna gente se llego El dicho negro y Rezibio el sanctissimo Sacramento y aquella tarde la muger de sifuentes harriero que dize no save Como se llama estubo en casa de la madre deste que declara que se dize Ana de Peralta . . . y dixo la dicha muger de çifuentes Arriero A la dicha madre deste que havia bisto Aquella mañana a su negro Pedro A comulgar y Aquella noche su madre deste llamo Al dicho negro Pedro y le Pregunto si havia Aquel dia comulgado en Santo Augustin y le rrespondio que si y la dicha madre deste le dixo pues confesaste primero y le rrespondio que no y le rreplico la dicha su madre Pues Como te llegastes [sic] A comulgar no te aviendo Confesado Primero y rrespondio El dicho negro Pedro que ya El havia confesado el dia de Sant Juan y que se llego A comulgar como hazian otros y entonçes La dicha madre deste llamo a este y le dixo mira lo que dize este negro Pedro que comulgo oy en Sant Augustin y este que declara Pregunto Al dicho negro Si hera berdad que havia Comulgado en Sant augustin sin confesarse y Le rrespondio que si torno A rreferir las mismas palabras que havia dicho A su madre y Pareçiendole que tiene obligacion de denunçiar deste Casso a benido a hazerlo Por descargo de su Conçiençia y todo Lo que a dicho es la berdad Para El juramento que tiene fecho y siendole leydo como es escrito en ello se afirmo e rratifico e lo firmo su nombre y se le encargo El secreto y prometiolo

Preguntado que tiempo Abra que bautizaron Al dicho negro Pedro

dixo que como dos o tres meses despues que se compro le bautizaron Porque su madre deste tubo muy Particular Cuydado en Enseñar la doctrina Al dicho negro y la deprendio En breve y Reza bien aunque muestra ser muy boçal en su proceder y que su hermano deste que dize Alonso Rodriguez deposar bien por que se Allo presente quando este que declara Pregunto al dicho negro Pedro si havia comulgado y todo lo que a dicho es la verdad

El canonigo santiago   Alonso de peralta   Paso Ante mi Pedro de yrala

Document 67: 1606—Lucía takes communion[4]

In the city [Puebla] of the Angels, March 29, 1606, before Canon Alonso Fernández de Santiago, commissary of the Holy Office of the Inquisition, in my presence, Pedro de Irala, notary of the said Holy Office. A man who said his name was Antonio Díaz, cobbler, native of Ciudad Rodrigo [in Spain] and *vecino* of this city, thirty-two years old more or less, presented himself willingly and without being summoned. He took

---

4. Archivo General de la Nación, Inquisición, Vol. 471, Exp. 40, f. 140r.

the oath in proper form, under which he promised to tell the truth in what he comes to declare in order to discharge his conscience.

He said that on the first day of Easter, which was last Sunday, at around eight o'clock in the morning, this deponent sent a Black woman slave of his, named Lucía, who is more *bozal* than ladina because he bought her about six months ago, to listen to mass at the main church. The said Black Lucía entered the sanctuary of the said church and as she saw that many people were taking communion, she received the most holy sacrament, bringing with her a certificate of communion and giving it to her "master" [sic]. He asked her how she had taken communion if she had eaten. She responded that she did not remember that she had eaten, and had taken communion in this way. This deponent knows that the said Black Lucía had eaten before going to mass, because he saw her eat. Knowing that he was obligated to give notice to the Holy Office of the Inquisition about the case, he has come to discharge his conscience. What he has said is the truth, according to the oath he took. He affirmed and ratified [his statement] and signed his name. He was charged with keeping the secret and he promised to do so.

| Canon Santiago | Alonso de Peralta | passed in my presence, Pedro de Irala |

[in the left-hand margin, "Antonio Díaz, cobbler, against Lucía, Black woman who took communion after eating"]

[Spanish transcription]

En la çiudad de los Angeles A Veynte Y nuebe de marzo de mill y seisçientos y seis Años ante El Canonigo Alonso Fernandez de Sanctiago, Comisario del santo oficio de la ynquisicion en presencia de mi Pedro de yrala notario del dicho santo officio parecio sin ser llamado y de su propia Voluntad Vn honbre que dixo llamarse Antonio Diaz çapatero natural de Çiudad Rodrigo [en España] Vezino desta çiudad que dixo ser de hedad de treynta y dos años Poco mas o menos del qual fue Reçibido Juramento en forma de derecho So cargo del qual Prometio de dezir berdad En lo que biene A declarar Por descargo de Su conçiencia.

Y dixo que El Primer dia de Pasqua de rresurrecion que fue El domingo Pasado Este que declara Envio como a las ocho de la mañana a Vna negra sclava suya que se dize Luzia que es mas bozal que Ladina por que abra seis meses que la conpro a oyr missa a la Yglesia mayor y la dicha negra Luzia se Entro en el sagrario de la dicha yglesia oyr missa y Como bio que Comulgaba mucha gente se llego y Reçibio El Sanctissimo Sacramento y traiendo çedula de la Comunion y dandosela a su "amo" [sic] Le dixo que Como havia Comulgado aviendo almorzado y le rrespondio que no se acordo que havia almorzado y asi havia Rezibido El Santissimo Sacramento y este que declara save que la dicha negra Luzia havia almorzado Antes que fuese a missa Porque la bido almorzar y Saviendo que tiene obligacion de dar notiçia al Santo officio de la ynquisicion del casso Lo a benido a hazer Por descargo de su conçiencia y lo que a dicho es la verdad para El juramento que hisso y En ello se afirmo e rratifico e lo firmo de su nombre y se le encargo El Secreto y prometiolo

El canonigo Santiago   Antonio Diaz   Paso ante mi Pedro de yrala

[al margen izquierdo, "Antonio Diaz çapatero contra Luçia negra comulgo aviendo almorzado"]

Document 68: 1609—Charges of cohabitation against Esperanza and Lorenzo Loriga[5]

In the city [Puebla] of the Angels, on June 9, 1609, before Alonso de Rivera Barrientos, court justice and justice of the holy brotherhood by His Majesty in this city. He has received news that Lorenzo Loriga, a free mulatto man, the son of Juana de Escobar, a Black woman who owns a warehouse, and Esperanza, a free Black woman, have been publicly cohabiting, offending God, Our Lord, with no regard for justice. In order to investigate the truth and proceed to a punishment against them, I received the following information. . . .

And then, immediately, on the said day, month, and year, the said court justice summoned Juana de Escobar, a free Black woman, who took an oath by God Our Lord and with the sign of the cross. Under this charge she promised to say the truth and was asked about the initial decree. She said that this witness knows Lorenzo Loriga, the free mulatto man, because she is this witness's mother and she knows Esperanza, the free Black woman. She knows that for seven months they have been cohabiting with each other in offense to God Our Lord, and they act and communicate with each other [in this manner], because both and each of them have confessed as much to this witness. Her son goes about restlessly and disorderly. This witness has reproached him for this, but [her son] replies that the said Black woman Esperanza has blinded him and bewitched him and that [he] will kill her. In effect, the said cohabitation is public and notorious. This is the truth under oath. She declared herself to be more than fifty years old and that although she is the said Lorenzo Loriga's

---

5. Archivo Histórico Judicial de Puebla, Exp. 741, ff. 1r–1v.

mother, she has told the truth and ratified [her testimony]. She did not sign because she does not know how to.

> Before me, Juan Andres de Torres, His Majesty's scribe

[Spanish transcription]

En la çiudad de los angeles en nueve dias del mes de Junio de mill y seiscientos y nueve años Alonso de Rivera Barrientos alcalde ordinario y de la santa hermandad Por su magestad en esta ciudad dixo que aora se le a dado notiçia que Lorenço Loriga mulato libre hijo de Juana de Escobar negra que tiene bodegon y Esperança negra libre estan amansevados Publicamente mucho tiempo en ofenssa de Dios Nuestro señor y sin temor de la Justicia y Para averiguar la verdad y proceder al castigo contra ellos rrecivo la ymformacion siguiente . . .

E luego yncontinente en este dicho dia mes y año dicho el dicho alcalde hizo Parecer ante si a Juana Descovar negra libre de la qual rrecivio Juramento y lo hizo Por dios Nuestro señor y por la señal de la cruz y so cargo del Prometio de dezir verdad y Preguntada por la caveza de proceso = dixo que esta testigo conoçe a Lorenço Loriga mulato libre por ques hijo desta testigo y Conoçe a Esperanza Negra libre y save que de siete messes a esta parte estan el uno con el otro amansevados en ofenssa de dios Nuestro señor y se tratan y comunican porque vetra [verá?] de que asi se lo an confesado a esta testigo ambos y cada uno de por si, el dicho su hijo anda ynquieto y alvorotado y rreprehendiendoselo esta testigo le da por rrespuesta que la dicha Esperança negra le a degado siego y que le tiene enhechizado y la a de matar y en efeto es publico e notorio el dicho amacevamiento y esta es la verdad so cargo del juramento que hizo declaro ser de hedad de mas de cinquenta años y aunque es madre del dicho Lorenço Loriga a dicho verdad y rratifico se en ello y No firmo Por no saver.

> Ante my Joan Andres de Torres scrivano de su magestad

Document 69: 1625—Charges of blasphemy against Antonia[6]

In the city [Puebla] of the Angels on April 5, 1625, before the Lord Doctor Pedro García de Herencia, canon of the sacred scriptures for the Tlaxcala cathedral and commissary of the Holy Office of the Inquisition in this said city and its bishopric. A Black woman presented herself without being summoned. She said that her name was Antonia and she serves in the San Jerónimo nuns' convent of this said city. She is a slave of Mother Leonor de Santa Ana, professed nun of the said convent. She said

---

6. Archivo General de la Nación, Inquisición, Vol. 303, Exp. 1, f. 20r.

that she was twelve years old. Upon taking the oath in proper form, she promised to tell the truth under the oath. She said, denouncing herself, that about six months ago when her said mistress was beating her, she renounced God twice, so that her mistress would not beat her anymore. A *mestiza* named María was present, along with an Indian woman also named María. As soon as she [Antonia] said this [her blasphemy], she repented and has been suffering from pain and sorrow, and thus, she comes to accuse herself of this crime. She will be subjected to any penitence she is given. This is what happened and nothing else. This is the truth by the oath she has sworn. [Her statement] was read to her and she said it was well-written and entered. She was charged with keeping the secret in proper form, which she promised to do. And she did not sign because she does not know how to. The said lord commissary signed on her behalf.

Doctor Herencia   Before me, *bachiller* Pedro Fernández de Solis, notary of the Holy Office

[in the left-hand margin, "Denial: Antonia, Black woman, accused herself of having denied God"]

[Spanish transcription]

En la çiudad de los angeles en çinco dias del mes de abril año de mill y Seisçientos y veinte y çinco ante el señor Doctor Pedro Garçia de Herençia canonigo de Sagradas scripturas de la cathedral de Tlaxcala, y comissario del Sancto officio de la inquisiçion en esta dicha çiudad, y su obispado paresçio sin ser llamada vna negra que dixo llamarse Antonia y servir en el convento de monjas de San Hieronimo desta dicha çiudad, y ser esclava de la madre Leonor de Sancta Anna monja profesa del dicho convento de edad que dijo ser de dose años la cual aviendo Jurado en forma prometio desir verdad so cargo del Juramento fecho y dize, y denunçia contra si que abra seis meses que estandola asotando la dicha su ama dijo dos beses que Renegava de Dios porque no la asotara mas, y que estavan presentes a esto una mestisa llamada maria, y otra india asimesmo llamada maria y = que luego que lo dijo se arrepintio, y [h]a estado con dolor y arepentimiento, y asi se biene acusar deste delicto, y esta sujeta a la penitensia que se le diere, y esto paso y no otra cosa y es la verdad por el Juramento que tiene fecho y siendole leydo dixo estava bien escrito, y asentado encargosele el secreto en forma prometiolo, y no firmo por dezir no saber firmolo por ella el dicho señor comisario

Doctor Herencia   Paso ante mi, El Licenciado Pedro Fernandez de Solis notario del santo officio

[al margen izquierdo, "Reniego, Antonia negra delato contra Si que havia renegado"]

Document 70: 1631—Will of Marta Rodríguez, a free Black woman[7]

In the name of Almighty God, amen = May all who see this letter know that I, Marta Rodríguez, free Black woman, neighbor, and native of this city, am currently sick in bed and in my full judgment and capacity. . . . I grant by this letter that my will be made and ordered in the following manner.

First, I trust my soul to God Our Lord who raised and redeemed it by his precious blood, death, and passion. And when God sees fit to take me [from this life], I want to be buried in the hospital of Our Lady in this city, in the tomb where my son Miguel Geronimo is buried. The priest of the Holy Church Cathedral of Tlaxcala and twelve clerics will accompany my burial if it takes place at a decent time. If not, the next day a mass will be sung with my body present. . . .

I order that fifty masses be prayed for my soul and another fifty for the souls of my deceased [relatives] and for [the souls of] purgatory.

I declare that I am a member of this city's Holy Charity and Our Lady of the Rosary brotherhoods. Their members will be notified of my death.

I order that Juan de la Cruz, free Black man and neighbor of this city, be given fifty gold pesos . . .

I order that Ana Santos, free mulatto woman and my daughter-in-law, be given three hundred pesos . . .

I order that Ana de Santiago, free mulatto woman, widow, and my niece, be given fifty pesos for the love I have for said Ana de Santiago.

I send Nicolás, the blind boy whom I am raising and who stays by my door, twenty-four pesos for his upbringing.

I send one peso to the customary and obligatory [charities], which I separate from my estate.

I declare the following as my estate. . . . Some houses and an inn, in which I live, which consist of two buildings, one of which is new. They are located in this city's Analco neighborhood and are free of any lien or mortgage.

---

7. Archivo Histórico Judicial de Puebla, Exp. 1622, ff. 1r–5v.

Two Black women, the first named Juliana, forty-five years old, and the other Magdalena, twenty years old, more or less, and a little mulatto boy named Diego, four years old, more or less, and a little Black girl named Ana, who is fourteen months old and whom I send to Juana Bautista.

I order that said mulatto named Diego be given to this city's convent of Our Lady of Mercy so that he will serve said convent all the days of his life . . .

I send the said Black woman, Magdalena, my slave, to the Licenciado Juan Díaz, so that she might be his, because this is my will. And in order to fulfill and pay for this testament, my orders and bequests, from this day forth I name the Licenciado Juan Díaz de Estalaya as my executor. . . . And since I have no legal ascending or descending heir, I leave my soul as my heir. . . .

This is done in the city [Puebla] of the Angels, on September 12, 1631. And I, the scribe, affirm that I know the testator and that she did not sign because she said she did not know how to. A witness signed on her behalf.

I made my sign in testimony of the truth, Alonso Corona, public scribe
eighteen [silver] reales, and no more, I affirm

[Spanish transcription]

En el nombre de dios todo poderoso amen = Sepan quantos esta carta vieren como yo marta Rodrigues negra libre vezina y natural de esta civdad estando enferma En cama y en mi libre Juicio y Entendimiento . . . otorgo por esta carta que hago y ordeno mi testamento en la manera siguiente.

Lo primero encomiendo mi alma a Dios Nuestro Señor que la crio y rredimio por su preçiosa sangre muerte y pasion y quando Dios fuere servido de llevarme quiero ser enterrada en el hospital de Nuestra Señora desta ciudad en la sepultura adonde esta enterrado Miguel Geronimo mi hijo y me acompañen el cura de la santa igleçia Cathedral de Tlaxcala y doze clerigos acompañados y el dia de mi entierro siendo hora decente y no siendo El siguiente se diga por mi alma misa cantada de cuerpo pressente . . .

Mando se digan Por mi alma çinquenta misas rrezadas y otras çinquenta por las almas de mis Difuntos y de purgatorio.

Declaro soy cofrade de las cofradias de la Santa Caridad y de Nuestra Señora del Rosario desta ciudad y asi se de avisso de mi falleçimiento a los hermanos de ellas.

Mando se den a Joan de la Cruz negro libre vecino desta ciudad çinquenta pesos de oro comun. . . .

Mando a Ana Santos mulata libre mi nuera trecientos pesos de oro comun de mis bienes.

Mando se den a Ana de Santiago mulata libre viuda mi sobrina çinquenta pesos de oro comun de mis bienes por el amor que tengo a la dicha Ana de Santiago.

Mando a Nicolas niño cegado a mi puerta que estoy criando veinte y quatro pesos para su crianza.

Mando a las mandas forsosas y acostumbradas vn peso con que las aparto de mis bienes.

Declaro por mis bienes . . . Unas casas y meson de mi morada que hazen dos viviendas la una nueva que son en el barrio de Analco desta ciudad y estan libres de censo y de otra hipoteca . . .

Dos negras llamadas la una Julliana de edad de quarenta y çinco años y la otra Magdalena de edad de veinte años poco mas o menos y un mulatillo llamado Diego de edad de quatro años poco mas o menos y vna negrita llamada Ana de edad de catorze meses que mando a Juana Bautista.

Mando se de al combento de Nuesta Señora de la Merced desta çiudad el dicho mulato llamado Diego para que todos los dias de su vida sirba en el dicho Convento . . .

Mando al Licenciado Joan Dias de Estalaya a la dicha Magdalena negra mi esclava para que lo sea suya porque ansi es mi voluntad y para cumplir y pagar este mi testamento y las mandas y legados desde hoy nombro por mi albacea al dicho licenciado Joan Dias de Estalaya . . . Y atento a que no tengo heredero forsoso asçendiente y ni descendiente dexo por mi heredera a mi Alma . . .

Fecho en la ciudad de los Angeles en doze dias del mes de septiembre de mill y seiscientos y treinta y un años y la otorgante a quien yo El escrivano doy fee que conozco no firmo porque dixo no saber a su rruego firmo un testigo . . . ante mi alonso corona scrivano publico

>Hize mi signo en testimonio de Verdad, Alonso Corona, escrivano publico
>dies y ocho rreales y no mas doy fee

Document 71: 1640—Dance Performed by the Black Creole Women of Mexico City[8]

Dance Performed by the Creole Black Women of the Most Noble and Most Loyal City of Mexico for the Reception and Entry of the Most Excellent Marquess of Villena, Duke of Escalona, Viceroy of this New Spain[9]

Composed by Nicolás de Torres[10]

Dedicated to Don Enrique Pacheco y Ávila,[11] Knight of the Order of Saint James, Captain of His Excellency's Guard, and Sergeant Major of this Kingdom [Printed] with License in Mexico [City] at the Press of Francisco Robledo, on San Francisco Street, in the year 1640

Dedication

Natural inclination leads us to undertake simple, home-loving tasks. This is one of those indeed, yet, knowing that my subject is the due festivities for our Prince and Lord [i.e., the viceroy] (may God keep him), it was enough to animate my smallness, beseeching Your Lordship to receive my affectionate love, which is enclosed in this little diversion. And I beg Your Lordship to look at it in your convalescence, because if it pleases thee, I shall be justified. May Our Lord keep Your Lordship in ever greater grace as Your Lordship deserves and your smallest servant desires.

Nicolás de Torres

Prologue

Dear reader, I pray to God that you are a friend, especially today when I expose my body to you with my muddled work, giving you occasion to carry out your hidden vengeance with your gossip. I have provoked you, I have given you occasion; take advantage of the opportunity. I only ask you to pay attention to my subject, for guided by loving praise, I have submitted myself to the whip of your criticism. Yet I find solace in the fact that, if you criticize me, it will be at your expense; and your

---

8. Biblioteca General Histórica, Universidad de Salamanca, "Festín hecho por las morenas criollas de la muy noble y muy leal ciudad de México," no folio. Transcription and translation courtesy of Professor Miguel Valerio.
9. Diego Roque López Pacheco Cabrera y Bobadilla (1599–1653), 7th duke of Escalona, 7th marquess of Villena and 7th count of Xiquena, etc., 17th viceroy of New Spain, first duke and grandee of Spain named an American viceroy.
10. Secular cleric and theology professor at the University of Mexico. Nothing more is known of him.
11. A relative of the viceroy.

money will pay me for knowing you. This dance was undertaken under my care. It is a humble act, yet exalted for being devoted to such a heroic prince [i.e., the viceroy]. May this act serve me as protection and these dancers as a sign of their appreciation. Since I committed myself to the risk, you will say that I erred of my own volition. Like it if you like; if not, take your vengeance, for you are alone, and this saves me from your complaints and keeps you from satisfaction. May God keep you.

Dance

Amidst sonorous instruments and an agreeable assembly, a select number of Black women gathered in a prepared dance. These women were stars who, born on American soil, demanded the preeminence of their influence.[12] Inspired by the greatest majesty this monarchy has seen,[13] these women prepared themselves for an extraordinary dance. Their leader carried a standard of silver fabric, whose shining colors led the way for her companions, who followed it like butterflies. On one side of this standard were the arms of His Excellency [i.e., the viceroy], which looked, with its gold embroideries and silk colors, like it wanted to represent spring itself, and many thought it florid May. On the other side was Solomon enthroned, equally adorned, loving and grateful for the gifts the Queen of Sheba laid at his feet, with this motto: *Omnia sub pedibus tuis* [Everything under your feet]. The Spanish motto was:

Prudent Sheba,
Who once surrendered her scepter to Solomon,[14]
Today, with her whole nation,
Surrenders the same to the marquess of Villena,
For being the most exalted of the house of Girón.[15]

The others, who followed the lead dancer's rays like a shining black sun, carried different hieroglyphs, which, kneeling with due reverence, they joyfully presented to His Excellency [i.e., the viceroy].

The first carried a placard with a portrait of angelic Teresa,[16] playing a bugle, the king and prophet of the instruments, who, like a goldfinch of the heavens, related

---

12. It was believed in early modern astrology, as it is today, that each person's destiny is influenced by the star of their birth. It is rarely applied, as in this case, to a group.
13. As a duke and grandee of Spain, Diego López Pacheco was the highest-ranking noble appointed an American viceroy up to that point.
14. This story is told in 1 Kings 10 and 2 Chronicles 9.
15. Diego López Pacheco belonged to this noble dynasty, which wielded great power in medieval Castile.
16. Marginal note: "It corresponds to His Excellency through blood and patronage." Diego López Pacheco was a distant relative of St. Teresa of Avila, who was also the patroness of the house of Villena.

this motto: *Misericordia Domini aeternum cantabo* [I will sing of the Lord's mercy forever].[17] And in Spanish:

[SONNET]

The celestial swan of Palestine sings
on the sweet lyre, in sonorous meter,
the greatness of him who, in himself glorious,
leads armies of archangels.

It does not cease, no, because its divine
voice is accompanied with the harmony of
that Carmel, fruitful in virtues,
that reaches, touches heaven.

Sing, Teresa, for to her ardent flight
eternal crown is promised;
raise the pitch, for heaven is obliged

To connect her to Villena's honor,
his divine zeal enjoying the laurel
of his patron and of Escalona's glory.

This first dancer was followed by a second who, no less gallantly, showed on a hieroglyph the flames of her love among the hazy aroma of a censer set on a silver-clothed table. It had this line: *Usque ad aras* [Friends till death do us part]. The Spanish:

Excellent lord, proud Pacheco,
Catholic patron,
of whom fame,
If she reached a brush,
Would paint a thousand pictures:
in the most distant lands
envy speaks of you, noble Pacheco,
your glorious renown
celebrates your deeds,
and in foreign regions,
my dark cloud adores
your light as a bright sun.
Receive from Africa

---

17. Psalm 89:1.

this perfume that in your light rises,
for although whiteness is denied me,
it [i.e., the incense] may be like my love,
yet not cloud it.

In third place, equally admirable, was another placard, which showed a jet-black fig hand,[18] whose golden bracelet had this line: *Ne timeat qui mecum servit* [Those who are with me need not fear]. And in Spanish:

Beautiful son of the Sun, proud Prince,
youth that Narcissus envies;
whose body houses a strange soul;
of free will, spirited master;
curly long hair, lordly countenance;
whose hair was guilded by Nature the artist;
smiling lips, proud gallantry:
if my jet-blackness forces me
to be an amulet to your highness,
take as spoils
this fig hand against the evil eye.

The foregoing dancer would have taken the prize if not for the angelic miracle of a Seraph, which, holding the arms of Portugal,[19] had this motto: *Signum coeli dedit ei* [Heaven gave him a sign[20]]. The Spanish motto:

The grateful disciple acknowledges
the learned hand of his master,
when he finds a sovereign paranymph
Who admires his imitation.

---

18. The fig hand (usually made of jet lignite) is an ancient African fertility object that has been popular in the Iberian world since antiquity, when it was introduced by the Romans. Still popular in Latin America, Iberians used it as an amulet against the evil eye.
19. Marginal note: "It corresponds to His Excellency for the house of the lords [dukes] of Vergáça" [sic]; should be Bragança; likely typesetter error. López Pacheco was the first cousin once removed of the duke of Braganza. This proved fateful, as the duke of Braganza declared himself king of Portugal, as John IV, in 1640, in what amounted to a declaration of war against Philip IV of Spain, since Portugal had been under Spanish rule since 1580. These events, augmented in Philip's ears by López Pacheco's enemies, especially the archbishop of Puebla and his eventual successor, Juan de Palafox y Mendoza, led Philip to withdraw his trust from López Pacheco and recall him to Spain in 1642, after which he was sent as viceroy to Navarre, where he died in 1653.
20. Possibly also "A heavenly sign was given (unto) him."

not otherwise, oh sovereign Duke,
are you in the arts, so generous and diligent,
that heaven commands, with divine effort,
that you teach a wise man one thing or two.

In fifth place was a brilliant sun that, rising over some roses, allowed an eagle to glimpse its light. This eagle, fortified against a rock, tried to look out through a dark cloud, anxiously orienting itself, with this motto: *Post tenebras spero lucem* [I hope for light after the darkness]. The Spanish motto:

Eagle of the roses,
that attentively looks for the dimmest ray
of the sun's splendor,
perpetual proof of your lasting honor:
my dark ink does not blur, great lord,
your sight of my succinct nation.
Let not my love, lord, be doubted,
may it not live, for being black, in distrust,
when in your florid sun
dawns the affable and wise.

The sixth dancer advancing, conquering art in the natural, was Hercules, that tethered to his columns and his wings of love outstretched, bore this motto: *Non plus ultra* [Go no further]. And in Spanish:

Through splendid seas I followed stars,
with strong oars I toiled in the spume,
I stomped up recondite provinces with my footprints,
I weaved the regions of the wind in feather,
to plant these two beautiful columns.
And in American soil, oh supreme joy!,
I found a Pacheco, from whose great sagacity
one cannot expect a greater fortune.

Challenging the public and richly adorned, in seventh place was an anagram, which showing a starry sky, imitated the moon in spirit, which assuring its continuous changes, if there is any certainty in women's words, had this motto: *Non mutabor* [I will not change]. And in Spanish:

My sanity is in doubt,
Glorious Duke, my lord,
if there could be some
black venture in love,
but firmness assures me
in so much sorrow
that in congratulating thee,
if sun I am to see thee
like a moon I am to adore thee
for thine I saw full.[21]

The eighth dancer, in quick twirls, was more eminent, carried a hieroglyph showing a crown, which keeping itself from both sea and land storms, had two anchors,[22] one on land, the other in the sands of the sea, with this motto: *Firma sunt in mare, et in terra* [I am firm on sea and land]. And in Spanish:

May the southern wind open dark heavens,
may the sea blare, roar with thirst,
for I fear no storm,
with the anchors of a Cabrera.

The ninth hieroglyph, as challenging to the mind as admirable to the eye, revealed to the eye a cup illumined by the loyal mark of a golden and colorful crown,[23] with this motto: *Debita redatur fidelitati* [Due loyalty is owed]. The Spanish motto:

If my greatness deserves
a gift from such majesty,
my loyalty can say
that it could not ask for more.

With general enjoyment this would have gotten the applause, if we forgot the two outstanding captives, who, breaking their prisons—although becoming captives of love—had this motto: *Redimius quot accepimus* [We receive as much as we redeem].[24] The Spanish:

---

21. The Spanish plays with of one of López Pacheco's titles, Villena, rendered as "*Vi llena*" (I saw full).
22. Marginal note: "It corresponds to His Excellency for the House of the lords marquesses of Moya." Symbols of the House of the marquesses of Moya, to which López Pacheco also belonged as a Cabrera.
23. Marginal note: "It corresponds to His Excellency for the House of the lords marquesses of Moya."
24. Marginal note: "It corresponds to His Excellency for his seniority," as a grandee of Spain. The motto is an allusion to the two forms of servitude, forced and voluntary.

Youthful don Diego, proud imitation
of the lover who adored the beautiful deity,
polished ruby, snowy rose,
lord served by a favorable star.
The slave leaves his sad prison
when your power imparts freedom
and whosoever sees your gallantry
is captivated by the sight of your bravery.

The reputation of the last woman would be in danger if she did not carry an ingenious placard with a bright sun, which, igniting the desires of a phoenix,[25] shows its reflections, in death's arms, pride itself in being eternal, trusting her rebirth to this motto: *Post nubila Phoebus* [Behind the clouds, the sun]. And in Spanish:

Burning light of the Pachecos,
first ceremony of the dawn,
fourth planet[26] adored by your sphere
where, like a Phoenix, it burns in love,
turned red by the fire,
where my love ordains
that I deliver myself to Villena's embers,
being black coal
either an affront on my lineage or a blot;
because, burning in your flame,
I will live in fame as coal with a soul.

With this, ingenious resonances, admiration to the eyes, applauses to the ears put an end to the event. Such appropriate matter, short festivities for such a great prince, great audacity in so humble a people, modest pen for such high flight: if I resemble Icarus, it is due to my affection. The prize is justified, for I feared not the danger. The end.

---

25. Marginal note: "It corresponds to his excellency for the House of the lords marquesses of Villena." The phoenix was the symbol of the House of Villena.

26. The sun in the geocentric model.

[Spanish original]

FESTIN[27]
HECHO POR LAS MORENAS CRIOLLAS DE LA MUY NOBLE, Y MUY LEAL CIUDAD DE MEXICO.

AL RECIBIMIENTO, Y ENTRADA DEL EXCELLENTISSIMO SEÑOR MARQUES DE VILLENA, DUQUE DE ESCALONA, VIRREY ES ESTA NUEVA ESPAÑA[28]
COMPUESTO POR NICOLAS DE TORRES[29]
Y
DEDICADO A DON ENRIQUE PACHECO Y AVILA[30], CAVALLERO DE LA ORDEN DE SANTIAGO, CAPITAN DE LA GUARDIA DE SU EXCELLENCIA, Y SARGENTINO MAYOR DESTE REYNO

Con licencia en Mexico, en la Imprenta de Francisco Robledo, en la calle de S. Francisco, año 1640.

DEDICACION

Natural inclinacion emprende caseras llanezas; esta lo es muy grande: mas conociendo, que el assumpto es debidos festijos à nuestro Principe, y Señor (que Dios guarde,) fueron bastantes à dar alientos â mi pequeñez, suplicando à v.m. reciba mi efectuoso amor, que va cifrado en este pequeño juguete, y en los ratos de su convalescencia le examine, que siendo á gusto de v.m. tendrè yo disculpa. Guarde nuestro Señor â v.m. en los augementos que merece, y su menor criado dessea. *Nicolas de Torres.*

PROLOGO

Lector amigo, ruego à Dios que lo seas: y mas oy, quando con el desaliño mis obras te descubro el cuerpo, para que executes con las murmuración tus encubiertas venganças. Yo te busco, yo de doy ocasion; aprovechate pues la tienes: mas solo te advierto, atiendas à mi assumpto: pues guiado de un amoroso aplauso, me entreguè

---

27. Del francés *festin*, y este a su vez del italiano *festino*: diminutivo de fiesta. *Autoridades* lo dará como: "Festejo particular que se hace en alguna casa, concurriendo mucha gente a divertirse con báiles, música, y otros entretenimientos."
28. Diego Roque López Pacheco Cabrera y Bobadilla (1599-1653), VII Duque de Escalona, VII Marqués de Villena, VII Conde de Xiquena, etc., XVII virrey de Nueva España, fue el primer duque y grande de España nombrado virrey americano.
29. Clérigo secular y profesor de teología en la Universidad de México. No se sabe nada más de él.
30. Pariente del virrey.

al suplicio de tu correccion. Mas consuelome con que si murmurares, serà á costa de tu dinero; y yo con èl grangearé[31] el conocerte.

Este festin se librò à mi cuidado; accion humilde, si levantada por ser para tan heroyco Principe[32]: sirvame à mi de amparo, si á ellas[33] de agradecimiento. Yo me obliguê al riesgo: y assi dirás que fue errar por mi gusto. Tenle si quieres, y si no vengate, que á solas estás, con que me escusas á mi de una quexa, y â ti de una satisfacion. Dios te guarde.

De instrumentos sonoros, y dulces turba en prevenida dança, se dispuso un corto numero de Negras, Estrellas, que produzidas en este Indiano suelo[34], solicitavan la predominancion de su influencia[35]: y llevadas de la mayor grandeza[36] que ha visto esta Monarquia, se prevenieron para un celebre festin. La Capitana que en acorde concierto llevava un estandarte de lama de plata[37], cuyos cambiantes eran Norte, á quien mariposas buseavan por los reflexos lo restante de su compañía. Ocupava la haz, las armas de su Excellencia[38], que con realces de oro, y matices de sedas, parece que se quería levantar con titulo de Primavera: y, no fue mucho, quando hubo quien le acreditara por florido Mayo. Hazia ygualda á sus espaldas en Regio Trono el Rey Salomon, no con menos ornato, tan amante como agradecido á los dones, que postrada á sus plantas le offrecia la Reyna Sabbà, con este mote: *Omnia sub pedibus tuis.*[39] La letra Castellana fue la siguiente.

Sabbá su cetro anágena
Por prudente á Salomon,
Y oy con toda su nacion,
Se le rinde al de Villena,
Por ser de mejor Girón.[40]

Las que como á sol de azabache seguian sus rayos de abalorio, llevavan distintos geroglificos, que hincadas de rodillas, con la devida reverencia los offrecian á su Excellencia, con ayroso desenfado.

---

31. Lo mismo que ganaré.
32. En el sentido más amplio de persona principal.
33. Las morenas criollas.
34. América.
35. En lenguaje astrológico, la influencia de las estrellas bajo las cuales nacieron las morenas criollas.
36. López Pacheco fue el primer duque y grande de España nombrado virrey americano.
37. Tela de plata.
38. López Pacheco.
39. "Todo bajo tus pies."
40. La casa de Girón, a la que pertenecía López Pacheco, era una antigua casa de Castilla, muy poderosa en el medioevo.

Llevava la primera en una tarja⁴¹ pintada al Cerubin Teresa⁴², que en acordes consonancias animava [f2v] el instrumento del clarin, Rey, y Propheta musico, y qual silguero⁴³ de los cielos referia este mote: *Misericordias Dimini aeternum cantabo.*⁴⁴ La castellana.

SONETO

Canta el Cisne Emperial de Palestina,
    En dulce lyra, en metro sonoro
    Las grandezas de aquel, que en si glorioso,
    Exercitos de Archangeles destina.
No cessa, no, porque à su voz divina,
    El contrapunto lleva numeroso
    Aquel Carmelo, que em virtud frondoso,
    Con el cielo se abraça, y se avezina.
Cante Teresa, que à su ardiente buelo
    Inmortal se previene la corona;
    Levante el punto, que obligado el cielo
A el honor de Villena la eslabona,
    Gozando el lauro su divino zelo,
    De Patron suyo, y gloria de Escalona.

Seguia á esta primera la segunda, que no menos bizarra⁴⁵ ostentava en un geroflifico, lo abrasado de su amor, y entre las aromas de un humoso pebete⁴⁶, à quien de basa [sic]⁴⁷ servia una compuesta mesa de plata: llevava este mote: *Usque ad aras.*⁴⁸ La Castellana.

Excellente Señor, Pacheco ayroso;
Catholico Mecenas,
De quien la fama, llenas
Tablas ocupa, si pincel anima:
El mas distante clima

---

41. Placa, plancha.
42. Nota marginal: "Tocale á su Excellencia por sangre y patronazgo." López Pacheco tenía cierto parentesco con Santa de Jesús, que también era santa patrona de la casa de Villena.
43. Jilguero en español moderno.
44. "Cantaré eternamente el amor del Señor" (Salmo 89,1).
45. Gallarda, lozana.
46. Composición aromática.
47. Base. Tiene que ser una mesa con la tela de lama.
48. "Hasta la muerte."

Te discanta[49], la invidia generoso,
El renombre glorioso
Celebra tus azañas,
Y en regiones estrañas,
Adora tu arrebol

Mi negra nube por luciente sol:
Recibe de Guinea
Este pebete, que en tu luz humea,
Que aunque el blanco color se me limite,
Si le yguala[50] a mi amor, no le compite.

Tuvo el tercer lugar con no menos admiracion otra tarja; la cual enseñava[51] una mano en forma de higa[52] de azabache, á cuya axorca[53] de oro adornava este mote: *Ne timeat qui mecum fuerit.*[54] La Castellana.

Hijo galan del Sol, Principe ayroso
Garçon de quien Narciso està invidioso,
Que el cuerpo alientas de bizarras almas,
De libre accion el ademan brioso,
Crespa gue [sic][55] deja, señoril semblante,
Que artista el natural dorò el cabello,
Coral tisueño [sic][56], ayrosa bizarria,
Si el azabache obliga
A que â tu gentileza sirva de higa;
Recibe por despojo
La de mi mano, contra el mal de ojo.

---

49. Canta.
50. El pebete.
51. Mostraba.
52. La mano en forma de higa (normalmente diminuta y hecha de azabache) originó como un amuleto africano de fertilidad que fue popular en Iberia (fue introducido por los romanos, quizás por su parentesco con un símbolo obsceno de estos) y aún lo es en Latinoamérica, donde se usa ponérselo a los recién nacidos en un brazalete, como protección contra el mal de ojo.
53. Brazalete.
54. "Los que están conmigo no necesitan temer."
55. Que.
56. Risueño.

Pudiera llevarse la gala la referida, â no oponersele el milagro angelico de un Serafin, que haziendo ostenacion de las Quinas de Portugal[57], tenia por timbre este mote: *Signum coeli dedit ei.*[58] La Castellana.

El ser conoce de la docta mano,
El discipulo grato á su maestro,
Hallando un Paranimpho soberano,
Que de su imitacion le atienda diestro.
No de otra suerte, liberal y presto,
Mandando el cielo con divino ahinco,
Que al docto le expliqueys quantas son cinco.

Hazia galante ostentacion el quinto lugar un Sol que haziendo oriente de unas rosas, dexava examinar sus luces de los desvelos de un águila, que haziendo fortaleza una peña, atalyava la vista por los resquicios de una negra nube, donde ansiosa le buscava, con este mote: *Post tenebras spero lucem.*[59] La Castellana.

Aguila de las flores,
Que atenta le examinas rayo à rayo
Al Sol los mas dormidos resplandores,
De tu durable honor continuo ensayo:
No turba gran señor mi negra tinta
Tu vista a clara en mi nacion sucinta,
No quede, no, señor, mi amor dudoso,
No viva por ser negro escrupuloso,
Quando en tu sol florido
Amanece lo afable, y lo entendido.

La que en sexto lugar parece se adelantava, venciendo el arte con lo adquirido en lo natural, fue Hercules, que abraçado con sus columnas, y tendidas las alas de su amor, era pregonero deste more: *Non plus ultra.* La Castellana.

---

57. Armas de Portugal, compuestas de cinco escudos, *quinas*.
58. "El cielo le dio una señal" o "Se le fue dada una señal celeste." Nota marginal: "Tocale à su Excellencia por la casa de los señores Duques de Vergança." Debería ser Bragança. López Pacheco era pariente del Duque de Braganza que se declaró rey de Portugal, como Juan IV, en 1640, en lo que implicaba declararle la guerra a Felipe IV, ya que Portugal estaba bajo su dominio desde 1580. Este parentesco vino a truncar el virreinato de López Pacheco, ya que sus enemigos, particularmente Juan de Palafox y Mendoza, lo usaron para hacer que rey dudase de su lealtad y le retirara su confianza, reclamando a España y despachándolo como virrey de Navarra, donde murió en 1653.
59. "Después de la oscuridad, espero la luz."

Por mares de explendor naveguè estrellas,
Con fuertes remos fatigué la espuma,
Las Provincias ocultas herî á huellas,
Las regiones del viento bordé en pluma,
Por fixar estas dos columnas bellas
Y en el Indiano suelo, ò dicha suma,
Hallé un Pacheco, que á su gran cordura,
Fuera hierro esperar mayor ventura.

Con oposicion publica, y bizarros arreos, ocupó el séptimo lugar un Anagrama, que haziendo gala de un estrellado cielo, parece que por coraçon le animava la Luna, que assegurando sus continuas mudanças, si ay seguridad en palabras mugeriles, llevava este mote: *Non mutabor.*[60] La Castellana.

Dudosa està mi cordura
Duque excelso, y mi señor,
Si puede aver en amor
Alguna negra ventura:
Mas la firmeza assegura
Mi recelo en tanta pena,
Que al daros la enorabuena:
Si Sol he de contemplaros,
Como Luna é de adoraros
Porque la vuestra Vi llena.

La que el octavo lugar en breves giros se tuvo por mas eminente fue un geroglifico, que demostrando una corona, que assegurandose de las inclemencias de mar y tierra, se afiançava de dos ancoras[61], la una fixa en la tierra, quando la otra estriba en las arenas del mar, llevando por mote: *Firma sunt in mare, & in terra.*[62] La Castellana.

Rompa el Austro negra esfera,
Cruxa el mar, brame sedienta,
Que no rezelo tormenta,
Con ancoras de un Cabrera.

---

60. "No cambiaré."
61. Anclas.
62. "Firme en mar y en tierra." Armas de los marqueses de Moya, a cuya casa pertenecía López Pacheco como pariente de los Cabreras. Nota marginal: "Tocale á su Excellencia por la casa de los señores Marqueses de Moya."

Contenia el noveno heroglifico, no menos suspension al antedimiento, qe admiraciones à la vista, haziendo jueces à los ojos, para una admirable copa que esmaltes de su oro, y timbre de su lealtad, la ilustrava una corona, con este mote: *Debita redatur fidelitati.*[63] La Castellana.

POE:Si à mi grandeza le toca
Premio de tal magestad,
Podrà dezir mi lealtad,
Que viene á pedir de boca.

Con general gusto se llevara esta los aplausos de los circinstantes, si se olvidara le celebre de dos cautivos, que despeciando sus prisiones, si bien para nuevos empeños de aficion referían este mote: *Redimius quod acepimus.*[64] La Castellano.

Galan don Diego, imitacion ayrosa,
Del que amante adorò la deidad bella,[65]
Embotado rubi, nebada rosa:
De que sirve señor, afable estrella.
Dexe el cautivo su prision penosa,
Si ya tu Imperio libertades huella;
Y al que llega à notar tu gallardia,
La cautiva el mirar tu bizarria.

Peligrara el cuidado de la que ocupava el ultimo lugar, à no apadrinarla lo curioso de una tarja, cuyo luzido adorno era un Sol, que haziendo brasas los deseos de un Fenix, se dexava numerar sus reflexos, y margenando su espacio en braços de la muerte, blasonava de eterna, fiando el renacer en este mote: *Post nubila Phebus.*[66]

Roxa iluminacion de los Pachecos,
Primero besamanos de la Aurora,
Quarto Planera [sic][67] que tu esfera adora,

---

63. "Debida es la lealtad correspondida." Nota marginal: "Tocale á su Excellencia por la casa de los señores Marqueses de Moya."
64. "Redimimos lo que recibimos." Una alusión a las dos servidumbres, la forzada (la esclavitud) y la voluntaria. Nota marginal: "Conviene a su Excellencia por mayorozgo [sic]" (debe ser mayorazgo), o sea por duque de Escalona, que es grande de España.
65. Venus.
66. "Detrás de las nubes, el Sol." Debería ser *Phoebus*. Nota marginal: "Toca á su Excellencia por la casa de los señores marqueses de Villena." El fénix (que dice Plinio el joven es de África) es el símbolo de la casa de Villena.
67. Cuarto planeta, el Sol en el modelo geocéntrico.

Donde qual Fenix arde enamorado,
Y del fuego encarnado,
Donde mi amor ordena,
Que me entregue à las brasas de Villena
Siendo negro carbon,
Ya de mi estirpe injuria, ó ya borron,
Pues ardiendo en tu llama,
Carbon con alma viviré á la fama.

Con esto dieron discreto fin curiosas consonancias admiracion à los ojos, aplauso â los oydos, tan conforme assumpto; festejo corto para tanto Principe; audacia grande en tan pequeña humildad; corta pluma para tan alto vuelo: si Icaro pareciere, cupla serà de mis afectos; disculpa el premio, pues no temió el peligro. FIN.

Document 72: 1642—The life story of Sebastián Domingo, alias Munguía[68]

In Mexico City, on May 16, 1642, during the morning audience, the lord inquisitors Licenciado Domingo Veles de Assas y Argo and Doctor Don Bartolomé González Soltero, bishop-elect of Guatemala, ordered Sebastián Domingo de Munguía, an imprisoned Black man in the jails, to be brought to them. Once present, they received his oath in due form. He promised to speak the truth in this audience as in all others until the conclusion of his cause . . . and he is willing to receive the punishment he may be given with humility. He begs that they consider that he has not sinned out of malice, and that he has experienced many hardships, imprisonments, and punishments which he has suffered and still suffers under the said Luis Mesquita. To declare all this, he has asked for this said audience.

Asked if he is Christian, baptized, and confirmed. If he attends mass, confesses, and takes communion during the occasions ordered by the Holy Mother Church.

He says that by the mercy of God he is a baptized Christian. He was baptized in the city of Mérida, by a cleric in that city's parish. He was confirmed by the bishop of Mérida, who was a cleric and lame. At the time [of his confirmation] he would have been sixteen years old, more or less. He confesses and takes communion during Lent and he fasts. This past Lent he confessed to a cleric in the Santa Veracruz parish, but he did not take communion, because they did not send him to church during Holy Week.

---

68. Archivo General de la Nación, Inquisición, Vol. 399, Exp. 2, 295r, 296r–297v, 299r.

He made the sign of the cross and blessed himself. He said the Our Father, Hail Mary, Credo, and Salve Regina well, and he did not know more of the Christian doctrine.

Asked for his life story, he said that as a fifteen- or sixteen-year-old youth, he was brought from Congo, in Guinea, where he was born, by a Portuguese man along with other Black *bozales*. He came straight to Campeche and from there he went up to the city of Mérida, where he was sold to Don Juan de Montejo Maldonado, in whose service he remained for about fifteen years. [Montejo Maldonado] sold him to Juan Ortuño de Olano in Campeche and he stayed with him for about a year and a half. [Ortuño de Olano] sold him in Veracruz to a Biscayan grant-holder named Juan de Guicochea, whom he served for two years before he was sent to this city of Mexico. Juan Caballero, *vecino* of Querétaro, bought him. He served him for about four years, and then he was sent to Veracruz with a son of his named Don Sebastián Caballero, who was going to Hispaniola. There [in Veracruz] he was married to the said Black woman, Felipa. They were married and veiled by Doctor Juan Matías Flores, who was the priest and beneficiary of the parish church of Veracruz. Their wedding godparents were Pedro Martín, Congo, who is deceased, and Pascuala, a Black woman, a slave of His Majesty in that city's fortress. He served Diego Tomás de Castañeda, who was the reeve,[69] and because of this, the said Don Sebastián Caballero sold him to Francisco Hernández, magistrate of the jail in the said city. He served Hernández for about two years, before he was sent to this city [Mexico City] to be sold, but no one wanted to buy him because this deponent said he was married. So they took him to the city of Tlaxcala, where Luis de Mesquita, a Portuguese man, was a *vecino* and had his textile mill. The latter bought this confessant with a power of attorney held by Gaspar de Arteaga, *vecino* of Mexico City, who had gone to the city of Tlaxcala. He [Sebastián Domingo de Munguía] has spent fifteen or sixteen years in Tlaxcala and in the Fresneda textile mill [in Atlixco], and lately in Puebla, for over a year and three months, because the said Luis de Mesquita bought a textile mill in the said city.

Asked if he knows, presumes, or suspects the reason for which he was brought imprisoned to the secret jails of this Holy Office, he said that he thinks that it is because he married a second time, to the said Black woman, Isabel, while the said Felipa, his first wife, was still alive. But in no manner was this done with malice. When he married for the second time, he was certain that the said Felipa had died, because they told him so. He feels weak and sick. It is certain that he will not flee or absent himself, because he spent so many days serving the said commissary in his house. If he had wanted to absent himself he would have already done so.

... and then, immediately, the said lord inquisitors having seen the good confession made by Sebastián Domingo, the Black man, and in consideration of what he

---

69. *corregidor*: this was the direct royal representative at the local level. The reeve presided over municipal councils, heard appeals cases, and remained a powerful figure until the late colonial period.

asked, as he is old, ill, so naked, and gravely affected by the jails' humidity, said and indicated that he be placed in the magistrate's room while this investigation continues and comes to its conclusion.

Before me, Eugenio de Saravia

[Spanish transcription]

En la Çiudad de Mexico biernes dies y seis dias del mes de mayo de mill y Seisçientos y quarenta y dos años estando es Su audiencia de la mañana los Señores Inquisidores Licenciado Domingo Veles de Assas y Argo y Doctor Don Bartolome Gonzalez Soltero electo obispo de Guatemala Mandaron traer a ella de las Carseles a Sevastian Domingo de Mungia negro Preso en ellas y siendo pressente fue del Resevido Juramento en forma de derecho so cargo del qual Promettio de dezir berdad asi en esta audiencia Como en las demas que con el se tubieren Hasta la conclusion de su caussa: Y que Guardara Secretto de todo lo que viere y entendiere y Con el pasare hasta la conclusion della. . . . . y esta dispuesto a Resevir con humilldad el castigo que se le diere y suplica se attienda a que no a pecado de malisia y a los muchos travajos prisiones y Castigos que a padesido y Padese en poder del dicho Luis de Mesquita y que Para declararlo a pedido esta dicha audiencia

Pregunttado si es cristiano baptisado y Confirmado y si oye missa confiessa y Comulga en los tiempos que Manda la Santa madre Yglesia

Dixo que Por la misericordia de Dios es cristiano baptizado y le bautizaron en la Çiudad de Merida un clerigo en la Parrochia de aquella Çiudad, y le confirmo el obispo de Merida que era clerigo y cojo y seria enttonses de edad de desiseis años Poco mas o menos, y Confiessa y Comulga las quaresmas y ayuna y esta quaresma pasada se confesso con vn clerigo en la Parrochia de la Santa Veracruz Pero no comulgo Porque no lo embiaron la Semana Santa a la yglesia.

Signose y Santtiguosse y dixo el pater noster, ave maria, credo y salve Regina vien dicho Y no supo mas de la dotrina cristiana.

Preguntado por el discurso de su vida dixo que siendo muchacho de quinze a desiseis años Le truxo de Congo de donde es natural en guinea un porttugues con otros negros vosales y vino derecho a campeche y de alli subio a la Çiudad de merida donde lo bendio a Don Juan de Montejo Maldonado en cuyo servisio estubo como quinze años el qual se bendio en Campeche a Juan Ortuño de Olano con quien estubo como año y medio el qual lo bendio en la Veraruz a un encomendero Vizcayno llamado Juan de Guicochea al qual sirvio como dos años el qual lo embio a esta Çiudad de Mexico y lo compro Juan Caballero vezino de Querettaro al qual sirvio como quattro años y despues lo embio a la Veracruz con vn hijo suyo llamado Don Sebastian Caballero que iba a Española y alli se caso como tiene confesado con la dicha negra Felipa y los casso y velo el Doctor Juan Mathias Flores que era Cura y benefisiado de la yglesia Parrochial de la Veracruz y fueron sus padrinos Pedro Martin Congo que ya es difunto y Pascuala negra esclava de Su Magestadd en la fuerza de aquella çiudad y servia a Diego Thomas de Castañeda, que era corregidor y por esta causa el dicho Don Sevastian Caballero lo bendio a Francisco Hernandes alcaide de la carsel en la dicha Çiudad al qual Sirvio como dos años el qual lo embio a esta Çiudad a bender y nadio lo quiso Comprar por dezir este declarante como era casado y lo llevaron a la Çiudad de tlaxcala a donde era vezino, y tenia su obraje Luis de Mesquita Porttugues el qual Compro a este confesante con poder que tubo para benderlo Gaspar de Arteaga vezino de esta Çiudad, que a la sazon avia ydo a Tlaxcala y en poder del dicho Luis de Amesquita a estado Como quinze o desiseis años en tlaxcala y en el obraxe de la fresneda y ultimamentte en la Puebla mas de un año y tres messes Por haver comprado el dicho Luis de mesquita un obraje en la dicha Çiudad.

Pregunttado si save Presume o sospecha la causa porque a sido traido Preso a las carseles secrettas de este santo officio dixo que le parese sera por Haverse cassado Segunda vez con la dicha negra Ysavel siendo viva la dicha Felipa su Primera muger Pero que en ninguna manera tubo malisia quando se casso Segunda ves porque tubo por siertto que era muertta la dicha Felipa como lo dixeron y se siennte flaco y enfermo y es seguro y no se huira ni ausenttara pues estubo tanttos dias en casa del dicho Comisario sirviendoloe y si quisiera ausenttarse lo Huviera hecho.

. . . e Luego ynconttinenti los dichos señores Inquisidores haviendo visto la buenna confision de Sevastian Domingo negro, y lo pedido Por el y bisto ser viejo enfermo, y estar ttan desnudo y hazerle mucho mal la humedad de las carseles, dixeron que sea Puesto en el quartto del alcaide, mientras se sigue y fenese esta causa y lo señalaron.

Ante mi Eugenio de Saravia

Document 73: 1655—The *chino* confraternity of Our Lady of Guadalupe[70]

May all who see this letter know that we, the brothers of the *chino* confraternity of our Lady of Guadalupe, established in the church of Santa Veracruz in this city [Puebla] of the Angels, are gathered in the residence of Don Alonso de Ayala, [who is a] merchant and administrator for the confraternity of Santa Veracruz, located in the said church. It is worthwhile to know that [we are] Simón de la Cruz, founder, who has been the administrator of the confraternity; Domingo Juárez, who has been the administrator three times, and a founder; Ventura Flores, I was also administrator and founder; Francisco Lorente, founder and former deputy; José Flores, I have been

---

70. Archivo General de Notarías del Estado de Puebla, Notaría 4, Alonso Corona, Box 181, ff. 559r–559v.

deputy; José de la Cruz, I have been the confraternity's rector; Diego Pacheco, Juan Francisco, Andrés de Carabajal, Felipe de Soberantes, and Felipe de Frias, past deputies, all of them free *chinos* and *vecinos* of this city; Luis de Trujillo, slave of Luis de Trujillo [sic], and Juan de Zapata, slave of Alonso Carrillo, also *chinos* and brothers of the said confraternity.

For ourselves, and in the name of the confraternity, and of the other brothers and members for whom we speak, we state that we presented a document to the most illustrious and most excellent lord Don Juan de Palafox y Mendoza, bishop of Osma, when he was bishop of Puebla of the Angels. We asked him to designate a space in the cemetery of the said church of Santa Veracruz for a chapel [in honor] of our confraternity's image of Our Lady of Guadalupe. He referred this matter to the lord Doctor Don Alonso de Salazar Varona, governor of this bishopric, to designate a plot if it was convenient and caused no damage of any sort. The lord Doctor determined that we could be given the said license after awarding a writ that we would pay and satisfy the said confraternity of Santa Veracruz 7 pesos and 4 tomines each year, in perpetuity, as alms for said location. [The Doctor also determined] that all the *chinos*, or other persons of whichever [skin] color, who were buried in the said chapel or church, would pay for its construction, just as the Blacks of the confraternity of Our Lady of Consolation, established in the church, paid. And that from alms gathered at all the festivities celebrated by the *chino* brothers in the said chapel or the said church of the Spaniards, they were to give a third of the alms they gathered to the Santa Veracruz confraternity.

We, the said Simón de la Cruz, Domingo Juárez, Ventura Flores, Francisco Lorente, José Flores, José de la Cruz, Diego Pacheco, Juan Francisco, Andrés de Caravajal, Felipe de Soberano, and Felipe de Frias commit jointly with them . . . that they and we will pay the said Santa Veracruz confraternity, its administrators, or whomever represents it, 10 common gold pesos as alms and pension for each year, in perpetuity, starting today, in this city, wherever we be asked for them, with the expenses of the debt. The alms for the site of the chapel were adjusted to 7 pesos and 4 tomines, with [an additional] 2 pesos and 4 tomines for the site given for the said sacristy. . . . And I, Don Alonso de Ayala, administrator of the said Santa Veracruz confraternity, am present. I accept this writ in the confraternity's name and that of its other brothers and deputies, to make use of it as may be needed. This letter is done in the city of the Angels on June 28, 1655. I, the scribe, attest that I know the grantors. The said Don Alonso de Ayala signed as a grantor and a witness signed for the rest, who said that they did not know how to sign. Witnesses, Tomás de Cárcamo, Nicolas Álvarez, Francisco de Torija, *vecinos* of this city.

Witness, Tomás de Cárcamo   Don Alonso de Ayala   before me, Alonso Corona, public scribe

[Spanish transcription]

Sepan quantos esta carta vieren como nos los hermanos cofrades de la cofradia de nuestra Señora de guadalupe de los chinos fundada en la yglecia de la santa beracruz de esta ciudad de los Angeles juntos y congregados en las cassas de la morada de Don Alonso de ayala, mercader y mayordomo de la cofradia de la santa beracruz sita en dicha yglecia conviene a saver Simon de la Cruz fundador y mayordomo que a sido de dicha cofradia = Domingo Juarez mayordomo que asido tres veces y su fundador en ella Ventura Flores que tambien fui mayordomo y fundador = Francisco Lorente fundador y diputado antiguo = Joseph Flores que e sido diputado Joseph de la Cruz que e sido rector de dicha Cofradia = Diego Pacheco y Juan Francisco Andres de Carabajal y Phelipe de Soberantes y Phelipe de Frias diputados passados todos chinos libres vecinos de esta ciudad = y Luis de Trujillo esclavo de luis de trujillo = Juan Çapata esclavo de Alonso Carrillo tambien chinos y cofrades de dicha cofradia todos

    por nos y en nombre de ella y demas ermanos y cofrades por quienes prestamos vos y causion Decimos que por Memorial que dimos al Yllustrisimo y excelentisimo señor Don Juan de Palafox y Mendoça obispo de Osma siendolo de este de la Puebla de los Angeles pedimosle nos señalase para capilla de la Ymagen de nuestra señora de guadalupe de nuestra cofradia sitio en el simenterio de la dicha yglesia de la santa beracruz que se remitio al Señor Doctor Don Alonso de Salazar Varona governador de este obispado para que siendo conveniente y sin perjuicio alguno se señalase dicho sitio y aviendolo visto determino el dicho Señor Doctor se nos podia Dar la dicha lisensia otorgandose por nuestra parte escritura de pagar y satisfacer a la dicha cofradia de la santa beracruz siete pesos y quatro tomines cada año perpetuamente de limosna por dicho sitio y que todos los chinos u otras perssonas de qualquier color que fuessen y se enterrasen en dicha capilla o en la Yglesia pagassen a la fabrica della según y como lo pagavan los negros de la cofradia de nuestra señora de consolacion fundada en ella y que de todas las festividades que selebrassen los ermanos chinos assi en dicha capilla como en la dicha Yglesia de españoles de la limosna que Juntassen avian de dar el terçio a la cofradia de la santa Veracruz . . .

    y nos los dichos Simon de la Cruz Domingo Juarez Ventura Flores Franisco Lorente Joseph Flores Joseph de la Cruz Diego Pacheco Juan Francisco Andres de Caravajal Felipe de Soberanos y Phelipe de Frias nos obligamos juntamente con ellos . . . a que pagaran y pagaremos a la dicha cofradia de la santa beracruz y sus mayordomos o en su nombre y a quien por ella fuere parte Diez pesos de oro comun de limosna y penssion cada un año de los que corriesen desde oy perpetuamente en Reales en esta ciudad o en la parte que se pidan a fin de cada año con costas de la cobrança los siete pesos y quatro tomines en que se comuto la limosna de el sitio de la dicha capilla y los dos pesos y quatro tomines de el sitio que se nos señalo para la dicha sachristia . . . y estando prescente yo el dicho Don Alonso de Ayala mayordomo de dicha cofradia de la santa beracruz en su nombre y de los demas cofrades y diputados de ella porque en presto caussion aseto esta escritura para usar de ella como le convenga que es fecha la carta en la ciudad de los angeles A Veinte y ocho dias del mes de junio de mill y seiscientos y cinquenta y cinco años e yo el escrivano doy fee conosco a los otorgantes de los quales firmo el dicho Don Alonso de Ayala y por los demas que dijeron no saber firmo un testigo a su ruego testigos Thomas de Carcamo Nicolas Alvarez y Francisco de Torija vecinos de esta ciudad =

testigo Thomas de Carcamo   Don Alonso de Ayala   ante my Alonso Corona,
                                                                       scrivano publico

Document 74: 1691—Marriage license for Magdalena de Santiago, White mulatta[71]

I, the provisor of this bishopric of Puebla of the Angels, authorize the priest or vicar of the new parish of Santa Cruz in this city, to post banns, according to the Holy Council of Trent, for Magdalena de Santiago, White mulatta, free, damsel, native and *vecina* of this city, who belongs to that parish. She is the legitimate daughter of Juan Lopez and Anna María, his deceased wife. [This information is to be verified] so that she may contract matrimony with José Ramos, *mestizo*, single, tailor journeyman, native and *vecino* of this said city, who belongs to the parish of the Holy Cathedral Church. He is the legitimate son of Miguel Francisco and Josefa Anna, his wife. If they can verify that the aforementioned man has been a parishioner of their parish, and if there is no canonical impediment against either party, they are to be married and veiled according to the order of our Holy Mother Church. Given in the city [Puebla] of the Angels, June 30, 1691.

Don Jerónimo de Luna   By order of the lord provisor
Fernando Pérez de Soto, notary public

[Spanish transcription]

El Provisor deste obispado de la Puebla de los Angeles, Doy Licencia al Cura o Vicario de la nueba parochia de Santa Cruz de esta Ciudad para que amonesten conforme al Santo conçilio de Trento a Magdalena de Santiago mulata blanca libre donzella Natural y Vezina de esta Ciudad a essa feligressia Hija lexitima de Juan Lopez y de Anna Maria su muger difunta para efecto de contraer Matrimonio con Joseph Ramos mestizo soltero ofizial de sastre natural y vesino desta dicha Ciudad a la feligressia de

---

71. Archivo del Santo Ángel Custodio (Analco), Informaciones Matrimoniales de Españoles y Castas, Caja 16, no folio.

la Santa Iglessia Cathedral de ella Hijo lexitimo de Miguel Francisco y de Josepha Anna su muger y constandoles de que el susodicho lo ha sido en su feligresia y no resultante ympedimento Canonico contra ninguna de las partes los Cassen y Velen segun horden de nuestra santa Madre Iglessia Dada en la Ciudad de los Angeles a treinta dias del mes de Junio de mil seiscientos y noventa y un años

Don Geronimo de Luna   Por mandado del señor Provisor
Fernando Perez de Sotto, Nottario Publico

Document 75: 1698—The brotherhood of Santa Efigenia and its constitutions[72]

Lázaro Merlo, Nicolás de Villegas, Manuel Flores, Rodrigo de Rojas, Felipe García, Francisco Vergara, Miguel de la Cruz, *vecinos* of this city of San José de Toluca. We say that for greater service to God, and honor and glory to the glorious Martyr Virgin Santa Efigenia, we intend to establish and institute a brotherhood in the church of Our Lady of Guadalupe and the glorious patriarch San José, which belongs to the hospital of the glorious San Juan de Dios in this said city. So that we might meet, manage, and confer the constitutions that the brotherhood will have, in order to govern and rule said brotherhood, we ask and beg Your Grace to concede us his license and permission to gather in the said church to gather, manage, and confer the constitutional rules. We have agreed to follow these constitutions as a foundation of Blacks and mulattos. With their collection of alms, those [brothers] contained in this petition, along with many other believers and devotees of the said Holy Virgin and Martyr, have placed a very decent altar with its effigy [of Santa Efigenia]. In this we hope to receive permission from Your Grace's greatness and in what is necessary, etcetera. Manuel Flores, Nicolás de Villegas, Rodrigo de Rojas, Miguel de la Cruz.

In the city of San José de Toluca, February 8, 1698. Those contained in this petition presented it before me, so that it might be read and acknowledged before the lord provisor and general vicar of this archbishopric. The bachiller Don Antonio de Samano Ledesma, the presbyter Francisco Sánchez Pichardo, and Luis de Betancur were witnesses and are known to the petitioners, to which I attest, bachiller José de Áviles Valdés, receiving notary.

* * *

---

72. Archivo de la Parroquia de San José (Toluca), Cofradías, Caja 85, Vol. 1, ff. 2v–5r. Courtesy of Professor Rafael Castañeda García.

In Mexico City, on February 13, 1698, this petition was read before the lord bachiller Don Antonio de Aunzibay Anaya, canon of the Holy Church cathedral of the Holy Catholic Church of this city, provisor judge and general vicar in it and its archbishopric, etcetera. Having been seen by His Grace, he said that he conceded and concedes license to Lázaro Merlo and the others contained in said petition. . . .

* * *

[in the left-hand margin, "Constitutions"]

In the city of ~~Mexico~~ San José de Toluca, March 6, 1698. In virtue of the conceded license [and gathered] in the room where meetings are held in the convent and newly established hospital of the lord San Juan de Dios, in the said city. . . . In the presence of the preaching father Friar Sebastián de Arriga, chaplain of the said hospital and all the brothers listed in the petition from the page before. All together, they made and requested the constitutions for the foundation of the Confraternity of the Glorious Virgin and Martyr Santa Efigenia. They are and will be followed as follows.

First, it is a constitutional rule that we may establish an altar for the glorious saint [Efigenia] in the church of the said hospital. On May 3, we are to elect an administrator, a rector, and four deputies, who are to govern the said confraternity and brotherhood. The said administrator is to keep three books: one for the meeting minutes and elections; another for the brothers, living and deceased; and another to enter the expenses and receipts of the alms received. If re-elected, the said administrator must give accounts of these tasks.

2nd, it is a constitutional rule that each year on the first day of Easter of the Holy Spirit, the feast of the confraternity will be celebrated. The confraternity shall give the convent of the said hospital twelve pesos for a sung mass, a sermon, and a procession.

3rd, it is a constitutional rule that each month a mass shall be sung for the brothers, living and deceased. Twelve reales will be given to the said convent for alms.[73]

4th, it is a constitutional rule that each brother who joins as a member of the confraternity shall give four reales in alms. Upon his death, a prayed mass will be said in his name.

5th, we request as constitutional rules that each year, on the afternoon of Holy Monday, we be obligated to lead a blood procession with a small bell, standard, cross, and the steps of the Glorious Saint [Efigenia]. To accompany the procession, the chaplain

---

73. One peso was the equivalent of eight reales.

priest should be dressed in religious garments and [will prepare] a sermon. Twelve pesos will be given for alms.

6th, it is a constitutional rule that each brother who enters the confraternity will give half a real each week to assist with the confraternity's expenses.

7th, it is a constitutional rule that each year during the eight days of prayer commemorating the deceased, on the day indicated by the father prior, an anniversary will be celebrated for the deceased brothers with a mass and vigil. The convent will be given five pesos for alms.

With this, we finish and conclude the said constitutions for the said confraternity. By means of the license given by the said lord provisor, we have, all together, agreed and conferred on the said constitutions. We ask Your most illustrious Lordship and the lord general provisor to approve and confirm them as we hope. All of us, the said founders, are committed to observing and following said constitutions and we are not to change any of them, without giving notice to the present or future lord provisor. We signed, among those who knew how to, with the said preaching father on the aforementioned day, month, and year. Fray Nicolás Flores de Espinosa, Manuel Flores, Francisco Roa Mejía, Nicolás de Villegas, Antonio Ariza, Juan Marcha Guerrero, Lázaro Merlo, Miguel de la Cruz.

Friar Sebastián González, chaplain of the convent of Our Lady of Guadalupe and Our Lord San José of the hospital of Our Lord San Juan de Dios, in the city of Toluca, in virtue of and conformity with the order issued by the lord bachiller Don Antonio de Aunzibay Anaya, provisor judge and general vicar of Mexico City and its archbishopric, on February 13 of this present year. I attended the meeting that took place on March 6 of this present month on the elaboration of the constitutions for the government of the confraternity of the Martyr Virgin Santa Efigenia. In Toluca, at the convent of the hospital of Our Lord San Juan de Dios, March 14, 1689. Fray Sebastián González.

[Spanish transcription]

Lasaro Merlo = Nicolas de Villegas, Manuel Flores = Rodrigo de Roxas, Phelipe Garcia = Francisco Bergara = Miguel de la Cruz, Vezinos de la Ciudad de San Joseph de Toluca = Dezimos que para mas servicio de Dios, honra y Gloria de La Gloriossa Virgen Martir, Santa Efiguenia [sic], tenemos yntencion De fundar e instituir, Vna hermandad En la Yglesia de Nuestra señora de Guadalupe y El Glorioso Patriarca San Joseph de la hospitalidad del Gloriosso San Juan de Dios, de esta dicha Ciudad y Para podernos Juntar, tratar y conferir las constitusiones que a de tener; por donde se a de goberna y rreguir [sic, regir] dicha hermandad. A Vuestra merced Pedimos y Suplicamos sea servido de Concedernos Su Lizencia y permisso para podernos Juntar en dicha Yglessia a hazer, tratar [y] Conferir las reglas Constitusiones que Siendo fundacion de Negros y Mulatos Como lo tenemos pactado, asi los Contenidos en esta peticion, Como otros muchos afectos y devotos, a dicha Sancta Virgen y Martir Con Cuias Limosnas Se a puesto y Colocado Vn altar mui desente, con su efigie que En lo haci hazer Esperamos Resevir Merzed de la Grandessa de Vuestra merced y En lo nessesario etcetera = Manuel Flores = Nicolas de Villegas Rodrigo de Roxas = Miguel de la Cruz.

En la Ciudad, de San Joseph de Toluca, a ocho dias del mes de febrero de Mill Seiscientos y nobenta y ochos años. Los contenidos en esta peticion la pressentaron ante mi Para que se lea y Provea ante el señor Provisor y Vicario General, de este Arçobispado Siendo testigos y del Conossimiento de las partes El Lizensiado Don Antonio de Samano Ledesma, Presvitero Françisco Sanches Pichardo y Luis de Vetancur de que doi fee ante mi Bachiller Joseph de Abiles Valdes Notario Receptor.

* * *

En la Ciudad de Mexico a tresse dias del mes de febrero de Mill Seiscientos y nobenta y ocho años, Ante el Señor Lizenciado Don Antonio de Aunzibay Anaya, Canonigo de la Sancta Yglesia Cathedral de la Sancta Yglesia Catholica de esta Ciudad, Juez Provisor y Vicario General en ella y Su Arçobispado etcetera se leyo Esta petision. Y Por su Merced Vista Dijo que consedio y consedio Lizencia â Lazaro Merlo y demas contenidos en dicha petision . . .

* * *

[al margen izquierdo, "Consttituciones"]

En la Ciudad De ~~Mexico~~ San Joseph de Toluca á Seis Dias del mes de Março de Mill Seiscientos y nobenta y ocho años Estando En la Sala donde se hazen las Juntas En el Combento y hospital nuebamente fundado En esta dicha Ciudad de el señor San Juan de Dios En Virtud de La lizencia Consedida . . . Pressente El Padre Predicador fray Sebastian de Arriga, capellan de dicho hospital, y todos Los Hermanos Contenidos En la petision de la foxa antes de esta. Todos Juntos hicieron y pidieron Las constituciones que para la fundacion de La Cofradia de la Gloriossa Virguen [sic] y Martir Sancta Efiguenia [sic] han de Guardar y Son En la forma siguiente.

Primeramente, Es constitusion que hemos de Poder fundar Vn altar de la Gloriossa Santa En La Yglesia de dicho hospital y El dia tres de Mayo se a de Eleguir [sic] Mayordomo, Rector y quatro Diputados Los quales an de Governar dicha cofradia y hermandad, y dicho Mayordomo a de tener tres Libros. Vno En que asienten Los Cabildos y Elecciones. Otro Para los Hermanos Vivos y Difuntos, y otro Para hazentar Los gastos y Resivos de las Limosnas que persiviere; y si se rreligiere dicho Mayordomo sea Haviendo dado quentas de lo que hubiere sido a Su cargo.

2ª. Yten Es constitusion que el Primero dia de Pasqua de Espiritu santo, Cada Vn año se a de Selebrar La fiesta de dicha cofradia Y Se a de dar de limosna â El Combento de dicho Hospital dosce [sic] pessos para missa Cantada, Sermon y Prosecion.

3ª. Yten Es constitusion. Se a de cantar Vna Missa Cada mes por Los Hermanos Vivos y Difuntos y Se a de dar de Limosna a dicho combento dosse Reales.

4ª. Yten Es constitusion. Que El Hermano que se asentare Por cofrade a de dar de Limosna quatro Reales y Luego que ffallesca se le a de desir Una Missa Resada.

5ª. Yttem Pedimos Por Constitucions que Cada Vn año El Lunes Sancto Por la tarde hemos de ser obligados a sacar Vna prosecion de sangre que conste de Campanilla Estandarte, Cruz y Los Passos de El martirio de la Gloriossa Sancta y Por el acompañamiento de El Capellan Saserdote que fuere Rebestido y Sermon Se an de dar de Limosna dosse pessos.

6ª. Iten Es constitucion que El Hermano que se asentare En dicha Cofradia a de ser obligado a dar medio Real Cada Semana para aiuda de los Gastos de dicha cofradia.

7ª. Ytten Es constitucion que cada año En la octaba de la commemoracion de los Difuntos el dia que Señalare El Padre Prior de dicha octaba, Se a de Hazer anibersario por los Hermanos Difuntos Con Su Missa y Vigilia Y sea a de dar de limosna a dicho combento Cinco pessos.

Con lo qual acabamos y fenesemos dichas constituciones para el Vsso de dicha cofradia que mediante La lizencia dada de dicho Señor Provisor hemos Tratado y Conferido Todos Juntos y Mediante las dichas constituciones Pedimos a Su Señoria Illustrisima y Señor Provisor General Se sirva de aprobarlas y confirmarlas que asi lo Esperamos y nos obligamos todos los dichos fundadores Referidos en dicha petision â Cumplir y Guardar dichas Constitusiones y no poder mudar ningunas sin que primero Se de quenta a dicho señor Provisor que a el presente es o en adelante fuere y lo firmamos, lo[s] que Supimos con el dicho Padre Predicador dicho dias mes y año arriba dichos ~~Fray~~ Nicolas Flores de Espinossa, Manuel Flores = Francisco Roa Mexia = Nicolas de Villegas = Antonio Arisa, Juan Marcha Guerrero = Lasaro Merlo = Miguel de la Cruz

Fray Sebastian Gonzales capellan del combento de Nuestra Señora de Guadalupe y Señor San Joseph de la hospitalidad de El Señor San Juan de Dios de la ciudad de Toluca En Virtud y Conformidad del auto del Señor Lizenciado Don Antonio de Aunzibay Anaya, Juez Provisor y Vicario General de la ciudad de Mexico y su Arçobispado, Proveido a los Tresse de febrero de este presente año En la Junta que se hiço a los Seis de Março de Este pressente mes asisti a la formacion de las Constitusiones para el Gobierno de la cofradia de la Virgen Martir, Santa Efinegia [sic, Efigenia] Conbento del hospital del Señor San Juan de Dios y Toluca catorze de Março de mill seiscientos y nobenta y ocho años Fray Sebastian Gonsales

Document 76: 1710—Prayers in Mexico City to San Benito de Palermo[74]

Arguments for these eight days of prayer.
I had read, mostly out of curiosity, in order to see and take note of the style in which it was written, the life and virtues of the incomparable man, the humble saint, SAN BENITO OF SAN FRATTELO, commonly known as of PALERMO; a beautiful mole [facial birthmark] that does not make things ugly, but rather brings grace to the always penitent, mortified, and, above all, poor religion of my dear father, the beloved Saint Francis Assisi. . . .

In following such learned teachers, I complain, and I say *that I feel and am very troubled that all people do not know this man as he deserves* [to be known]; because the devotion to this saint is not widely practiced. I place before your eyes an admirable man, not descended from kings, not of the lineage of princes, not with the blood of nobles, but a descendant of a humble people, two poor Blacks, one of them in the condition of a slave, the other free. My saint was born of this lineage (as God makes great works from such low foundations). They raised their son with a holy fear of God, so that his customs would be the example for nobles, a model for great [people]. The parents knew well that houses are made more noble through exemplary acts than by keeping the papers of noble descendants. . . .

If you have need, or find yourself ill, and need remedy, turn to BENITO, who appears to be the only physician, so admirable is he in granting health to the sick because his intercession and invocation is admirable for this. If you are afflicted by lumbago, what they call a kidney stone, turn to BENITO, and stop wasting time searching for chemicals and foreigners. Because invoking him, or having some contact with a printed image or a relic of his, is enough to rid yourself of this. I will not give you other cases of this disease as proof, in order to keep this volume short,

---

74. Fondo Antiguo Biblioteca Franciscana, excerpts from *Octava de san Benito de S. Fradelo, llamado vulgarmente de Palermo. Por las ocho Bienavenuranças. Dispuesta por el Br. Don Juan Francisco de Dios Medina, Presbytero, Su devoto* (En Mexico: 1710), no folio.

otherwise it would go from an eight-day plan of prayer to a full narrative, but it is not because I am lacking in admirable examples from his life. . . .

[Benito] gives feet to the lame, and hands to the maimed, as happened to a boy named Joseph Lomenaco, who was unable to take a step, or move, unless he was carried. His parents decided to turn to this saint. In a holy manner, they applied a relic of his habit to the child's crippled parts. The boy, feeling in them an extraordinary spirit, immediately left the crutches, going about with such agility and firmness, that he also ran and leaped as if he had never had [an ailment]. Though his relics heal a great amount, his printed images and invoking his name are also enough to expel evil spirits. Devoted person, these are the examples my mind has been able to understand in order to encourage you to become very devoted to this Black saint, because I can tell you what the beloved wife told her husband: I am Black, but I am a beautiful woman: *Nigra sum, sed formosa*. He is Black, but beautiful: *Niger sum, sed formosus*. Search for him so that you may place yourself in his trust, and by his means reach what you want from God. Therefore, I refer you to these prodigies so that stimulated by these signs, this illustrious city [Mexico City] and you may experience his favors and assistance. With affection, I desire that all would search for [Benito] so that they would know him through his works. This has been my main motivation, along with giving multiple intercessors, so that you may reach what you need of God as you intend. May the saint inflame your will and light your desire in such a way that you persevere in his devotion and do not desist as in all the other things. I ask this of you, and that God give his blessing, and that I be made a better person, so that we may all enjoy it in glory. Farewell.

Method of carrying out the eight days of prayer.
This can be done any time of the year at church before [Benito's] altar or at home before an image of his. However, those who esteem themselves as devout followers of the saint should begin on March 28, in order to finish [the eight days of prayer] on April 4, the day that the saint died. I do not specify the exercises that are to be followed, because these are voluntary and the spiritual priests are tasked with that. I only ask that these eight days of prayer begin with a good confession, thinking of all your sins, and that you receive God sacramented [consecrated as a communion host?] on the first and last day, so that you may achieve more efficiently the things you ask of this saint's intercession. . . .

[Spanish transcription]

Motivos a la octava.
Aviendo leìdo mas por curiosidad de vèr, y notar el estilo que traìa la Vida, y virtudes del incomparable Varon, del humilde Santo SAN BENITO DE SAN FRADELO, conocido vulgarmento por el de PALERMO; lunar hermoso que no afea, sì que

agracia la siempre penitente, mortificada, y mas que otra pobre Religion de mi querido Padre, y amado Santo San Francisco de Assis . . .

Yo siguiendo tan doctos Maestros assi me quejo, y digo: *que siento, y llevo muy á mal que no conoscan todos á este Varon como merece;* pues no está muy estendida la devocion de este Santo, pongote à los ojos vn hobre admirable, no descendiente de Reyes, no de linaje de Principes, no de sangre de Nobles sí descendiente de vna gente humilde, como son dos pobres negros, por la condicion esclavo el vno, y el otro libre, de éste pues linaje nació mi Santo (que de tan bajos cimientos haze Dios obras grandes) criaron estos à su hijo en el temor Santo de Dios para que fuessen sus costumbres el exemplo de nobles, y dechado de grandes, bien sabian los Padres, que mas se ennoblecen las cassas con exemplares acciones, que con guardar papeles de nobles descendencias . . .

Tienes necessidad; en enfermedad, y necesitas de remedio, acude à BENITO, que parece el vnico medico, porque es admirable en esta gracia de dar salud à enfermos porque su intercesion, y invocacion, es admirable para esto; si te aflige el mal de hijada, que llaman piedra de orina, acude con BENITO; y quitate de andar gastando el tiempo en buscar quimicos, y Estrangeros: porque su invocacion, ò contacto de alguna estampa, ò reliquia suya es bastante para que la arrojes de tì, no te pongo para prueva de esta enfermedad otros casos por no hazer mas largo este volumen, porque pasara de Octava á narracion; no porque me falten en su vida admirables. . . .

Dà pies á cojos, y manos á mancos, como le sucedió à vn niño llamado Joseph Lomenaco, que no pudiendo dar paso, ni moverse; sino era llevandole, acordaron sus Padres de acudir á este santo, y aplicandole santamente vna reliquia de su habito en la partes tullidas, y sintiendo en ellas el muchacho vn extraordinario aliento, dexò luego las muletas andando con tanta agilidad, y firmeza, que tambien corria, y saltaba como si nunca huviera tenido nada, que mucho que sus reliquias sanen, pues son bastantes tambien, como sus estampas, é invocacion de su nombre, basta para desterrar los malignos espiritus. Estos son, devoto, los que mi capacidad ha podido comprehender para excitarte â que seas muy devoto de este Santo Negro, porque te puedo decir lo que á el Esposo le dixo su amada: Negra soy, pero hermosa: *Nigra sum, sed formosa*, Negro es pero hermoso: *Niger sum, sed formosus*: que le busques para encomendarte à èl, y por su medio alcanzar de Dios lo que desseas, par esto con cuydado te refiero esso prodigios para que estimulado con essas señas experimente esta Ilustre Ciudad, y tu, sus favores, y auxilios: bien quisiera mi afecto, que todos lo buscaran para que todos lo conocieran por sus obras, este ha sido el mayor motivo, y el dar abogados multiplicados, para que alcanzes de Dios lo que pretendes, el Santo te inflamme la voluntad, encienda el desseo de tal manera, que perseveres en su devocion, y no descaëscas, com en las demâs cosas, yo assi te lo pido, y â Dios que dè su gracia, y a mi me haga bueno para que todos le gozemos en la gloria: Vale.

Modo de hazer la Octava.

En qualquier tiempo del año se puede hazer, en la Iglesia delante de su Altar, ó en su casa delante de vna Imagen suya; pero los que se preciaren devotos del Santo han de empezar el dia veinte y ocho de Março para acabarla el dia quatro de Abril, dia en que falleció este Santo, no pongo los exercicios que han de hazer porque estos son voluntarios, y esto toca darlos á los padres espirituales; solo encargo el fin que pretendo en esta Octava, y es que dè principio á ella, con vna buena Confession, pensando todos sus pecados, y que recivan â Dios Sacramentado el primero, y vltimo dia, para que con mas eficacia consigan lo que por intercecion de este Santo piden.

Document 77: 1725—Nicolás Palomino Arias responds to accusations of bigamy[75]

Based on an extract taken from the books of said parish and given to bachiller Don Manuel Calvo de Alegría, as ordered by the commissary of [the Inquisition in] Guatemala . . . it appears and is evident that on February 24, 1713, after reading the wedding banns, the said bachiller Calvo, as the most senior priest, held a license of the local ecclesiastical authority. He authorized the marriage of Nicolás Arias, native of Guatemala and mulatto slave of the said Governor Francisco Rodríguez, to Simona de la Rosa, free mulatta and native of this city; and veiled them in front of the church. The [wedding] godparents and witnesses are the same that she names in her preceding statement. . . . [She] only added and adds, a few more physical marks of this accused person, her husband, such as two missing teeth in the upper part of his mouth.

To the accusation, [Nicolás Palomino Arias] confesses as he has said and will refer to later on. The extract is correct with regard to the marriage that was contracted, as stated by the godparents and the parish priest. He only denies using the last name of Arias, and he denies being anyone's slave.

María de la Trinidad, mother-in-law of the accused and sixty years old; José Rodríguez, mulatto 26 years old; María Ventura Rodríguez, over 22 years old, who served as godmother to the marriage; and bachiller Manuel Calvo de Alegría were examined and [their statements] completely ratified according to the tribunal's commission during the month of July 1723. They declared and declare that they were present at the marriage that the accused contracted with the said Simona about ten years ago in the parish of the city of San Miguel. They say that he led a married life with her for about three years. He had one or two children with her, until he left her after committing some faults and disorders against his master, Don Francisco Rodríguez, who

---

75. Archivo Histórico Nacional (España), Inquisición, 1730, Exp. 7, ff. 4v–7r, 10v–11r.

owned him as a slave. As the godparents and witness who were referred to, they all explained and specified his personal marks and how the said bachiller married them.

To this accusation, he confesses what has been said and what is insinuated later on. He openly confesses that what these witnesses say is true about his marriage to the mulatta Simona and that he married her at the time and under the circumstances that are expressed. He only denies ever having been a slave and administrator of Captain Rodríguez. He denies having led a married life with her for more than six months, insisting that he only left her pregnant. He says that he has never changed his last name and has always called himself Nicolás Palomino. He says that he left her because she fled from him, as he has stated, but not because he stole or wrongly sold what he is imputed to have done, since he was not an administrator, just a servant on the hacienda.

Based on an extract taken from the book of marriages celebrated in the town of Tapachula, as ordered by the said Commissary Reyes on December 19, it appears and is evident that on February 12, 1720, after having read the three wedding banns, as ordered by the Holy Council of Trent, and no impediment to [the marriage] having been raised, the bachiller Gregorio Canzino, in front of the church and with license from the provincial vicar of that province, married this accused man, Nicolás Palomino, mulatto and single, to Rosa de Chages, *mestiza* widow of Lucas Barranco, as *vecinos* of that town. Blas García and María Nicolasa, mulattos and *vecinos* of Chiltepeque, were godparents [to the marriage]. The witnesses were Juan de la Cruz, Diego Palomeque, and Francisco Javier de la Cruz. This extract is completely verified.

To this accusation he confessed as is said. He confessed that the statement is certain and true, and that he contracted the second marriage as it declares.

According to a petition presented by this accused man before the bachiller Gregorio Canzino Barba, the priest of the Tuxtla region, and in accordance with the depositions of three witnesses named Eugenio Méndez, mulatto, 40 years old, and *vecino* of the town of Tapachula, where the information was being received; Cristóbal Ortíz, Spaniard, *vecino* of Guatemala, 50 years old; and Francisco de Cueto, resident of the said town of Tapachula, and 33 years old, it is evident and appears that the accused took the last name of Palomino and carried on as a free mulatto, single, and native of the city of Guatemala, as the son of Lorenza de Ocampo, mulatta of the same city. The first two witnesses, Eugenio Méndez and Cristóbal Ortíz, swore that they had known the accused from Guatemala. They knew that he was a free and single man. Ortíz added that he had known him from his childhood in the company of his mother. However, none of [these witnesses] signed [their depositions] because they say they do not know how to. Nor was this information received before a judge or notary. It seems that the bachiller Gregorio Canzino Barba sent it to the provincial vicar, Juan Román de Meneses, as ecclesiastical judge of the province of Soconusco. The latter considered the information sufficient [for a marriage] and granted the license for the Tuxtla priest, or his representative, to marry them after the wedding banns if no impediment surfaced. This was done by the said bachiller Gregorio Canzino Barba, as is evident from the certifications at the end of the said information. It appears that the third witness, Francisco de Cueto, deposed truthfully, because he knew the accused man for five years in that location as a single man. Unlike the other two witnesses, who swore what is said, [Cueto] was in the service of Don Pedro de los Reyes, beneficed priest and commissary [for the Inquisition].

In response to the accusation and its third section, [Nicolás Palomino Arias] denies ever having induced the witnesses to present false testimony. He confesses that one of them, the Spaniard whose name he cannot even remember, died fifteen days after presenting the information. . . . With regard to the published statement, he confesses that it is true that he gave that information. But it is false that he was accompanied, or that he even went with any of the witnesses who deposed. He does not know if it is true that one of them knew his mother, because one of the witnesses affirmed that he had accidentally [?] come from Guatemala to the town of Tapachula, and not with the accused. Therefore, the accused comes to confess that he does not know either of the two witnesses, nor did he know of them until then. He does not know why they swore that they had known him from Guatemala and since his childhood. However, whatever may come up against these witnesses must be ratified, so that everything is stated clearly and distinctly.

* * *

[This file] was received by the tribunal, reviewed on November 9, 1725, and voted on by inquisitors and the ordinary of the Chiapa bishopric. [The accused] is to process in a particular auto-da-fé to the church indicated by the commissary, should there be no Dominican church. He is to process with the insignias of a person married two times, where his sentence will be read with merits, *abjure de levi*.[76] The next day, as a sign of justice, he will be given two hundred lashes in the usual streets and he will be banished for eight years from the province of Soconusco, Mexico, Madrid, and six leagues surrounding [these places]. During the first four years, his service will be sold to one of the textile mills in Guatemala, whichever the commissary indicates and chooses. The profits of his service will be delivered to his master, after discounting the costs of transporting him to Guatemala and any other costs. After these four years of service in the textile mill, his master must be given notice to retrieve this accused person. During the first year, the accused is to pray a part of the rosary to Our Lady, and within two months he is to make a general and sacramental confession. With regards to the marriage bond, he is to be sent to the ordinary ecclesiastic who may and should know about this cause.

---

76. An abjuration was a formal renunciation of heresy. Inquisitors could condemn a Catholic suspected of a slight heresy with a charge of *abjure de levi*.

On November 22 of the said year, the sentence with merits, the order, and the instruction for its execution were sent to the commissary of Ciudad Real de Chiapa. The commissary confirmed receipt of these [documents] in the letter of February 5, 1726, and is entrusted with carrying them out.

[Spanish transcription]

Por vna partida sacada en toda forma de los Libros de dicha Parrochia y dada por el Bachiller Don Manuel Calbo de Alegria de orden del Comisario de Goatemala . . . consta y pareze como el tal Bachiller Calbo en 24 de febrero de setezientos y treze, como cura rector mas antiguo con Lizenzia del ordinario y leidas las amonestaziones desposo y velò *Ynfacie eclesie* a este Reo Nicolas Arias natural de Goathemala y mulato esclabo de dicho Gobernador Francisco Rodriguez, con Simona de la Rosa mulata libre natural de aquella Ciudad siendo Padrinos y testigos los mismos que ella nombra en su declarazion Antezedente . . . y solo añadio y añade, mas señas personales de este Reo su marido, y como le faltaban dos dientes en la parte superior de la boca.

A la acusazion lo confiesa como queda dicho, y adelante se refiere, y a la Publicacion confiesa ser cierta la partida de haver contraydo el Matrimonio que en ella se refiere, siendo Padrinos y Parroco los que se expresan; y solo niega el Apellido de Arias y el aver sido, ni ser esclabo de persona alguna = [fin margen]

Maria de la Trinidad, suegra de este Reo y de hedad de sesenta años, Joseph Rodriguez mulato de 26, María Ventura Rodriguez de mas de 22 y Madrina que fue del Matrimonio, y el Bachiller Manuel Calbo de Alegria, examinado y ratificados en toda forma y según la comission del tribunal por dicho mes de Jullio y año de [17]23 Dixeron y Dizen averse hallado el Matrimonio que este Reo contrajo abria como diez años en la Parroquia de aquella Ciudad de San Miguel, con la tal Simona, y como hizo vida maridable con ella como tres años y tuvo vno, v dos hijos asta que la dejo por las faltas y desordenes que cometio para con dicho su Amo don Francisco Rodriguez de quien hera esclabo explicando y expresando todos, o, los mas sus señas personales y como los caso dicho Bachiller, y fueron Padrinos y testigos los que quedan referidos . . .

A la Acusazion lo confesó como queda dicho y adelante se insinua; Y a la Publicazion confiesa llanamente ser cierto lo que dizen estos testigos en orden a su Casamiento con la mulata Simona y que se casó con ella por el tiempo y en las circunsancias que expresan; negando solo el haver sido esclabo y mayordomo del capitan Rodriguez, y el haver hecho vida maridable con ella mas de seis meses; insistiendo en que solo la dejó preñada y nunca se â mudado el apellido llamandose siempre Nicolas Palomino, y en que la dejo por lo que tiene dicho sobre abersele huydo, y no por haver el hurtado ni malbaratado lo que se le imputa pues no fue mayordomo sino sirbienta [sic] de la hazienda

Por una partida sacada de los Libros de casamientos zelebrados en el Pueblo de Tapachula de orden de dicho Comisario Reyes, y en 19 de Diziembre consta y pareze como en doze de febrero del año de [1]720, corridas las tres amonestaziones segun lo ordenado por el Santo Conzilio de Trento y no haviendo resultado ympedimento alguno el Bachiller Gregorio Canzino con Lizenzia del Vicario Probinzial de aquella (Probinzia los) Casô *in fazie eclesie* à este Reo llamado Nicolas Palomino mulato soltero con Rosa de Chages mestiza viuda de Lucas Barranco vezinos de aquel Pueblo, siendo Padrinos Blas Garzia y Maria Nicolasa mulatos y vezinos del de Chiltepeque y testigos Juan de la Cruz, Diego Palomeque, y Francisco Jabiêr de la Cruz, la qual se halla concordada en toda forma.

A la Acusazion lo confeso como bá dicho; y a la Publicazion confiesa ser cierta y verdadera y el haver el, contraydo el 2º Matrimonio según y como en ella se expresa

Por vna petizion que en siete de Diziembre de [1]719 presentô este Reo Ante el theniente de Curâ del partido de Tustla [Tuxtla] Bachiller Gregorio Canzino Barba y por las deposiziones de 3 testigos llamados Euxenio Mendez mulato, de hedad de quarenta años y vezino del Pueblo de Tapachula donde se rezivia la Ynformazion, Christobal Ortiz español vezino de Goathemala y de hedad de cinquenta años y Francisco de Cueto morador de dicho Pueblo de Tapachula y de hedad 33 años. Consta y pareze como este Reo tomo el apellido de Palomino, y se dio por mulato Libre, soltero y natural de la Ciudad de Goathemala, e hixo de Lorenza de Ocampo mulata de la misma ciudad, y los dos primeros testigos Euxenio Mendez, y Christobal Ortiz, Juraron haverlo conozido desde Goathemala, y que savian hera libre y soltero, añadiendo el Ortiz averle conozido desde sus tiernos años en compañía de su Madre, pero ninguno de ellos firma por dezirse no saver; ni la tal Ynformazion se hizo Ante mas Juez, ni Notario, que el tal Bachiller Gregorio Canzinp Barba el qual pareze la remitio al Bicario Provinzial Juan Roman de Meneses como Juez eclesiastico de aquella Probinzia de Soconusco, y que la dio este por bastante y conzedio lizenzia para que el cura de Tustla, y su theniente lo pudierse casar corridas las Amonestaziones y no resultado ympedimento como lo executo dicho theniente Bachiller Gregorio Canzino Barba como consta de las zertificaziones puestas al final de dicha Ynformazion en la qual dicho 3º testigo Francisco de Cueto, pareze depuso solo con verdad, en orden a, aver conozido â este Reo, de cinco años, â aquella parte soltero, y en servizio del Venefiziado y Comisario Don Pedro de los Reyes â diferenzia de los otros dos que Juraron lo que queda dicho.

A la Acusazion y Capitulo 3º de ella niega haver induzido a los testigos para que Jurasen falso y confiesa que uno de ellos, español que no se nombra, ni sabe como se llama, y que murio a los 15 dias despues de la Ynformazion. . . . Y a la publicazion confiesa ser cierto haver dado esta Ynformazion pero que es falso haverle acompañado, ni hido con el alguno de los testigos que la componen y que no sabe si es cierto que alguno de ellos conoziere a su Madre, pues el uno de ellos que lo afirma vino accidentalmente [¿?] de Goathemala al Pueblo de Tapachula, y no en su compañía. Con que biene en sustanzia â confesar que a ninguno de los dos conozia, ni conozio asta entonzes, ni sabe por que Juraron le conozian â el desde Goathemala y sus tiernos años; Aunque se deverá ratificar en lo que contra ellos resulta según estilo, y para que diga con toda claridad y distinzion =

* * *

Y rezivida en el Tribunal se Vio en consulta de 9 de Noviembre de 1725 y fue Votado por los Inquisidores y ordinario del obispado de Chiapa; â que salga â Auto particular de fee â la Yglesia que señalare el Comisario, no haviendola de Santo Domingo, con insignias de Casado dos Vezes donde se le Lea su sentenzia con meritos, *Abjure de Levi*, y al otro dia le sean dados en forma de Justizia Duzientos azotes por las calles acostumbradas, y sea desterrado por tiempo de ocho años de la Provincia de Soconusco, y de Mexico, y Madrid y seis leguas en contorno, y los quatros primeros se venda su servizio en Vno de los obrages de Goathemala el que dicho Comisario señalare y dispusiere cuyo importe rebajados los gastos de su conduzion â Goathemala, y los demas que puede haber causado, se entriegue [sic] â su Amo, avisandoselo para que ocurra a recaudar la Persona de este Reo cumplidos que sean los quatro años de obrage, y que el primer año reze los savados Vna parte de Rosario a Nuestra señora, y que dentro de dos meses se confiese general y sacramentalmente. Y en quanto al Vinculo del Matrimonio fuese remitido al ordinario eclesiastico que de la causa pueda y deva conozer =

Y en 22 de Noviembre de dicho año se remitieron al comisario de Ciudad Real de Chiapa la sentencia con meritos, y la orden e Ynstrucçion combeniente para su execuzion, de cuyo rezivo avisò en carta de 5 de Febrero de este año de 1726, y de quedar en quenta de executar su contenido.

Document 78: 1731—Lázaro del Valle's marriages in Acámbaro and Chihuahua[77]

Presented in the Holy Office of Mexico City on July 9, 1732.

Inquisitors Navarro and Tagle.

Most Illustrious Sir,

The inquisitor attorney has seen the charges filed against Lázaro del Valle, alias García, who was a mulatto slave of Don José Carrillo, now deceased, and a native of the town of Acámbaro. He contracted a legitimate marriage in the said town with

---

77. Archivo General de la Nación, Inquisición, Vol. 832, Exp. 2, 60r, 66r–67r, 99r, 100v.

Efigenia de la Cruz, alias de los Dolores, on December 28, 1723, and lived with the said Efigenia. He contracted a second marriage before the church with Juana del Carmen, a *coyota* woman,[78] in the village of San Felipe el Real, on October 28, 1730. The first marriage is sufficiently proven with the marriage certificate, the deposition of the witnesses who were godparents, and others. It is certain that the said Efigenia still lives, and she was also examined. The second marriage is evident by the marriage certificate and the commissary's account, which states that [Lázaro del Valle] is with the said Juana del Carmen, having her as wife. The commissary adds that he has yet to receive the depositions of witnesses for further justification. The identity of the [accused] person is proven by the statement of a witness who says that he saw and knew him. This is the person who denounced him. In addition, he is identified by personal marks. To this effect, Your Grace should order that the commissary of the village of San Felipe el Real arrest the said Lázaro del Valle and embargo his money, if he has any. After receiving the information on his marriage to the said Juana, he is to be sent, at the first opportunity, to the secret jails of this tribunal and placed in them. I will provide further information in due form. Your Lordship will decide what is best. Mexico City, July 8, 1732.

Licenciado Don Diego Mangado y Clavijo

* * *

In the town of Acámbaro, on December 28, 1731, at nine in the morning, before the lord bachiller Don José Reyes y Ortega, commissary of the Holy Office of this said town. A man who said his name was Luis Díaz, muleteer by trade, native of this said town, presented himself without being summoned and took the oath to tell the truth. He is a *vecino* of the San Bartolomé valley, lessee of the ranch named El Rosario in the jurisdiction of the bishopric of Guadiana. He is 49 years of age. In order to discharge his conscience, he says and denounces that as a local of this said town he knows for certain how he saw Don José Carrillo de Figueroa, deceased *vecino* of this said town, raise a mulatto slave. The latter is the son of Juana del Valle, mulatta slave of the said [Carrillo de Figueroa]. This deponent saw the said slave, named Lázaro, three times in the town and mines of Chihuahua. The last time he the confessant knew of him was October 4th of this present year and he gave notice to his master, so that he could send for him. Giving notice to his master on today's date, his master confirmed that it is common knowledge that Lázaro del Valle is married here to Efigenia de la Cruz, mulatta slave of the said Don José Carrillo. She is currently under the domain and in the house of Don Pedro de Balbuena y Figueroa, owner of the La Concepción hacienda, in this jurisdiction. The said mulatto slave Lázaro is certainly married in the said town and mines of Chihuahua to a woman whose name

---

78. A caste label used to describe a person of mixed ancestry, typically a person of Indigenous and African descent.

he [Luis Díaz] does not know. She was raised by Don Joseph Barriaya, *vecino* of the said mining town. [Lázaro] lives in the house of Don Juan Joseph de Urrutia, *vecino* of the said mining town, and is a bricklayer by occupation. He pretends to be a free person. And this is the truth by the oath he has made. [His statement] was read to him and he said it is well-written. He does not state this out of hate and promised to keep the secret. He does not know how to sign, the said lord commissary signed on his behalf. Bachiller Don Joseph Reyes de Ortega. Passed before me, Antonio de Robles, the named notary.

[The document] accords with the original that is held in this Inquisition's Chamber of the Secret, to which I refer, certify, and sign.

Don Francisco de los Ríos y Cosío

* * *

Lord,

In virtue of Your Lordship's order to identify the person known as Lázaro del Valle, alias García, alias José de Galavis, who has a denunciation and cause in the Holy Office, I solicited this information in the Conchos garrison and found that he had fled. However, relying on some news, I learned that he had gone to the Real de Oro [Indebé, the mining town in Zacatecas?], more than 130 leagues[79] removed from this village. To apprehend him more securely, I exhorted the lord governor of that kingdom [to arrest him]. The governor, with catholic zeal and prudence, investigated the case, apprehended and brought [Lázaro] to this village where he is imprisoned. . . . January 24, 1746.

Licenciado Antonio Feliz Valdéz Lavandera

Note. In the document of April 27, 1747, that was presented in this tribunal by order of the lord inquisitor Tagle, the commissary of Chihuahua says that this prisoner fled, with others, from the jail where he was being held.

[Spanish transcription]

Pressentada en el santo oficio de Mexico en nuebe de Julio de mil Setezientos y treinta y dos años

Inquisidores Navarro, y Tagle

---

79. A Spanish league measured 2.6 miles (4.3 kilometers), although there was often considerable variation in local measurements.

Yllustrísimo Señor

El Ynquisidor fiscal ha visto los autos seguidos contra Lazaro del Valle alias Garcia mulato esclavo que fue de Don Joseph Carrillo ia difunto, natural del Pueblo de Acambaro, sobre que aviendo contrahido legitimo matrimonio en dicho Pueblo con Efigenia de la Cruz alias de los Dolores en 28 de Diciembre de 1723 viviendo la dicha Efigenia, contraxo segundo matrimonio in facie Ecclesia con Juana del Carmen coiota [sic, coyota] en la Villa de San Phelipe el Real en 28 de Octubre de 1730. esta provado el 1.º matrimonio en vastante forma por la fe de cassamiento, desposiciones de los testigos que fueron Padrinos, y otros, y es cierta la supervivencia de la dicha Efiginia, por estar tambien examinada, y el 2.º matrimonio consta por la fe de cassado, y relacion del Comissario, que dice esta con la referida Juana del Carmen teniendola como muger, y añade este Comissario que queda entendiendo en recibir las deposiciones de los testigos para maior justificacion, y la identidad de la Persona se prueva por el dicho de un testigo, que ocularmente lo vio y conozio, que es el que lo denuncio, y ademas desto le convienen las señas personales; por lo qual se servira Vuestra Señoría dar orden al Comissario de la Villa de San Phelipe el Real para que aprenda la Persona del dicho Lazaro del Valle envargandole el peculio, si lo tuviere, y que recivida la informacion en que conste el matrimonio con la referida Juana, lo remita en primera ocasión a las Carceles secretas deste Tribunal, y puesto en ellas protesto pedir mas en forma Vuestra Señoría acordara lo mexor. Mexico y Julio 8 de 1732.

Lizenciado Don Diego Mangado y Clavijo

* * *

En el Pueblo de Acambaro a veynte y ocho dias del mes de Diziembre año de mill setezientos y treynta y uno a las nuebe oras de la mañana ante el Señor Bachiller Don Joseph Reyes y Ortega Comisario del santo oficio de este dicho Pueblo, Parezio sin ser llamado y Juro en forma que dira verdad un hombre que dixo llamarse Luys Diaz de oficio Arriero natural de ese dicho Pueblo y vezino de la Jusidizion del Valle de San Bartholome arrendatario de un rancho nombrado el Rsoario en dicha Jurisdizion del obispado de Guadiana de hedad de quarenta y nuebe años el qual por descargo de su Conzienzia Dize y Denunzia: que como oriundo de este dicho Pueblo conoze ciertamente como que le vio criar a un mulato esclabo de don Joseph Carrillo de Figueroa difunto vezino que fue de este dicho Pueblo, hijo de Juana del Valle mulata esclava del susodicho y que aviendo visto tres vezes al dicho esclavo que se llama Lazaro en el Real y minas de Chiguagua y la ultima el dia quatro de octubre de este presente año observo el ~~confesante~~ conosimiento de dicho esclabo para avisar a su amo que embiara por el y que aviendo dado la notizia oy de la fecha con zertidumbre de su mismo Amo y de publico estar aquí casado con Efigenia de la Cruz mulata sclava de dicho Don Joseph Carrillo que actualmente se halla en poder y casa de don Pedro de Balbuena y Figueroa Dueño de la hazienda de la Conzepcion en esta Jurisdizion y que el dicho mulato esclavo Lazaro ziertamente esta casado en el dicho Real y minas de Chiguagua con una muger cuio nombre ignora la qual crio Don Joseph Barriaya vezino de dicho Real y que vibe en la casa de Don Juan Joseph de Vrrutia vezino de dicho Real con oficio de Albañil dicho esclavo y corriendo por libre y que esta es la verdad por el Juramento que tiene echo y siendole leydo dixo que esta bien escrito y que no lo dize por odio prometio el secreto y por no saver escribir lo firmo por el dicho Señor comisario = Bachiller Don Joseph Reyes de Ortega—Paso Ante mi Antonio de Robles notario nombrado

Concuerda con su original que para en la Camara del Secreto de esta Ynqqusicion a que me remito Zertifico y firmo.

Don Francisco de los Rios y Cossio

* * *

Señor,

En virtud del mandato de Vuestra Señoría por lo que toca â identficar la persona de Lazaro del Valle, alias Garcia, alias Joseph de Galavis, con la que ay denuncia y causa en el Santo Oficio; habiendola solicitado en el Presidio de Conchos, halle que habia hecho fuga, pero valiendome de noticias supe que se habia ido al Real de Oro [¿en Zacatecas?], distante de esta villa mas de 130 leguas, y para cogerlo con mas seguridad exorte al Señor Governador de esse Reino quien con catholico Zelo, haziendo con toda Prudencia las diligencias aprehendio y traxo á esta villa donde se halla preso. . . . Henero 24 de 1746 . . .

Licenciado Antonio Feliz Valdez Lavandera

Nota. En Escrito de 27 de Abril de 1747, Que presento en este Tribunal, de mandato del señor Ynquisidor Tagle el Comisario de Chiguagua, participa como este Reo hizo fuga, con ôtros, de aquella Carzel Donde se hallava preso.

Document 79: 1787—Priest of Huazolotitlán, Oaxaca demands obedience[80]

Most Illustrious Sir, Doctor, Don José Gregorio Alonso y Ortigosa

There is much remorse that weighs down my heart, as I am obligated to give account of the heavy task that I have before myself and which I cannot verify as

---

80. Archivo General de la Nación, Instituciones Coloniales, Policía y Empedrados, Vol. 8, 350/6, Exp. 6, ff. 92r–93r.

I should, but especially because I cannot even find the way to do so, due to how ill-taught and coddled these mulattos are. They are in possession of freedom, as is promised by their scattered dwellings, that are distant from this head town, four, five, and six leagues away. My travel to their quarters has been of little use, even with the help of the lord magistrate, on roads more fit for beasts than for rational beings due to the current rainy season. I have not experienced this with my poor Indians, who obediently and promptly have come forth to confess and take communion. . . .

Each day there are new families, and I do not think I will be able to complete the census over the course of this year. This is not just because of the outsiders, who come here because they can find absolute liberty here more than in any other place, but because of the same Creoles in the church throughout the year. After certifying the attached census, I have found out about two married [people] and three widows, with their respective families. These are now noted in the original [census], which I keep bound and lined to govern this parish, and will use to verify all those I uncover by means of church banns and specific investigations. . . .

Nicolás B_____ [illegible] is in this district and the justice asks for him to be delivered alive or dead. I have sent a message to a trustworthy person who lives next to him, telling [Nicolás] to come when and however he would like to be confessed. I have given him signals for how to call me, if at night, but have received no response. Moreover, he lives permanently with his concubine, which I bring to Your Most Illustrious Grace's attention.

There are many who are listed as not confessed in the attached letter, who have now gone to confession, but they have not presented their certificate. There are others who do not know the doctrine. There are very few of those, but they are the most rebellious and live in a state of cohabitation. They have been used to not going to confession for two, three, or more years, as we are experiencing every day. With respect to the children, their parents answer that at the age of twelve or thirteen they are too young to go to confession, but I make them come to confess from age ten on up.

This is the news I have to share with Your Most Illustrious Grace, for your administration and the fulfillment of my obligations. I refer to the certifications I have been given and to whatever precepts Your Most Illustrious Grace sees well to order and impose. In the meantime, I ask the Almighty to grant you prosperous life. Huazolotitlán, July 23, 1787. . . . I kiss the hands of Your Most Illustrious Lordship,

Your most humble servant and captain, Francisco González de Sarralde

[Spanish transcription]

Yllustrisimo Señor Doctor Don Josef Gregorio Alonso y Ortigosa . . .

Son muchos los Remordimientos, que oprimen mi corazon, viendome precisado a dar cuenta de la pesada obligacion que tengo sobre mi, y no poderlo verificar, no como debo, pero ni aun como pudiera hacerla, à Causa de lo mal enseñados y consentidos que estan estos Mulatos, apoderados de la libertad, que prometen sus habitaciones dispersas, y distantes de esta Cabecera, como lo son quatro, cinco, y seis leguas, sin haverme ^{bastado} el bajar a sus Rancherias, con todo el Auxilio del Señor Alcalde mayor, por Caminos mas propios de Bestias que de Racionales en la presente Estacion de Aguas; lo que no he experimentado con mis Pobres Yndios, que obedientes, y prontos han concurrido, tanto a Confesar y Comulgar . . .

Cada dia ban saliendo nuebas familias, y Creo, no se podra cerrar el Padron en el discurso de este año, no solo por los forasteros, que Cada dia se introducen, por hallar aqui, mas que en ninguna otra parte, quanto puede apetecer una absoluta libertad, sino tambien por los mismos criyollos [sic] en la Yglesia, en todo el año: Despues de certificado el adjunto Padron, he averiguado dos Casados, y tres viudas, Con sus respectibas familias, los que quedan anotados en el Orijinal, que reservo encuadernado, y forrado p[ara] Gobierno de este Curato, lo mismo que verificar quantos vaya descubriendo con continuas amonestaciones, y diligencias particulares. . . .

Se halla en este distrito Nicolas B_____, pedido por la Justicia vivo, ó muerto, a quien he mandado recao [sic] con persona de satisfaccion que vive junto à el, que venga quando, y como quiera a confesarse, dandole señas por donde me debera llamar, si fuere de noche, y no me ha respondido, y a mas vive con su concubina continuamente lo que pongo en noticia de Vuestra Señoria Yllustrisima.

De los que ban por no confesados en el adjunto papel hay muchos, que ya lo han hecho, pero no han presentado sus cedulas hay otros que no saben la doctrina, pero son mui pocos, pero mas son los rebeldes, y amancebados, acostumbrados à no confesarsen [sic] en dos, tres, y mas años, como cada dia lo estamos experimentandos: por lo que toca a los Niños, responden Comunmente Sus Padres, que de doze, y trece años son chiquititos para confesarsen, pero io les obligo à venir de diez para arriba.

Es quanto tengo que poner en noticia de Vuestra Señoría Yllustrisima, para su Govierno y Cumplimiento de mi obligazion y Remitiendome a la Certificacion que llebo dada, y preceptos que Vuestra Señoria Yllustrisima se sirva mandar, imponerme; pido en el interim al todo Poderoso, prospere su vida felis años Huasolotitlan y Julio 23 de 1787 años. . . . Beso las manos a Vuestra Señoría Yllustrisima

        Su mas Humilde Servidor y Cappitan, Francisco Gonzalez de Sarralde

CHAPTER 7

Freedom Papers

This chapter features documents from 1581 to 1780 that detail how enslaved people formally acquired their freedom. Whereas members of maroon communities could lead autonomous lives without such documentation, free and formerly enslaved people led lives entangled with paperwork. For those whose ancestors or parents had been enslaved, acquiring documents that proved their freedom was an extraordinarily expensive, but necessary. This was all the more true for individuals who actively sought to purchase their own manumission document (*carta de libertad*) or who could demonstrate their freedom through a final will or royal decree. In this regard, the 1581 decree in favor of Benito represents a rare case of the Spanish monarch ordering the freedom of an enslaved individual.

In colonial Mexico, it was far more common for a group of friends and relatives to pool resources in order to purchase a manumission letter from a slaveholder. Often, the representative of this effort was the mother or father of an enslaved child, who also represented the will of a larger (if often unnamed) community. Because slavery was transmitted by the maternal line, it became especially important for enslaved communities to secure the freedom of young girls. Freeing enslaved boys was also of paramount importance, but it did not have the same urgency as guaranteeing the freedom of enslaved girls. The 1621 manumission of baby Constansa, although costly, ensured that she would never in her life give birth to enslaved children. Other cases featured in this chapter—such as María receiving her freedom papers in 1650—reveal the consequences of not being able to liberate enslaved children from a young age.

In other cases, free individuals had to state and restate their free status because their liberty was constantly challenged by local officials and corrupt patrons. The four Huexotzingo men who presented their 1641 complaint evidently had a very different everyday experience from Clara de la Cruz, a free woman of Asian and Indigenous descent. The latter case is especially telling in that even as the daughter of a Native woman, de la Cruz felt the need to formalize her status as a free person. Nonetheless, their cases are linked by the everyday treatment that Indigenous people and their descendants received (or expected to receive) even decades after the New Laws of 1542. Indeed, these are sobering reminders of how theoretically free people had to continuously resist the demands of a society heavily invested in slavery.

Most of the documents in this chapter also reveal the constant negotiation that was required in everyday interactions between people in bondage and their enslavers *after* writing a letter of manumission. The "promise" of an eventual freedom features prominently in these documents. Just as evident are the delaying tactics of enslavers who promised to liberate an individual or family at a future moment. The 1696 and 1714 cases speak to that elusive freedom, which owners conditioned with the "after my days" formula. Countless slaves perished waiting for the fulfillment of such conditional manumissions. Alternatively, slaveholders often retained their enslaved workers during the entirety of their productive lives, before freeing them once the latter could no longer sustain themselves. Perhaps to reduce the likelihood of such a scenario, in 1780 María Antonia Mariscal actively sought a different owner for her daughter in a process known as *pedir papel*, literally "asking for paper." Collectively, all the documents included here speak to the costly and lengthy process of securing freedom papers.

Document 80: 1581—A royal decree for the freedom of Benito[1]

To the Count of Coruña, our relative, viceroy, governor, and captain general of the New Spain, and in your absence, to the person or persons in charge of the government of that land. Benito, Creole, has given us an account of how he is our slave and has been serving us in the ongoing construction of the port and island of San Juan de Ulúa in that land. Aware that he has served us ~~to order freedom be given to him~~ as he is thirty-six years old, is married to a free woman, and is usually sick, he begs us to order that freedom be given to him in exchange for another and better slave so that [the latter] may serve us in his place if this were our inclination. In regards to this matter and according to those in our council of the Indies, we consider it good and, therefore, we order that you see to the aforementioned [request] and procure it, as we have indicated. Done in Elvas on February 3, 1581. I, the King . . .

[annotation in the left-hand margin, "To the viceroy of New Spain, that he should look into and see to it that Benito, Creole slave of His Majesty, of those who work in the construction of San Juan de Ulúa, be given freedom in exchange for another slave, given that he is sick and married to a free woman."]

---

1. Archivo General de Indias, México, 1091, L.9, ff. 245v–246r. http://pares.mcu.es/ParesBusquedas20/catalogo/show/12696105?nm

[Spanish transcription]

Conde de Coruña pariente nuestro virrey governador y cappitan general de la Nueva España y en vuestra ausençia a la Persona o personas a cuyo cargo fuere el gobierno de essa tierra por parte de Benito criollo nos a sido fecha Relaçion que es nuestro esclavo y como tal nos esta sirviendo en la obra que se haze en puerto e ysla de San Juan deluba [sic, San Juan de Ulúa] de essa tierra y si nos ha suplicado atento a lo que nos havia servido de mandar le dar livertad y que es de hedad de treynta y seis años y se havia casado con muger Libre y andava de ordinario enfermo fuesemos servido de mandarle de livertad dando otro tal esclavo y mejor que el Para que en su lugar nos sirva de como la nuestra merced fuese e visto por los del nuestro consejo de las Indias acatando lo suso dicho, lo havemos tenido Por Bien y asi os mandamos que Beais lo susodicho y lo Procurais que nos os lo Remitimos fecha en Elvas a tres de hebrero de mill y quinientos y ochenta y un años yo el Rey . . .

[nota al margen izquierdo, "Al virrey de la nueva españa que bea y probea lo que pide Benito criollo esclavo de Vuestra Magestad de los que travajan en la obra de San Juan de Lua [sic] sobre que se le de livertad dando otro esclavo atento a que se a casado con muger libre y anda enfermo"]

Document 81: 1621—Conditional manumission for baby Constansa[2]

May those who see this letter know that I, Doña Isabel Pacheco de Villapadierna, widow, and *vecina* of this city [Puebla] of the Angels in New Spain, grant this letter. I say that I hold Constansa, a mulatta girl who must be eight months old, more or less, as a captive slave. [She is] the daughter of Inés Pacheco, a Black woman, my slave, who has served me well and loyally, as I have received good deeds from her the entire time that she has been in my power. Because the said girl Constansa was born in my house and because her father, Juan de Aya, native of the Philippine Islands, a hosier by trade and *vecino* of this city, has given me one hundred common gold pesos in silver which I have received . . . I state that I free and release the said mulatta girl Constansa from the subjection and captivity into which she was born and in which she has lived until now. I empower her so that as such a free person she may appear in court, make her testament, send her goods to whomever she pleases, and so that she may do everything else that a free person could and should do. I am committed that now and at all times this will be true according to the said [letter of] freedom. No

---

2. Tulane University, Latin American Library, Puebla Notarial Collection, Box 4, Folder 21, no folio.

one will impose an obstacle or impediment on her and if anyone should, I will take it upon myself to defend and follow said cause. She is to be left in quiet and pacific possession of said liberty and for that purpose I commit my person and my present and future goods. . . . I renounce the laws in my favor and the general law. Done in this city of the Angels on October 29, 1621. The grantor that I, the scribe, attest to know, signed it. Witnesses, Sancho de Yarza, Francisco Ruíz el Viejo, Matías de los Ríos, *vecinos* who were present. And then the said grantor said that she awards this writ of freedom with the condition and clause that the said mulatta Constansa may not leave this kingdom, but must remain and live in it for the rest of her days . . . and with this clause and charge, she awards this [letter of] freedom and signs it.

Doña Isabel Pacheco

[Spanish transcription]

Sepan cuantos esta carta vieren como yo Doña Ysabel Pacheco de Villapadierna viuda vezina desta ciudad de [Puebla de] los angeles de la nueva españa otorgo por esta carta y digo que por quanto yo tengo por mi esclava cautiva a Constansa niña mulata que sera de hedad de ocho meses poco mas o menos Hija de Ynes Pacheco negra mi esclava la qual en todo el tiempo que a estado en mi poder me a servido bien y ffielmente y e rresivido della buenas obras dignas de rrenumerasion y ansi por esto como por que la dicha Constansa niña nasio en mi cassa y por que Juan de Aya su padre natural de las Yslas Filipinas oficial de calsetero vezino desta dicha civdad me a dado cien pesos de oro comun en rreales de plata de que me doy por entregada . . . otorgo [que] ahorro [y] liberto a la dicha Constansa niña mulata de la sujesion y cautiberio en que nasio y a estado Hasta hoy y le doy poder para que como tal persona libre pueda pareser en juicio y hazer su testamento mandando sus vienes a quien le paresiere y hazer e haga todo lo demas que como tal persona libre puede y debe hazer y me obligo de que ahora y en todo tiempo le sera cierta y segun a la dicha libertad y a ella no le sera puesto embargo ni ynpedimiento por ninguna persona y si se le pusiere tomare a mi cargo la defensa y seguire la dicha causa. Han de le dexar en quieta y pasifica possession la dicha libertad y para ello obligo my persona y bienes avidos y por aver . . . renuncio las demas leyes de mi favor y la general del derecho que es fha en esta dicha ciudad los angeles en veinte y nueve dias del mes de octubre de mill y seis cientos y veinte y un años y la ottorgante que yo el scruiano doy fee que lo firmo siendo testigos Sancho de Yarça y Francisco Ruiz el Viejo y Matias de los Rios, vecinos y pressentes y luego la dicha ottorgante dixo que esta escriptura de libertad ottorga con calidad y condicion que la dicha Constansa mulata no salga fuera de este reyno sino que antes ha de esttar y vivir en el todos los dias de su vida . . . y debaxo desta condicion y obligacion le da y otorga la dicha libertad y lo firmo

Doña Isabel Pacheco

Document 82: 1625—Cathedral council manumits Juana de la Cruz's children[3]

In the name of God Almighty, amen. May all who see this letter know that we, the dean and council of the vacant seat of the holy cathedral church of Tlaxcala . . . are gathered and congregated in the room and site of our council [meetings] as patrons and administrators of the Hospital of the Immaculate Conception of Our Lady, under the spiritual protection of San Juan de Letrán of this city [Puebla] of the Angels. We say that the hospital held as its slave one Juana de la Cruz, a mulatta woman, currently free, who had Ana de la Cruz, who still lives, and Francisco, who is deceased, as her natural children. With the approval and permission of the lord bishop Don Diego Romano, may he be in glory, the said Juana de la Cruz gave and paid three hundred common gold pesos to the hospital's administrator at the time for her children's freedom. This charge was recorded in the hospital account book that Juan Pérez de la Fuente, the current administrator and supervisor of the hospital, showed [us]. A part of this entry was copied for her petition, suggesting and asking in due form for the liberty of her said daughter as appears as follows.

I, Juana de la Cruz, free mulatta, am the mother of Ana de la Cruz. In the best manner and form allowed by law, I come before Your Grace and say that when I was a slave of the Hospital of Our Lady in this city, I gave birth to the said Ana de la Cruz and to Francisco, who is already dead. I took them out of the servitude and slavery into which they had been born, giving, as I effectively gave and paid, three hundred pesos in reales cash, with the approval and permission of the lord bishop Don Diego Romano, may he be in glory. The administrator of the hospital at the time received [this sum] and entered it in the hospital account books. And so that Your Grace might verify the truth of what is reported, it is in the best interest of Ana de la Cruz, my daughter, that the said Juan Pérez de la Fuente exhibit before the current secretary the book or books where this entry might be found, on account of the said three hundred pesos that I paid for the freedom of my said children. So that having been seen, a letter of freedom be given in due form to my said daughter, therefore,

I ask and beg Your Grace to decree and order that in doing so, Your Grace will render justice ordering that the said freedom letter be prepared, so that at all times it may be evident that my daughter is free and not subject to slavery or servitude, and for this matter and what is necessary, etcetera. . . .

In accordance with what is requested by the said Juana de la Cruz, and executing and complying with what is requested by the said is contained in the said entry, in the best form and manner according to the law, we, as patrons of the said hospital, state that we free the said Ana de la Cruz, mulatta, daughter of the said Juana de la Cruz, from the subjection and captivity into which she was born on account

---

3. Archivo General de Notarías del Estado de Puebla, Notaría 3, e Diego Corona, Box 50, ff. 1698r–1700v.

of the said three hundred pesos she gave and paid for both her children . . . done in the city [Puebla] of the Angels, October 24, 1625. I, the scribe, attest that I know the grantors, who signed. Witnesses, Antonio de Otamendi, Ambrosio Gutiérrez, and José de Silva, *vecinos* of this city. Attested, requested by the said woman.

Doctor Don Juan de Vega	Doctor Don Luis de Monzón
Doctor Gaspar Moreno	Doctor Herencia
Doctor Don Alonso de Salazar Barona	
Licenciado Don Francisco de la Torre y Escobar	
Doctor Pedro Manrique de Lara	Licenciado Don Agustín de Sedaño
Don Luis de Góngora	Juan de Ocampo
Doctor León Castillo	Diego Bravo, prebendary
Doctor Juan Nieto de Ávalos	Doctor Francisco del Río
	Doctor Don Juan del Castillo Cabeza

Before me, Diego Corona Vásquez, public scribe

[Spanish transcription]

En el nombre De dios todo poderoso amen sepan quantos esta carta vieren como nos el dean y cabildo sede vacante de la santa yglesia catedral de Tlaxcala . . . estando Juntos y congregados en la sala y Lugar diputado de nuestro cabildo como patronos y administradores del ospital de la Limpia consepçion De nuestra señora adbocaçion de San Juan de Letran de esta ciudad de los angeles dezimos que teniendo por su esclaba el dicho ospital a Juana De la cruz mulata que al presente es Libre tubo por sus Hijos naturales a ana de la cruz que oy vive y a ffrancisco ques ya difunto y la dicha Juana de la Cruz que conbeneplasito y permiçion del señor obispo don diego rromano que se en gloria dio y pago por la Libertad de los dichos sus Hijos al mayordomo que entonses Hera del dicho ospital trezientos pesos de oro comun en rreales de que se le Hiso cargo en el libro de sus quentas que exzibio Juan Perez de la ffuente mayordomo y administrador que al pressente es del dicho ospital cuya partida se saco De su pedimyento ynsinuando y pidiendo en forma La liberttad de la dicha su Hija como de ella parese que su tenor es como se sigue.

Joana de la Cruz mulata libre como madre que soy de ana de la cruz en la mexor bia y forma que de derecho Lugar aya paresco ante vuestra señoria y digo que es ansi que siendo yo esclava del ospital De nuestra señora De esta ciudad pari a la dicha ana de la cruz y a ffrancisco ques ya muerto a los quales saque de la servidunbre y esclabitud en que naçieron Dando como en efecto di y pague por su Libertad al dicho ospital con beneplaçito y permiçion del Señor obispo Don diego rromano que sea en gloria trezientos pesos en Reales de contado y en nombre del dicho ospital Los rrecibio el mayordomo que entonses Hera y de ellos se Hiso cargo en los Libros de su administraçion del dicho ospital y para que a vuestra señoria conste de la berdad de su rreferida conbiene al derecho de la dicha ana de la Cruz mi Hija que el dicho Juan Perez de la Fuente exziba [sic] ante el pressente secretario el Libro o Libros Donde esta asentada la partida de los dichos trezientos Pesos que pague por rrason de la libertad de los dichos mis Hijos para que bista se de carta de libertad en forma a la dicha mi Hija atento a lo qual

a vuestra señoria pido y suplico ansi Lo probea y mande que en Hazerlo ansi vuestra señoria administre Justicia mandando Hazer la dicha carta de libertad para que en todo tiempo conste que la dicha mi Hija es Libre y no sujeta desclabitud y serbiumbre y para ello y en lo nessesario etcetera. . . .

y en conformidad de lo pedido Por La dicha Juana de la Cruz y poniendo en execucion y cumplimiento Lo ~~pedido por La dicha~~ contenido en el dicho auto por la pressente en la mexor bia y forma que aya lugar de derecho otorgamos por esta carta que como patronos del dicho ospital ahorramos a la dicha Ana de la cruz mulata Hija de la dicha Juana De la Cruz De la sugecion y captiberio con que naçio por rrason de los dichos trezientos pesos que dio y pago por anbos Los dichos sus Hijos . . . fecha en la civdad de los angeles a Veinte y quatro diass del mes de otubre de mill y seiscientos y veinte y cinco años E Yo el scrivano doy fe que conozco a los otorgantes que lo firmaron testigos Antonio de Otamendi, Ambrosio Gu.o [¿Gutiérrez?] y Joseph de Silva y del Portillo vecinos desta ciudad testado pedido por la dicha.

Doctor don Juan de Vega	Doctor Don Luis de Monzon
Doctor Gaspar Moreno	Doctor Herencia
Doctor don Alonso de Salazar Barona	
Licenciado don Francisco de la Torre y Escobar	
Doctor Pedro Manrique de Lara	Licenciado Don Augustin de Sedaño
Don Luis de Gongora	Juan de Ocampo
Doctor Leon Castillo	Racionero Diego Bravo
Doctor Juan Nieto de Avalos	Doctor Francisco del Rio
	Doctor don Juan del Castillo Caveça

Ante mi Diego Corona Vasquez scrivano Publico

Document 83: 1626—María Salomé sues for her freedom[4]

María Salomé, a Black woman, as is most convenient by the law . . . I appear before Your Grace and say that as follows in the message that I present with all the necessary solemnity, I came to an agreement with Diego García de Paredes, my deceased

---

4. Archivo Histórico Judicial de Puebla, Exp. 1341, ff. 1r–2r.

master. He would give me freedom and promised it to me for one hundred fifty pesos of common gold, which he asked for. In this agreement, during his lifetime I gave him ninety-three pesos and four tomines, for which he awarded me a letter of receipt. After his death, I gave Juan de Yarza Zubiate, his executor, other sums of money with which I arrived at the said one hundred and seventy pesos [sic]. As I wanted to demand my freedom and begin a suit for it, the said executor told me to give him another seventy pesos and he would award [my freedom] without a lawsuit or any contradiction. To avoid this, I have given and paid him [these sums] and he has also given me a letter of receipt, so that from my end I have satisfied all that I was asked to do. The said executor must now give and award my letter of freedom, releasing me of all servitude.

Therefore, I ask and beg Your Grace to accept the said message and summon the said executor to recognize the said receipts and declare if it is true that these were preceded by the agreements to which I refer. And that in these agreements, I was paying the said pesos. If he declares this [to be true] as it is, order him to award me the said freedom letter in due form. May Your Grace formalize this judicial decree by means of your authority. If he denies this, then may he be called to address the information that I offer. I ask for justice and expenses and I swear to God and on the cross that this is true and not of malice.

Carvajal Arteaga

[Spanish transcription]

Maria Salome negra Como mejor aya lugar de derecho . . . paresco ante Vuestra merced y digo que como consta deste Recado que presento Con la solemnidad necesaria yo me conserte con Diego Garcia de Paredes mi amo defunto = en que me diesse libertad y el me la prometio por çiento y cinquenta pessos de oro Comun que me pidio por ella y en esta conformidad le di en su vida noventa y tres pessos y quatro tomines de qual me otorgo carta de pago = y despues de muerto entregue a Juan de Yarça Çubiate su alvaçea testamentaria otras cantidades con que llegue a los dichos pesos a ciento y setenta [sic] y queriendo demandar mi libertad y poner pleito a ella me dijo el dicho alvaçea que le diesse otros setenta pesos mas y que me la daria sin pleito ni contradision y por evitarlo se los he dado y pagado y de ellos tambien me tiene dada carta de pago de suerte que de mi parte e satisfecho con todo lo que se me pidio. y el dicho alvacea de la suya esta obligado a darme y otorgarme carta de libertad en forma librandome de toda serbidumbre.

Por tanto, A Vuestra merced Pido y supplico aya por pressentado el dicho Recado y mande parescer ante si al dicho alvaçea y que Reconosca las dichas cartas de pago y declare si es Verdad Como lo es que preçedieron los consiertos que Refiero en este pedimiento y en essa conformidad le fui pagando los dichos pesos y si declarare le mande que luego me otorgue y de la dicha carta de libertad en forma interponiendo vuestra merced en ella su authoridad y decreto Judiçial y si negare se çite para informasion que ofresco y pido Justicia y Costas y Juro a dios y a la Cruz ser sierto y no de malicia.

Carvajal Arteaga

Document 84: 1630—Temporary freedom for Ana de la Cruz and her children[5]

In the name of God, amen. May all who see this letter know that I, Juan Tomás, *vecino* of this city of Cholula, say that I have as my slaves Ana de la Cruz, a mulatta woman, twenty-five years old, whom I received and bought from Diego Ruíz, *vecino* of this said city, and Juan and Nicolás, mulattos, her sons, this one four years old and that one two years old. I am about to travel to the kingdoms of Castile and I have goodwill for the said mulatta and her sons for having served me well. In consideration of this and during the time of my absence and no other time, I free and release the said Ana de la Cruz and her two named sons from the subjection and captivity in which they have been, so that from this day forward they may be and appear in court, make deals and contracts, and dispose of their goods by testament or in another manner as free people not subject to captivity, with the condition that every time that I return to this kingdom [of New Spain], the said mulatta and her children are to subject themselves to my service and be slaves as they currently are. I will be able to dispose of them as their master and owner, so that their use of liberty will be and shall be entered only for the time that I may be absent and no more . . . but if I should not return to [New Spain], then this [letter of] liberty is to be considered perfect and will be free and permanent and should be kept and followed in all time without contradiction. And they should use it in virtue of this title and in compliance, I commit my person, goods, rights, and power of attorney to His Majesty's justices so that they may compel me, as if this were a definitive sentence, passed in a judged matter. I renounce the laws in my favor and the general [law]. Done in the city [Puebla] of the Angels on January 17, 1630. I, the scribe, attest that I know the grantor, who signed. Witnesses, Juan Guerra, Juan de Bique, Pedro Leonardo, *vecinos* of this city.

Juan Tomás   Before me, Alonso Corona, public scribe

---

5. Archivo General de Notarías del Estado de Puebla, Notaría 4, Alonso Corona, 1630 Enero, Box 137, no folio.

[Spanish transcription]

En El nonbre De dios amen sepan quantos esta Carta vieren Como yo Joan Tomas vezino de la ciudad de Cholula digo que tengo por mis esclavos a Ana de la Cruz mulata de Hedad de veinte y cinco años que ube y compre de Diego Ruiz vezino de la dicha civdad y Joan y Nicolas mulatos Sus hijos Este de quatro años y aquel de dos años y estoy de partida para los Reynos de Castilla y tengo Buena boluntad a la dicha mulata y Sus hijos por aberme Servido vien En cuya consideraçion y durante el tiempo de mi aussencia y no mas ni de otra Suerte otorgo que Ahorro y liverto a la dicha Ana de La Cruz y sus dos Hijos nonbrados de la Sujecion y Cautiverio en que an estado para que de oy en adelante puedan estar y parecer en Juicio Hacer tratos y haser contratos y disponer de sus vienes por testamento y En otra Manera como personas libres no Sugetas a esclavitud Con Calidad que cada y quando que buelba a este rreyno [de Nueva España] La dicha mulata y sus Hijos an de rreducirse a mi Servizio y Ser mis esclavos como agora lo son y E de poder disponer dellos como amo y Dueño suyo de Suerte que El vso de la dicha livertad a de ser y se entre de por el tiempo que yo estubiere aussente y nomas . . . pero si no biniere a el a de quedar Esta livertad perfeta y a de ser libre y permanente Guardarse y Cumplirse en todo tiempo sin contradicion y an de ussar della En birtud deste Titulo y a cumplimiento obligo mi persona bienes y derechos y poder a las Justicias de su magestad para que en ello me apremien como por Sentencia Difinitiva pasada en cosa Juzgada rrenuncio leyes de mi favor y La general fecha en la ciudad de los Angeles a diez y siete dias del mes de Henero de mill y seyscientos y treynta años E yo el scrivano doy fee conozco al otorgante que lo firmo testigos Juan Guerra, Juan de Bique, Pedro Leonardo vezinos de Esta ciudad =

Juan thomas   Ante mi Alonso Corona Scrivano publico

Document 85: 1641—Huexotzingo natives demand not to be treated as slaves[6]

Juan Andrés, José Gabriel, Juan Lucas, and Juan Bernal, Indian men and *vecinos* of this province of Huexotzingo, we come forth before Your Grace and declare that we and our wives were enjoying our freedom when Juan Guerrero Pedraza, farmer in the Tlaxcala jurisdiction, hired us to serve on his hacienda as we did. Yet for no reason, the said Juan Guerrero Pedraza, his sons, overseers, and servants beat us and mistreated us verbally and physically with no fear of God Our Lord and thinking nothing of royal

---

6. Bibliothèque nationale de France, Manuscrits, Espagnol 460, ff. 114r–115r.

justice. They made us work against our will day and night, locking us in on feast days to this effect. They did not want to pay us for our work, nor would they settle our account, so that we would serve them perpetually as if we were their slaves.

Although we sought the royal justice to make us free, this never took place because the said Juan Guerrero is a powerful person and influential with the justices of the Tlaxcala jurisdiction. Seeing that we were so oppressed about a year ago, we left his [Guerrero's] hacienda and came to this jurisdiction [of Huexotzingo], where we have been working on the hacienda of Captain Cristóbal Martínez de Zerdio. Here we have found shelter, protection, good treatment, and pay for our work. We have been well-fed, clothed, and our royal tributes have been paid for us. We had enjoyed our own will until a few days ago, when the said Juan Guerrero, his sons, and servants, following their evil attempt, have disturbed us. They have sought to return us to their hacienda by force and violence as if we were their slaves and have sent Indians from their hacienda to trick us and take us [back] to his service. Seeing so many wrongs, we appeal to the most excellent lord marques of Villena, duke of Escalona, viceroy of this New Spain, and we complain of the mentioned parties so that His Excellence might issue orders of protection so that the justices protect our freedom and notify the said Juan Guerrero, his sons, overseers, and servants that they may not make us serve them against our will, whether we owe them money or not. . . .

[It has come to] our attention that in seeking to avenge the hate and passion that he has for us, the said Juan Guerrero Pedraza has presented a lawsuit against us with a sinister account before the governor of the city of Tlaxcala. He has claimed that we owe him money and that we fled his service because an arrest warrant was issued against us and presented before Your Grace. And it was agreed that [the warrant] could not be fulfilled because the decrees prevent this from taking place. . . .

Having presented the said decrees in obedience and compliance, we ask and beg Your Grace that Juan Guerrero, his sons, and overseers be notified that they must comply with them and allow us to freely demand our justice before His Excellency. . . . and we swear to God and on the cross that this writ is certain and true and not out of malice. We do not sign as we do not know how to.

[Spanish transcription]

Joan Andres, y Joseph Gabriel, y Juan Lucas, y Juan Bernal, yndios, Vezinos desta provinzia de Guexotzingo como mejor aya lugar En derecho Parescemos ante Vuestra merced y desimos que estando nosotros y nuestras mugeres gosando de nuestra libertad, Juan Guerrero Pedraza labrador en [la] Jurisdizion de Tlaxcala nos alquilo Para que sirvieramos En su haçienda Como lo hisimos Y sin ocazion alguna el dicho Juan Guerrero Pedraza y sus hijos mayordomos y Criados Con poco temor de dios nuestro señor y menosprezio de la rreal Justiçia nos aporreavan y maltratavan, de obra y de palabra hasiendonos trabajar Contra nuestra boluntad de dia y de noche, Y dias de fiesta ençerrandonos Para Este efecto sin querernos Pagar nuestro trabajo ni ajustar nuestra quenta Para que perpetuamente les sirvieramos Como si fueramos sus sclavos

Y aunque procuramos que la Real Justiçia nos pusiese en nuestra libertad nunca tuvo efecto Por ser el dicho Juan Guerrero persona Poderosa y balida Con las Justiçias de la dicha Jurisdizion de Tlaxcala y biendonos tan oprimidos abra tiempo de Vn año Que nos Salimos de su hacienda y nos benimos a esta Jurisdizion donde Emos estado trabajando en haçienda del Capitan Cristobal Martinez de Zerdio donde hallamos abrigo anparo y buen tratamiento y Paga de nuestro trabajo dandonos muy bien de Comer y bestir y Pagando Por nosotros Los Reales tributos y gosando de nuestra boluntad hasta que de poco dias a esta parte El dicho Juan Guerrero, hijos y Criados, En prosecusion de su mal yntento nos an ynquietado Procurando bolbernos a su haçienda con fuerza y biolenzia como si fueramos Sus sclavos, Y echandonos indios de su haçienda para que nos engañasen y llebasen a Su servizio y biendo tantos agravios Ocurrimos ante el Excelentísimo Señor marqués De Villena, duque de escalona, Virrey desta nueba españa y nos quejamos de los susodichos a que fue servido su Excelencia de librarnos mandamientos de anparo Para que las Justiçias nos anparasen nuestra Libertad y que se notificasen al dicho Juan Guerrero, Sus hijos mayordomos y Criados. No se sirvan de nosotros contra nuestra boluntad quier le devamos dinero o no . . .

[Ha venido] a nuestra notiçia que el dicho Juan Guerrero Pedrasa Procurando bengar El odio y Pasion que nos tiene Con siniestra Relazion Se querello de nosotros ante el gobernador de la ciudad de Tlaxcala dando a Entender que le debemos dineros y que nos huimos de Su servizio Porque se libro Carta de Justicia Para prendernos la qual se presento ante Vuestra merced y fue servido de declarar no aver lugar El Cumplimiento Por la prebenzion de dichos decretos . . .

A Vuestra Merced Pedimos y suplicamos que aviendo Por presentados los dichos decretos en su obedesimiento y Cumplimyento mande se notifique a dicho Juan Guerrero hijos y mayordomos, Pudiendo ser avidos en esta Provinzia Para que por lo que les toca los Cunplan Y nos dejen con libertad Pedir nuestra Justiçia ante Su excelencia . . . y Juramos a dios y a la cruz Este escrito ser çierto y verdadero y no de maliçia Y no firmamos Por no Saver.

Document 86: 1650—María receives her freedom papers[7]

My brother, the bachiller Juan de Olmedo, may he be in glory, left me a little mulatta named María with the condition that she would be a slave for my use for the rest of

---

7. Archivo General de Notarías del Estado de Puebla, Notaría 3, Box 101, Melchor Fernández de la Fuente, Junio 1650, ff. 21r–22v.

the days of my life. She has been serving me for twenty-eight years and I find myself aged and in poor health. Her mother wants to settle her [into a marriage or convent] and has offered to give me eighty pesos so that she may take [her daughter]. So that I may renounce my rights [to her] and the young woman be protected after my days, I ask Your Grace to grant me permission for what has been said and so that I may alleviate my many needs with the eighty pesos. I have been in the infirmary [of the convent] for three years suffering many [ills]. The bearer [of this letter] is the mother of the little mulatta. She carries with her a writ that certifies the truth of what I have said: I ask Your Grace to grant me permission to award her freedom. She is from the convent of Our Lady of the Immaculate Conception. [Puebla] of the Angels, June 17, 1650.

> Your subject, I kiss Your Hands, Jerónima de los Angeles, president
> Leonor de la Cruz

Given that the licenciado Juan de Olmedo awarded this writ in this city before Alonso Corona, public scribe, on December 17, 1619, it is certified that by this document he awarded freedom to María, a mulatta, who was then two years old, with the charge and condition that she would serve Mother Leonor de la Cruz, the sister of said licenciado Juan de Olmedo, for the rest of the days of [the nun's] life. The said María, mulatta, has served her for more than thirty-one years, and the said Mother Leonor de la Cruz finds herself very old and in continual sickness. And because Mariana de la Cruz, a free Black woman and the mother of the said mulatta María, wants to settle her [into a marriage or convent] and aid the needs of Mother Leonor de la Cruz, she offers eighty pesos to aid [the nun] and serve her for the time that she may. I give permission to the said Mother Leonor de la Cruz to deliver the said mulatta María to the free Black woman Mariana de la Cruz, so that she may be free. [I give permission] that [the nun] may receive eighty pesos in reales, so that she may spend them on her clothing and needs. I award her permission and faculty for all this. Ángeles, June 18, 1650.

> Doctor Don Alonso Salazar Varona

[Spanish transcription]

A mi me dejo mi hermano el licenciado Juan de Olmedo que en gloria sea una mulatilla llamada Maria con condision de que fuese esclaba a mi uso por los dias de mi vida a beynte y ocho años que me sirbe y yo me hallo con edad y poca salud quiere su madre ponerla en estado y por que se la dege llebar me da ochenta pesos en que hago la premuta [sic] de mi derecho y mas quedara anparada La mosa despues de mis dias; Vuestra merced sea servido de conçederme lisensia para lo dicho y para que con los ochenta pesos socora mis nesesidades que son muchas por que a tres años que estoy en la enfermeria padesiendo muchas - la portadora que es madre de la mulatilla lleba la escritura por donde consta la berdad de lo que digo: y deme Vuestra merced lisensia para otorgarle libertad. es de La linpia conçepcion de nuestra señora Angeles y Junio dies y siete de 1650 años

> subdita de vuestra merced que su Mano Beso, Gerónima de los Angeles presidenta
> Leonor de la Crus

v. Atento a que el Licenciado Joan de Olmedo otorgo escritura en esta ciudad ante Alonso Corona escrivano Publico en diez y Siete dias del mes de diziembre de mill y seisçientos y diez y nueva años y consta por ella aver dado Livertad a maria mulata de edad entonces de dos años con cargo y calidad que estubiese a el usso de La madre Leonor de la Cruz hermana de dicho Licenciado Juan de Olmedo por los dias de su vida y por que a mas de treinta y un años que dicha maria mulata La sirve y allarse dicha madre Leonor de la cruz en mucha edad, y continua enfermedad, y que Mariana de la Cruz negra Libre Madre de dicha Maria mulata, quiere ponerla en estado y para socorrer Las neçesidades de La madre Leonor de la cruz Le da Luego ochenta pesos y por el tienpo que puede aver de servirla = Doy Liçençia para que dicha madre Leonor de la Cruz entregue a Mariana de la Cruz negra libre, La dicha Maria mulata con que llega el quedar Libre, y reçiva Los ochenta pesos en reales y los pueda gastar en su vestuario y neçeçidades que para todo le conçedo Liçençia y facultad. Angeles diez y ocho de Junio de mill y seisçientos sinquenta años.

> Doctor don Alonso de Salazar Varona

Document 87: 1650—Gabriel frees his wife and infant son[8]

In the name of God Almighty, amen. May all who see this letter know that I, the bachiller Antonio de Peralta Goni, clergyman priest, *vecino* of this city [Puebla] of the Angels, declare that I own Dominga, a Black woman from the land of Angola, forty years old, more or less, as a slave. I bought her from Gaspar de Laris and Luisa de Rojas, his wife, by a writ that they awarded in this city on March 28, the past year of 1642, before Juan Guerra, who was [one of the city's] public scribes. [I also own] her small son, a little Black boy, a year old, who was born in my house. And because she has served me punctually and loyally, and because other Black people, her relatives, and Gabriel, a Black slave of Esteban Alonso and the husband of the said Black woman Dominga, have promised to give me four hundred and sixty pesos

---

8. Archivo General de Notarías del Estado de Puebla, Notaría 4, Nicolás López Gallegos, Box 174, 1650 Julio, f. 484v.

of common gold in reales, I have decided to award her and her son freedom. Putting this into effect in the best manner and form by law, they have indeed satisfied the four hundred and sixty pesos in cash reales. I renounce the laws of the delivery and the proof and acceptance of the money and declare that I free and release the said Black woman Dominga and Lorenzo, her little Black son, from the subjection and captivity they are in, so that from this day forward they or their attorneys may be and present themselves in court, enter contracts and their testaments, dispose of their goods, and other things that a free person is allowed to do. I ask the present scribe to give them the copies they requested of this document . . . in the spirit of said freedom, which I promise to hold firm and will not revoke by testament or public writ, nor will I go against [this document], its tenor or form by any other contract. . . . Done in the city [Puebla] of the Angels on July 13, 1650. I, the scribe, attest that I know the grantor [of this document], who signed it. Witnesses, Nicolás Álvarez, Alonso de Soria, and Nicolas Amaro, *vecinos* of this city.

Antonio de Peralta Goni   before me, Nicolás López Gallegos, public scribe

[Spanish transcription]

En el nombre de dios todo poderoso amen sepan quantos esta carta vieren como io el lisensiado Antonio de Peralta Goni clerigo presvitero vecino de esta ciudad de los angeles digo que tengo por mi esclava a Dominga negra de tierra angola de edad de quarenta años poco mas o menos que huve y compre de Gaspar de Laris y Luisa de Rojas su muger por escritura que otorgaron en esta ciudad a Veinte y ocho de março de el año pasado de mill y seiscientos y quarenta y dos ante Juan Guerra scrivano publico que fue de ella y un ijuelo suio negrillo de edad de un año que nacio en mi casa y por haverme servido con puntualidad y fidelidad y porque otros negros sus parientes y Gabriel, negro esclavo de esteban alonso marido de la dicha Dominga negra me an prometido dar quatrocientos y cecenta pesos de oro comun en reales e determinado darle libertad y a el dicho su ijo [sic] y poniendola en efecto por la precente en aquella via y forma que mejor lugar tenga en derecho respecto que con efecto se me an satisfecho los dichos quatrocientos y secenta pesos en reales de contado de que me doy por entregado renuncio leies de la entrega y su prueva y acepcion de la pecunia otorgo que ahorro y liberto a los dichos Dominga negra y Lorenco negrillo su hijo de la sujecion y cautiverio en que estan para que de oy en adelante puedan por si o sus procuradores estar y pareser en juicio hazer tratos y sus testamentos y disponer de sus vienes y lo demas que a persona libre es permitido y pido a el precente escrivano les entregue los traslados que pidieron de esta escritura . . . en son de dicha libertad la qual prometo aver por firme y no revocarla por testamento scritura publica ni otro contracto ni ir contra su tenor y forma . . . fecha en la ciudad de los angeles a trece dias del mes de jullio de mill y seiscientos y sinquenta años e io el escrivano doi fe que conosco al otorgante que lo firmo testigos Nicolas Alvarez Alonso de Çoria y Nicolas Amaro, Vezinos desta ciudad

Antonio de Peralta Goni   ante mi, Nicolas Lopez Gallegos, scrivano publico

Document 88: 1668—Clara de la Cruz, free *china*, ratifies her liberty[9]

Clara de la Cruz, *china* and legitimate wife of Alonso Pérez Galván, Spaniard, absent in the Philippine Indies. I appear before Your Grace, as best fits my rights, and say that as I am about to make a trip outside of this city, and so that no justices in any way impede me from doing so, I ask Your Grace to receive [the following information]: that I am a free person, not subject to slavery, as I am the legitimate daughter of Antonio de la Cruz, a free *chino* man, and Magdalena Luisa, an Indian woman, his deceased wife. [I was] born and procreated during their marriage and I am likewise the legitimate wife of the said Alonso Pérez Galván. Said man is absent from this kingdom and [has been] in the Philippine Islands for more than sixteen years. Given this information, may this be enough to grant me permission, in the absence of my said husband, to appear in court, enter deals and contracts, sell and purchase goods, and the rest that I may find fitting.

I ask and beg Your Grace to order this information be received in this writ. . . .

By His Majesty, this petition was read as presented by the aforementioned woman. The magistrate ordered that the information given by the said Clara de la Cruz be received according to its tenor . . . and it was signed.

Nicolás de Bañuelos   Before me, Nicolás Álvarez, royal and public scribe

[Spanish transcription]

Clara de la Cruz china muger Legitima de Alonso Perez Galban español ausente en las yndias Philipinas. Parezco ante Vm como mejor de mi derecho combiene y Digo que por quanto estoy para hazer viage fuera de esta Ciudad Y para que en ninguna manera se me pueda poner ympedimento por ninguna Justiçias sea de servir vuestra merced mandar se re meciva ynformaçion de como soy Libre y no sugetta a esclavitud Por ser como soy hija Legitima de Antonio de la Cruz chino libre y de magdalena Luisa yndia su muger difuntta avida y procreada durante su matrimonio y asi mesmo de como soy mujer Legitima del dicho Alonso Perez Galvan y que el susodicho esta ausente de este reino y en las Yslas Philipinas mas tiempo ha de diez y seis años y

---

9. Archivo Histórico Judicial de Puebla, Exp. 2276/1749, ff. 1r–1v.

Dada en la parte que baste me conçeda lizencia mediante a la ausencia del dicho mi marido para estar y pareçer en Juicio hazer tratos y contratos vender y comprar vienes y lo demas que me pareçiere.

A Vuestra merced pido y suplico mande se me reçiva dicha informaçion al thenor de este scripto . . .

Por su magestad Se leyo esta petticion Que presento la contenida. El alcalde mando se le ressiva a la dicha clara de La crus La Ynformassion Que ofrese al tenor de Su escrito . . . y lo firmo =

Nicolas de Bañuelos   Ante my Nicolas Alvarez scrivano Real y publico

Document 89: 1696—Manumission promise for Catarina de San Juan[10]

In the name of God Our Almighty Lord, amen. May all who see this letter know that I, Doña Josefa Martínez de la Carrera, widow of José Rodriguez, [am] a *vecina* of this very noble and loyal city [Puebla] of the Angels in the Alto de San Francisco neighborhood. I say that I own Catarina de San Juan, a mulatta *cocha*, who is also called Catarina Rodriguez, as my slave. She is forty years old, more or less, and is the legitimate wife of Juan García, a *chino* man and pork butcher by trade. Because the said mulatta woman has accompanied me in my widowhood, was born in my parents' house, has served me with particular affection and care, has procreated four children while under my power, and for other causes and reasons worthy of gratitude, I have decided to award her freedom for the time and in the manner that will be declared. Putting this into effect in the best manner and form by law, I free and release the said Catarina Rodríguez, mulatta, my slave, so that after my days and from the day of my death she may be free and enjoy her liberty as if she had been born with it. From [that day forward] she may be and appear in court for herself or through her attorney, enter deals and contracts, trade and dispose of goods through testament or in the manner that she may find best. Therefore I renounce and set aside from now until that day all the rights, personal and royal deeds, dominion, and other [claims] that I have over said slave and I yield, renounce, and transfer them to her. With the explicit condition that she is to assist and serve me until I die, as she has done up to now, and should she fail in this requirement, this freedom [letter] will be declared null. . . .

I, the scribe, attest that this is done in the very noble and loyal city [Puebla] of the Angels on July 23, 1696. I, José de Meneses, scribe of the King Our Lord (may God

---

10. Archivo General de Notarías del Estado de Puebla, Notaría 3, Joseph de Meneses, 1696 Julio, no folio.

keep him) and a *vecino* of this said city, attest that I know this grantor, who awarded [this writ] and signed. Witnesses, Pedro Pérez del Castillo, Juan Muñoz de Alaras, Pedro Sánchez de Ortega, *vecinos* of this city who were present.

Josefa Martínez de la Carrera   before me, José de Meneses, His Majesty's scribe

[Spanish transcription]

En el nombre de Dios nuestro señor todo poderoso amen Sepan quantos esta carta vieren como Yo Doña Josepha Martinez de la Carrera viuda de Joseph Rodriguez vezina desta muy noble y muy leal Ciudad de los angeles al varrio Alto de San Francisco digo que tengo por mi esclava a Catarina de San Juan, mulata cocha que tambien se llama Catarina Rodriguez, y sera de hedad de quarenta años Poco mas o menos que es muger lexitima de Juan Garsia chino de ofisio tosinero y Porque dicha mulata me a acompañado en mi Biudes y haver nascido en la cassa de mis Padres y servidome con particular afecto y cuidado y haver Procreado en my poder quatro hijos y por otras causas y rasones dignas de agradesimiento tengo determinado el darle livertad Para el tiempo y en la forma que yra declarado y poniendolo en efecto Por la Presente en aquella via y forma que mejor lugar tenga en derecho, otorgo que aorro y liberto a la dicha Catarina Rodrigues mulata mi esclava para que la sussodicha despues de mis dias y desde el dia de mi fallesimiento sea libre y gose de dicha su liverttad como si huviesse nascido con ella y desde entonses pueda estar y pareser en juisio por si o por su procurador haser tratos y contratos granjear bienes y disponer de ellos por testamento o en la forma que le Paresiere para lo qual me desisto y aparto desde ahora para entonses de todos los derechos acsiones Reales y Perssonales de proprios señorio y otros que a dicha sclava tengo y se los sedo renunsio y transfiero para que la susodicha devajo de Condizion expresa de que me a de asistir y servir hasta que yo falleszca como hasta aqui lo a echo y faltando a esta requisito a de ser nula esta livertad que le hago . . .

Yo el esscribano doy fee que es fecha en la muy noble y muy leal ciudad de [Puebla] de los Angeles a veinte y tres dias del mes de Jullio de mill seizcientos y noventa y seis años e Yo Joseph de Meneses escrivano del Rey Nuestro Señor (que Dios guarde) vesino de esta dicha Ciudad doy fee conosco a la otorgante la qual hasi [sic] lo otorgo y firmo siendo testigos Pedro Perez del Castillo, Juan Muñoz de Alaras y Pedro Sanchez de Ortega vesinos de esta dicha Ciudad presentes

Josepha Martines de la Carera   ante my Joseph de Meneses escribano de su magestad

Document 90: 1714—Freedom for Micaela de la Cruz, of the Caravalí nation[11]

May all who see this letter know that I, Doña Rosa de Monforte Díaz, maiden, *vecina* of this city [Puebla] of the Angels, legitimate daughter of Luis Díaz and Antonia Nuñez, his deceased wife, confess myself to be more than thirty years old and am aware of my rights as I am beyond guardianship and others' managing of my affairs.

I say that I have and possess Micaela de la Cruz of the Caravalí nation, who is fifty years old, more or less, as a slave subject to servitude. I received her as part of my parents' estate and in payment of my paternal and maternal inheritance. During the time that she has been in my domain and during my father's life she has served me well, with much love, loyalty, and willingness, caring for me in my sicknesses as if she were my mother [with] acts worthy of repayment. Therefore, in the best manner and form by law, I free and release the said Micaela de la Cruz of all captivity, servitude, and subjection after the days [of my life] and not before, so that she may do as she might please, and decide what might be best. [She] may be and appear in court, make her testament and codicils, and do everything else that a free person can do, with the condition that during the time of my life she is to serve and assist me as she has done up to today. By this current letter, I desist and renounce all the rights and deeds that I have against her, and I promise and commit to following it firmly. . . . Done in the city [Puebla] of the Angels, February 10, 1714. The grantor, whom I the scribe attest that I know, signed. Witnesses, bachiller Don Joseph Pérez Aguayo, deacon clergyman; Miguel Gregorio de Lavanda, and José de Quevedo, *vecinos* of this said city.

Doña Rosa Monforte Díaz

I, Francisco de Castro, scribe for His Majesty Our Lord, may God keep him, and notary public in the Indies . . .

[Spanish transcription]

Sepan quantos esta carta vieren como yo Doña Rosa de Monforte Dias donzella Vezina desta Çiudad de [Puebla] de los Angeles hija lexitima de Luis Diaz y Antonia Nuñes [Antonia Nuñez] su muger difunctos, mayor que Confieso ser de mas de treinta años Savidora de mi derecho fuera de tutela y ajena administracion.

Digo que por quanto Yo tengo y poseo por mi esclava subjetta de Servidumbre a Michaela de la Cruz de naçion Caravali que sera de hedad de sinquenta años poco mas o menos y se me aplico por vienes de dichos mis padres en quenta y pago de mi lexitima paterna y materna, y durante el tiempo que a estado en mi poder y en vida del dicho mi padre me a servido vien con mucho amor lealtad y Volumptad

---

11. Archivo Municipal de Puebla, Documentos Varios, Tomo 4, ff. 103v–104r.

Cuidandome en mis enfermedades Como si fuera mi madre [con] obras dignas de remunerazion por tanto En aquella via y forma que mejor lugar tenga en derecho otorgo que ahorro y liverto de todo captiverio Servidumbre y subjesion a la dicha Michaela de la Cruz para que despues de mis dias y no antes, pueda hazer de si lo que quisiere y por vien tubiere y estar y parezer en Juiçios aser su testamento y Codisilios y todo lo demas que persona libre puede hazer con la Calidad de que durante el tiempo de mi vida me a de servir y hasistir [sic] como lo a echo hasta hoy. Y por esta presente Carta me desisto y aparto de todo el derecho y accion que contra la sussodicha tengo y prometo y me obligo de lo haver por firme . . . que es fecha en la Ciudad de los Angeles a dies dias del mes de febrero de mil Setesientos y Catorze años y la otorgante que Yo escrivano de su magestad doy fee Conosco lo firmo siendo testigos el Bachiller Don Joseph Perez Aguayo clerigo diacono Miguel Gregorio de Lavanda [de la Vanda o de la Banda] y Joseph de Quevedo vezinsos desta dicha Ciudad

doña Rosa Monforte Dias

Yo Francisco de Castro escrivano del Rey Nuestro Señor que Dios guarde y su Notario Publico de las yndias . . .

Document 91: 1780—María Antonia Mariscal finds an owner for her daughter[12]

Mexico, July 1, 1780.
To the Lord Prosecutor,

Most Excellent Sir,
María Antonia Mariscal, a free mulatta, *vecina* of the city of Puebla and resident in this one [Mexico City], legitimate mother of Petra Cecilia, also a mulatta. By this written petition in the best form by law, I say that when I was a slave of Doña Paula Migueles, *vecina* of the said city of Puebla, I had my said daughter, who was therefore born a slave of said lady.

Once I had received my freedom papers and my daughter being eleven years old, more or less, I asked my said mistress permission to search for a [new] master for my daughter. She gave me this paper with no set timeline, and while I was absent dealing with these affairs, she sold [my daughter] to Don Francisco Adorno, also a *vecino* of Puebla, for eighty pesos.

---

12. Archivo Histórico Judicial de Puebla, Exp. 4649, ff. 4r–4v.

I was unaware of this sale, as I had found someone who could buy my daughter. This was Don Juan Dionisio Mantilla, lieutenant of the town of Tilapa, [in the] jurisdiction of Izúcar. He sent my mistress one hundred pesos for the price of my daughter: [My mistress] answered that [my daughter] was already sold to the said Adorno.

A year elapsed during which time my daughter was under Adorno's power, because he would not let me communicate with or even see her. I resorted to the lord governor of Puebla with this complaint, and he ordered that I be allowed to see my daughter, which greatly offended her master. To avoid [further] disturbances, I asked for permission to search for a new owner, which was granted. But having found [a new potential owner] in Doña Nicolasa de Oropesa, also a *vecina* of Puebla, the said Adorno inhumanely and arbitrarily raised the price of my daughter to one hundred and ten pesos, which the said Doña Nicolasa paid for her.

With this in mind, I appeal to Your Excellence's reasoning to order that the said Adorno return the thirty extra pesos to Doña Nicolasa by which he raised my daughter's price, on a whim and without a preceding valuation, despite the fact that he had owned her for less than a year. Therefore, because it is not licit to impose slavery on servants and reduce their freedom, and because if my daughter remains sold for eighty pesos, it will be easier for her and for me to gather [this sum] for her ransom and liberty, or to seek another master, in case things do not go well with her current one. Thus, for both reasons I ask Your Excellency to defer to this my petition and pass along the case to the lord prosecutor, as is ordered in the document that I duly present on folio 2. Therefore, I beg Your Excellency to order this in this manner, as is just and what is necessary, etcetera.

Licenciado Francisco Guerra y Vega de Manzanares

[Spanish transcription]

Mexico 1° de Julio de 1780.
Al Señor Fiscal

Excelentísimo Señor

Maria Antonia Mariscal mulata libre vezina de la ciudad de la Puebla y residente en esta, Madre legitima de Petra Cecilia tambien Mulata; por el ocurso que mas haya lugar en Derecho Digo: Que siendo yo esclava de Doña Paula Migueles vezina de dicha ciudad de Puebla huve â la expresada mi hija, que, de consiguiente nació esclava de dicha Señora

Siendo ya mi hija de once años poco mas, ô menos; y haviendose me dado mi carta de libertad; pedí a la citada mi Ama Papel para buscar Amo para mi hija. Diómelo sin plazo alguno, y entre tanto hacia yo mi Diligencia, ausente yo, la vendió aquella a Don Franciscco Adorno vecino tambien de Puebla en ochenta pesos

Ignorante yo de dicha venta, encontré quien comprara á mi hija, que fué Don Juan Dionysio Mantilla Teniente del Pueblo de Tilapa, Jurisdiccion de Yzucar, quien haviendo embiado á mi Ama cien pesos por precio de mi hija; respondió aquella, que ya estaba vendida á dicho Adorno.

Haviendo corrido como un año, que estuvo mi hija en poder de Adorno, porque este no me dexaba comunicarla, ni aun verla, ocurrí al Señor Governador de Puebla con esta queja; y porque mandô, que me permitieran veer [sic] á mi hija, se indignó mucho Su Amo; y yo para evitar disturbios le pedí Papel; que me dio para buscar otro Dueño. Pero haviendo encontrado a doña Nicolasa de Oropesa tambien vezina de Puebla; subió inhumanamente y á su arbitrio el citado Adorno, el precio de mi hija hasta ciento, y diez pesos que dio por ella dicha Doña Nicolasa.

En esta atencion ocurro â la Justificacion de Vuestra Excelencia para que se sirva mandar, que el referido Adorno debuelba a Doña Nicolasa los treinta pesos mas, en que sin preceder valúo, y solo por su antojo, aumentó el precio de mi hija, aun no haviendola poseido mas que un año poco menos; asi porque no es licito gravar la esclavitud, y extrechar la libertad á los siervos; como porque quedando vendida mi hija en los ochenta pesos mas facil le será á ella, y â mi el juntarlos para su rescate, y libertad, ô el solicitar otro Amo, caso que no lo pase bien con la que tiene motivos ambos para que Vuestra Excelencia se sirva deferir á mi pedimiento, dando previamente vista al Señor Fiscal, como está mandado en el documento que presento debidamente en folio 2. Por tanto A Vuestra Excelencia Suplico: asi lo mande, que es Justicia y lo necesario etcetera

Licenciado Francisco Guerra y Vega de Manzanares

CHAPTER 8

Debt and Belonging

The documents in this chapter focus on how free and enslaved people dealt with patrons and creditors as well as with the relatives, friends, and allies who were willing to assist them financially and materially. Securing money, or rather debt, was a crucial facet of the lives of free and enslaved people in Mexico. This was especially true for the city of Puebla, whose archives are the source for most of the documents in this chapter. Borrowing funds from relatives, patrons, and potential employers could have positive generational consequences for those seeking freedom papers. Debt, however, could also saddle individuals with unpayable accounts or force entire families into collective repayment plans. Simón de Mesa's 1590 debt contract also speaks to the ways in which free people navigated debt and, at times, literally escaped their obligations. The 1605 case of Diego de Valencia and Magdalena reveals how free Afro-Indigenous families navigated the threat of debt collection and even imprisonment. In other cases, enslaved people often found themselves securing debts for their owners. The 1621 document included here reveals how a free woman of African descent used an enslaved African woman as collateral for a payment.

Debt was not all negative. As the colonial period advanced, more and more people of African, Asian, and Indigenous descent established their belonging to a particular town, village, or city by claiming others' debts. For instance, Gaspar Hernández, a free man from the Canary Islands, firmly rooted himself in Puebla through his work as a baker during the 1620s. His testament sheds light on a vast network of clients, but also on meaningful personal relationships. For other free people, securing debt was necessary to everyday life. The master printer Lázaro Rodríguez de la Torre was an exceptional character due to his profession. However, like most other urban residents, he also had to enter into a debt agreement in order to lease his living quarters, a common situation among free people of African descent (*afrodescendientes*). The archival record also shows that free families of African descent cultivated relations of belonging in peripheral Indigenous neighborhoods, such as Santa María Xonacatepec. Agustina Mónica's 1681 testament serves as a useful example of this process of neighborhood formation and its generational impact. The case of José de Peralta's burial arrangements speaks to a different kind of debt and belonging. Here, the powerful Dominican order acknowledged its debt to an influential and wealthy patron of African descent. Peralta had managed to accrue such wealth that in 1690 he contributed financial resources to the construction of the Capilla del Rosario, perhaps the most exuberant example of Mexican Baroque architecture.

For most residents of eighteenth-century Mexico, however, day-to-day life was not one of opulence. While slavery was definitely on the decline, free people encountered increasingly aggressive taxation in the reforms advanced by Spain's Bourbon rulers (1700–1808). Decreasing one's tax obligations became a crucial strategy for common people. Gertrudis Caballero's husband requested his Spanishness to be formally acknowledged—not in order to claim some lofty social status, but rather to relieve his family's tribute payments. Even the smallest advantage in a person's fiscal status could have important consequences decades later. Similarly, the 1735 inventory produced after Pascual de Vela's death opens a window into the small profit margins and debts that a middling merchant could expect to hold, even in a flourishing city like Zacatecas. Drafted shortly after a prolonged silver boom (and at the start of a long economic decline), the listing speaks to the constant pressures of debt and the difficulties of balancing the books of a small business.

Document 92: 1590—Simón de Mesa, free and imprisoned[1]

May all who see this letter know that I, Simón de Mesa, free mulatto and currently a resident of this city [Puebla] of the Angels of New Spain, declare that I entered into a service contract with Ginés de Cárdenas, *vecino* of the city of Tlaxcala, to serve him for two years in anything he ordered, for five and a half pesos each month. On account of this service, I received 51 pesos and 4 tomines of common gold from the said [de Cárdenas] as was accounted and declared in the writ that was entered in the city of Cholula on April 15, 1589. I refer to this document to state that I served him for some time and received more money, but after a few days I absented myself from his service and went into the service of Juan de Herrera, *vecino* of Mexico City, from whom I received 58 pesos in reales. When the said Juan de Herrera came to this city, Ginés de Cárdenas had me arrested and thrown into its public jail due to the said service contract. When I was in jail, Juan de Herrera interceded on my behalf with the said Ginés de Cárdenas and gave him 77 pesos of common gold. This was the sum of my account that I ended up owing him for the contract. . . . Therefore, I award and recognize by this letter that I am committed to serving the said Juan de Herrera, who is present, the said 133 pesos of said gold . . . and he is to discount six and a half pesos of common gold for each month [of service]. . . . Likewise, he is to give me food to eat, and in this manner I commit to entering said service and I will not absent myself, under pain of being brought from wherever I might be in shackles and at my expense. . . .

---

1. Archivo General de Notarías del Estado de Puebla, Notaría 4, Box 36, 1590 Septiembre, ff. 415r–416r.

... Done in the city [Puebla] of the Angels, September 17, 1590. I, the scribe, know the said Juan de Herrera. Witnesses, Ginés de Cárdenas and Juan de Cárdenas. They swore to God in proper form that they know the said Simón de Mesa, mulatto, and that he is named thus and is the person referred to in this writ. Because both grantors said that they do not know how to sign, a witness signed. Jerónimo de Salazar, *vecino* of this city, also was a witness. Both parties declared that if the said Simón, mulatto, should give and pay the said Juan de Herrera the 133 pesos or what remains of this debt, the latter is obligated to receive them and free the former from this writ.

Before me, Alonso de León, his majesty's scribe
On behalf of the grantors and as a witness, Juan de Cárdenas

[Spanish transcription]

Sepan quantos esta carta vieren como yo Simon de Mesa, mulato libre rresidente que soy al presente en esta ziudad de los angeles de la nueba España digo que por quanto yo hiçe escritura de servicio a Gines de Cardenas, vezino de la ciudad de Tlaxcala para le servir en lo que me mandasse tiempo de dos años por rrazon que en cada un mes me avia de pagar çinco pesos y medio e para en quenta del dicho servycio rrecebi de el susodicho zinquenta y un pesos y quatro tomynes de oro comun como se quenta y declara por la escritura que se otorgo en la ciudad de Cholula a quince dias del mes de abril de myll y quinientos e ochenta y nueve años que me rremyto en cumplimyento de lo qual le servi çierto tiempo y fui rrezibiendo mas dinero y al cabo de ciertos dias me aussente del dicho su serviccio y me fui al de Juan de Herrera, vezino de la ciudad de Mexico y del rreszibi çinquenta y ocho pesos de oro commun en rreales y abiendo benido con el dicho Juan de Herrera a esta ciudad el dicho Xines de Cardenas me hizo prender y poner en la carcel publica de ella en virtud de la dicha scriptura y estando en ella a mi rruego e ynterçession el dicho Juan de Herrera dio al dicho Xines de Cardenas setenta y sinco pesos de oro comun que aberiguada mi quenta conmigo le quede debiendo asi por la dicha scriptura ... por tanto otorgo y conozco por esta carta que me obligo de servir al dicho Juan de Herrera que esta presente los dichos çiento y treynta y tres pesos del dicho oro ... me a de descontar en cada un mes seys pesos y medio de oro comun ... asimysmo me a de dar de comer y de esta manera me obligo de hazerle dicho servycio e no me ausentare del so pena que a mi costa sea traydo de donde estubiere y con prisiones ...

... es fecha en la ciudad de los angelez en diez y siete dias del mes de septiembre de myll y quinientos e noventa años e yo el dicho scrivano conozco al dicho Juan de Herrera. Siendo testigos Xines de Cardenas y Juan de Cardenas. E juraron a dios en forma conozçer al dicho Ximon de Messa mulato y nombrarsse asi y ser El referido en esta scriptura. E porque ambos otorgantes dixeron no saber firmar, lo firmo un testigo y asi mysmo fue testigo Jeronimo de salazar, vezino desta dicha ciudad. E declararon anbas partes que si el dicho Ximon mulato diere y pagare al dicho Juan de Herrera los dichos çiento y treynta y tres pesos e los que dellos le rrestare debiendo sea obligado a los rreszibir y a le dar por libre desta scriptura.

Paso ante my, Alonso de Leon Scrivano de su magestad
A ruego de los otorgantes y por testigo, Juan de Cardenas

Document 93: 1605—An indebted Afro-Indigenous family from Cholula[2]

In the city [Puebla] of the Angels on October 11, 1605, before Nicolás de Villanueva, magistrate of this city and before me, the scribe, and witnesses. Diego de Valencia, of mulatto color, and Magdalena, an Indian woman fluent in our Castilian language, presented themselves as the principal debtors. Juan Francisco, an Indian man, Mariana Hernandez, his wife of mulatta color, and Maria Castilan Suchil, widow and mother-in-law of the said Diego de Valencia, [presented themselves] as *vecinos*, natives of the city of Cholula, and guarantors of the said Diego de Valencia and payers, in order that no confiscation of goods or other actions be taken against the principal debtors. . . .

We, the said Magdalena, ladina Indian, and Mariana Hernandez, of mulatta color, in the presence of their said husbands and with their license, which they requested and demanded from them and which the said men conceded in form. Using the licenses for the said union, all the aforementioned said that Diego de Valencia is imprisoned and arrested in this city's public jail because he did not pay four pesos from the remainder of a debt of a hundred and six pesos and two reales that he owes for a horse that he had bought from Francisco Hernández Alconero. The latter took [de Valencia] out of jail and paid his sentencing fees, a bay-colored horse, and some other things, all of which amounts to the remaining sum that he owes. Because at present de Valencia cannot pay this debt until he is released from the said jail, he asks for payment to be delayed in the following manner. The debt will be discounted four pesos each month for Valencia's service, and two pesos for the service of the said Magdalena Hernández, his wife. The main debtors confessed and declared that they owe this sum of ninety-four pesos to Francisco Díaz de Vargas. . . .

The said debtors and their guarantors, under the said union, are committed to paying the said Francisco Díaz de Vargas, the said ninety-four pesos, which will be discounted through the service of Diego de Valencia and Magdalena, Indian, his

---

2. Archivo General de Notarías del Estado de Puebla, Notaría 4, Box 58, 1605 Octubre, Juan Francisco, no folio.

wife. . . . They will do this service for however many months are needed, beginning on November 1, this coming year, and will do whatever they are ordered by the said Francisco Díaz de Vargas, his agent, or administrator in this city or in any other part without fail in this said service . . . and we, the said Magdalena, Indian woman, and Maria[na] Hernández, mulatta, accepted this writ, and swore to God and on the cross in due form that they understand the implications of this writ. They have not made or entered any oath, claim, or protest against this writ, and if any should appear, they revoke it. At no time, will they act against this writ . . . on the said day, month, and year before the said lieutenant, who certified his authority and judicial decree, by means of Alonso de Ora, court interpreter for this hearing. The said interpreter signed for the granting parties who said they did not know to sign. Witnesses, Francisco Pacheco, Fernando de Rosas, Luis Av. [Ávila?], *vecinos* of this city.

Before me, Juan Francisco, public scribe.

[Spanish transcription]

En la ciudad de los Angeles en onze dias del mes de otubre de mill y seiscientos y cinco años ante nicolas de villanueva theniente de alcalde mayor desta ciudad e por ante mi El scrivano e testigos paresçieron presentes Diego de Valencia de color mulato e Madalena yndia ladina en nuestra lengua castellana Prencipales deudores y Joan Françisco yndio, e Mariana Hernandez, su muger de color mulata y Maria Castilan Suchil biuda suegra del dicho Diego De Valençia e todos vezinos y naturales de la ciudad de Cholula Como sus fiadores del dicho Diego de Valençia e principales pagadores y sin que contra el prencipal sea fecha ni se haga execucion de bienes ni otra deligencia alguna . . .

e nos las dichas Madalena yndia ladina y Mariana Hernandez de color mulata en presençia y con lisençia de los dichos sus maridos que tales les pidieron y demandaron y los susodichos se la conçedieron en forma y ussando della devaxo de dicha mancomunidad todos los susodichos otorgantes Dixeron que Por quanto en la carçel publica desta ciudad esta Presso y envargado el dicho Diego de Valençia por no ventar [sic] quatro pesos que le deve de rresto de çiento y seis pesos y dos reales de un cavallo que lo que avia Pagado por El a Françisco Hernandez Alconero sacandole de la Carçel y de lo que pago por El por condenaçion y de un cavallo bayo y de otras cosas que todo Ello monto La dicha cantidad de rresto de la qual le debe la dicha cantidad e porque de presente no se la puede pagar ya por bien questa suelto de la dicha Carçel y esperarle por ella al plaço que de yuso sera conthenido con que se los baya subiendo a Razon de quatro Pesos cada mes el servicio de Valençia y la dicha Madalena Hernadez su muger de dos pesos cada mes por tantos en la mas bastante fforma que al derecho del dicho Francisco Dias de Vargas, confesaron y declararon los dichos prencipales ser deudores de los dichos noventa y quatro pesos . . .

se obligaron los dichos prençipales y fiadores debaxo de la dicha mancomunidad que los dichos Diego de Valençia e Madalena yndia Su muger pagaran al dicho Francisco Diaz de Bargas los dichos noventa y quatro pesos desquitandolos en su servicio . . . los meses que bastaren para Ello comensando a Correr desde primero dia del mes de novienbre Primero que verna [sic] deste año haziendo el dicho officio en todo aquello que se les mandare por el dicho Francisco Diaz de Vargas, o su agente o mayordomo en esta ciudad o en otra parte sin hazer ffalta alguna en el dicho serviçio . . . e nos las dichas Madalena Yndia e Maria[na] Hernandez mulata por ser aseptada Juraron a dios y a la cruz en fforma que entienden el effeto desta scritura y que contra ella no tienen ffecho Juramento rreclamaçion ni protestacion en contrario y si Paresçiere lo rrevocan, y en ningun tiempo yran ni veran contra esta scritura . . .

en el dicho dia mes y año, dichos ante el dicho teniente, que Ynterpuso en ella su autoridad y decreto Judiçial y mediante Alonso de Ora Ynterprete de juzgado desta audiencia e lo firmo el dicho ynterprete e por los dichos otorgantes que dixeron no saber siendo testigos Francisco Pacheco, Fernando de Rosas, y Luis A.v [¿Ávila?] vezinos desta ciudad

Ante my, Jhoan Francisco, scrivano publico

Document 94: 1621—A free Acapulco woman pawns Juana de Terra Nova[3]

May all who see this letter know that I, Juana Sánchez de Mescula, free mulatta and *vecina* of the port of Acapulco, resident in this city [Puebla] of the Angels, state that I owe and am committed to paying one hundred pesos to Esteban Pérez, *vecino* of the said port of Acapulco, or whomever holds his power of attorney. This [debt] is for another one hundred pesos that the aforementioned man willingly gave me in cash reales as an act of friendship, which I certify that I received, to help prepare my way to the port of Acapulco . . . and I commit to repaying him the said one hundred pesos in reales in this city or anywhere I might be asked for them four months after the date of this writ, along with the expenses of recovering them.

For surety of this debt, I truly give and pawn a Black woman, my slave named Juana de Tierra Nova [Terranova], thirty-four years old, more or less. So that if, at the end of the said term, I have not paid the said pesos, the said Esteban Perez will be able to sell her in or out of auction, without citing or calling me, although of course I understand that I am cited and called [to this commitment]. With the price he receives for her, he may cover this payment and if it is not enough, he may charge

---

3. Archivo General de Notarías del Estado de Puebla, Notaría 4, Box 103, 1621 Septiembre, f. 2262r–2262v.

me, with a simple sworn statement with no further proof needed. In the meantime, I commit not to sell or alienate her to any person, and if I did, the said sale would be revoked, so that he could remove [my slave] from the possession of a third party. To this effect and to award a bill of sale for her, I give Esteban Pérez power of attorney, as required by the law, and by his consent, I will retain the said Black woman. I commit my person and my present and future goods and I award power of attorney to His Majesty's justices, in particular those in this city and in the said port of Acapulco, to whose charter and jurisdiction, I submit. . . . Done in the city [Puebla] of the Angels on September 25, 1621. The said grantor did not sign because she said she does not know how to. A witness signed on her behalf and she presented a witness known to her; to Juan de Zamora, his majesty's scribe; and to Cristóbal Martínez de Serdio, *vecinos* of this city. They swore to God and on the cross that they know the said woman, and that she is named as seen in the writ. Witnesses to the grant, Juan Bautista Romero, Juan Guerra, and Alonso Vásquez de Dueñas, *vecinos* of this city.

As a witness, Alonso Vásquez de Dueñas   Before me, Alonso Corona, public scribe

[Spanish transcription]

Sepan quantos esta carta vieren como yo Juana Sanchez de Mesqula mulata libre vezina del puerto de Acapulco residente en esta ciudad de los angeles otorgo que devo E me obligo a pagar a Estevan Perez vezino del dicho puerto de acapulco y a quien su poder ubiere cien pesos de oro comun que le devo y son por otros cien pesos que el susodicho por me haçer amistad y buena obra me presto en rreales de Contado para abiarme al dicho puerto de acapulco de que me doy por entregada . . . y me obligo de pagarlos dichos cien pesos del dicho oro en rreales en esta ciudad u donde se me pidan para de la fecha de esta escriptura en quatro meses cumplidos primeros siguientes con las costas de la Cobranza =

y para seguridad de esta deuda doy y enpeño Real y verdadero y por via de fiança una negra mi esclava llamada Juana de Tierra Nova [Terranova] de hedad de treinta y quatro años poco mas o menos para que si cumplido el dicho plazo no pagare los dichos pesos sin citar me ni requerirme por que desde luego me doy por citada y Requerida pueda el dicho Estevan Perez benderla en almoneda o fuera della y de su precio se haga pago y por lo que no alcansare me execute con su Juramento sinple con que lo dijere sin otra prueva y en el ynterin me obligo a no la vender ni engenar a ninguna persona y si la bendiere no balga la dicha venta y el suso dicha la pueda sacar de poder de tercero posehedor para El dicho Efecto y para otorgar Escriptura de venta della le doy al dicho estevan perez mi poder cumplido El que de derecho se rrequiere y de su consentimiento queda en mi poder la dicha negra y para Ello obligo mi persona y bienes avidos y por aver y doy poder a las Justicias de su magestad en especial a las desta ciudad y a las del dicho puerto de Acapulco a cuyo fuero y juridiçion me someto

... es fecha en la ciudad de los angeles en veinte y cinco dias del mes de septiembre de mill y seiscientos y veinte y un años y la otorgante no firmo porque dixo no saver firmo a su rruego un testigoo y presento por testigo de su conozçimiento a Juan de Çamora escrivano de su magestad y a Xpoval Martinez de Serdio vecinos de esta ciudad juraron a dios y a la Cruz en forma de derecho conozcer a la susodicha y ser la contenida y llamarse del nombre que en su escriptura se a nombrado testigos del otorgamiento Juan Baptista Romero, Juan Guerra, y Alonso Vasquez de Dueñas, vezinos de esta ciudad

Por testigo, Alonsso Vasquez de Dueñas   ante mi Alonso corona, scrivano publico

Document 95: 1626—Will of Gaspar Hernandez, free man from the Canary Islands[4]

In the name of God, amen. May all those who see this letter know that I, Gaspar Hernandez, free mulatto, *vecino* of this city and native of the island of La Palma in Gran Canaria, am the legitimate son of Simón González and Catalina Díaz, who are deceased. I am sick in bed and in my free judgment, understanding and in full memory, which God Our Lord was willing to give me, believing, as I firmly believe, in the mystery of the Holy Trinity and all the other things that our Holy Mother Roman Catholic Church holds and confesses. I fear death, which is a natural thing, and I choose the most Serene Queen of the Angels, Our Lady Mother of God, as my intercessor and patroness. I state that I am making and ordering my last testament and final will in the following manner.

First, I trust my soul to God, Our Lord, who raised and redeemed it. Upon my dying of the present illness, I order that my body be buried in this city's Convent of Santo Domingo or in the main church, in the manner and place that my executors think best. I ask that the alms be paid out of my estate and that on the day of my burial ... a mass with my body present be celebrated with the [church] ministers.

I order that twelve masses be celebrated for my soul and my parents' souls. In addition, ten sung masses are to be celebrated for my soul and another nine masses for Our Lady of Consolation and another nine for Our Lady of Altagracia.

I declare that I owe nothing to anyone, unless it is for Francisco Gil, the miller, to whom I owe twenty pesos. He orders that these be paid.

I declare that Juan de Carmona Paredes, presbyter, owes me the gold pesos that will appear in the promissory notes that I have in my possession. ... The said notes are currently held by Felipe de Torres, attorney, for which I have received two loads

---

4. Archivo General de Notarías del Estado de Puebla, Notaría 1, Pedro de Mendoza, Box 4, 1626, no folio.

of wheat, at two pesos per bushel. I order that the rest be charged from the aforementioned [Carmona].

I declare that Captain José de Rivas, *vecino* of this city, owes me one hundred and five pesos of common gold for bread I have given him. For surety of this debt, he gave and pawned a chain, which I understood to be made of gold, although later I found out it was an alloy [of copper and zinc]. I order that the chain be given back to him and the amount charged.

I declare that Amador de Hita, the elder, *vecino* of Tlaxcala, owes me twenty-four pesos for bread that I have given him. I order this to be charged.

I declare that Pedro de Hita owes me four pesos for bread. I order this to be charged.

I declare that Amador de Hita, the younger, owes me forty-six pesos, that I order be charged for the bread I have given him.

Sebastian de Bocanegra, *mestizo*, owes me twenty-nine pesos for bread and barley from my garden. I order that this be charged.

Lorenzo de Sepúlveda, *vecino* of this city, owes me ten pesos. I order that this be charged.

In addition, Gaspar González, Spaniard, owes me one hundred pesos for bread, tiles, mules, and hats I gave him.

Martin Pérez, Indian baker, owes me one hundred and fifty pesos as will be demonstrated.

I order that Bernabe, an Indian man, who lives in my house, son of the deceased Diego de Santiago, be given ten pesos, a mattress, and a sack cloth.

I order that Francisca, an Indian woman, be given a *guanpie* [clothing item?] and some petticoats worth ten pesos, for the good service she has given me.

I state that I was married legitimately, according to the orders of the Holy Mother [Church], to Juana Flores, who is deceased. I did not receive anything in dowry from the said woman, nor did I have children with her during our said marriage.

Diego de Olivera, estate manager, owes me fifty-four pesos. I order that these be charged.

I order that forty pesos be given to the city's brotherhood of Nuestra Señora del Rosario, that should be charged from the debts that are owed to me.

I leave and name father Friar Juan de Alcalá, legal representative of this city's Santo Domingo convent, and Acasio de la Cruz, nephew [?], as my executors for this my will. So that each of them, *in solidum* (jointly), may take my goods and sell them at auction or outside of it, as they see best.

After finishing and paying this, my testament, orders, and bequests, I leave and name Juana de Salazar, whom I have raised in my house since she was a little girl, as my universal heir, given that I have no mandatory heirs, so that she may have and inherit my goods with God's blessing. Moreovoer, I revoke, annul, and declare with no value or effect any other testaments, orders, codicils or powers of attorney that I may have made, so that they have no validity, except for this my testament. . . .

Done in the city [Puebla] of the Angels on November 3, 1626. The said grantor, whom I, the scribe, attest that I know, said that he does not know how to sign. A witness signed. Witnesses. Antonio de Bonilla, Juan Chacón, Juan de Leiba, Domingo de Torres, Lorenzo de Sepúlveda, Alonso de Espinosa de los Monteros, *vecino*, and I, Pedro de Mendoza, His Majesty's scribe, and all [of the above] *vecinos* of this city.

As witness, Alonso de Espinosa de los Monteros

[Spanish transcription]

En El nombre de dios amen Sepan quantos Esta carta bieren como yo Gaspar Hernandez mulato Libre vezino desta ciudad y natural de la ysla de la Palma En gran Canaria hijo ligitimo de Simon Gonzales y Catalina Dias diffuntos estando Enffermo En cama y En mi libre Juisio Entendimiento y cumplida memoria tal qual dios nuestro señor ffue servido de darme creiendo como firmemente creo El misterio de la Santisima Trenidad y todo lo demas que tiene y conffiesa la santa madre yglesia catolica rromana temiendome de la muerte que es cosa natural y Eligiendo por mi Yntersesora y abogada a la Serenisima reina De los angeles madre de dios señora nuestra otorgo que hago y ordeno mi testamento vltima y ffinal boluntad En la manera siguiente

Lo primero Encomiendo mi anima a dios nuestro señor que la crio y rredimio y ffalesiendo de la presente Enffermedad mando que mi cuerpo sea sepultado en el conbento de Santo Domingo desta ciudad o En La yglesia mayor como y En la sepultura que a mis albaceas paresiere y se pague la limosna de mis bienes mando se diga El dia de mi Entierro . . . vna misa de cuerpo presente con sus ministros

Mando se digan por mi anima doce misas y por las de mis padres y mas se digan por mi anima diez misas resadas y otras nuebe a Nuestra Señora de Consolacion = y otras nuebe a Nuestra Señora de Altagrasia

declaro que no devo cosa alguna a nadie si no es a Francisco Xil molinero que debe veinte pesos manda se paguen

declaro que me debe Juan de Carmona Paredes presvitero los pesos de oro que paresera por los bales que tengo juros En mi poder . . . Los quales dichos bales tiene En su poder Felipe de Torres procurador y a quenta dellos a rresevido dos caizes [sic, caixas] de trigo a dos pesos fanega mando que lo demas se cobren del suso dicho

declaro que El capitan Joseph de Rivas vezino desta ciudad me es deudor de ciento y cinco pesos de oro comun de pan que le e dado y me dio para emprenda y seguridad vna cadena la qual Entendi que era de oro y despues paresio ser de alquimia mando se le buelba y se cobre del la dicha cantidad

declaro que me debe Amador de Yta El biejo vezino de Tlaxcala veinte y quatro pesos de pan que le e dado mando se cobren declaro que me debe Pedro de Yta de quatro pesos de pan que le e dado mando se cobren

declaro que me debe Amador de Yta El moso quarenta y seis pesos mando se cobren del que son de pan que le e dado

deveme mas Sevastian de Bocanegra mestizo veinte y nuebe pesos de pan y sevada de mi huerta mando se cobren del

deveme Lorenzo de Sepulbeda vezino de esta ciudad diez pesos mando se cobren

Mas me deve Gaspar Gonzales español cien pesos de pan losa y mulas y sonbreros que le di

debe me Martin Perez yndio panadero ciento y cinquenta pesos como paresera

mando se le den a Bernave yndio hijo de Diego de Santiago diffunto que Esta En mi casa diez pesos y vn colchon y vna jerga

mando se le den a Francisca yndia por El buen servisio que me a hecho vn guanpie [¿prenda de vestir?] y unas naguas que cueste diez pesos

declaro que ffui casado Lijitimamente segun orden de la santa madre [iglesia] con Juana Flores diffunta y no rresevi En dote con la susodicha cosa alguna ni tube hijos ningunos della durante El dicho matrimonio

debe me Diego de Olivera estansiero cinquenta y quatro pesos mando se cobren

mando que se den a la coffradia de Nuestra Señora del Rosario de esta ciudadd quarenta pesos de lo que se cobrare de las deudas que me deven

dexo y nonbro or mis alvaseas testamentarios y executores de este mi testamento a el padre frai Juan de Alcala procuador del convento de Santo Domingo desta ciudad y Acasio de la Cruz sonbreno [¿sobrino?] y a cada vno ynsolidum para que Entrren En mis bienes y los bendan y rrematen En almoneda o ffuera della como Le paresiere

y cumplido y pagado Este mi testamento mandas y legados En el contenidos dexo y nonbro por mi vnibersal heredera atento a que no tengo erederos fforsosos a Juana de Salazar que E criado en mi casa desde chiquita para que aya y Erede mis bienes con la bendision de dios y a mas, rreboco y anulo y doy por ninguno y de ningun balor ni Efecto todos y qualesquier testamentos mandas codisilios poderes para los otorgar que aya ffho para que no balga salvo Este testamento . . .

fecha En la Civdad de los angeles a tres dias del mes de novienbre de mill y seiscientos y beinte y seis años y El otorgante que yo El scrivano doy fee que conosco dixo no saber firmar a su rruego lo firmo vn testigo siendo testigos Antonio de Bonilla y Juan Chacon y Juan de Leiba y Domingo de torres y Lorenzo de Sepulbeda y Alonso Despinosa de los Monteros bezino e yo Pedro de Mendoça scrivano de su magestad y todos bezinos desta civdad.

                 por testigo, Alonso Despinosa de los Monteros

Document 96: 1640—Francisco López's many, many debts[5]

In the city [Puebla] of the Angels, on May 10, 1640, Francisco López, free mulatto, muleteer, and *vecino* of this city, whom I attest that I know, appeared before me, the public scribe, and witnesses. He [López] said that he owes and is committed to paying three hundred and four pesos and four tomines to Diego de Padilla Matamoros, owner of a mule train and *vecino* of this city, whom I attest I know or to whoever holds the power of attorney that he awarded in this city on June 21 of year, 1635, before this scribe . . . in addition to forty pesos that he owed for a payment to Sebastian M.ha [?], and the expenses that resulted from an investigation led against him by Don Juan Calderón, administrative judge of the two percent [tax]. This is in addition to the expenses caused by the denunciation of Francisco Melgarejo, the constable, against him for carrying a knife. López also owes ten pesos of His Majesty's royal tributes for when he was imprisoned, and the rest de Padilla Matamoros has given him in reales to dress himself and support Inés de la Cruz, mulatta, his wife, so that the said sum was adjusted to three hundred and four pesos and four tomines. . . .

López committed to paying these pesos, and will do so by serving the said Diego de Padilla with his mule train as a muleteer, at a rate of nine pesos [a month] of the said gold, which the latter is to give him for his work, although they did not come to an agreement on this. De Padilla is to pay him at the end of each month the necessary pesos to discount the three hundred pesos and four tomines, with a statement that the said nine pesos are to reduce the debt only by four pesos and four tomines [each month]. The other four pesos and four tomines will be given during the course of the month for Lopez's clothing, to support his said wife, and other needs and expenses that may come. Likewise, the said Diego de Padilla is to give the said grantor a riding mule for his travel and is to feed him during all the time necessary to pay off the said debt. With this, López commits not to absent himself until he has finished paying the said three hundred and four pesos and four tomines. . . .

The said Diego de Padilla Matamoros, whom I, the scribe, attest that I know, was present and awarded this writ with the clauses contained in it, and committed to pay the said Franciso López, mulatto, four pesos and four tomines at the end of each month of service. He is also obliged to give him, each successive month, reales for the expenses of the debt, and he will not fire López, under punishment of paying the full amount at once. De Padilla Matamoros committed his person and word to this. Both parties gave permission to the royal justices, in particular those of this city, to compel them as in a past sentence in a judged matter. They renounce the laws in their favor and the general law. Diego de Padilla signed the writ and Antonio Suárez, a witness,

---

5. Archivo General de Notarías del Estado de Puebla, Notaría 4, Box 164, Alonso Corona, 1640 Mayo, ff. 401r–402r.

signed for the mulatto, who says that he does not know how to. Witnesses, Alonso Tinoco, and Juan de Jerez, *vecinos* of this city. I attest that I know them all.

Diego de Padilla Matamoros   Antonio Suarez de Vargas, as a witness
                                   Before me, Alonso Corona, public scribe

[Spanish transcription]

En la çiudad de los angeles En dies dias del mes de mayo de mill y Seis Y quarenta años ante mi el escrivano Publico y testigos pareçio Francisco Lopez mulato libre harriero vezino desta çiudad que doi fee conosco; Y otorgo que deve y se obliga de pagar a Diego de Padilla Matamoros dueño de Recua vezino desta dicha Ciudad a quien ~~doi fee que conosco~~ su poder vbiere; tresçientos y quatro pessos y quatro tomines de oro comun que le deve los dusientos y doçe pesos Por escriptura otorgada En esta çiudad a veinte y uno de Junio del año Pasado de mill y seisçientos y treinta y çinco Por este scrivano . . . y los de mas a mas quarenta pesos que por el pago a Sebastian M.ha [¿?] a quien los devia; Y las costas que se le causaron en Vna caussa que le hiço don Juan Calderon Juez administador del dos por çiento añadido, Y las de otra que Por denunsiasion de Francisco Melgarejo, alguacil se siguio contra el Por traer cuchillo, Y asimismo dies pesos de los Reales tributos de su magestad Por questava preso y lo demas que le a dado en Realess Para bestirsse y Sustentar a Ines de la Cruz mulata su muger con que se ajusto a la dicha cantidad de los dichos tresçientos quatro pesos y quatro tomines . . .

y sse obligo a la paga de ellos; y a que la hara sirviendo al dicho diego de padilla en la dicha su rrequa de harriero; Por Rasson de nueve pesos del dicho oro que le a de dar el sussodicho por su trabaxo que es la cantidad e no se consertaron; y le a de Pagar Por fin de cada mes de los que fueren nesesarios, Para el desquite de los dichos tresçientos quatro pesos y quatro tomines, con declarasion que de los dichos nueve pesos Sean de Yr discontando tan solamente quatro pesos y quatro tomines por quenta de la dicha deuda y los otros quatro pesos y quatro tomines que le a de ir dando En el discurso del dicho mes Para bestirse, sustenta a la dicha su muger y otras nesesidades y gastos que tubiere; Y asimesmo le a de dar el dicho Diego de Padilla a el dicho otorgante mula de caballeria en que ande; Y de comer todo el tiempo que nessesario fuere para el dicho desquite; con lo qual se obliga a no ausentarse hasta aver acabado de pagar los dichos tresçientos quatro pesos y quatro tomines . . .

y estando Presente el dicho Diego de Padilla Matamoros a quien asimemso yo el escribano doi fee conosco; otorgo aseta [sic] esta escriptura segun y como en ella se contiene, y se obligo de pagar a el dicho Francisco Lopez mulato Por fin de cada mes los que Sirviere los dichos quatro pesos y quatro tomines que asi tiene obligacion a darle vn mes subsesivo a otro en Reales con las costas de la cobrança; y a no despedirlo Pena de pagarle de basio y a ello obligo su perssona y boz y ambos dieron para las

Justicias Reales en especial a las desta ciudad donde son vezinos Para que les apremien como por sentencia pasada en cosa Jusgada rrenuncian leies de su favor y la general y lo firmo el dicho Diego de Padilla y por el mulato que dixo no saver, un testigo Antonio Suarez Alonso Tinnoco y Juan de Xeres, vezinos desta çiudad todos doi fee que conosco

Diego de Padilla Matamoross	Por testigo Antonio Suarez de Vargas
ante mi	Alonso Corona, scribano publico

Document 97: 1640—Lorenzo del Puerto's examination[6]

In the very noble and very loyal city [Puebla] of the Angels of New Spain, December 31, 1640. Juan de Amaya de Obando and Diego Cordero, judge and inspector, examiners in the office of shoemaking this year by their election and nomination, appeared before Pedro Fernández de Lasprilla, court justice, and the regent Don Francisco de Aguilar and Velasco, judge, as deputies and faithful executors in the city. I, the municipal scribe, attest to [Amaya and Cordero's role as examiners]. They said that they have examined Lorenzo del Puerto, of mulatto color, who said that he was native to this city, a free person, a man currently thirty-two years old, of good body, thin, with a scar on his left hand. To examine him as an expert shoemaker, they asked him to make and cut, and with his hands he had made and cut everything in relation and pertaining to said occupation by his accord and reasoning. And having asked him once and again all relevant questions, he responded and satisfied them as a good, skilled, and sufficient journeyman. As such they declared, then and now, that he may be ordered, awarded, and granted a letter of examination to use in his said office in a public store with journeymen and apprentices. They swore to God and on the cross in the appropriate form that they had conducted the exam well and faithfully in conformity with their ordinances.

Having seen this statement and oath, said judges hold the said Lorenzo del Puerto as examined. As such they granted him license and faculty to use it freely in his public store with journeymen and apprentices, in this city as in all of His Majesty's other cities, villages, and places of the kingdoms and manors. No one, regardless of their quality or condition, may impede him [from using this license]. On behalf of the King, Our Lord, all and any of his judges and justices ask and plea that the aforementioned [Lorenzo del Puerto] be held as such an examined master in the said office. . . . The judges ordered that he be given this sealed letter, with a copy of it and the city's seal, and corroborated by me, the scribe. As such, they establish their

---

6. Archivo Municipal de Puebla, Expedientes, Tomo 220, Cartas de Examen, ff. 34r–34v.

authority on this matter. The said Juan de Amaya signed and the said Diego Cordero said that he did not know how to sign. A witness, Juan Hernández de la Parra, signed on his behalf. Pedro Meléndez and Antonio Maya, *vecinos* of this city.

Pedro Fernández de Lasprilla   Don Francisco de Aguilar   Juan de Maya de Obando
As witness Juan Hernández de la Parra

[Spanish transcription]

En la muy noble y muy leal çiudad de los Angeles de la Nueba España en treinta y un dias del mes de diziembre de mill y sseisçientos y quarenta años ante Pedro Ferrnandez de Lasprilla alcalde ordinario y el rregidor don Francisco de Aguilar y Belasco Justiçia diputados fieles executores en ella por El Rey nuestro Señor pareçieron Joan de Amaya de Obando y Diego Cordero, alcalde y beedor, exsaminadores del oficio de çapatero este presente año por eleccion y nombramiento en ellos fecho de que yo El escribano de cabildo doy fee y dixeron que ellos an exsaminado en el dicho oficio de çapatero de obra prima a Lorenço del Puerto de color mulato natural que dixo ser desta çiudad Libre que es un hombre de hedad al presente de treinta y dos años de buen cuerpo çençeno con una señal de herida sobre la mano izquierda para lo qual le abian mandado hazer y cortar y el avia fecho y cortado por Sus manos todo lo tocante y perteneçiente en el dicho ofiçio de çapatero de obra prima todo con Su cuenta y rrazon y que abiendole fecho Las preguntas y rrepreguntas al caso tocantes a todoabia rrespondido y Satisfecho como bueno abil y suficiente ofiçial y por tal lo declaraban y declararon y que se le puede mandar dar y librar carta de exsamen para usar El dicho oficio en tienda publica con oficiales y aprendiçes y Juraron a dios y a la cruz en forma de derecho aber fecho el dicho exsamen bien y fielmente en conformidad de sus ordenanças =

E bisto por los dichos Juezes la dicha declaracion y Juramento ubieron por exsaminado al dicho Lorenço del Puerto y como a tal Le dieron liçençia y facultad para que lo pueda usar Libremente en tienda publica con ofisiales y aprendices asi en esta dicha ciudad como en todas las demas ciudades villas y Lugares de los rreynos y señorios de su magestad sin que se le impida por persona alguna de qualquier calidad y condiçion que sea y de parte del Rey nuestro Señor rrequieren a todos y qualesquier sus Juezes y Justiçias y de la suya rruegan y piden por merced ayan y tengan al sussodicho por tal maestro exsaminado en el dicho ofiçio y no consientan que en el uso del se le ponga ympedimiento alguno antes le mande dar y que se le de todo favor y ayuda para que goze de todas las graçias y preeminençias que gozan y deben gozar los demas maestros exsaminados en todas Las çiudades villas y Lugares de los reinos y señorios de su magestad donde el sussodicho fuere y asisitere y para ello Le mandaron dar esta carta sellado el traslado della con el sello desta ciudad y rrefrendada de mi El escrivano en la qual interponen su autoridad y lo firmaron El dicho Joan de Amaya y por El dicho Diego Cordero que dixo no saber a su rruego lo firmo un testigo siendolo Juan Hernandez de la Parra Pedro Melendez y Antonio Maya vezinos desta çiudad.

Pedro Fernandez Delasprilla   don Francisco de Aguilar   Juan de Maya de Obando
                                              Por testigo Juan Hernandez de la Parra

Document 98: 1675—Lázaro Rodríguez de la Torre, free master printer, leases a house[7]

May all who see this letter know that I, Lázaro Rodríguez de la Torre, free mulatto, master printer and *vecino* of this city [Puebla] of the Angels, state that I commit to pay forty-eight pesos to bachiller Alonso de Gamboa, secular priest of this bishopric, and to the person who holds his power of attorney for the lease of a house on the corner of the street that goes from the San Agustín convent to Acuña's textile mill. On one side, the house abuts with houses owned by the said bachiller Alonso de Gamboa and on the other side, it abuts with the house of bachiller Macario de Anzures. The lease is for next year, 1676, from the beginning of January through the end of December and for the price agreed. Therefore, I renounce any contrary argument of this matter, the laws of delivery, and the previous. I will pay the said forty-eight pesos in reales in this city or wherever I might be asked for them in three installments during the said year. I will pay the third part of the lease after every four months, and the third part will include the expenses of the debt. I will not abandon the said house during the said time, under punishment of paying the entire year's rent. I firmly commit my person and goods, and empower His Majesty's justices, especially those of this city, where I am a *vecino*, and where I am subjected by law to be compelled as in a past sentence in a judged matter. I renounce the laws in my favor and the general law. Done in the city [Puebla] of the Angels on December 30, 1675. I, the scribe, attest that I know the grantor who signed the letter. Witnesses, Juan Godinez, His Majesty's scribe, Joseph de Trujillo, and Ignacio López, *vecinos* of this city.

Lázaro Rodríguez de la Torre   before me, Tomás de Ortega, royal and public scribe

[Spanish transcription]

Sepan quantos esta carta Vieren como Yo Lasaro Rodrigues de la Torre Mulato libre Maestro Ympressor vesino de la ciudad de los angeles otorgo que Me obligo de pagar al licenciado Alonso de Gamboa presvitero domisiliario de este obispado Y a la perssona

---

7. Archivo General de Notarías del Estado de Puebla, Notaría 4, Tomás de Ortega, Box 209, f. 1182r.

que tubiere Su poder quarenta y ocho pesos de oro comun por el arendamiento de Vna cassa en esquina de la calle que ba de el convento de San Augustin al obraje de Acuña linde por vna parte cassas de el dicho Licenciado Alonso de Gamboa y por otra de el Licenciado Macario de Ansures por tiempo de vn año que es el que viene de Mill y seiscientos y setenta y seis desde principio de henero asta fin de disiembre de el en dicha cantidad por cuia Raçon Renunsiando poder alegar cossa en conttrario leyes de el entrego y la previa pagare dichos quarenta y ocho pesos en Reales en esta ciudad o en la parte que se me pidan por los tercios corridos de dicho año al fin de de cada quatro meses la tercera parte con costas de la cobransa y no dejare la dicha cassa durante dicho tiempo pena de pagar la renta del año y a la firmeza obligo Mi perssona y vienes y doy poder a las Justisias de su magestad en especial a las de esta ciudad donde soy vecino y por derecho estoy sometido para que a ello me apremien como por sentencia passada en cossa Jusgada renuncio leyes de mi favor y la general de el derecho que es fecha en la ciudad de los Angeles a treinta dias de el mes de disiembre de mill y seiscientos y setenta y cinco años e yo el sscribano doy fee conosco al otorgante que lo firmo testigos Juan godines sscribano de su magestad Joseph de trujillo y Ygnacio Lopes vesinos de esta ciudad

Lazaro Rodriguez de la Torre   ante mi Thomas de ortega, scrivano Real y Publico

Document 99: 1681—Will of Agustina Mónica, free *parda*[8]

In the name of God Almighty, amen. May all who see this letter know that I, Agustina Mónica, free *parda* and *vecina* of the Santa María Xonocatepec neighborhood in this city [Puebla] of the Angels, native of Mexico City, and the widow of Juan Sánchez, a free *pardo*, am healthy and in full judgment and natural understanding, which God Our Lord has given me. I firmly and truly believe in the mystery of the Holy Trinity, Father, Son and Holy Spirit, three distinct persons and one True God. I believe in everything else Our Holy Mother Catholic Church of Rome believes, holds and confesses. I have lived by this faith and will die by it, choosing as my defender and intercessor in the Divine Tribunal the most Serene Queen of the Heavens, the Virgin Holy Mary, Mother of God and Our Lady Conceived in Grace and Glory since the first instance of her being, so that she might pardon me for my sins, thus I make and order my testament in the following manner.

First, I trust my soul to God Our Lord for having raised it in his likeness and redeemed it with his precious blood, passion, and death, so that at the time of my

---

8. Archivo General de Notarías del Estado de Puebla, Notaría 4, Box 141, Antonio Gómez de Escobar, ff. 23r–24v.

death His Divine Majesty will place it in those places where it may be most useful and I am, of course, satisfied with his most holy will. I want my body to be buried in the church, place, and with the [funerary] accompaniment that my executors see best. I leave this choice to them.

I order that twenty masses be said for my soul, giving a fourth to the holy parish church of Our Lord San José, where I am a parishioner, and other masses be distributed by my executors among the priests that they see fit. The alms for all these masses will be paid from my estate as part of the ordinary pittance.

I order two reales from my goods be given to the mandatory and usual charities, and I exempt these mandatory bequests from any other claim they might have on my estate.

I declare that I owe nothing to any person, blessed be God, and no one owes me anything.

I declare that I was married according to the laws of the Holy Mother Church to the said Juan Sánchez, and at the time of our marriage I brought no dowry to the marriage. Likewise, he had no capital. During our marriage we had and procreated as our legitimate children Juan Andrés, more than fifty years old and muleteer by trade = Catarina de Medina, widow of Lorenzo de Guadalajara = Lucía de Santiago, legitimate wife of Agustín Rodríguez, *vecino* of this city = Antonia de los Ángeles, more than thirty-four years old = and Valerio de Santiago, thirty-two years old. I declare them as mine and my husband's legitimate children.

I declare that my husband and I gave Juan Andrés, our son, a piece of land in the Santa María Xonacatepec neighborhood that borders the water conduit that goes from this city's San Francisco convent. The plot is about thirty yards long and wide, and we bought it from Lorenzo Diego, Indian. The lot was barren [at the time of purchase] and is worth thirty gold pesos; I declare it so that it may be known.

I declare that my husband and I gave the said Lucía de Santiago, our daughter, a house in the said Xonacatepec barrio as her dowry on her marriage to the said Agustín Rodríguez. The house borders the piece of land mentioned in the clause above, which we gave to the said Juan Andrés. We also gave another piece of land to the said Antonia de los Ángeles, our daughter. The house we gave to Lucía de Santiago consists of a living room and two shacks, a patio, and a corral. It cost one hundred pesos to build it. I declare this so that it may be known.

I declare that in the previous clause I declared that we gave Antonia de los Ángeles, our daughter, a plot and in this clause I declare it once again. Said piece of land is in the Xonacatepec barrio and borders the house that we gave to the said Lucía de Santiago. A roofed room and a wooden-slotted kitchen are built on this piece of land given to the said Antonia de los Ángeles. The plot is thirty yards long and wide and worth fifty pesos in fair and common judgment. I declare this so that it may be known.

I declare that my husband and I gave the said Catarina de Medina, our daughter, at the time of her marriage to Lorenzo de Guadalajara, another piece of land in the

Xonacatepec neighborhood, which is barren and thirty yards long and twenty wide. It abuts the house we gave the said Lucía de Santiago, and is worth thirty pesos. [We also give her] another twenty pesos, so that one quantity and the other amount to fifty pesos. I declare this so that it may be known.

I declare as my goods a piece of land in the Xonacatepec barrio, which borders the water conduit that goes to the San Francisco convent. The plot is forty yards long and thirty wide and features two shacks, which cost me fifty pesos to build. Since I am aware that I have given my children the real estate declared in the preceding clauses, I apply and adjudicate this plot to my son, Valerio de Santiago, so that it may be his property. He will do as he wishes with this piece of land, and I make this grant as what is owed to him by his paternal and maternal inheritance rights.

I declare as my goods the furniture and goods in my house, which are of little consideration, and an inventory will be made of them by my executors.

And for the execution and fulfillment of this my testament and everything contained in it, I leave and name the said Juan Andrés = Catarina de Medina = Lucía de Santiago = Antonia de los Ángeles = and Valerio de Santiago, my children, as my executors . . . and I name and institute my said legitimate children and *vecinos* of my husband [sic] as my universal and mandatory heirs, so that they may have and inherit for themselves [my estate] in equal parts ~~as this is my will~~ with God's blessing and my own. . . . Done in the city [Puebla] of the Angels, June 9, 1681. I, the scribe, attest that I know the grantor, who did not sign because she said that she did not know how to write. A witness signed on her behalf. Witnesses, José de Meneses, Antonio Camacho de Aguilar, and Alonso Damián, *vecinos* of this city.

José de Meneses   Before me, Antonio Gómez de Escobar, royal and public scribe

[Spanish transcription]

En el nombre de Dios Todo Poderosso Amen Sepan quantos esta carta Vieren como yo Agustina Monica, Parda libre Vezina desta çiudad de los Angeles Al barrio de Sanctta Maria Jonacatepeque [Xonacatepec] y Nattural de la de Mejico Viuda de Juan Sanchez pardo Libre estando sana Y en mi libre Juiçio Memoria y entendimiento Natural qual Su Magestad de Dios Nuestro Señor a ssido Servido de darme Creyendo como firme y Verdaderamente Creo El misterio de la Sanctissima trinidad Padre hijo y espiritu Sancto tres Perssonaz distintas y vn solo Dios Verdadero y en todo lo demas que tiene Cree y confiesa Nuestra Sancta Madre Yglesia Catholica de Roma debajo de cuia fee Y Creençia he vibido y protesto vibir y morir Elijiendo Como elijo por mi Abogada e ynterçessora A la Serenissima Reina de los cielos La Virgen Sancta Maria Madre de Dios y Señora nuestra Conçebida en graçia y Gloria desde el primer ynstante de su Ser Para que lo sea por mi en el Tribunal Divino y me alcançe perdon de mis pecados otorgo que hago y ordeno mi testamento en la manera siguiente.

Lo primero encomiendo mi Alma a Dios Nuestro Señor por Haverla Criado a su hechura y semejança y Redimidola Con su Preçiosa sangre Passion y muerte para que en falleziendo su Divina Magestad La heche a aquellas partez donde mas se sirba con cuya Voluntad Sanctissima desde luego me comformo, Y El cuerpo quiero sea enterrado en la Yglesia parte y lugar en la forma y con el acompañamiento que paresiera a mis Albaçeas a cuya elecçion lo dejo.

Ordeno se digan por mi Alma Veinte misas Rezadas dando la quarta a la Sancta Yglesia Parrochial del Señor San Joseph donde soy feligrez y las demas se Repartan por mis albazeas entre los saçerdotes que les paresiera y la limosna de todas se pague de mis Vienez por la pitança hordinaria.

Ordeno se den de Mis Vienez Dos Reales a las mandas forzossas y acostumbradas, A todas ellas con que las aparto del derecho que tienen a mis Vienez.

Declaro que no debo cossa alguna a ninguna Perssona, sea Dios Benditto, ni a mi se me debe nada.

Declaro fui Cassada segun orden de nuestra Sancta Madre Yglesia Con el dicho Juan Sanchez y al tiempo y quando contrajimos dicho nuestro matrimonio no llebe a su poder dote ninguno ni el susodicho Assimesmo tenia Capital y durante nuestro Matrimonio hubimos y procreamos por nuestros hijos Legitimos A Juan Andres de ofizio harriero de mas de sinquenta Años = a Catarina de Medina viuda de Lorenzo de Guadalajara = A Lucia de Santiago, muger Legitima de Agustin Rodriguez, vezino desta çiudad = Y a Antonia de los Angeles de mas de treinta y quatro años = Y a Valerio de Santiago de treinta y dos años, declarolos por mis hijos Legitimos y del dicho mi marido.

Declaro que yo Y el dicho mi marido Dimos al dicho Juan Andres nuestro hijo vn pedaso de tierra en dicho barrio de Santa Maria Jonacatepeque que linda con la Cañeria del agua que ba a el convento del señor San Francisco desta çiudad que tendra treinta baras de largo y ancho que hubimos y compramos a Lorenzo Diego Yndio, El qual estaba heriasso y baldra treinta pessos de oro comun, declarolo para que conste.

Declaro que yo y el dicho mi marido dimos a la dicha Lucia de Santiago nuestra hija en dote con el dicho Agustín Rodríguez, una cassa en dicho barrio de Jonacatepeque que linda con el pedaso de tierra que llebo declarado en la Clausula antez que dimos al dicho Juan Andres; y con otro pedaso de tierra que declaro asimesmo dimos a la dicha Antonia de los Ángeles nuestra hija que se compone la dicha cassa que assi dimos a la dicha Lucía de Santiago, de una sala y dos Jacales, su patio y corral que costó zient pessos de labrarlo, declarolo para que conste.

Declaro que en la Clausula antezedente llebo declarado dimos a la dicha Antonia de los Angeles nuestra hija vn pedasso de Solar y en esta Clausula lo buelbo a hazer y que dicho pedasso de tierra es en dicho barrio de Jonacatepeque a la linde de la Cassa que dimos a la dicha Lucia de Santiago y en este pedaso de tierra dado a la dicha Antonia de los Angeles esta fabricado vn Aposento de techo y su cozina de Jacale de tajamanil [sic, tejamanil] que tendra treynta baras de largo y de ancho y a justta y comun estimassion Valdra çinquenta pesos, declarolo para que Conste.

Declaro dimos Yo y el dicho mi marido a la dicha Catarina de Medina nuestra hija al tiempo que contraho matrimonio con el dicho Lorenzo de Guadalajara otro pedaso de tierra en el dicho barrio de Jonacatepeque que se compondra de treinta baras de largo y beinte de ancho eriaso a la linde de la Cassa que asi dimos a la dicha Lucia de Santiago que baldra treynta pesos, con mas beinte pesos en realez que una y otro cantidad monta çinquenta pesos declarolo para que conste.

Declaro por mis Vienez un pedaso de tierra en dicho barrio de Jonacatepeque que Linda con dicha Cañeria de el agua que ba a dicho convento del Señor San Francisco que tendra quarenta baras de largo y treinta de ancho en que estan fabricadas dos xacales que me costaron zinquenta pesos El qual atento a tener dado a los demas de mis hijos los Vienez Raizes que ban declarados en las clausula antezedentez lo aplico y adjudico al dicho Valerio de Santiago mi hijo para que sea suyo en propriedad y como tal disponga de dicho pedaso de tierra como mas bien Visto le fuere cuya aplicassion le hago por lo que a de haver de Sus legitimas paterna Y materna.

Declaro por mis Vienez El mueble y o menaje de mi cassa que es de muy poca Considerasion de que por menor se ara ymbentario por mis albaseas.

Y para la ejecuzion y Cumplimiento deste mi testamento y lo en el conthenido dejo y nombro por mis albazeas testamentarios a los dichos Juan Andres = Catarina de Medina = Lucia de Santiago = Antonia de los Angeles = Y Valerio de Santiago = mis hijos . . . Ynstituyo y nombro por mis Universales herederos a los dichos Juan Andres, Catarina de Medina = Lucia de Santiago = Antonia de los Angeles Y a Valerio de Santiago mis hijos Legitimos vezinos [sic] de el dicho mi marido que lo son forzossos Para que lo que ymportare lo ayan y hereden para ssi por Yguales partez por ser esta mi Voluntad con la bendiçion de Dios y la mia. . . . fecho en la çiudad de los Angeles a nuebe diaz de el mez de Junio de mill seiszientos y ochenta y vn Años e Yo el escribano Doy fee que Conozco a la otorgante que no firmo por que dijo no saver escrevir A su rruego Lo firmo vn testigo, testigos Joseph de Meneses, y Antonio Camacho de Aguilar, Y Alonso Damian vezinos de esta Ciudad

Joseph de Meneses   ante my, Anttonio Gomez Descobar, Scrivano Real y Publico

Document 100: 1690—Burial arrangements for José de Peralta and his descendants[9]

May all who see this letter know that I, Friar Bernardo de Andia, Master [in Theology], priest of the order of preachers, member of the convent . . . of the glorious patriarch of the lord Santo Domingo, of this city [Puebla] of the Angels, by virtue of the power of attorney that I hold in the name of the reverend prior priest and the religious men of said convent, whose tenor is as follows . . . [the document authorizing de Andia to make decisions for the Dominican convent follows].

Using said power of attorney in the name of this city's convent of Our Lord Santo Domingo and in the name of the reverend prior priest and the religious men who form part of it now and in the future, I assign and designate a crypt that is in the main body of the Chapel of Our Lady of the Rosary, next to the well, for the burial and grave of José de Peralta, of *pardo* color, free *vecino* of this city, and for his children, grandchildren, and descendants. This is in remuneration and gratitude for the gift of alms that he made with the silver rods that he purchased for the canopy of Our Lady of the Rosary's image, in addition to thirty pesos that he has given and delivered to me complete in cash reales of which I am content and satisfied in the name of the said convent. . . .

So that the said burial and grave be known in future centuries and the memory of its property not be lost, the said José de Peralta will place a sculpted earthenware cover with his name and the letters or characters that he prefers and are permitted for his renown and that of his children, wives, heirs, and successors. Because truly from this day forward and in perpetuity, I remove and separate the convent from all rights and actions, real and personal property, dominion and any other claim over the said burial place. . . .

And for this same matter, I approve and authorize this writ for greater perpetuity and with force and firmness and the important requisites and validation, to which I commit the said convent's present and future goods and rents. In the convent's name, I empower the corresponding justices knowledgeable in this cause, to compel the convent as in a past sentence in a judged matter. I renounce the laws in its favor and the general law. And I, the said José de Peralta, being present, accept this writ and state that I will use the rights and actions by virtue of acquiring the said sarcophagus and burial. Done in the city [Puebla] of the Angels on May 23, 1690. I, the scribe, attest that I know the grantors, who signed. Witnesses, Domingo de Herrera, Francisco de Herrera Calderón, Diego de Neira, *vecinos* of this said city.

Friar Bernardo de Andia

José de Peralta
Before me, Miguel Zerón Zapata,
public and municipal scribe

---

9. Archivo General de Notarías del Estado de Puebla, Notaria 4, Box 230, Miguel Zeron Zapata, ff. 857r–858v.

[Spanish transcription]

Sepan cuantos esta carta vieren como yo el padre maestro Fray Bernardo de Andia del orden de predicadores conventual . . . del glorioso patriarca del Señor Santo Domingo desta ciudad de los Angeles y en virtud de poder que tengo en del Reverendo Padre Prior y Religiosos de dicho convento con que su tenor a la letra es el siguiente. . . . [sigue la carta poder del convento dominicano a favor de Andia]

    Y de dicho poder usando otorgo que en nombre de dicho convento del señor Santo Domingo desta ciudad y del Reverendo Padre Prior y religiosos de el cual presente son y adelante fueren asigno y destino por entierro y sepultura de Joseph de Peralta de color pardo libre vecino de esta ciudad y para sus hijos, nietos, y descendientes un cajon que esta en el Cuerpo de la Capilla de Nuestra Señora del Rosario, junto del posso que esta en ella en remuneracion y agradecimiento de la limosna que hizo de las varas de plata que costeo para el palio de la Imagen de nuestra Señora del Rosario con mas treinta pesos que me ha dado y entregado en reales contado en numero caval a mi contento y satisfaccion de que en nombre de dicho convento . . . para el conocimiento de dicha sepultura y entierro y que en los siglos venideros no se pierda la memoria de su propriedad. Ha de poder poner el dicho Joseph de Peralta una loza esculpida en ella su nombre con las letras y caracteres que le pareciere y fueren permitidos para la notoriedad de ser suyo dicho entierro y de sus hijos, mujeres, herederos, y subscesores como realmente desde hoy lo es y lo ha de ser perpetuamente para cuyo efecto desisto y aparto a dicho convento de los derechos y acciones, reales y personales de propiedad señorio y otros que a dicho sitio de sepultura tiene . . .

    y por el mismo caso queda aprobada y prevalidada esta escriptura que para ser de mayor perpetuidad hago con las fuerzas y firmezas y requisitos importantes y a su validacion a cuya firmeza obligo los bienes y rentas de dicho convento habido y por haber y en su nombre doy poder a las justicias a quienes competa el conocimiento de sus causas para que ello le apremien como por sentencia pasada en cosa juzgada, renuncio leyes de su favor y la general de derecho. Y presente yo el dicho Joseph de Peralta acepto esta escritura y protesto usar de los derechos y acciones que en virtud he adquirido a dicho sarcofago y sepultura que es fecha en la ciudad de los Angeles a veinte tres dias del mes de mayo de mil y seiscientos y noventa años y los otorgantes a quienes yo el escribano doy fe que conzco. Lo firmaron siendo testigos Domingo de Herrera, Francisco de Herrera Calderon, y Diego de Neira, vecinos de esta dicha ciudad.

Fray Bernardo de Andia   Joseph de Peralta
                                                                                               ante mi Miguel Zeron Zapata,
                                                                                               escribano publico y de cabildo

Document 101: 1728—Antonio de Amaya accused of adultery with María de la O[10]

Miguel Rodríguez, Spaniard and *vecino* of this city, as husband of Doña María de la O, and as a person juridically joined to her, following the requirements and solemnities of the law, I present a criminal lawsuit against Antonio de Amaya, apparently a *chino*, and *vecino* of this city, blacksmith by trade. On Tuesday night, on the 27th of this month, around eight-thirty, I caught the mentioned man, with disregard for royal justice and with grave damage to his conscience, in the house of my dwelling place, with the said María de la O, my wife, with whom he has committed adultery [against] me. In an act of fury, I attacked him, and the said Amaya gave me four wounds with a hand spindle, injuring my left arm in three places and my abdomen. Seeing that I was injured, he took my said wife and is hiding her. Before this happened, because I had suspicions, I had warned the said Antonio de Amaya on several occasions not to enter my house, as I was worried that I would experience what has happened. I suspected this for more than three years and warned him several times during that span, even throwing him out of my house. So that such an unholy crime be punished according to the law and so that under the punishments they will incur it might serve as punishment and example for others, I ask Your Grace to order the said Antonio de Amaya to be arrested and imprisoned in the public jail, charging your magistrate with this task. With respect to my said wife, in following the solemnities of the law, I also present a lawsuit and ask that she be placed in this city's Santa María Egipciaca women's retreat.[11] I am prepared to justify all of the above, and protest that I will accuse them further, therefore,

I ask and beg Your Grace to accept this lawsuit, and in its tenor, to examine the witnesses that I will present. I ask that you order and determine everything as I have requested, as it is just. I ask and protest for damages and I swear to God Our Lord, on the sign of the holy cross, according to the law, that this lawsuit is true and not done out of malice, and in the necessary, etcétera.

Also, I say that Your Grace should order that the present scribe certify the wounds that the said Antonio de Amaya gave me, after this order, as I request above.

Miguel Rodríguez

In the very noble and loyal city [Puebla] of the Angels, on July 30, 1728. Before the lord bachiller Don Francisco Antonio de Bustamente, lawyer for this kingdom's royal audience, chief justice, and captain general in this city, by His Majesty. This petition and its contents were read.

---

10. Archivo Histórico Judicial de Puebla, Exp. 3070/0469, ff. 1r–1v.
11. *recogimiento*: a place of forced reclusion for women.

Document 101: 1728—Antonio de Amaya accused of adultery with María de la O

[Spanish transcription]

Miguel Rodriguez español Vezino de esta ciudad Marido y conjunta persona de Doña Maria de la Ô Premissos los requisitos y solennidades del Derecho me querello criminalmente de Antonio de Amaia, al parecer chino, Vezino de esta Ciudad de ofizio herrero, ên razon del que el sussodicho, con poco temor de Dios nuestro señor en menosprecio de la Real Justicia, y Grave daño de su consiencia el dia martes en la noche que se contaron Veinte y siete del corriente, como a las ôcho y media lo coji, en la casa de mi morada, con la dicha Maria de la O, mi mujer, con quien, me ha cometido adulterio, y llevado del acto primo, colerico le embesti, y el sussodicho, con vn malacate, me dio quatro heridas, tres en el brazo Yzquierdo, y Vna ên el Bacio, y Viendome herido, se llevo consigo a la dicha mi muger a quien tiene oculta, y antes de haver sussedido lo referido, por tener Yo malicias, en Varias ôcaciones le he amonestado, al dicho Antonio de Amaia, no entrara en mi cassa, temiendome de que no sussediera lo que he experimentado, y dichos requerimientos le he hecho Varias Vezes ên el êspacio, de mas de tres años ha que tengo las malicias, hasta llegar a correrlo de mi Cassa, y para, que tan Ynsecrable delicto sea castigado conforme â la ley, y devajo de las penas, en que han Yncurrido, que a ellos les sirva de castigo, y a otros de exemplo, se ha de servir Vuestra merced Justicia mediante de mandar, se ha aprehenda [sic] al dicho Antonio de Amaia, y se ponga presso ên la carzel publicca de reo adentro, êncargandosele por tal â su Alcayde, y a la dicha mi muger de quien assi mismo, premissas, las solennidades del Derecho, me querello, se ponga en el recojimiento de Santa Maria Ejipciaca de esta Ciudad que estoy presto a Justificar todo lo referido, devajo de la protexta de acussarlos mas en forma, por todo lo qual

A Vuestra merced, pido y suplico se sirva de admitir esta querella, y que a su thenor se examinen a los testigos que precentare, y mandar hazer y determinar en todo como llevo pedido, que es de Justicia que pido protexto costas y Juro por Dios nuestro señor y la señal de la santa Cruz segun forma de Derecho, ser esta querella Cierta, y no de Malicia y en lo nessessario etcetera

Otro si Digo, Que se ha de Servir Vuestra merced de mandar que el pressente escrivano a continuacion del auto, que a este escripto se proveiere, ponga certificacion de las heridas, que me dio el dicho Antonio de Amaia. pido *vt supra*

Miguel Rodriges

en la mui noble y mui leal ciudad de los Angeles a treynta dias del mes de Julio de mil settecientos y veinte y ocho años ante el señor Lisenciado Don Francisco Anttonio de Bustamante Abogado de la Real audiencia de este reino Justicia maior y theniente de Capitan General en esta ciudad por su Magestad se leyo esta peticion que presento el contenido en ella

Document 102: 1734—Genealogy and education of a philosophy student[12]

Domingo de Araballes, free *pardo*, *vecino* of this city [Puebla], I appear before Your Grace, in the best recourse to the law, and say: It is in my best interest to have the following information, which I offer, received. I am the legitimate son of Francisco de Araballes and Ana de Castañeda, his deceased wife, who had and procreated me during their legitimate matrimony. In this opinion and renown, I was and am commonly held. I am legitimately married and veiled, by order of our Holy Mother Church, to Teresa de la Encarnación Ortiz, natural daughter of Gertrudis de la Cruz, who is deceased. During our marriage, we have had and procreated Juan Manuel de San Roque y Araballes, among others. He is presently sixteen years old, as seen in the certificate of baptism that I present in due form. He has studied philosophy at the College of ~~the Spirit~~ San Ildefonso of this city's Jesuit Society. Later on, he studied surgery with father friar Manuel Rodríguez, of the sacred order of Our Lord San Hipólito, prior of his convent in the town of Xalapa. We have raised, fed, and recognized him as our legitimate son, and the said [San Roque y Araballes] has recognized us as his parents without any contradiction. [I also state] that I, my parents, my wife's parents, and our child, we were and are all free *pardos*, old Christians, of honest living, customs, and good actions, without calling attention to ourselves. We are all and also have been old Christians, clean of [taint of the] bad race of Moors, Jews, and of those newly converted to the guild of our holy Catholic faith, nor have we been punished by the Holy Office of the Inquisition, or another tribunal. By giving this information, I ask that Your Grace order that I be given the authorized testimonies that I may request in the form and manner so that they may be attested. To this end, I beg Your Grace to order what I have referred to above, as it is justice. I swear in due form, and in what is necessary, etcetera.

Domingo Antonio Araballes

[Spanish transcription]

Domingo de Araballes, pardo libre vezino de esta ciudad por el mejor recurso de derecho paresco ante Vuestra merced y Digo: que al mio combiene se me reçiba informaçion que ofresco al tenor de este escrito de ser como soi hijo legitimo de Francisco de Araballes, y Anna de Castañeda su muger difuntos, havido, y procreado constante su legitimo matrimonio, en cuia opinion, y fama fui, y soi comunmente reputado, y de como me hallo casado y velado legitimamente segun orden de nuestra Santa Madre Yglecia con Theresa de la Encarnaçion Ortis hija natural de Gertrudis de la Cruz difunta, y durante nuestro matrimonio hemos havido, y procreado por nuestro

---

12. Archivo Histórico Judicial de Puebla, Exp. 3242/0642, f. 2r.

hijo legitimo entre otros a Juan Manuel de San Roque y Araballes, que al presente sera de hedad de Dies y seis años, contenido en la certificacion de Baptismo que en debida forma presento, el qual se hâ hallado Cursando Phylosophia en el Colegio de el espiritu san Yldefonso de la compañia de Jesus de esta ciudad y despues cyrugia con el Padre frai Manuel Rodrigues del Sagrado orden de Señor San Hypolito, y Prior de su combento de el Pueblo de Xalapa, a quien hemos estado criando, alimentado, y reconosçiendo por nuestro hijo legitimo, y el susodicho a nosotros por sus Padres sin haver cossa en contrario, y tambien de como yo mis Padres, los de la dicha mi muger, y nuestro hijo somos, y fueron pardos libres, christianos viejos, de onesta vida, costumbre y buenos proçederes sin dar nota de nuestras personas, y que todos somos, y tambien fueron christianos Viejos limpios de toda mala raza de Moros, Judios, y de los nuebamente combertidos al gremio de nuestra Santa fee catholica, ni menos castigados por el Santo ofiçio de la Ynquisission, ni otro Tribunal alguno. Y dada dicha Ynformacion en la parte que vaste se ha de servir Vuestra merced mandar se me den los testimonios que pidiere authorisados en forma y manera que hagan fee; y para ello. A Vuestra merced suplico se sirba de mandar hazer como refiero, que es Justicia que perjuro en forma, y en lo nesessario etcétera.

Domingo Anttonio Araballes

Document 103: 1735—Inventory of a merchant in Zacatecas[13]

In the city of Our Lady of the Zacatecas, on July 10, 1734. The lord bachiller Don Juan Antonio de Ahumada, lawyer for the royal council and audiences of these kingdoms, captain general of this said city and its district, its Crown representative by His Majesty, said that as it is now nine o'clock in the morning on this day, His Grace received news that a man of broken color, apparently a mulatto widower, named Pascual de Vela, had died without a testament. He owned a small store, which was supported by Don Antonio Ruíz de Quirós, *vecino* and merchant of this city, in front of the city's main parish. This was communicated verbally to His Grace, along with the passing of the said Pascual. In consequence, His Grace should and did order that the said small store be closed off and an inventory be made of its contents immediately and without any delay. With respect to the intestate death of the said man, the present scribe will produce a certificate of the dead body and will

---

13. Archivo Histórico del Estado de Zacatecas, Civil, Bienes de Difuntos, Caja 29, ff. 1r–1v, 5r–5v. Courtesy of Professor Norah Gharala.

take charge of closing the small store, so that everything may be disposed of, and thus it was decreed, ordered, and signed.

Don Juan Antonio de Ahumada
Before me, Alonso de Coronado, royal and public scribe

[in the left-hand margin, "certificate of a dead body"]

And then, immediately, I, the scribe, visited the small store owned by Pascual de Vela, according to the order on the previous page. I attest and give true testimony, as I am permitted by law and nothing more, to have seen the deceased cadaver which seemed to be that of the said Pascual, apparently without breath or vital spirit, according to the knowledge that I had of him while living. He was lying on a *petate* mat, and at his sides four tallow candles were burning. I certify this, so that it is evident, in this city of Our Lady of the Zacatecas on July 10, 1734. Witnesses, Felipe González Calderón, Miguel Hernández, and Felix de Salazar, who were present.

And I sign it, Alonso de Coronado, royal and public scribe

. . .

[list begins with an extensive inventory of cloths]

• A small silver jewelry box from Father Zesati's house, for four reales	0 p. 4
• A cross and a small jewelry box, for three reales	0 p. 3
• A little piece of cloth for decorating, for a real and a half	1 p. 1 ½
• Some little breeches made of coarse cloths, for a real and a half	0 p. 1 ½
• A coral choker from Paulín, for a real	0 p. 1
• A ribbon from the *santera* [female healer?], for two reales	0 p. 2
• Two silver spoons from Don Juan Zesati, for four reales	0 p. 4
• Four ounces of old silver-copper alloy, for two reales	3 p. [sic]
• A silver spoon, for two reales	0 p. 2
• A jewelry box of the good shepherd, for one real	0 p. 1
• A shell with the Virgin of Dolores, for two reales	0 p. 2
• A small silver cross, for three reales	0 p. 3
• An old cloth shawl, for five reales	0 p. 5
• A piece of black woolen stuff from Castile	0 p. 4

- Six pesos and three reales from various small items 6 p. 3
- Four reales for other small items 0 p. 4
- A silk scarf, for two reales 0 p. 2
- A gold and copper alloy [pendant?] from La Laguna, for a peso and one and a half reales 1 p. 1 ½
- A pair of used silk stockings 1 p. 4
- An ordinary hat, for three reales 0 p. 3
- A glazed blue linen lining for a large petticoat, for a peso 1 p.

[in the left-hand margin, "Debts in favor of the creditors"]

To Don Antonio Ruíz de Quirós, fifty-eight pesos, five reales and a half	58 p. 5 ½
To Don Cristóbal Ramírez, twenty-three pesos for bread	23 p.
To Esteban Ramírez, Alcántara's cashier	23 p.
To the landlady, seven pesos and a real and a half	7 p. 1 ½
	<u>111 p. 7</u>

[in the left-hand margin, "Debts in favor of the estate]"

Master Simón, the dulcian player, owes the remainder of eighteen pesos and five reales	18 p. 5
Don Francisco de Castro owes twelve pesos	12 p.
Señora Gertrudis owes nine pesos	9 p.
Joseph Rodriguez owes one peso	1 p.
Felipe *entierra muertos* [gravedigger?] owes three pesos and four reales	3 p. 4
Lorenzo de Santiago owes seven reales	0 p. 7
The landlady owes four pints of wine, at four reales each, which comes to two pesos, these are discounted from the nine [pesos], one real and a half, which are owed for the house rent, seven pesos and a real and a half are left	2 p.
Juan de Zamora owes six reales and a half	0 p. 6 ½
Urbina owes two reales	0 p. 2
Domingo owes one peso three reales	1 p. 3
Manuel owes one peso one real	1 p. 1

Master Quintero owes two pesos and a real and a half	2 p. 1 ½
Miguel Capitán owes two pesos and half a real	2 p. 0 ½
Joseph Telles owes four pesos	4 p.
Bartolomé owes three pesos five reales	3 p. 5
Bonilla, the son of the elder Bonilla, owes a peso five reales	1 p. 5
Juan, the gilder, owes four reales	0 p. 4
Oaxaca [sic] owes two pesos	2 p.
Doña María Ignacia, the wife of Francisco de Escobar, owes the remainder of six pesos	6 p.
Juan de Soto, the husband of la Nava, owes the remainder of seven pesos six reales	7 p. 6
Doña Catarina, "the Zarazua," owes five pesos six reales	5 p. 6
	<u>91 p. 1 ½</u>

With this, the inventory of pawned items and clothing was concluded.

[Spanish transcription]

En la Ciudad de Nuestra Señora de los Zacatecas en Diez de Jullio de mill Setecientos treinta y quatro años. El Señor Lizenciado Don Juan Antonio de Ahumada Abogado de los Reales Consejo y Audiencias de estos Reynos Theniente de Capitan General de esta dicha Ciudad y Su Districto y Corregidor En ella por Su Magestad = Dixo que por quanto ahora que Serán las nuebe horas de la mañana De este Dia se le ha dado â dado a Su Merced notiçia de haver falleçido Sin disposiccion thestamentaria Vn hombre de Color quebrado al pareser mulato Viudo nombrado Pasqual de Vela quien tenia Vn tendejoncito Escaso frente de la Yglecia Parroquial mayor de esta Ciudad a Expensas de Suplemento que le tenia Don Antonio Ruiz de Quiros Vezino y mercader en esta dicha Ciudad, lo que assi Verbalmente Se le ha notiçiado â Su Merced Como el de el fallecimiento de el dicho Pasqual, en Cuia consequençia Devêra Mandar y su Merced Mandô Se passe luego y sin dilacion algunâ Sercar dicho Tendejon interin Se haze Ymbentario de lo que en el Exisitiere. Respecto de la muerte intestada de el dicho â Cuia diligencia passe el presente Escripano [sic] y puesta Zertificacion de fee del Cuerpo Muerto y Diligençia de Serrarse el tendejo Con Vista de todo Se Providençiarâ y assi lo Proveyo, Mando y firmo =

Don Juan Antonio de Ahumada   Ante mi Alonso de Coronado
                                                                        scribano Real y Publico

[al margen izquierdo, "fee de Cuerpo muerto"]

Y luego incontinenti, Yo el Escribano estando en el tendejoncito que tenia a su Cargo Pasqual de Vela en conformidad de el Autho de la buelta Zertifico y doy fee y Verdadero testimonio en quanto por Derecho me es permitido y no En mas haver Visto Vn difunto cadaver al pareser Sin respiracion ni aliento Vital que parecia Ser el de el dicho Pasqual Según el Conosimiento que en Vida tuve de el, el que estaba puesto en Vn petate y â sus lados quatro belas de Sebo ardiendo, y para que Conste assi lo Zertifico en esta Ciudad de nuestra Señora de los Zacatecas en dies de Jullio de mill Setecientos treinta y quatro años Siendo testigo Phelipe Gonzalez Calderon, Miguel Hernandez, y Felix de Salazar presentes =

    Y Lo signo Alonso de Coronado scrivano Real y Publico

* * *

[sigue un extenso inventario de telas]

Ytten. Vn relicario de plata de en casa del Padre Zesati, en quatro rreales	0 p. 4
Ytten. Vna Cruz y un relicario en tres rreales	0 p. 3
Ytten. Vn pedazito de franja en real y medio	1 p. 1 ½
Ytten. Vnos Calzositos [sic] de Pañete en real y medio	0 p. 1 ½
Ytten. Vna gargantilla de Corales de Paulín en un real	0 p. 1
Ytten. un liston de la santera en dos rreales	0 p. 2
Ytten. dos cucharas de Plata de Don Juan Zesati en quatro rreales	0 p. 4
Ytten. Quatro onzas de plata vieja ligada a seis rreales	3 p. [sic]
Ytten. Vna cuchara de Plata en dos rreales	0 p. 2
Ytten. Vn Relicario del buen pastor en un Real	0 p. 1
Ytten. Vna concha con Virgen de Dolores en Dos rreales	0 p. 2
Ytten. Vna cruzesita de plata en tres rreales	0 p. 3
Ytten. Vn Revozo Viejo atelado en cinco rreales	0 p. 5
Ytten. Vn pedazo de Vayeta negro de Castilla	0 p. 4
Ytten. Seis pesos y tres rreales de Varias menudencias	6 p. 3
Ytten. Quatro rreales de otras menudencias	0 p. 4
Ytten. Vna mascada de Seda en dos rreales	0 p. 2

Ytten. Vna tumbaga de La Laguna en un peso real y medio	1 p. 1 ½
Ytten. Vn par de medias de Zeda muescas vsadas	1 p. 4
Ytten. Vn sombrero ordinario de tres rreales	0 p. 3
Ytten. Vn forro de mitan azul de Pollera en un peso	1 p.
[al margen izquierdo, "Ditas a favor de los Acrêhedores]	
a Don Antonio Ruiz de Quiros cinquenta y ocho pesos cinco reales y medio	58 p. 5 ½
a Don Christobal Ramirez de pan Veinte y tres pesos	23 p.
a Estevan Martinez Cajero de Alcantara	23 p.
A la casera siete pesos real y medio	7 p. 1 ½
	<u>111 p. 7</u>
[al margen izquierdo, "Ditas a favor de los Vienes"]	
Deve el Maestro Simon el Bajonero de resto dies y ocho pesos y cinco reales	18 p. 5
Deve Don Francisco de Castro Doze pesos	12 p.
Deve Señora Gertrudis nuebe pesos	9 p.
Deve Joseph Rodriguez un peso	1 p.
Deve Phelipe Entierra Muertos tres pesos y quatro rreales	3 p. 4
Deve Lorenzo de Santiago siete rreales	0 p. 7
Deve la casera quatro quartillos de Vino a quatro rreales son dos pesos que esfalcados de los nueve [pesos] y real y medio, que se le deven de casa sale restan siete pesos y real y medio	2 p.
Deve Juan de Samora seiss rreales y medio	0 p. 6 ½
Deve Vrbina dos rreales	0 p. 2
Deve Domingo un peso tres rreales	1 p. 3
Deve Manuel un peso un real	1 p. 1
Deve el Maestro Quintero dos pesos real y medio	2 p. 1 ½
Deve Miguel Capitan dos pesos y medio real	2 p. 0 ½
Deve Joseph Thelles quatro pesos	4 p.
Deve Bartholome tres pesos cinco rreales	3 p. 5

Deve Bonilla el hijo del Biejo Bonilla un peso y cinco rreales	1 p. 5
Deve Juan el Dorador, quatro rreales	0 p. 4
Deve Guaxaca [sic] dos pesos	2 p.
Deve Doña Maria Ygnacia, Muger de de [sic] Francisco de Escobar de resto seis pesos	6 p.
Deve Juan de Soto Marido de la Nava de resto siete pesos y seis rreales	7 p. 6
Deve Doña Catharina la Zarazua cinco pesos y seis reales	5 p. 6
	91 p. 1 ½

Con lo qual se concluyo este Ymbentario de Prendas

Document 104: 1788—Gertrudis Caballero's husband taxed unfairly[14]

Mexico [City], September 19, 1788

To the lord fiscal attorney of the royal treasury

Miguel de Torres, Spaniard and *vecino* of the Hacienda de la Concepción in the jurisdiction of Tlaxcala. In the best possible form, I say that I am currently serving Don Lorenzo Domínguez in the said hacienda. I am married to Gertrudis Caballero, mulatta and a widow of another subject from the same vicinity. Since I have been serving my master, I have been forced to pay tribute for my said wife for five years. My said master has satisfied [these tribute payments], as is evident by the receipts that I hold. With this issue in mind, I turn to Your Excellency's justification and beg to have my *calidad*[15] as a Spaniard certified, so that I may be relieved from the payment of tribute that I pay to the tax collector for vagrants for my said wife. It is public and well-known that I am Spanish, which I will prove if necessary, and for this motive I have not paid the royal tribute. Therefore, I ask that Your Excellency order that the decree serve as a dispatch with regard to my well-known insolvency and my occupation as a poor muleteer.

---

14. Archivo Histórico Judicial de Puebla, Exp. 5247, ff. 1r–2r.
15. *Calidad* was a social category that took into account a person's physical appearance, standing in society, reputation, and ancestry. As such, it was a complex and highly subjective category of identification that could be contested.

I humbly beg Your Excellency to order and determine as I have requested, etcétera.

He does not know how to sign

* * *

Most Excellent Sir

I have requested the current tax roll for the Tlaxcala jurisdiction from the chamber of the royal audience, in order to determine whether Gertrudis Caballero, the wife of Miguel de Torres, is in fact listed, as argued in this case file. I have not received the tax roll because it was sent to the lord intendant of Puebla, whose district is responsible for that area [of the Concepción hacienda]. I should only say that, because he is a Spaniard, as stated, the wife is not supposed to pay tribute, although she belongs to tribute-paying *calidad*. In this, her [tribute status] was improved as a result of her marriage, which is in following with practice. Your Excellency will determine what is just on this matter. Mexico City, October 24, 1788.

Riva

[Spanish transcription]

Mexico 19 de Septiembre de 1788

Al Señor Fiscal de Real Hazienda

Miguel de Torres Español y vecino de la Hazienda de la Concepcion en Jurisdiccion de Tlaxcala; como mas haya lugâr = Digo: Que en la actualidad me hallo sirviendo en dicha Hazienda a Don Lorenzo Dominguez, y Casado con Gertrudis Caballero Mulata, viuda que fué de otro sugeto de la misma vecindad: Desde que estoy sirviendo â dicho amo, me hân hecho pagàr Tributo por dicha mi Muger ha tiempo de cinco años, que lo ha satisfecho el referido mi Amo, como consta por los recivos que paran en mi poder. En esta atencion ocurro â la Justificacion de Vuestra Excelencia suplicandole se sirva mandar, que haciendo constar ser de calidad Español se me reelebe de la paga de los Reales tributos que pagò al recaudador de vagos, por la nominada mi Muger; por sêr publico y notorio sêr yô español, lo que en caso necesario harè constar y de no habêr pagado dicho Real derecho. por este motivo: para lo que se ha de servir Vuestra Excelencia assimismo mandâr que el decreto sirva de despacho respecto â mi notoria insolvencia y sêr mi exercicio pobre Arriero.

A Vuestra Excelencia rendidamente suplico se sirva mandar hacer y determinar como pido &.a

No sabe firmar

* * *

Excelentisimô Señor

Haviendo pedido por la Matricula corriente de la Jurisdicion de Tlaxcala al oficio de Camara de la Real Audiencia para reconocer si efectivamente se halla empadronada Gertrudis Caballero muger de Miguel de Torres que ha promovido este Expediente, no se me ha pasado por tenerla remitida al Señor Yntendente del Puebla à cuyo distrito toca aquel Partido; y unicamente devo decir, que siendo èl Español, como expresa, no corresponde tribute la muger aunque esta sea de calidad contribuyente de que salio por haver mejorada de suerte con el matrimonio, lo qual es con arreglo à la practica sobre que determinarà Vuestra Excelencia lo que estimare Justo. Mexico 24 de Otubre de 1788.

Riva

CHAPTER 9
Fragile Freedoms

The documents in this chapter evidence the constant difficulties that free-born and recently freed people experienced in Mexico. The caste system established shifting sets of limitations that affected almost everyone, even if they could produce a letter of manumission or a baptismal entry demonstrating a long lineage of free ancestors. The elite Spaniards who controlled city councils benefited from the caste system and wielded disproportionate influence over local affairs. Some of these local regulations were meant to establish control over working people generally, affecting both free and enslaved populations. The 1615 restrictions on *Carnestolendas* celebrations offer a glimpse into elite anxieties during popular celebrations, but also into the differentiated punishments handed out according to caste categories. The 1610s and 1620s, in particular, were decades of considerable racial anxieties, which culminated in the persecution of African-descended communities throughout Mexico. Black town criers were a common feature of the colonial landscape, yet the role of free *pardos* and mulattos as interpreters and scribes (and thus producers of information) was frequently contested. The documents from 1623 and 1686 speak to those dynamics.

It is important to emphasize that even people who managed to formally secure their freedom encountered all sorts of restrictions on their personal lives. The 1658 selections speak to a vast community of 123 men who had sexual relations with other men in Puebla, Mexico City, and surrounding towns. Serge Gruzinski published a ground-breaking article based on his analysis of this case, "Las cenizas del deseo: Homosexuales novohispanos a mediados del siglo XVII" (1985), which has been translated as "The Ashes of Desire: Homosexuality in Mid-Seventeenth-Century New Spain" (2003). The documents from this case are included here as a reminder of the violent limitations that both enslaved and free people encountered when it came to questions of sexuality. The text reveals the ruling elite's deep anxieties surrounding the clothing, behaviors, and nicknames of men who loved other men, and the affective ties between them.

In other cases, free families in rural settings found themselves combating a profoundly corrupt judicial system. The 1783 case of the Ávalos family in Colima speaks to the injustice and despair that free people often encountered when pitted against powerful overseers and their patrons. The petition also sheds light on the musical culture that must have animated many gatherings in the late eighteenth century. A year later, the demands of an Izúcar family expose the system of deceit that sugar plantation owners used to extend their control over individuals, families, and communities that were legally free.

This chapter also features the 1829 abolition act proclaimed by President Vicente Guerrero. Crucially, the abolition decree was proclaimed by a man of African descent, who at the time served as the leader of a conflicted, newly independent nation. The internal debates surrounding individual freedoms and opportunities and the dismantling of the caste system can also be seen in Spain's 1812 lifting of caste restrictions and in José María Morelos's 1813 "Sentiments of the Nation." The version of the "Sentiments" presented here, with numerous corrections and emendations, is meant to highlight the internal tensions and debates among Morelos's circle. Finally, the tangible consequences of independence are evident in a fascinating 1826 document from Teotitlán del Camino, Oaxaca. This mass manumission contributes a valuable local case through which to imagine the last days of slavery in Mexico.

Document 105: 1612—Restrictions on Black socialization in Puebla[1]

In the very noble and loyal city [Puebla] of the Angels of New Spain, on April 7, 1612. The said city entered its council and town hall as is customary . . . and in my presence, the council scribe, the following was agreed upon. . . .

This day the city said that as it has heard news that in Mexico City it has been decreed and ordered by the lords of the royal audience in this New Spain that Blacks and mulattos, free and slave, shall not bear swords, daggers, knives, nor other public weapons. They will not have brotherhood meetings, nor gather for song, nor at dances, nor in other places, under certain punishments, because that is what appears to be most convenient for the service of God Our Lord and His Majesty. As this city wants to do the same, it was agreed and ordered that it be publicly proclaimed from this day forward that the said Blacks, mulattos, free or slave, those belonging to the *vecinos* of this city or to foreigners who may come, with no regard to their status, condition, or standing, may not in any manner have brotherhood meetings publicly or secretly, nor may they gather for songs or dances, nor may three of them go on the streets [together] to any given place. A punishment of two hundred lashes will be applied for each thing in which they exceed themselves. The weapons that may be taken from them will, of course, be given to the officer or officers who apprehend them. In addition, a [fee of] four reales will be imposed for the imprisonment of any Black or mulatto [person] that might be apprehended for the above. And to investigate the things above, the arresting officer will be believed by a simple statement, with no further investigation needed; of this they must be aware. The magistrate and municipal court justices of this

---

1. Archivo Municipal de Puebla, Actas de Cabildo, Vol. 14., ff. 220/219v.

city are charged to observe this without exception, and will not admit nor accept the requests of any person, because this is convenient to the service of God Our Lord and His Majesty, until something further is decreed and ordered.

[Spanish transcription]

La muy noble y muy leal çiudad de los angeles de la nueva españa en siete dias del mes de abril de mill y seisçientos y doze años. La dicha çiudad entro en su cabildo y ayuntamiento como lo tiene de costumbre . . . por pressençia de mi el escrivano de cabildo en el qual se acordo lo siguiente . . .

Este dia la dicha çiudad dixo que por quanto se a tenido notiçia que en la çiudad de Mexico se a hordenado y mandado por los señores de la Real audiençia desta nueva españa que los negros y mulatos libres y esclavos no traygan espadas, dagas, cuchillos ni otras armas publicas, ni hagan juntas de cofradias, ni en cantillos, ni en bayles ni otras partes so çiertas penas porque assi a paresçido convenir al serviçio de Dios nuestro señor y de su magestad y queriendo esta dicha çiudad hazer lo mismo se acordo y mando se pregone publicamente que desde hoy en adelante los dichos negros ni mulatos libres ni esclavos assi de los vezinos desta çiudad como de los forasteros que a ella vinieren de qualquier estado condiçion y calidad que sean no puedan en manera alguna hazer las dichas juntas de cofradias publica ni secretamente ni estar en cantillos ni en bayles ni yr por las calles publicas tres dellos a qualesquier parte que sea, so pena de dozientos açotes por cada cosa que excçedieren de los susodicho y de perdimiento de las armas que les fueren quitadas las quales se aplican desde luego para el alguaçil, o alguaçiles que los prendieren y mas quatro reales de prision de qualquier mulatto o negro que aprendieren por lo suso dicho y para averiguacion de [ilegible] cosa de las Referidas sea creydo el alguazil que los prendiere por su simple argumento sin otra diligençia alguna sobre que se les encarga la conçiençia y que los señores Alcalde mayor y ordinarios desta çiudad lo executen yrremisiblemente sin admitir ni respectar aceptaçion ni ruegos de persona alguna porque assi conviene al serviçio de Dios nuestro señor y de su magestad hasta que otra cosa se hordene y mande.

Document 106: 1615—Controlling *Carnestolendas* or Mardi Gras[2]

In the very noble and very loyal city [Puebla] of the Angels of New Spain, on February 20, 1615. . . .

---

2. Archivo Municipal de Puebla, Actas de Cabildo, Vol. 15, ff. 56/55.

This day, the said city [council] said that in the days near *Carnestolendas* [Mardi Gras] each year and on the same day, there are groups and gatherings of Spaniards, *mestizos*, Blacks, mulattos, and Indians, who throw oranges, limes, and other things at each other. Aside from this being an impertinent thing that causes noise and restlessness, there have been deaths, injuries, and many other disgraces as a result. So to avoid this, it was agreed that it will be publicly proclaimed that on the said day of *Carnestolendas* or on other days close to it, no persons shall throw oranges, limes, nor any other thing at each other under pretense of game or entertainment. Neither will the said groups form in the said barrios, nor in any other part of this city, under punishment of six pesos and three days of jail for the Spaniards. For the *mestizos*, three pesos and ten days of jail. The said pesos will be applied to the construction and repairs of the Atoyac river bridge. A hundred lashes will be given to the Blacks, mulattos, and Indians along the public and customary streets of this city, in addition to paying the constable a common gold peso for each imprisoned person.

[Marginal note: "that there be no groups, nor that they throw oranges during *Carnestolendas*."]

[Spanish transcription]

En la muy noble y muy leal çiudad de los Angeles de la Nueva España en veynte dias del mes de Febrero de mill y siesçientos y quinze años . . .

Este dia la dicha çiudad dixo que por quanto en los dias cercanos al de carnestolendas de cada un año y en el mismo dia, en los barrios desta çiudad calles reales y plaças publicas della ay bandos y juntas de personas españoles mestizos negros mulatos e yndios y unos a otros se tiran con naranjas limas y otras cosas. Y demas de ser cosa ynpertinente y de ruydo y alboroto an sucedido muertes, heridas y oras muchas desgraçias y para lo evitar se acordo se pregone publicamente que en el dicho dia de carnestolendas ni en demas cercanos a el ningunas personas so color de juego o entretenimiento ni en otra manera se tiren unos a otros con las dichas naranjas limas ni otra cosa ni hagan los dichos bandos en los dichos barrios ni en otra parte alguna desta çiudad so pena a los españoles de cada seis pesos y tres dias de carzel y a los mestizos tres pesos y diez dias de carçel aplicados los dichos pesos para la obra y adereço que se haze en la puente (sic) del rrio de Atoyaque y a los negros mulatos e yndios cada çient açotes por las calles publicas y acostumbradas desta çiudad demas de pagar a el alguazil que hiziere la prission un pesso de oro comun de cada persona.

[Al margen, "que no aya bandos, ni se tiren con naranjas en las carnestolendas"]

Document 107: 1618—Ordinance against Black gatherings, dances, and games[3]

In the very noble and loyal city [Puebla] of the Angels of New Spain, on May 18, 1618, the said city entered its council and town hall meeting as is customary . . . and, thus, in the presence of me, Nicolás Fernández de la Fuente, scribe for Our Lord the King and the said council, the city agreed to the following. . . .

On this day, the regent Pedro de Uribe, the city's legal representative, said and proposed that many and various times it has been ordered that Black and mulatto gatherings are not to be allowed in the plazas, on the royal streets, or in the Indians' neighborhoods. And that they should not be allowed to have dances, games, or other forms of entertainment and noise that have resulted and result in fights, injuries, deaths, and other damages that could be even greater. Because they attend these events, those who are slaves miss many days from their masters' service and absent themselves. So that this ceases, it is convenient to decree a greater remedy and this should be made into an ordinance.

The city [council] seeing this said that after carefully considering the aforementioned and using Our Lord the King's mercy and authority, it decreed and ordered that, for the good and the peace of their Republic, that from here on there shall be no gatherings, dances, ring games, nor other entertainments or merrymaking for the said Blacks or mulattos, whether free or slave, in the said plazas, neighborhoods, streets, nor in other public or private places. Nor are they to walk around at night throwing stones at windows, making noise, or singing and playing music. For those who are free, the punishment will be ten common gold pesos for each, which will be applied in four parts to his majesty's chamber, the city's funds, the judges, and the accuser, and one hundred lashes to be given in public. For the slaves, the said corporal punishment, and the magistrate, court justices, judge, deputies, and loyal executors of this city and whoever noted it first will execute the said punishments without any pardon. Any constables who arrest them in the act will put them in the public jail to be punished. The said constables will receive one common gold peso for every slave they apprehend for the said crime, considering that as slaves, they are not to be condemned to a monetary punishment.

The said city, council, and its regiment ask the Most Excellent Lord Viceroy of this New Spain to confirm this order and have it publicly proclaimed so that all of this may be known and the said justices may execute it.

---

3. Archivo Municipal de Puebla, Actas de Cabildo, Vol. 15, ff. 190/189.

[Spanish transcription]

En La Muy noble y muy Leal çiudad de Los Angeles de la nueva españa a diez y ocho dias del mes de Mayo de mill y siesçientos y diez y ocho años. la dicha çiudad entro en su cabildo y ayuntamiento como lo tiene de costumbre . . . y assi por pressençia de mi Nicolas Fernandez de la Fuente, escrivano del Rey nuestro señor y del dicho cabildo la dicha çiudad Acordo lo siguiente . . .

En este dia el Regidor Pedro de Urive Procurador mayor desta dicha çiudad dixo y propuso que muchas y diversas vezes se a mandado que no aya juntas de negros y mulatos en las plaças y calles Reales ni en los barrios de los yndios. Y que no hagan bayles danças juegos ni otros entretenimientos y Ruydos de que an Resultado y Resultan Riñas, enemistades, heridas, muertes y otros daños y amagan a otros mayores y los que son esclavos por acudir a esto faltan muchos dias del serviçio de sus amos y se aussentan. Y para que esto çesse conviene se provea de mayor Remedio y que sobre ello se haga ordenança =

Y visto por la dicha çiudad dixo q usando de la merçed y facultad que tiene del Rey nuestro señor por el tenor de la pressente aviendo bien mirado y considerado lo susodicho para el bien y quietud de su Republica ordena y manda que de aqui adelante no se hagan las dichas juntas, danças, bayles, juegos "de sortijas", ni otros entretenimientos y huelgas por los dichos negros ni mulatos libres ni esclavos en las dichas plaças, barrios, calles ni otras partes publica ni secretamente ni anden de noche tirando piedras a ventanas ni haziendo Ruydos ni dando musicas so pena a los que fueren libres de cada diez pesos de oro comun aplicados por quartas partes camara de su magestad, Propios de çiudad, juezes y denunçiador y que les sean dados çien açotes publicamente y a los esclavos la dicha pena corporal y el alcalde mayor y ordinarios y justiçia diputados fieles executors desta çiudad y quien primero previniere executen las dichas penas sin remission alguna y cualesquiera alguaziles los prendan en infragante y pongan en la carzel publica para que se castiguen. Y de cada esclavo que prendieren por el dicho delicto lleven los dichos alguaziles un peso de oro comun de prission por su trabajo supuesto que estos por ser esclavos no an de ser condenados en pena pecuniaria =

Y la dicha çiudad cabildo y Regimiento della pide al excelentisimo señor Virrey desta nueva españa lo mande confirmar y que se pregone publicamente para que venga notiçia de todo y las dichas justicias lo executen.

Document 108: 1623—Charges against Francisco Manzanedo, mulatto interpreter[4]

In Chapultepec, Most Excellent Lord, on July 20, 1623

Francisco Ponce, *vecino* of the city of Tepeaca. I say that Francisco Manzanedo, who is mulatto, is in this city and carries out the office of interpreter in this province. And there are laws, royal ordinances, that prohibit him from being an interpreter and carrying out said office. Therefore,

I ask and beg Your Excellence to order that he no longer carry out the office of interpreter nor any other royal office, since he is forbidden from having such [positions], and that he should pay the tributes that he owes His Majesty. In this I will receive good and grace.

Francisco Ponce

Most Excellent Sir, if Your Excellence is so disposed, you may order that if the said account in this report is true, the justices may not allow this Francisco Manzanedo to carry out the office of interpreter, or any other royal office, and that he should pay tribute. July 29, 1623.

Doctor Luis de Sifuentes

[Spanish transcription]

En Chapultepec, Excelentisimo Señor A 20 de Julio de 1623

Francisco Ponçe vezino de la ciudad de Tepeaca digo que en ella esta Francisco Mançanedo el qual es mulato y usa oficio de ynterpete en la dicha probinçia y pues las leyes hordenanças Reales esta prohibido el poderlo ser ni usar el dicho oficio atento a lo qual

A vuestra excelencia pido y suplico se sirba de mandar no use el dicho oficio de ynterpete ni otro Real pues le esta prohibido el poder los tener y que pague tributos que deve a su magestad en que Reçevire bien y merced

Francisco Ponce

Excelentisimo señor siendo Vuestra excelencia servido, puede mandar que siendo çierta la Relaçion que por este memorial se haçe, la Justicia no consienta que este Francisco Mansanedo use offiçio de interpetre ni otro Real y que pague tributo. 29 de Julio. 623.

Doctor Luis de Cifuentes

---

4. Archivo General de la Nación, Indiferente Virreinal, Caja 4380, Exp. 28, ff. 1r–1v.

Document 109: 1646—Juan Martín and Luisa Hernández accused of cohabitation[5]

In the city [Puebla] of the Angels, on July 5, 1646, Juan de Vargas de Inostrosa, this city's magistrate by His Majesty, said that today at around eleven at night, more or less, he was making his rounds when he was told that for more than five years Juan Martín, a free mulatto, single, *vecino* of this city, and journeyman tailor, has been and is publicly cohabiting with Luisa Hernández, a free mulatta, single. The aforementioned Juan Martín has entered her house at all hours of the day and they have been eating and sleeping together as if they were a legitimate husband and wife. From this cohabitation there has been and is scandal and gossip in this city, so to address what has been reported and the damage that could come from this before me, the public scribe, he [Vargas de Inostrosa] went to the houses where the said Luisa Hernández, mulatta, lives. Entering the house, he found the aforementioned Luisa and the said Juan Martín, mulatto, in a room together, naked and lying in bed. As a result, the said magistrate ordered and made opening charges against them. . . . I, the scribe, attest regarding the said arrest and, accordingly, I received their oath in the presence of His Grace. The aforementioned swore by God Our Lord and on the sign of the cross, according to the law, and promised to tell the truth. They were each asked secretly and apart and both said and confessed that it was true that they had been cohabiting for five years, more or less. . . . And the said magistrate ordered that the said Juan Martín, mulatto, be imprisoned and placed in this city's public jail and delivered to it. And, thus, it was done. . . .

Juan de Vargas de Inostrosa   Before me, Alonso de Bonilla, scribe for His Majesty

[Spanish transcription]

En la ciudad de los Angeles a cinco dias del mes de Julio de mil seiscientos y quarenta y seis años Juan de Vargas de Inostrosa alcalde ordinario de esta ciudad por su magestad dixo que oy que seran las onse de la noche poco mas o menos yendo su merced de rronda se le dio noticia de que Juan Martin mulato libre soltero vezino desta ciudad oficial de sastre de mas de cinco años a esta parte a estado y esta publicamente amancevado con Luisa Hernandez mulata libre soltera entrando el susodicho en su caza a todas oras comiendo y durmiendo Juntos como si fuesen marido y muger lijitimos y que de dichos amasevamiento a avidos y ay nota escandalo y murmuracion en esta ciudad y para obrar lo rreferido y el daño que se puede rrecreser su merced por ante mi el escrivano fue a las casas donde bive la dicha Luisa Hernandez mulata y aviendo entrado dentro della fue hallada la susodicha y el dicho Juan Martin mulato en vn aposento Juntos y desnudos y acostados en cama por lo qual el dicho alcalde

---

5. Archivo Histórico Judicial de Puebla, Exp. 1961/1434, ff. 1r–1v.

mando hazer y hizo contra ellos esta caveza de proseso . . . que yo el escrivano de por fee la dicha aprehencion y en esta conformidad yo el dicho escrivano rrecevi Juramento en presencia de su merced de los susodichos los quales lo hisieron Por dios nuestro señor y por la señal de la cruz en forma de derecho y prometieron de decir verdad y siendo Preguntados a cada vno de por si secreta y apartadamente anbos dixeron y confezaron hera verdad que de tiempo de cinco años a esta parte Poco mas o menos an estado amansevados . . . y el dicho alcalde mando que el dicho Juan Martin mulato fueze prezo y Puesto en la carzel publica desta ciudad y entregado en ella por tal y se hizo asi . . .

Juan de Vargas de Hinostrosa

Ante mi, Alonso de Bonilla,
scrivano de su magestad

Document 110: 1658—Investigation into men who loved other men[6]

I, Esteban de Mugarrieta, commissioned scribe, one of the scribes for Mexico's royal audience of this New Spain, for His Majesty Our Lord, and for the case which will be described below. I certify that on September 27 of this year [1658], the lord bachiller Don Juan Manuel de Sotomayor, Knight of the Calatrava Order of His Majesty's Council and a magistrate in this court, was informed that some men had committed the nefarious sin. [This took place] one afternoon this very month by this city's stone walls in the field.

His Grace summoned Juana de Herrera, a *mestiza* washerwoman, whose oath was taken. She said that the previous Thursday, September 26, she was washing clothes by the stone wall, which is toward San Lázaro, outside of this said city. Some boys approached her hastily and shouted that she should go see some men who were playing like dogs. The said woman rose and went a certain distance from where she was washing, a good stretch away from her post. She saw that two men were committing the nefarious sin, one on top of another, both without their trousers. The man on top was covering the man below with a cape he was wearing. The said woman said she did not dare to get any closer, for fear that they would kill her. Due to this fear, she was only able to recognize Juan de la Vega, mulatto. The other seemed to her to be a *mestizo*, this was the man that was on the bottom.

His Grace immediately began an investigation to find where the said Juan de la Vega lived. It was discovered that he lived in Doña Melchora de Estrada's house, which is in the San Pablo neighborhood. His Grace went to the said Doña Melchora's

---

6. Archivo General de Indias, México, 38, n. 57b, no folio.

house, but the said Juan de la Vega had moved from there. [His Grace] received information from the people who lived in the said house where the said Juan de la Vega had lived. He found out that [Juan de la Vega] was an effeminate mulatto, who was called *Cotita*, which is the same as pansy. The said mulatto would switch his hips and on his forehead usually wore a little cloth, called a *melindre*, that women use. In the openings of the sleeves of a white doublet, he wore many hanging ribbons. He would sit on the floor like a woman and make tortillas, wash [clothes], and cook. Some youths, whom he called "my soul, my life, my heart," would visit him. They would sit with him and sleep together in a room. And the said Juan de la Vega was offended if they did not call him Cotita.

Likewise, an Indian named Tomás de Santiago was examined. He said all of the things above and said that one night he had stayed in the room of the said men in Doña Melchora's house. As there was [moon]light that night he saw that José Durán, a *mestizo* youth from the city [Puebla] of the Angels, committed the nefarious sin with Jerónimo Calbo, a native of this city. With the investigation and news given in Doña Melchora's house, the [location of] the house to where the said Juan de la Vega had moved was identified. The said man was sought out at midnight and found in said house. Upon entry, the said Juan de la Vega, José Durán, Jerónimo Calbo, Miguel Jerónimo, *mestizo*, and Simón de Chavez, Indian, were found naked and apprehended.

They were brought to the court's jail and were visited by all the court's judges on October 3 of this present year. Following the lord magistrates, the case was received within a certain term and [the accused] were charged. His Grace, the said lord bachiller Don Juan Manuel de Sotomayor, was tasked with taking their confessions, arresting the other criminals and taking their confessions, and conducting further investigations until the case against the said criminals was established and against any others who might be offenders.

Then immediately, His Grace, the said lord magistrate, took the confessions of the said men. At first, they denied [the charges]. Yet with the said Juana de Herrera, *mestiza*, and Tomás de Santiago's face-to-face depositions (*careo*) and additional questioning, the said Juan de la Vega, Jerónimo Calbo, José Durán, and Simón de Chavez confessed to committing the nefarious sin an infinity of times with many and different people, indicating the place, time, day, month, year, and other specific details. [They all confessed] except for Miguel Jerónimo, who denied the charges. Nonetheless, the referred parties—as eyewitnesses—accused him, yet he persevered in denying the charges.

As a result of the confessions of the accused, Juan de Correa, an old *mestizo*, more than seventy years old, was arrested. Initially he denied the charges, but with the face-to-face deposition he confessed to committing the nefarious sin for more than forty years. He declared [the names of] many people with whom he had done this and it was proven that he had committed the nefarious sin since he was seven years old. He boasted that the current century was finished, because people did not enjoy themselves as much in this century as in the last one, which he said was before this city flooded.[7] Because the said Juan de Correa said that back then he was a pretty girl and that he dressed as a woman with other men. And they enjoyed themselves committing the nefarious sin. He taught the accused persons and other youths during these gatherings and spent his wealth on them. He would host them at his house, telling them that although he was old, he was a pretty girl and should be eaten like a frog, from the waist down.

Likewise, it was investigated that the said Juan de Correa and other old men were in a house in [the neighborhood of] San Juan de la Penitencia, almost beyond this city's walls, where they were visited by another old man and youths. [Here] they met as women and they called themselves girls, and they gave each other nicknames for the beautiful women of this city. In these visits, they would give each other gifts and commit the nefarious sin one with another.

And the said Miguel Jerónimo, who is referred to as the one who denies the charges, was one of those who made these visits and committed the nefarious sin. They called him "la Zangarriana," because everyone thought that he resembled a well-known courtesan who lived in this city.

Likewise, it was investigated that there was another house in the San Pablo neighborhood where an Indian named Juan, a tanner, lived. Here, a feast was held for San Nicolás in a private chapel in his house, where many gathered to commit the nefarious sin. They would dance as women, call on each other for other women's visits in other places, and these men were complicit in this crime.

The said Juan de Correa, more than seventy years old, would take provisions for said gatherings. He would dance with the aforementioned men. He would put the cape he was wearing on his hip, and switching his hips, he would complain, saying that he was ill and suffering from *mal de madres*.[8] At this, the said men would give him gifts and give him chocolate and he would call them "my soul, my life," and other compliments. They called the said Juan de Correa *la Estampa* [the Print], which was the name of a very beautiful lady who lived in this city.

This information led to the arrest of Nicolás de Pisa, a Black man more than sixty years old, who had committed the nefarious sin and was complicit with the referred men. There had been jealous quarrels among them, because the said Black man had another lover.[9] This is how those mentioned called the others with whom they committed these blunders. The said Black man denied the charges, but later, with the eyewitnesses' face-to-face depositions, he confessed to it.

---

7. Mexico City experienced catastrophic flooding between 1629 and 1634.

8. *mal de madres*: a variety of pains experienced by women after childbirth.

9. *guapo*: typically, *guapo* means "handsome," but in this context means lover or boyfriend.

Likewise, this investigation revealed that Cristóbal de Victoria, a Spanish man, was an accomplice. He was more than eighty years old, was missing an eye, and was half-blind in the other. He was short, bald, and hunchbacked. He had been convicted by the Holy Office [of the Inquisition] for presenting false testimony. Initially, he denied the charges, but confessed after the face-to-face deposition of Jerónimo Calbo, a twenty-three-year-old *mestizo* with whom he had committed the nefarious sin and whom he called his lover. He also condemned other persons who were accused by the aforementioned men and declared that he had committed the nefarious sin continuously in this city since before the flood, more than thirty years ago. He said that he had ruined this city with the people he had taught to commit this sin and that Juan de Correa had done the same harm by teaching different people how to commit it.

After more than eight days, the prisoners' statements revealed that Benito de Cuevas, mulatto, was an accomplice, and he was arrested. He denied the charges, but then confessed to all the charges of which he had been accused by the referred people. He was arrested and declared that a day before he was apprehended, a man had come to his house while he was praying the rosary at night. The man told him to flee because his partners were being arrested for being *putos*[10] and that they were accusing him. [Cuevas] did not recognize the person who told him this, but it was a very handsome man, very well-dressed, and he had never seen him in his life. Another day, the said Benito went to mass at this city's cathedral and began to pray the rosary, offering [his prayer] to Our Lady, that she might remove him from this sin. As he left praying, he was arrested on the street. He has blamed many people with specific details; some of these have fled and others were arrested.

From the statements and confessions of all of the referred men, up to nineteen people were arrested, against whom the case has been established by His Grace alone [magistrate Sotomayor]. He carried out all the necessary investigations up until the sentencing and in this state the case was seen in the royal court on October 23, by the lords licenciados Don Juan Manuel Sotomayor, Knight of the Order of Calatrava, Don Antonio de Lara Mogrobejo, and Don Álvaro de Faez Valdés. The Most Excellent Lord Duke of Albuquerque, viceroy, governor, and captain general of this New Spain, attended the proceedings without interruption for two days. Another day, when the proceedings ended, His Excellency did not attend because he had gone to see the draining project. However, the proceedings were ended by all the referred lords, with the assistance of lord Don Luis de Mendoza Cataño, of His Majesty's council and attorney in this royal audience, who publicly acknowledged the case and informed on it. Likewise, for three days, the city's lawyers advocated

---

10. This is a loaded, controversial term. It was used in popular speech in colonial times (and is still used in the present). In this context, *puto* was used to refer "to someone *habitually* accustomed to having sodomitical relations" (emphasis in the original). See Zeb Tortorici, *Sins Against Nature: Sex and Archives in Colonial New Spain* (Durham: Duke University Press, 2018), 64.

for the aforementioned [accused men] without interruption. In the meantime, while this case was being sentenced against the nineteen criminals, other criminals were arrested as part of this case and proceedings. As the said criminals spontaneously confessed, fifteen prisoners were convicted and confessed. These were Juan de la Vega, Jerónimo Calbo, Miguel Jerónimo, José Durán, Simón de Chavez, Juan de Correa, Nicolás Pisa, Cristóbal de Vitoria, Benito de Cuevas, Domingo de la Cruz, Indian, Matheo Gaspar, Indian, Juan Martín, Indian, Miguel de Urbina, Indina, Juan de Izita, Indian, and Lucas Mateo, *mestizo*.

And the rest of the nineteen each had one complicit eyewitness and other evidence against them. More than one hundred and three absent criminals—Indians, mulattos, Blacks, *mestizos*, and Spaniards—were charged. Each of them has at least one eyewitness, others have two or three witnesses and other evidence against them.

The said Lucas Mateo is fifteen years old, according to the investigation, and thus, the sentence was given in the following manner: the said Lucas Mateo was condemned to two hundred lashes and six years of labor in a mining mill. The fourteen were condemned to death by fire, the confiscation of all their goods, and thus, the said punishment was carried out on the said men. All fifteen were taken to the place of execution, where they were burned [except Lucas]. The said Lucas was present and watched them burn, and so the punishment was carried out [affecting] him, as well. The one hundred and three referred men were called by edicts and proclamations. With those named by the fifteen on whom the sentence was carried out and with the nineteen whose cases have begun, [other confessions] are being heard and other men have been accused. There are nine prisoners left and their proceedings continue.

Likewise, I certify that during the investigation against the said Miguel de Urbina, an Indian who was executed, while his goods were being confiscated, a figurine of baby Jesus was found. The figurine of the holy child had its face, shoulder, and back parts burned. It was brought before His Grace, the said lord magistrate. In his confession, the said Miguel de Urbina declared that he was lying in bed with his wife a day after having a carnal act with her and regretted that this was not with a man with whom he communicated nefariously and carnally. Enraged, Urbina grabbed a lit candle and set fire to the holy child [figurine], leaving it with swollen arms, with bruise marks, blisters, and all the same marks as if he had set fire to a human body, according to what was declared by some experts. The said holy child was removed from His Grace, the said lord magistrate, and taken to His Excellency [the viceroy], who has it in his possession.

I likewise certify that each of the criminal bodies of all referred nineteen criminals was examined by two well-respected surgeons, who declared that they were very used and corrupt.

I likewise certify that the said Miguel Jerónimo denied the charges of seven eyewitnesses and other evidence against him. Later, the same day that he was taken to the place of execution, he spontaneously confessed before His Grace.

Likewise, I certify that all the referred men who were executed ratified their testimony against the absent [accused] men. In said ratifications and in many other statements made after their confessions, and once they were in the chapel, they ratified everything they had said in the confessions and statements, without any torture or the threat of it. I certify that the aforementioned men, as appears in the investigation, committed this sin explicitly during the days of Our Lady, of the holy apostles, and other Church festivities, because most of them had images of Our Lady and the referred saints in their private chapels. In order to celebrate their feasts, they invited one another, gathered there, and committed the nefarious sin. They identified the other houses where they would celebrate their feasts, and with this pretext they would commit [the sin]. They would call on each other and strengthen their clumsy and nefarious correspondence.

This, according to the investigation of the said case, where all the aforementioned is evident and appears in further detail, to which I refer. By order of His Grace, the lord magistrate, I submitted the present [document] in Mexico City on November 24, 1658. With Blas de Cubillas, Manuel de Heredia, Juan Martínez, *vecinos* of this city, as witnesses.

Esteban de Mugarrieta, commissioned scribe

[Spanish transcription]

Yo Estevan de Mugarrieta scrivano Receptor vno de los del numero de la Real audiencia de Mexico desta nueva españa por el Rey nuestro Señor Y de la Causa que de Yuso se hara mencion, Certifico que en veinte y siete de Septiembre pasado del año de la data deste, se dio noticia al Señor Lizenciado Don Juan Manuel de Sotomayor Cavallero del orden de Calatrava del conssejo de su Magestad su alcalde en esta corte de como vnos hombres havian Cometido el pecado nefando en la albarrada desta Ciudad que es en el Campo por el mesmo mes en un dia del siendo por la tarde

Su merced mando parecer ante si a Juana de herrera mestiza labandera y haviendosele Recevido Juramento dixo como el Juebes proximo pasado Veinte y seis de septiembre estando labando en dicha albarrada que es a la parte de San Lazaro fuera desta dicha ciudad havian llegado a ella Vnos muchachos Dando la gran priesa y diciendole a Vozes que fuese a Ver vnos hombres que estavan Jugando como perros y la dicha muger se lebanto y fue a una distancia de donde estava labando vuen trecho mas de su puesto y vio que estavan dos hombres Cometiendo el pecado nefando el uno encima del otro quitados los calzones anbos y el que estava encima tapaba al de debajo Con la Capa que tenia puesta. Y la dicha muger dixo que no se atrebio a llegar cerca porque no la matasen y que por este miedo solamente conocio a Juan de la Vega mulato y el otro le parezio que hera vn mestizo que hera el que estava debajo

Y luego al punto hizo su merced Diligencia de donde Vivia el dicho Juan de la Vega y se hallo Vivir en casa de doña Melchora de estrada que es al barrio de San

Pablo y su merced fue a casa de dicha Doña Melchora y se havia mudado della el dicho Juan de la Vega y Recivio en ella Ynformacion de las personas que Vivian en dicha casa de quien era el dicho Juan de la Vega Y se averiguo que hera mulato afeminado que le llamaban Cotita que es lo mismo que mariquita Y que el dicho mulato se quebrava de cintura y traia atado en la frente de hordinario vn pañito que llaman melindre que vsan las mugeres Y que en las aberturas de las mangas de vn Jubon blanco que traia puesto traya muchas Cintas pendientes y que se sentava en el suelo Como muger y que hacia tortillas Y lababa Y guisaba Y le visitavan vnos mozuelos a quienes el susodicho llamaba de mi alma mi vida mi corazon y los susodichos se sentaban con el y dormian Juntos en un aposento, Y el dicho Juan de la Vega se ofendia si no le llamaban Cotita =

Y asimismo se examino Vn Yndio llamado Thomas de Sanctiago que dijo de todas las cosas Referida Y como una noche se havia quedado a dormir en el aposento de los susodichos en casa de la dicha Doña Melchora y que vio en ella por haver luz que dicha noche cometieron el pecado nefando Vn mozo mestizo de la Ciudad de los angeles llamado Joseph duran con otro mozo llamado geronimo Calbo natural desta ciudad, y con esta aberiguacion y la noticia que se dio en casa de la dicha Doña Melchora de la casa donde se havia mudado el dicho Juan de la Vega se fue a buscar a el susodicho a las doze de la noche Y se hallo la dicha casa Y entrando dentro fueron apreendidos Juntos en cueros el dicho Juan de la Vega, el dicho Joseph duran, el dicho geronimo calbo, miguel geronimo mestizo, y simon de chaves Yndio.

Y fueron traidos a la Carcel de corte y se visitaron en sala plena en tres de Octubre deste presente año y por los señores alcaldes se Recivio la causa a prueva Con cierto termino se les hiço Cargo y se cometio a su merced del dicho señor lizenciado Don Juan manuel de sotomaior el tomarles las confesiones prender los demas Reos y tomarles las confesiones y hacer demas diligencias hasta poner la causa en estado Con los dichos Reos y con los demas que parecieren Culpados

Y luego Yncontinenti su merced de dicho señor alcalde tomo las confesiones a los susodichos. Y estando negatibos a los principios Con los careamientos que se les hicieron de la dicha Juana de herrera mestiza y el dicho thomas de Santiago y otras Repreguntas, Confesaron el haver cometido el pecado nefando Ynfinidad de Vezes con diferentes y muchas personas señalando lugar tiempo hora dia mes y año y otras circunstancias los dichos Juan de la Vega, geronimo calbo, Joseph duran, simon de chaves, menos miguel geronimo que estubo negatibo a quien asimismo Culparon los Referidos como testigos de Vista Contra el susodicho y estubo negatibo y persebero en estarlo =

Y de las confessiones De los susodichos Resulto el prender a Juan de correa mestizo viejo demas de setenta años el qual estando negatibo a los principios con los Careamientos Confeso que havia mas de quarenta años que cometia el pecado nefando declarando muchas personas Con quien le havia Cometido y se le probo que desde hedad de siete años le cometio y que se alabava de que el siglo presente estava acabado porque no se olgavan en este como en el pasado que el llamaba que era antes que esta ciudad se ynundase porque entonzes el dicho Juan de correa dijo que era linda niña y que andava Vestido de muger con otros hombres y que se olgaban cometiendo el pecado nefando y a las personas Referidas y a otros mozuelos los enseño con las platicas Referidas y gastava su hazienda con ellos y los tenia en su casa diciendoles que aunque hera Viejo era mui linda nina [sic] Y que se havia de comer como la Rana de cintura para abajo =

Y asimismo se aberiguo que el dicho Juan Correa con otros viejos estavan en una casa a [el barrio de] san Juan de la penitencia Casi estramuros desta Ciudad donde los yban a Visitar otro viejo Y mozos y se hacian las Visitas como mugeres y se llamaban niñas y se ponian los nombres de las mugeres hermosas desta ciudad y en dichas visitas se Regalaban vnos a otros y cometian el pecado nefando los unos con los otros = Y el dicho Miguel geronimo que es el negatibo Referido hera Vno de los que hacian las dichas Visitas Y cometia el pecado nefando y le llamaban la Zangarriana porque era comun a todos a semejanza de Vna muger de amores que hubo en esta ciudad muy Comun =

Y asimismo se aVeriguo que havia otra casa a san Pablo donde Vivia Vn Yndio llamado Juan Zurrador donde con ocasión de una festibidad que el susodicho hacia a san nicolas en un oratorio de su casa se Juntaban muchos que cometian este pecado nefando Bailavan Como mugeres se citaban para otras Visitas de mugeres en otras partes diferentes Y estos eran hombres Complices en este delicto =

Y el dicho Juan Correa De mas de Setenta años les llevaba los Recaudos de dichas Visitas y Bailava con los susodichos poniendose por la cintura la capa que traia puesta y quebrandose de cintura y quejandose Diciendo que Yba malo Y que llebava mal de madre a la qual los susodichos le Regalaban y davan chocolate diciendoles mi alma mi vida Y otros Requiebros Y a el dicho Juan Correa le llamaban la estanpa [sic, estampa] que era el nombre de una dama muy hermosa que hubo en esta ciudad; Y de esta Ynformacion Resulto el Prender a nicolas de pisa negro De mas de sesenta años que cometia el pecado nefando y hera el complize entre los Referidos entre los quales havia abido pendencia de Zelos porque el dicho negro tenia otro guapo que asi llamaban los susodichos a aquellos Con quien Cometian estas torpezas. Y el dicho negro estubo negatibo y luego con los careamientos de los testigos de Vista lo confeso =

Y asimismo Resulto desta averiguacion ser Complize Xpoval de Vitoria español hombre de mas de ochenta años, a quien le faltava vn ojo y el otro tenia medio tuerto, pequeño calbo Corcobado que fue penitenciado por el Sancto oficio por testigo falso el qual estubo negatibo a los principios y con el Careamiento que se le hizo con el dicho geronimo calbo mestizo de Veinte y tres años, con quien el dicho christoval de Vitoria havia cometido el pecado nefando Confeso haverles Cometido con el susodicho y ser su guapo, Y asimismo Condeno a otras personas que estavan Condenadas por los susodichos y declaro que havia cometido el pecado nefando continuadamente en esta ciudad desde antes de la Ynundacion mas de treinta años Y que tenia perdida esta Ciudad con las personas a quien el susodicho avia enseñado a cometer este pecado y que el dicho Juan correa havia echo el mismo daño enseñandole a cometer a diferentes personas =

Y Resulto de la declaracion de los Referidos ser Complize Benito de cuebas mulato que despues de mas de ocho dias de presos los susodichos fue preso y estando negatibo Confeso todos los delictos que le havian Ynputado las personas Referidas por los dichos delinquentes fue preso y declaro que Vn dia antes que le prendiesen fue Vn hombre a su casa del susodicho estando Rezando el Rosario por la noche y le dijo que se huiese porque estaban presos sus compañeros por putos y que le culpaban y que no conocio quien se lo dijo sino que hera vn hombre muy galan y de mui buen arte y no le avia Visto en su Vida y a otro dia el dicho Benito fue a oir misa a la cathedral desta ciudad y Comenzo a Rezar el Rosario ofreciendosele a nuestra señora porque le sacase de este pecado saliendole Rezando a la calle fue preso y ha culpado a muchos Con singulares Circunstancias que algunos dellos se havian huido y otros fueron presos =

Y de las declaraciones y confesiones de todos los Referidos Resulto el Prenderse hasta diez y nueve personas con quienes se puso la cavesa en estado por su merced que por si solo puso en el, y hizo todas las diligencias necesarias hasta ponerla en estado de sentencia y estando en este estado se vio en la Real sala en veinte y tres de octubre por los sseñores Lizenciados Don Juan Manuel de Sotomayor Cavallero del orden de calatrava, don Antonio de Lara Mogrobejo, y don Albaro de Faez baldes, asistiendo el excelentisimo señor duque de Albuquerque virrey y governador y Capitan general desta nueva españa dos dias arreo a la vista y otro dia en que se acabo de Ver no asisito su excelencia [el virrey] por haver ydo al desague mas se acabo de Ver por todos los señores Referidos con asistencia del señor don luis de mendoza cataño del consseo de su Magestad fiscal en esta Real audiencia que acuso e Ynformo en publico en esta causa, Y asimismo tres dias arreo estubieron abogando en favor de los susodichos los abogados desta ciudad y en el ynterin que se sentencio dicha causa fueron presos fuera de los diez y nueve reos con quien esta causa se vio otros que Resultaron de la Vista y que asimismo Yban confesando expontaneamente los dichos Reos de que Resulto que se hallaron Conbictos y confiesos quince Reos que fueron Juan de la Vega = geronimo calbo = Miguel geronimo = Joseph duran = Simon de chaves = Juan Correa = Nicolas pisa = christobal de Vitoria = Benito de Cuebas = Domingo de la Cruz Yndio = Matheo gaspar Yndio = Juan martin Yndio = Miguel de Vrbina Yndio = Juan de Ycita Yndio, y lucas Matheo mestizo =

Y los Demas hasta el dicho numero diez y nueve tubo cada uno de ellos contra si vn testigo de Vista Complize y otros Indicios y Culparon a mas de ciento y tres Reos ausentes Yndios mulatos negros mestizos y españoles y cada uno de ellos tiene el que menos contra si vn testigo de Vista y otros a dos y otros a tres testigos y otros Yndicios =

Y el dicho lucas matheo tiene quince años según pareze por los autos y asi salio la sentencia en la forma siguiente = el dicho lucas matheo fue condenado a docientos azotes y seis años de mortero y los catorce a pena de fuego y secreto de sus vienes sin embargo y asi se executo la pena en los susodichos y salieron todos quince en un dia y fueron llebados a el suplizio donde fueron quemados, y el dicho lucas se hallo a Verlos quemar executandose la pena con el, Y los ciento y tres Referidos fueron llamados a edictos y pregones Y con los que Van a decir de los quinze Con quien se executo la sentencia hasta los diez y nueve Con quien se puso en estado se les abrio el termino y se van oyendo y an caido despues aca otros y quedan presos nueve con quien se va siguiendo esta causa =

Y Certifico asimismo que según pareze de los autos a el dicho Miguel de Vrbina yndio que fue ajusticiado se le hallo en el embargo de Vienes vn niño Jesus quemada la cara y la espalda y las demas posterioridades del sancto niño el qual se trujo a presencia de su Merced dicho señor alcalde y declaro el dicho Miguel de Vrbina en su confesion que estando acostado en su cama con su muger vn dia acabando de tener con ella acto carnal arepentido de que no fuese con el hombre a quien comunicava el susodicho nefanda y carnalmente Cogio vna Vela encendida con rrabia, y pego fuego al sancto niño el qual quedo con los brazos ynchados y acardenalado y con Vejigas y con las mismas señales que si se hubiera ençendido el fuego en un cuerpo humano y lo declararon asi personas peritas y el dicho Sancto niño le llevo su excelencia y le tiene en su poder y lo saco del de su merced dicho señor alcalde =

Y asimismo certifico que a todos los diez y nueve Reos Referidos se les ajusto primero el Cuerpo del delicto viendolos a cada uno de por si dos cirujanos de mucho Credito y opinion que declararon estar muy vsado y corruptos =

Y certifico asimismo que el dicho miguel geronimo que estubo negatibo tubo Contra si siete testigos de Vista y otros Yndicios y despues el mismo dia que fue a el suplicio expontaneamente Confeso ante su merced =

Y certifico asimismo que todos los Referidos que fueron ajusticiados se Ratificaron como testigos contra los ausentes y en dichas Ratificaciones y en otras muchas declaraciones que hicieron despues de sus Confesiones y estando ya en la Capilla se Ratificaron en todo lo que tenian dicho en sus Confisiones y declaraciones, sin have Ynterbenido tortura ni conminacion a ello, Y certifico que los susodichos según pareze de los autos cometieron este pecado señaladamente los dias de nuestra señora, de los Sanctos apostoles y otras festibidades de la Yglesia porque los mas de ellos tenian en sus oratorios las Ymagenes de nuestra señora y demas sanctos Referidos Y con ocasion de Zelebrar sus fiestas se conbidavan los unos a los otros y alli se Juntavan y cometian el pecado nefando y señalaban las otras casas donde Zelebrar las fiestas y con este pretexto le yban cometiendo y se llamaban los unos a los otros y estrechavan su correspondencia torpe y nefanda =

Segun que todo lo susodicho mas largamente consta y pareze de los autos de dicha causa que pasaron ante mi a que me Remito. Y por mandamiento de su merced del señor alcalde di el presente en la ciudad de Mexico a Veinte y quatro dias del mes de noviembre de mill y seiscientos y cinquenta y ocho años, siendo testigos Blas de Cubillas, Manuel de Heredia, y Juan Martinez Vezinos desta dicha ciudad =

Estevan de Mugarrieta, Scrivano Receptor

Certificamos y damos fee que estevan de Mugarrieta de quien ba firmado el testimonio desta otra parte es tal scribano Receptor vno de los del numero desta Real audiencia. Y Como tal vsa y exerce el dicho oficio Y a los autos testimonios y demas Recaudos tal como este que ante el susodicho an pasado y pasan se les a dado y da entera fee y credito el Juicio y fuera del. Y para que dello Conste dimos la presente en la ciudad de Mexico A Catorze Dias del mes de diziembre de mill y seiscientos y Cinquenta y ocho años.

Juan Adame Montemayor	Pedro del Valle	Phelipe Fajardo
Scrivano Real	scrivano de su magestad	Scrivano Real

Document 111: 1658—List of men executed for and suspected of having sex with other men[11]

Memorandum of those executed for having committed the nefarious sin. Their case was prosecuted by Lord bachiller Don Juan Manuel de Sotomayor, Knight of the Order of Calatrava, of His Majesty's council, his magistrate in this court. The fourteen convicts and confessants were sentenced by the royal criminal court on November 4 of this year, 1658. Another convict confessed later on in the chapel. One of the convicts, being a minor less than fifteen years old, was sentenced to two hundred lashes and sold for six years to the mines. Their names are as follows:

Juan de la Vega Galiano, mulatto, by another name Cotita
Jerónimo Calvo, *mestizo*
José Durán, *mestizo*
Miguel Jerónimo, *mestizo*. This is the convict who confessed in the chapel
Simón de Chavez, Indian
Nicolás Pisa, Black
Domingo de la Cruz, Indian
Mateo Gaspar, Indian
Benito de Cuevas, mulatto
Cristóbal de Victoria, Spaniard

---

11. Archivo General de Indias, México, 38, N.57c, no folio.

Juan Martín, Indian
Juan de Izita, Indian
Miguel de Urbina, Indian. This one burned the figurine of the holy baby Jesus
Lucas Mateo, *mestizo*. This is the minor who was given two hundred lashes

Prisoners for this crime in the royal jail whose cases are being investigated
Juan del Castillo, *mestizo*
Francisco Melchor, Indian
Juan de la Cruz, Indian
Francisco Rodríguez, soldier
Simón de Morales, mulatto
José de Ahumada, mulatto
Nicolás, mulatto, mute
Lorenzo Rodríguez, *castizo* [person of Spanish and mixed descent], glovemaker
Don Antonio de las Casas

[List of] those called to the edicts and announcements for said case. Most of them have two eyewitnesses and others one eyewitness [implicating them]. None of those called have been summoned by hearsay. All of those included in the edicts are as follows:

A

Antonio Berrueco, Spaniard, son of the regent Berrueco of the city [Puebla] of the Angels
D. Agustín, Spanish youth
Agustín, Indian, butcher, tall-bodied
Andrés, *mestizo* soldier in Captain Cabrera's company
Alonso, *mestizo*, short-bodied, whom they call *la Conchita* [the little shell]
Agustín, *mestizo*, cobbler, whom they call the *mitre pulquero* [pulque (drink) miter]
Alonso, *mestizo* from Puebla, petticoat weaver. He is married to a mulatta
Antonio, raggedy Indian who serves in Puebla's Colegio de San Luis
Alonso, *morisco*, servant of Joseph Carrillo in the city [Puebla] of the Angels
Antonio, Portuguese, who sells fruit in Puebla's [main] plaza

B

Bernabé, free mulatto, pockmarked
Baltazar de los Reyes, Indian baker
Bernabé, Spanish, tailor, who is called *la Luna* [the moon]
Bartolomé, *mestizo*, fireworks-maker and tailor

C

Sebastián [*written* Çebastian] Perez, Spaniard, whom they call *Carrozas* [carriages]
Simón [*written* Çimon] de Morales, Spaniard, journeyman tailor

D

Diego de Anota, tailor, old
Diego, doublet tailor who makes suede bags
Diego de Loaiza, tailor
Domingo, Spaniard, blacksmith from Puebla
Diego de Mongayo [Moncayo?], student in Puebla
Diego, *mestizo*, gilder
Diego de Zamora, Indian
Diego Gutiérrez, *mestizo*, tailor
Domingo Ruíz, Spaniard, barber
Domingo, student in Puebla
Diego, ladino Indian, leather tanner in Puebla
Diego, Indian, pulque producer in Puebla
Diego, mulatto, puppeteer in Puebla

F

Francisco de Aguilar, free mulatto
Felipe, mulatto, branded
Francisco, *mestizo*, *ahitero* [?]
Francisco de Chavarría, Black
Francisco, Black Creole, who serves in the San Pedro hospital in Puebla
Francisco, *mestizo*, who serves in this city [Mexico City]
Felipe Delgado, *mestizo*, pulque carrier

G

Gaspar, Black, slave of Jacinto Dávila
Gaspar de los Reyes, Black, silversmith
Gaspar de los Reyes, Indian
Gaspar or Baltazar, regent Mancilla's mulatto
Gaspar de los Reyes, Indian

H

Hipólito, mulatto, who serves the count of Santiago

J

Juan, Indian, tanner
José de Robles, Spaniard from Puebla

Juan, Indian or Black
Juan de la Cruz, Indian, baker
Juan Diego, Indian
Juan Jacinto, Indian, tall
Juan Francisco, Spaniard, who comes and goes to the port of Acapulco
José, Spaniard, whom they call Shrimp
Juan Francisco, Spaniard, tailor, whom they call the king of France
José, *morisco*, whom they call little egg house
Juan del Castillo, mulatto
José, Indian, who serves in Tacuba and whom they call the reddish one
Juan Rodríguez, student in Puebla
José, *mestizo*, quarry worker
Juan García, Spaniard, barber in Puebla
José Carrillo, student in Puebla
José, young Spaniard from Puebla
José Bandera, student in Puebla
José de Cuevas, student in Puebla
José Carrillo, student, son of Juan Carrillo, butcher in Puebla
José, *mestizo*, who serves Franciso de Villa Arauz, student at Puebla's Colegio de San Juan
José Gomez, *mestizo*, glovemaker in Puebla
José, Spaniard, glovemaker in Puebla
José, *mestizo*, cobbler in Puebla
José Flores, *mestizo*, tailor in Puebla

L

Lorenzo, *mestizo*, tailor in Puebla
Luis de Vergara, Don Antonio de Vergara's Black man
Lucas Hernández, mulatto, cobbler in Puebla

M

Little Miguel, Indian from Puebla
Marcos, *mestizo*, whom they call *el conelo* [?] in Puebla
Martín, Indian, whom they call the Martina of the heavens (*la martina de los cielos*)
Mateo, mulatto, clothweaver in Puebla
Mateo, free mulatto from Oaxaca, journeyman blacksmith in Puebla
Martín de Córdova, Spaniard who serves in Puebla

N

Matías, *mestizo*
Nicolás Gutiérrez, free mulatto

Nicolás de Poblete, mulatto
Nicolás, Indian from Puebla
Nicolás, Indian from Cholula
Nicolás, *mestizo*, tailor
Nicolás, Black slave of the regent Don Andrés Navarro
Nicolás, White mulatto
Nicolás, Indian, cobbler

P

Pedro Vañón, Spaniard
Pedro, *mestizo*
Little Pancho, Indian, whom they call rattle [or rattlesnake]
Pedro de Solís, *mestizo*, harp player
Pedro, Black man who belonged to Doctor Hierro in Puebla

R
Ramón, mulatto from Puebla, who serves Don Juan de Mancilla

S
Esteban [*written* Stevan], Black slave of Moya

T
Tomás Sillo, mulatto slave of Doctor Alemán
Tomás de Molina, Indian, cobbler
Tomás, Indian, very long-bodied

V[12]

An Indian sweeper from the Colegio de San Luis in Puebla
An Indian, small-bodied and bleary-eyed, who serves in the Colegio de San Ramón
A very fat Black man whom they call *Morosa* [the slow woman]
A *mestizo* youth, who serves in the Convento del Carmen in Atlixco

[Spanish transcription]

Memoria de los ajustisiados Por aver cometido el pecado nefando cuia causa fulmino el Señor Lizenciado Don Juan manuel de Sotomayor Caballero de la orden de Calatrava del Consejo de Su magestad su alcalde en esta corte, que Sentensio la Real sala del crimen en quatro de noviembre deste año de mill Y seiscientos Y cinquenta

---

12. These individuals, whose names had not yet been identified, were listed in the "V" section because their physical description was preceded by the singular undetermined article "vn" or "un."

Y ocho. Los catorce convictos y confiesos Y otro convicto que despues estando en la capilla confeso y a uno Dellos Por menor de quinçe años se sentensio en doscientos açotes y bendido en minas Por tiempo de Seis años cuios nombres son los siguientes

 Juan de la vega galiano mulato por otro nombre Cotita
 Geronimo Calvo mestiso
 Joseph Duran mestiso
 Miguel Geronimo mestiso, este el el convicto que confeso estando en la capilla
 Simon de Chaves Yndio
 Juan correa mestiso
 Nicolas pisa negro
 Domingo de la cruz Yndio
 Matheo gaspar Yndio
 Benito de Cuevas mulato
 Xpoval de Victoria español
 Juan martin Yndio
 Juan de izita Yndio
 Miguel de urbina indio: este quemo la echura de vn santo ñiño Jesus
 Lucas matheo mestiso: este es el menor a quien se dieron dosçientos açotes

Presos por este delicto en la Real carzel cuyas causas se ban substansiando

 Juan del Castillo mestiso
 Francisco melchor indio
 Juan de la cruz indio
 Francisco Rodrigues soldado
 Simon de morales mulato
 Joseph de aumada mestiso
 Nicolas mulato mudo
 Lorenso Rodrigues Castiso guantero
 Don Anttonio de las cassas

v. Llamado a edictos Y pregones Por dicha causa y los mas dellos con dos testigos de vista y otros con un testigo de Vista, Sin que ninguno de los llamados sean con testigos de oidas Que todos los inclusos en los edictos son los siguientes

A

Anttonio berrueco español hijo del rregidor berrueco de La çiudad de los angeles
Don augustin español mosalbete
Augustin Yndio carnisero alto de cuerpo
Andres mestiso soldado de la compañía del cappitan Cabrera
Alonso mestisso, pequeño de cuerpo que llaman la Conchita
Aug.n mestiso sapatero que llaman el mitre pulquero

Alonso mestiso de la puebla tejedor de naguas casado con una mulata
Anttonio Yndio pilguanejo que sirve en el colexio de San luis de la çiudad de los angeles
Alonso morisco. Criado de Joseph carrillo de la çiudad de los angeles
Anttonio Portugues que bende fruta en la plasa de la Puebla

B

Bernave mulato libre picado de biruelas
Balthasar de los rreies yndio panadero
Bernave sastre español que llaman la luna
Bartolome mestiso coetero y sastre

C

Çebastian Perez español que llaman carrosas
Çimon de morales español oficial de sastre

D

Diego de anota Sastre Viejo
Diego Yndio coletero que ase bolsas de gamusa
Diego de loaisa sastre
Domingo español herrero de la Puebla
Diego de Mongaio [¿Moncayo?] estudiante en la puebla
Diego mestiso dorador
Diego de samora indio
Diego gutierrez mestiso sastre
Domingo Ruiz español barvero
Domingo estudiante en la puebla
Diego Yndio ladino surrador en la puebla
Diego Yndio pulquero en la puebla
Diego mulato titiritero en la puebla

F

Francisco de aguilar mulato libre
Fhelipe mulato herrado
Francisco mestiso ahitero [¿?]
Francisco de chavarria negro
Francisco negro criollo que sirve en el ospital de San Pedro en la Puebla
Francisco mestiso que sirve en esta çiudad [México]
Fhelipe delgado mestiso acarreador de pulque

G

gaspar negro esclavo de Jacinto davila
gaspar de los rreyes negro Platero
gaspar de los rreyes Yndio
gaspar o baltasar mulato del rregidor mansilla
gaspar de los rreyes indio

H

Hipolito mulato que sirve al conde de Santiago

J

Juan indio Surrador
Joseph de rrobles español de la puebla
Juan Yndio o negro
Juan de la cruz yndio panadero
Juan diego Yndio
Juan Jacinto yndio alto de cuerpo
Juan francisco español que ba i biene al puerto de acapulco
Joseph español que llaman Camarones
Juan francisco español sastre que llaman el rrei de Fransia
Joseph morisco que llaman de casita de guebo
Juan del castillo mulato
Joseph Yndio que sirve en tacuba y que llaman el alasan
Juan Rodrigues estudiante en la Puebla
Joseph mestiso Cantero
Juan garcia español barbero en la puebla
Joseph Carrillo estudiante en la puebla
Joseph español moso de la puebla
Joseph bandera estudiante en la puebla
Joseph de Cuebas estudiante en la puebla
Joseph Carrillo estudiante Hijo de Juan carrillo Carnisero en la Puebla
Joseph mestiso que sirve a francisco de villa arauz colexial en San Juan en la puebla
Joseph gomes mestiso guantero en la puebla
Joseph español guantero en la puebla
Joseph mestiso sapatero en la Puebla
Joseph flores mestiso sastre en la puebla

L

Lorenso mestiso sastre en la puebla
Luis de Vergara negro de Don anttonio de Vergara
Lucas hernandez mulato sapatero en la puebla

M

Miguelillo Yndio de la puebla
Marcos mestiso que llaman el conelo [¿conejo?] en la puebla
Martin indio que llaman la martina de los sielos
Matheo mulato texedor de Paños en la puebla
Matheo mulato libre de guaxaca ofisial de herrero en la Puebla
Martin de Cordova, español que asiste en la puebla

N

Matias mestiso
Nicolas Guttierrez mulato libre
Nicolas de Poblete mulato
Nicolas Yndio de la Puebla
Nicolas indio de cholula
Nicolas mestiso sastre
Nicolas negro esclavo del Regidor Don andres navarro
Nicolas mulato blanco
Nicolas yndio Sapatero

P

Pedro vañon español
Pedro mestiso
Panchuelo indio que llaman cascavel
Pedro de Solis mestiso tañedor de arpa
Pedro negro que fue del Doctor hierro en la puebla

R

Ramon mulato de la Puebla que sirve a Don Juan de mansilla

S

Stevan negro esclavo de Moya

T

Tomas sillo mulato esclavo del Doctor aleman
Tomas de molina indio sapatero
Tomas Yndio mui Largo

V

Vn indio barrendero del colexio de San luis de la puebla
Vn indio chiquillo de cuerpo lagañosso que Sirve en el colexio de San Ramon
Vn negro mui gordo que llaman morossa
Vn moso mestiso que sirve en el convento del Carmen de atrisco [Atlixco]

Document 112: 1686—A royal scribe and his family defect[13]

The King

President and civil court judges of my royal audience in the city of Guadalajara in the kingdom of Nueva Galicia. Francisco Martinez de Río Frío has conveyed to me that he is the natural son of Don Francisco de Río Frío and Teresa de Vergara, free mulatta, and that since the year 1674 he has held the office of notary for the ecclesiastical tribunal of that city. Precisely during that time he has served as secretary to the presidents of that audience, in light of which I gave him the title of scribe and notary for my Western Indies, trusting the [royal audience] with his examination. He has yet to enter into it because he needs my dispensation to hold this office, due to his mother's defect, and has begged me to concede it. This was seen by the chamber council of the Indies, where it was discovered that, when he asked and was given the decree, he hid his mother's said defect which he has now declared. So that (for his punishment and chastisement so that no one else incurs in similar fault and malice) his request has been denied. By the present letter, I order and command that once you receive this dispatch, you see to it that his title, as scribe and notary of my Western Indies, which I gave to Francisco Martinez de Río Frío, be removed and that a hundred-ducat fine be imposed on him, and you will not allow any appeal. You will remit the said ducats and title to my undersigned secretary, separately, in the customary form at the first opportunity. You will give an account of this action without omitting a single thing, as this is my will, and my accountants who reside in my royal council of the Indies will take notice of this present letter. Done in Madrid, February 27, 1686. I, the King. By order of the King Our Lord, Don Antonio Ortiz de Otalora. Marked by the chamber [council].

[in the left-hand margin, "To the audience of Guadalajara, so that it remove the title that was dispatched to Francisco Martínez de Rio Frío as my scribe and notary of the Indies, impose a hundred-ducat fine, and send it with the title, for the reason that is described."]

[Spanish transcription]

El Rey

Presidente y Oidores de mi Audiencia Real de la Ciudad de Guadalaxara en el Reyno de la nueva Galicia. Por parte de Françisco Martinez de Rio Frio se me ha representado que es hixo natural de Don Francisco de Rio Frio y de Teresa de Vergara mulata libre y que desde el año de mill seiscientos Setenta y quatro está ejerçiendo el ofiçio de notario del Tribunal eclesiastico de esa Ciudad y que Justamente a sido en

---

13. Archivo General de Indias, Guadalajara, L.6, ff. 32r–33r.

este tiempo Secretario de mis Presidentes de esa Audiencia en cuia considerazion el año de mill seiscientos y ochenta y dos le di titulo de escrivano y notario de mis Indias ocçidentales cometiendo a ella su examen del qual no a vsado todavia por haver sido que neçesita de dispensazion mia del defecto de Su madre para exerçer este ofiçio, suplicandome fuese servido de conçedersela. Y Visto en mi Consejo de Camara de Indias donde se ha reconoçido que quando pidio y se le despachó el fiat del cautelo y ocultó el defecto referido de Su madre que ahora ha declarado como quiera que (para castigo suyo y escarmiento de que ninguno yncurra en semejante culpa y maliçia) se le ha denegado su pretenssion Por la presente os ordeno y mando que luego que reçivais este despacho dispongais que se Recoja el titulo que en onçe de Junio de mill Seiscientos y ochenta y dos le di a Francisco Martinez de Rio Frio de escrivano y Notario de mis Indias ocçidentales y que se le saquen çien Ducados de multa sin admitirle replica ninguna los quales con el dicho titulo los remitireis dirigidos a mi Infrascripto secretario por quenta aparte en la forma que se acostumbra en la primera ocassion de cuia ejecuçion me dareis quenta sin que en ello haia la menor omision que asi es mi Voluntad y de la presente tomaran la razon mis contadores de quenta que residen en mi consejo Real de las Indias fecha en Madrid a Veinte y siete de febrero de mill seiscientos y ochenta y seis años = Yo el Rey, Por mandamiento del Rey nuestro señor, Don Antonio Ortiz de Otalora = Señalada de la Camara.

[al margen izquierdo, "A la Audiencia de Guadalaxara que recoxa el titulo que se despachó de mi esscribano y notario de las Indias a Francisco Martinez den Rio Frio natural de aquella Ciudad y le saque çien ducados de multa y los remita con el titulo por la causa que se le previene."]

Document 113: 1783—Music, violence, and corruption in Colima[14]

Don Matias de Galvez, etcetera. Before me the following writ was presented:

Most excellent lord, José María de Estrada, in representation of Asencio de Ávalos, mulatto, as father of Justo de Ávalos, and brother of Juan Antonio de Ávalos, before Your Excellency. In due form, I say that:

On account of it having rained on the morning of the [feast of] Saint James, July 25 [1783] past, at the time that the people of the Albarrada hacienda, from the

---

14. Archivo General de la Nación, Gobierno Virreinal, General de Parte, Vol. 64, 1005/235, Exp. 235, Año 1783, ff. 198–199.

Colima jurisdiction, were going to mass, several individuals entered the house of the said Juan Antonio de Ávalos to avoid the rain. Among them were Juan Ramón, José Antonio Regalado, the overseer of the hacienda, and Andrés León. To entertain themselves while it rained, the said Juan Antonio de Ávalos began playing a harp.

A disagreement took place between León and Juan Ramón, and the former was injured. Because my client's son [Justo] went to see what the racket was about, the overseer threw a stone at him, which missed, although he had done nothing to provoke or offend the overseer in any manner. As if this was not enough, the overseer took a small short sword he had unsheathed and cut him [Justo] on the head with it. As he struck him other times, one of my client's nephews struggled with the overseer to free Justo from death, which was near, due to the mortal wounds that the overseer was delivering. The magistrate of the said jurisdiction [of Colima] gave an account of this disgrace, ordering that Justo be healed and that Andrés León and Juan Antonio de Ávalos be sent to prison, the latter for having played his instrument.

My client, overcome with the rawest and most just emotion from seeing his son gravely wounded, presented a civil and criminal lawsuit against the overseer Regalado. However, despite the fact that he is not the perpetrator of this crime, the magistrate pressured my client to produce one hundred pesos to pay for the medical expenses and other affairs that needed to be taken care of: [My client] did not consent to this in any way. . . .

In truth, these are very irregular proceedings undertaken by the magistrate, putting the aggrieved in prison and leaving the perpetrators in freedom in order to placate (as he is instructed to do) the priest of the Convent of Our Lady of Mercy of Colima, to whom the hacienda belongs. This for having played [music] and engaged in a truly innocent activity. The chief magistrate wants my client to pay for his son's medical expenses and other affairs, yet [my client] did not injure him. Finally, the magistrate demonstrates that he wrongly intends to take considerable sums of money from my client, this being the strangest thing, to take this money from my client's misery.

For all these reasons it is a very suspicious and risky affair that they [the magistrate and his allies] continue supervising this cause. Therefore, this case is worthy of remedy and it is most opportune to resort to Your Excellency's superiority. In order to justly rectify this affair, I beg that you issue an order to whichever individual Your Excellence finds appropriate (recusing, as I recuse, the said chief magistrate in due form and not out of malice), as long as it is not the local magistrate of the said village, whom I also recuse from this case since he is partial to the chief magistrate. The order should notify this person to immediately present the charges that have been filed against Juan Antonio Ávalos and Justo Ávalos. If there are none, or it turns out that there is no just motive that requires the imprisonment of these unfortunate men, they should be set free. Likewise, this person should proceed to apprehend the overseer José Antonio Regalado, presenting charges against him and any others who are found guilty in due form, in accordance with the law.... Therefore I ask and beg Your Excellency to order what I have requested as I ask. I swear in due form, etcetera.

... By virtue of the present letter and after having reviewed this dispatch, I order the chief magistrate of Colima to send to my superior government all of the charges related to this case involving Asencio de Ávalos. This will be done without any protest, under a penalty of one hundred pesos, which will be demanded of the chief magistrate should he fail to do so. He is warned, as I warn him, that if Juan Antonio [de Ávalos] and Justo de Ávalos are not imprisoned for any cause other than that listed in the writ above, they are to be released ... and this dispatch will be recorded in the chancery.

Mexico City, September 27, 1783. Matías Galvez, by order of His Excellency. Don Juan Joseph Martínez de Soria. The reasoning above was followed.

This [document] concurs with the original.

[Spanish transcription]

Don Matias de Galvez, etcétera. Por quanto ante mi se precento el escrito Siguiente.

Excelentisimo Señor José Maria de Estrada, por Asencio de Abalos, Mulato, Como Padre de Justo de Abalos, y hermano de Juan Antonio de Abalos, ante vuestra excelencia como mejor proceda por Derecho Digo: Que Con motivo de haver llovido la mañana del dia de Santiago, veinte y cinco de Julio [1783], ynmediato, a tiempo que yba de bisita de oyr Missa la gente de la Hazienda de la Albarrada Jurisdiccion de Colima, se entraron varios Sujetos huyendo del Agua à la Casa del citado Juan Antonio de Avalos, y entre ellos Juan Ramon, Josef Antonio Regalado, Mayordomo de la Hazienda y Andres Leon, y para divertir el Rato, mientras pasaba el Agua Comenzó a tañer una Arpa, el mencionado Juan Antonio de Abalos =

Movido pleito entro Leon y Juan Ramon, salió herido aquel, y por haver ocurrido al Ruido el referido hijo de mi parte sin haver provocado, ni ofendido de alguna manera al citado Mayordomo, le tiró este una pedrada, y nó haviendole alcanzado, metió mano al espadin que traia desenbainado, y con él dio una cortada, en la caveza, y al tiempo de asegundarle otras se habrazó de el Mayordomo, un Sobrino de mi parte para livertar â su hijo Justo de la muerte, que le amagaban las mortales heridas que aquel le tiraba: de cuia desgrasedia [sic, ¿desgracia?] quenta à el Alcalde mayor de dicha Jurisdiccion, quien mandó Se pusiera en curazion à Justo, y se reduxeran à prision, à Andres Leon, y à Juan Antonio de Abalos, por haver tocado este Su Ynstrumento =

Penetrado mi parte del mas vibo, y Justo Sentimiento de ver mui gravemente erido â su hijo, se querelló Sivil, y criminalmente contra el Mayordomo Regalado, y sin embargo de ser esté el delinquente, y perpetrador de aquel delicto, extrechaba el Alcalde Mayor a mi parte a que le exhiviera cien pesos para costear la curacion y demas Diligencias que era necesario practicarse: A que de ninguna Manera concintió . . .

= Son á la verdad muy irregulares procedimientos del Alcalde Mayor el poner en pricion à los ofendidos , y deja[r] en livertad à los delinquentes por conplacer (segun Se Ynstruye) al Padre Commendador del Convento de Nuestra Señora de la Merced de Colima, à quien pertenece dicha Hazienda él puso preso à Juan Antonio Avalos, para haver puestose à tocar, y estar empleado en una diverción verdaderamente Ynocente, él quiere que mi parte consteé la curacion de Su hijo, y demas diligencias sin haver sido quien lo hirio, e finalmente demuestra una Yntencion dañada de llevar crescidos derechos siendo lo mas extraño quererlos sacar de la miceria de mi parte =

Por todas estas Raçones es asunto mui sospechoso, y areisgado el que sigan en el conocimiento de la Causa, y por tanto digno del devido remedio, y siendo el mas oportuno el favorable ocurso à la Superioridad de Vuestra Excelencia, Suplico à su recta Justificacion se sirva de mandar (recusando, como recuso en el todo al Yndicado Alcalde mayor cuya recusacion Juro en debida forma, no çer de malicia) librar despacho cometido al sugeto que fuere del Superior agrado de Vuestra Excelencia que no seá el Alcalde de primero voto de dicha Villa, a quien asimismo recuso, por ser parcial del Alcalde mayor para que notifique à este que inmediatamente se exhiva la causa que hubiere formado à Juan Antonio Abalos, y a Justo Abalos, y no exhiviendola, o que conste de la que le entregare, no haver Justo motivo que demande la pricion de estos Ynfelices, los ponga en livertad, y que asimismo proceda àprehender al Mayordomo José Antonio Regalado, siguiente de la causa contra este, y demas que resultaren culpados, en forma, y conforme à derecho y consultando quando deude con Asesor por tanto—A Vuestra excelencia Suplico se sirva mandar hacer como pido Juro en forma etcétera . . .

. . . y en su virtud por el precente Mando al Alcalde mayor de Colima que luego que con este despacho sea requerido, remita al oficio de mi Superior Gobierno todos los Autos que con el asumpto, que por parte de Asencio de Abalos se relacionan en el escrito inserto, tenga formados, lo que cumpla sin dar motivo de queja, vajo la multa de cien pesos, que se le exhijiran en su defecto; previniendole, como le prevengo, de que no estando Juan Antonio y Justo de Abalos, presos por otra causa de la que del citado escripto se especifica les relaje para àhora la carcelaria, vajo la fianssa . . . y de este Despacho se tomara Razon en la Chancilleria. Mexico y Septiembre veinte y siete de mil setecientos ochenta y tres. Matias Galvez = Por mandado de Su Excelencia. Don Juan Joseph Martinez de Soria. Y se tomo la Razon prevenida.

Concuerda con su original.

Document 114: 1784—An Izúcar family demands its freedom[15]

Excellent Lord   It is begged that everything be read to determine their right to liberty

Mexico [City], July 31, 1784.

To the lord general assessor, by the office of the superior government.

José Astacio, in my name, and for my mother Gertrudis, and my three siblings, Marcos Antonio, Fernando José, and Rose Gertrudis, all of us mulattos, and residents of the Señor San José hacienda, which belongs to Juan Sobreira, a *vecino* of this court, and is located in the Izúcar jurisdiction. I say, at Your Excellency's feet and in the best form before the law, that as is perceived and appears, a will was prepared under the necessary oath by Don José Leon y Heredia on six sheets [of paper] on October 13, 1729. My parents, Marcos, now deceased, and the said Gertrudis, [were] slaves of the mentioned Don José de León. The latter, in the last clause of the fourth sheet of his testament, stated that my parents were his slaves and noted that they would remain so during the lifetime of Doña Manuela de Toledo, his wife, but that upon her death my said parents would be freed and liberated, and that they should receive an abstract of this clause. Neither my father nor my mother were ever able to secure this [document], despite the fact that it has been a long time since the mentioned Doña Manuela died, by whose death they were freed. Afterward, our said parents procreated us, my siblings and myself. In consequence, we were conceived and born of parents who were already free on account of Doña Manuela de Toledo's passing. As my mother is free, we are also free. On this matter, Your Excellency, in your greatness, would be well served to order that the justice of the Izúcar jurisdiction efficiently investigate the certainty of the said Doña Manuela's death, as will be evident from the books of the Izúcar parish. And should her death turn out to be true, and our birth after her [passing], by that very same fact, my mother, as the rest of us, are to be declared free by the greatness of Your Excellency by giving us the corresponding document. In order that we be helped as poor people, by our notable misery, I beg Your Excellency to do as I request, as it is just. I swear in form, etcetera.

I do not know how to sign

---

15. Archivo Histórico Judicial de Puebla, Exp. 4894, f. 8r–8v.

Document 114: 1784—An Izúcar family demands its freedom

[Spanish transcription]

Excelentisimo Señor   Suplica se lea todo por conbenir a su derecho de libertad

Mexico 31 de Julio de 1784.

Al Señor Asesor General por el oficio de Superior Govierno à que toca.

José Astacio por mi, y por mi Madre Gertrudis, y mis tres hermanos Marcos Antonio, Fernando José, y Rosa Gertrudis, Mulatos todos, y recidentes en la Hacienda de Señor San José perteneciente a don Juan Sobreira vezino de esta Corte, y cita en Jurisdicion de Yzucar, a los pies de Vuestra excelencia y en la mexor forma que haya lugar por derecho: = Digo Que como se percibe y consta del testamento que con el Juramento necesario presento en f6 [seis fojas] utiles otorgado por don José Leon, y Heredia a los trece de Octubre de Setecientos veinte y nuebe, haviendo sido mis Padres, Marcos ya defunto, y dicha Gertrudis, esclabos del precitado Don José de Leon, este en la ultima clausula f4 de dicho su testamento declarandolo a los referidos mis Padres por tales sus esclabos, prebino que lo fuesen por el tiempo de la vida de doña Manuela de Toledo su muger y que fallecida esta quedasen dichos mis Padres horros, y libertos, y se les diese un tanto de esta clausula con pie y cabeza. esto jamas lo pudieron conseguir, ni mi Padre, ni mi Madre, no obstante de que ha mucho tiempo que fallecio la precitada doña Manuela por cuia muerte quedaron libres. Despues nos fueron procreando dichos nuestros Padres, á dichos mis Hermanos, y a mi, y consecuentemente como que ya fuimos concebidos, y nacidos de Padres que ya eran libres por el fallecimiento de doña Manuela de Toledo, lo es mi Madre, y lo somos tambien nosotros. en esta atencion se ha de serbir la grandeza de vuestra excelencia mandar que el Justicia del partido de Yzucar diligencie con eficacia la certesa de la muerte de dicha doña Manuela que constará en los Libros de la Parroquia de Yzucar, y que resultando ser cierta su muerte, y haver nacido nosotros despues de ella, por el mesmo echo asi a mi Madre como a nosotros se nos declare libres por la grandeza de Vuestra Excelencia dandosenos de ello el correspondiente recaudo, y que para todo senos ayude por Pobres, por nuestra notoria miseria. A Vuestra excelencia suplico haga como pido que es Justicia juro en forma etcetera

No se firmar

Document 115: 1812—Restrictions lifted for qualified people of African descent[16]

Don Francisco Javier Venegas de Saavedra . . . general of the royal armies, viceroy, governor and captain general of this New Spain, president of its royal audience. . . . The Supreme Ministry of Grace and Justice has communicated the following royal order, dated February 10, to me.

"Most Excellent Lord, the kingdom's regency has provided me with the following decree: Don Fernando VII, king of the Spains by the grace of God and the constitution of the Spanish monarchy, and, in his absence and captivity, the regency named by the extraordinary general courts. To all who may see or hear the present [decrees], let it be known that the courts have decreed what follows:

"The general and extraordinary courts desire to enable those Spanish subjects who, by any line, trace their origin to Africa, to study the sciences and to access an ecclesiastical career, so that they will be increasingly useful to the state. By the present decree, the courts have decided to enable those Spanish subjects who by any line trace their origin to Africa so that, should they be endowed with good qualifications, they may be admitted to university enrollments and degrees, be students in seminaries [for the priesthood?], take the habit in religious communities, and receive the sacred orders, as long as they satisfy the remaining requirements and circumstances established by the canons, laws of the kingdom, and the specific constitutions of the different corporations where they intend to be admitted. The present decree only invalidates the specific laws and statutes that are opposed to the qualification that is now conceded. The kingdom's regency will let this be known so that it will be done, and will have it printed, published, and circulated. . . . Given in Cádiz on January 29, 1812."

So that this news is known to all, I order that after publishing this proclamation in the capital and in the other cities, villages, and places of the kingdom, the usual copies be sent to the tribunals, magistrates, and chiefs responsible for understanding and observing it. Given in the Royal Palace of Mexico City on September 25, 1812.

Francisco Javier Venégas   By order of His Excellency

[Spanish transcription]

Don Francisco Xavier Venegas de Saavedra . . . Teniente General de los Reales Exércitos, Virey, Gobernador y Capitan general de esta Nueva España, Presidente de su Real Audiencia . . .

Por el Supremo Ministerio de Gracia y Justicia se me ha comunicado con fecha de 10 Febrero último la Real Orden siguiente.

---

16. Archivo General de la Nación, Indiferente Virreinal, Bandos, Exp. 16, f. 1r.

"Excelentísimo Señor = La Regencia del Reyno se ha servido dirigirme el Decreto que sigue = Don Fernando VII por la Gracia de Dios y por la Constitución de la Monarquía Española, Rey de las Españas, y en su ausencia y cautividad la Regencia nombrada por las Cortes generales extraordinarias, á todos los que las presentes vieren ó entendieren, sabed: Que las Córtes has decretado lo siguiente:

"Deseando las Córtes generales y extraordinarias facilitar á los súbditos Españoles, que por qualquiera línea traigan su orígen del Africa, el estudio de las ciencias, y el acceso á la carrera eclesiástica, á fin de que lleguen á ser cada vez más utiles al Estado, han resuelto habilitar, como por el presente Decreto habilitan, á los súbditos Españoles que por qualquiera línea traen su orígen del Africa, para que, estando por otra parte dotados de prendas recomendables, puedan ser admitidos a las matrículas y grados de las Universidades, ser alumnos de los Seminarios, tomar el hábito en las Comunidades religiosas, y recibir los órdenes sagrados, siempre que concurran en ellos los demas requisitos y circunstancias que requieran los Cánones, las Leyes del Reyno y las Constituciones particulares de las diferentes corporaciones en que pretendan ser admitidos, pues por el presente Decreto solo se entienden derogadas las Leyes ó Estatutos particulares que se opongan á la habilitacion que ahora se concede. Lo tendrá entendido la Regencia del Reyno para su cumplimiento, y así lo hará imprimir, publicar y circular. . . . Dado en Cádiz á 29 de Enero de 1812. . . ."

Y para que llegue á noticia de todos mando que, publicada por Bando en esta Capital y demas Ciudades, y Villas y Lugares del Reyno, se remitan los exemplares acostumbrados á los Tribunales, Magistrados y Gefes á quienes corresponda su inteligencia y observancia. Dado en el Real Palacio de México á 25 de Septiembre de 1812.

Francisco Xavier Venégas   Por mando de Su Excelencia

Document 116: 1813—José María Morelos and "The Sentiments of the Nation"[17]

Sentiments of the Nation

1. That America is free and independent of Spain and all other nation, government, or monarchy, and that this be sanctioned, giving reason of this to the world.

2. That the Catholic faith be the only religion, without tolerance for others.

---

17. Archivo General de la Nación, Acta de Independencia y Constituciones de México, Documentos del Congreso de Chilpancingo, Manuscrito Cárdenas, ff. 33r–34v.

3. That all ministers will survive on tithes and first-fruits taxes,[18] and that the people will not have to pay any other collections aside from their devotion and offering.

[in the left-hand margin of point 4, "Not this one."]

4. That the dogma be sustained by the Church hierarchy, which is the pope, the bishops, and the priests. So that any plant that God did not cultivate shall be rooted out: <u>*Omnis plantatio quam non plantabit Pater meus celestis eradicabitur. Matthew 15*</u>[19]

5. That sovereignty emanates directly from the people, who only want to deposit it ~~in the Supreme National American Congress, made up of representatives from the provinces in equal numbers~~ in their representatives, dividing its powers into the legislative, executive, and judicial [branches]. The provinces will elect their speakers; these and the rest must be wise and provident subjects

6. ~~That the Legislative, Executive and Judicial powers will be divided into compatible assemblies to exercise their power.~~

7. That speakers will serve rotating four-year terms, the oldest giving way to the newly elected.

8. That remuneration for speakers will be congruent, sufficient, and not superfluous, and will not exceed 8000 pesos.

9. That only Americans are to ^{obtain} jobs ~~to be obtained~~

10. That no foreigners are to be admitted, unless they are artisans capable of teaching their skills and are free of all suspicion.

11. ~~That States establish customs and, therefore,~~ the fatherland will not truly be free and ours unless the government is reformed, vanquishing the tyrannical, substituting the liberal, ~~and likewise~~ and throwing out of our land the Spanish enemy, who has so often declared itself to be against ~~our Fatherland~~ this nation.

12. That as all good law is superior to all men, our congress should dictate what these should be, that will commit to constancy and patriotism, moderate opulence and

---

18. *primicias*: a religious tax on first fruits that was supposed to be paid to the Catholic church in addition to the tithe (*diezmo*).
19. <u>"Every plant, which my heavenly Father hath not planted, shall be rooted up." Matthew 15:13, King James Version.</u>

idleness, in such a fashion that the day wages of the poor be raised, so that they may improve their habits and distance themselves from ignorance, theft, and pillaging.

13. That the general laws be applicable to everyone, without exception for privileged groups, and that these be privileged only with regard to the use of their ministry.

14. That there be a discussion in the congress when establishing a law, and that it be decided by a plurality of votes ~~That laws be drafted and discussed by as many wise men as possible, so that we may proceed correctly.~~

15. That slavery be proscribed forever, as well as the distinction of castes, leaving all equal so that only vice and virtue will distinguish one American from another.

16. That our ports be open to friendly foreign nations. However, these nations will not be allowed to enter the kingdom, regardless of how friendly they may be. There will only be a few ports open for this effect, prohibiting unloading in all the others, subject to a 10% levy or another duty on their merchandise

17. That each person will have their property protected and their house respected, as in a sacred asylum, and all offenders will receive punishment.

18. That torture shall not be permitted in the new legislation.

19. That in the same [legislation] a constitutional decree be established to dedicate December 12 to the patroness of our liberty, the most holy Mary of Guadalupe, to be celebrated in all the towns. A monthly devotion will be required of all towns.

20. That foreign troops, or those of another kingdom, should not step on our land, and, if they do so to render assistance, may not be where the supreme council [is located].

~~21.~~ That no expeditions beyond the nation's borders will be permitted, especially overseas expeditions; but those [expeditions] that are not of that kind will be allowed [in order to] spread the faith to our inland brothers.

22. That the infinity of tributes, levies, and impositions, which weigh us down, be lifted, and that each individual will pay an equal and light tax of 5% on ~~seeds and other property~~ ^{their earnings} or on another equally light charge that will not oppress as much as the sales tax, duties on royal monopolies, tribute, and others do. With this ~~light~~ ^{brief} contribution and the good management of the property confiscated from the enemy, the weight of the war will be managed and the employees' salaries paid.

Chilpancingo, ^{September} 14, 1813

José María Morelos

23. Likewise, that September 16 be commemorated every year, as the anniversary of the day when the voice of independence rose and our holy liberty began, because it was on that day that the Nation ~~unsealed~~ ᵒᵖᵉⁿᵉᵈ its lips to claim its rights ᵃⁿᵈ ᵇʳᵃⁿᵈⁱˢʰᵉᵈ ᵗʰᵉ sword ~~in hand~~ in order to be heard. [This day] will always commemorate the merit of our great hero, the lord Don Miguel Hidalgo and his partner, Don Ignacio Allende.

Amended on November 21, 1813 . . .

[Spanish transcription]

Sentimientos de la Nacion

1. Que la America es libre è independiente de España, y de toda otra Nacion, Gobierno ò Monarquia, y que asi se sancione ~~dan~~ dando al Mundo las razones.

2. Que la Religion catolica sea la unica, sin tolerancia de otras.

3. Que todos sus Ministros se sustenten de todo y solo los diezmos y Primicias, y el Pueblo no tenga que pagar mas obenciones que las de su debosion y ofrenda.

[al margen izquierdo, "Este no"]
4. Que el dogma sea sostenido por la Gerarquia de la Yglesia que son èl Papa, los Obispos, y los Curas, por que se debe arrancar toda planta que Dios no planto: <u>Omnis plantatio quam non plantabit Pater meus celestis eradicabitur. Mateo Capitulo XV</u>

5. Que la Soberania dimana inmediatamente del Pueblo èl que solo quiere depositarla ~~en el Supremo Congreso Nacional Americano compuesto de representantes de las Provincias en igualdad de numeros~~ en sus representantes dividiendo los poderes de ella en legislativo ejecutivo y Judiciario eligiendo las provincias sus vocales y estos a los demas que deven ser sujetos sabios y de providad

~~6. Que los Poderes Legislativo, Ejecutivo y Judicial esten dibididos en los cuerpos compatibles para Ejercerlos.~~

7. Que funcionarán quatro años los Vocales turnandose, saliendo los mas antiguos, para que ocupen èl lugar los nuevos electos.

8. La dotasion de los Vocales, será una congrua suficiente y no superflua, y no pasará por ahora de 8000 pesos.

9. Que los empleos ˡᵒˢ ᵒᵇᵗᵉⁿᵍᵃⁿ solo los Americanos ~~los ebtengan~~

10. Que no se admitan Extrangeros, sino son Artesanos capaces de Instruir, y libres de toda Sospecha.

11. ~~Que los Estados fundan costumbres, y por consinguiente la~~ Que la Patria no será del todo libre y nuestra, mientras no se reforme èl Gobierno, abatiendo èl tiranico, subsistuyendo èl liberal, ~~é igualmente~~ y luchando fuera de nuestro suelo ál Enemigo Español, que tanto se ha declarado contra ~~nuestra Patria~~ esta nacion.

12. Que como la buena Ley Es Superior a todo hombre, las que dicte nuestro congreso deben sér tales, que obliguen á contansia y Patriotismo, modere la opulensia y la indigensia; y de tal suerte se aumente èl jornal del pobre, que mejore sus Costumbres, ~~alexando~~ alexe la Ignoracia, la Rapiña y èl hurto.

13. Que las Leyes generales comprendan á todos, sin Ecepcion de Cuerpos pribilegiados: y que por estos solo lo séan en quanto èl uso de su ministerio.

14. Que para dictar una ley se discuta en el congreso, y decida a pluralidad de votos ~~Que para dictar una Ley, se haga Junta de Sabios, en el numero osible, para que proceda con mas acierto, y exonere de algunos cargos que pudieran resultarles.~~

15. Que la Esclavitud se proscriba para Siempre, y lo mismo la distincion de Castas, quedando todos Iguales, y solo distinguirá á un Americano de otro èl Vicio, y la Virtud.

16. Que nuestros Puertos se franquen á las Naciones Extrangeras amigas, pero que estas no se internen al Reyno, por mas amigas que séan, y solo ~~habrá~~ ʰᵃʸᵃ Puertos señalados para el efecto, prohibiendo èl desembarq~~ue~~ᶜᵒ en todos los demás, señalando èl diez por ciento. u otra gabela a sus mercancïas

17. Que á cada uno se le guarden sus propiedades, y respeto en su Casa, como en un asilo Sagrado, Señalando penas á los infractores.

18. Que en la nueba Legislacion no se admita la tortura.

19. Que en la misma se establezca por Ley Constitucionál, la celebrasion del dia doce de Diciembre en todos los Pueblos dedicado á la Patrona de nuestra Libertad Maria Santisima de Guadalupe, encargando á todos los Pueblos la debocion mensal.

20. Que las tropas Extrangeras, ó de otro Reyno, no pisen nuestro suelo, y si fuere en ayuda, no estarán donde la Suprema Junta.

21. Que no se hagan Expediciones fuera de los limites del Reyno, especialmente Ultramarinas, pero [sí las] que no són de esta clase, [para] propagár la fe, á nuestros hermanos de tierra dentro.

22. Que se quite la infinidad de Tributos, pechos, é imposiciones que nos abogian, y se señale á cada indibiduo un Sinco por ciento de semillas y demás efectos [en sus ganancias] ò otra carga igual [de] ligera, que no oprima tanto, como la alcabala, él Estanco, èl Tributo, y otros; pues con esta ligera [corta] contribucion y la buena administracion de los bienes confiscados al Enemigo, podrá llebarse él peso de la Guerra, y honorarios de Empleados.

Chilpancingo 14 [y Septiembre] de 1813

José Maria Morelos

23. Que igualmente se solemnice el dia 16 de Septiembe, todos los años, como él dia Anibers[ar]io en que se lebanta la Voz, de la independencia, y nuestra Santa Libertad comensó pues en ese dia fue en el que se desplegaron [abrieron] los labios de la Nacion para reclamár sus derechos [y enpeño la] con Espada en mano para ser oida recordando siempre el merito del grande Heroe él Señor Don Miguel Hidalgo y su compañero Don Ygnacio Ayende.

Respuestas en 21 de Noviembre de 1813 . . .

Document 117: 1826—A mass manumission in Teotitlán del Camino, Oaxaca[20]

In the capital of the free state of Oaxaca, on March 30, 1826. Before me, the national, public scribe assigned to [Oaxaca City] and witnesses, on one side the most excellent lord, vice governor, citizen Ramón Ramírez de Aguilar, who currently serves in the state government and on the other, the citizen Manual Saenz de Enciso, former representative of this sovereign congress. Both parties said that according to Article 7 of the constitution of this state of Oaxaca, it is required that all classes of people who existed as slaves in this state be given freedom, compensating their master or previous owners. On this matter, the government began proceedings which included the different appraisals that were given to the slaves of the Ayotla mill and sugarcane

---

20. Archivo Histórico de Notarías de Oaxaca, Vol. 577, ff. 135–135v, 140r–141r. Courtesy of Professor Sabrina Smith.

plantation.... On these particular issues the state has dealt favorably with the said Enciso as the agent of Don Matías Eduardo Valverde, the owner of that estate and lord of all his slaves. In everything, [Enciso] has proceeded and proceeds by virtue of the power of attorney that was conferred by the said Valverde. The tenor of this document follows the arrangement exercised by the citizen Mariano Almonte, trial judge of the jurisdiction of Teotitlán del Camino....

Accordingly, and based on the latest agreement on these issues, the most excellent lord vice governor and the party representing the owner of Ayotla and his slaves have agreed to the terms, manners, and forms as explained in the following articles.

1. First, the state manumits and frees all the slaves of the Ayotla mill, that is the property of the mentioned Matías Eduardo Valverde, for the quantity and compensation of only six thousand two hundred pesos, which the state will disburse from its own public funds.

2. Second, the state will promptly exhibit in timely fashion the two thousand two hundred pesos that Valverde needs for pressing matters after this writ is signed. His agent, of course, is satisfied with receiving this quantity and renounces the laws of non-delivery, their proof, and exception, and the *non numerata pecunia* (unpaid money). Valverde will receive and the state will supply the remaining four thousand pesos through payments of five hundred monthly pesos, or as much as is possible, starting from this date.

3. Third, Valverde's agent will present to the lord governor of Teotitlán del Camino any and all of the slaves that belonged to the said sugar plantation or mill, according to the form and terms that were agreed to in the appraisal carried out by the trial judge in Ayotla on January 6 of the past year. The appraisal is cited and inserted in this writ.

4. Fourth, if one or more of the individuals listed in the agreement and appraisal carried out by the citizen Almonte are missing, their value and price will be reduced from the six thousand two pesos following a rigorous accounting to the respective proportion. In the event that there is a larger number [of slaves] than that designated by the appraisal, the owner of Ayotla will be paid observing the same proportional rule.

5. Fifth, if one or several of those listed [in the appraisal] fled and the owner of the mill is able to present them in the future, or if they present themselves voluntarily, the state will increment the price as well, in fair proportion to the six thousand two hundred pesos of the agreement, just as now the compensation is reduced by those not currently present in that place.

6. Sixth, all of the slaves who fled before the appraisal carried out by the said Almonte was verified, and whose names are not listed, are also set free and are not subject to slavery. They also enter into the indemnification of the six thousand two hundred pesos, so that the said interested party of Ayotla may not ask or demand anything regarding their presentation or summoning.

On account of all this, the mentioned agent offers to comply thoroughly and perfectly with the previous articles with respect to his power. Likewise, the most excellent lord vice governor, with respect to the state, also agrees to follow this in the best manner and form according to his name. In fulfilling the mentioned Article 7 of the constitution that governs us, the vice governor declares as people free of all captivity, servitude, oppression, patronage, or any other horrific title, all the individuals listed in the inserted appraisal and all the others who have fled the said place, plantation, or sugar mill of Ayotla. So that enjoying their complete freedom, they may be esteemed as such [free people], and that they might exercise the abilities that are granted to citizens by conferring upon them all the power and faculties that are duly theirs. So that without limitation or hindrance they may use their liberty, by this instrument celebrated to their benefit, I ordered and order that each of them be given this document so that they will at no time return to slavery or servitude, nor recognize any dominion above them. The said agent understands this, and has guaranteed that he renounces, yields, and transfers to the state any excess or surplus in the value of the slaves, thus cooperating in the manner that he can with openness and humanity. In this manner, he makes a pure, perfect, and irrevocable donation through a firm contract . . . and by removing the lord and owners of the slaves, he renounces the action of property, dominion, and lordship that he has held over them. He consents that from this writ he will be given testimony that acknowledges his generosity and compassion and the agent of Ayotla commits to seeing through the sale [sic] and its security and guarantees, according to the law. . . . In testimony of which they awarded this writ and signed, witnesses the citizens Francisco Antonio Salgado, Vicente Santaella, Francisco Aragón, *vecinos* of this said capital.

Ramón Ramírez de Aguilar   Manuel Saenz de Enciso   Before me, José Ignacio
                                                                                Salgado

[Spanish transcription]

En la Capital del Estado livre de Oaxaca á treinta dias del mez de Marzo de mil ochosientos veinte, y seis años. Ante mi el Escrivano Nacional Publico de los del Numero de ella, y testigos de la una parte el Excelentisimo Señor Vice Governador Ciudadano Ramon Ramirez de Aguilar que actualmente funciona en el Gobierno del Estado: y de la otra el Ciudadano Manuel Saens de Ensiso Ex Diputado de este Soberano Congreso y dijeron. Que por quanto conforme al Articulo Ceptimo [sic] de la constitucion de este Estado de Oaxaca se de en Obligacion de livertad á toda Clase de personas que como Esclavos existan en el, indemnisando á sus amos, ó propietarios previamente; sobre Cuyo motivo se formó expediente por este Gobierno, en que se perciben los diversos aprecios que se dieron a la Esclavonia del Trapiche, e Ingenio de Aljotla . . . sobre cuyos particulares se han tratado con mas ventajas para el Estado diversos puntos con el citado Ensiso como Apderado [sic, apoderado] de Don Matias Eduardo Valverde Dueño de aquella Finca, y Señor que ha sido de toda su Eclavonia [sic, esclavonía], que en todo, y en la parte que le ha tocado ha prosedido; y procede á virtud del Poder comferido por dicho Valverde; cuyo tenenor [sic, tenor] con el de la Operación practicada por el Ciudadano Jues de primera Ynstancia de aquel partido de Totitlan del Camino, Mariano Almonte . . .

mediante lo qual, y lo ultimamente tratado en el particular se han comvenido el Excelentisimo Señor Vice Governador; y la parte del dueño de Ayotla, y su Esclavonia en los terminos, modo, y forma que esplican los Articulos Siguientes.

1º El primero. Que este Estado manumite, y liverta á todos los Esclavos del trapiche de Ayotla que es de la propiedad del referido Matias Eduardo Valverde por la Cantidad, é indemnisacion de solo seis mil doscientos pesos que sacará de sus propios fondos públicos.

2ª La segunda. Que á buena cuenta hara pronta exhibision de dos mil, doscientos pesos, que necesita Valverde para sus urgencias, luego que sea firmada esta Esriptura [sic], y de cuya cantidad desde luego se dá por resivido su Apoderado. Sobre lo que renuncia las Leyes del no entrego, su prueva, y excepción e la non numerata pecunia, y el resto de quato mil pesos lo hirá persiviendo, y enterandole el Estado, á razon de quinientos pesos mensales [sic], corrientes desde esta fecha, ó lo mas que le fuere posible.

3º El tercero. Que la parte de dicho Valverde precentará al Señor Governador de Teotitlan del Camino todos, y qualesquiera de los Esclavos que en Calidad de tal hallan pertenesido á dicho Yngenio, ó Trapiche, según en la forma, y terminos que refiere el abaluo hecho por aque[l] Jues de primera Ynstancia en el mismo Ayotla a seis de Enero de el año próximo pasado. Que ba citado, é inserto en esta Escriptura.

4º El quarto. Que si de los individuos Constantes en el abaluo, y operación echa por el Citado Ciudadano Almonte, faltaren uno, ó mas se rebajará su valor, y precio por rigorosa quenta de proporcion respecto, á los seis mil doscientos pesos que por livertarlos da el Estado; En la inteligensia de que haviendo mayor numero del que designa dicho abaluo se le pagaràn á la parte del dueño de Ayotla obserbandose la misma regla de proporcion.

5º El quinto. Que si se hubiesen fugado alguno, ó varios de los que resa dicho avaluo, y pudiere el dueño del Trapiche presentarlos en lo venidero, ó ellos se precentasen, boluntariamente, le bonificara el Estado su presio tambien, á justa proporcion de los seis mil doscientos en que se han combenido, como ahora se le rebajan por no estar existentes en aquel Lugar.

6º El sexto. Que todos los Esclavos que hayan fugado antes de verificarse el abaluo del referido Almonte, cuyos nombres no consten en el, quedan tambien livres sin sujecion, á esclavitud, entrando en la indemnisacion de los seis mil doscientos pesos, sin que por su precentacion, ó comparecensia pueda el interesado de Ayotla pedir, ni exigir cosa alguna.

Mediante lo qual ofreciendo el referido apoderado que seran Cumplidas bien Cabal, y perfectamente lo que respectivamente toca á su poder ante de los Articulos anteriores, y lo mismo el Excelentisimo Señor Vice Governador, por lo que respecta al Estado desde luego por la precente en la mayor [sic, mejor] via, y forma que halla á su nombre, y en cumplimiento del citado articulo septimo de la Constitucion que nos goviena, declara por personas libres de todo cautiverio, servidumbre, y oprecion, patronasgo, ú otro orendo [sic, horrendo] titulo, á los individuos que comprende el incerto abaluo, y á los demas que antes de el se hayan fugado de aquel lugar Yngenio, ò trapiche de Ayotla, para que gozando de su entera livertad, se les estime por tal, y puedan ejercer las funciones que les son concedidas á los ciudadanos confiriendoles todo el poder, y facultad que en echo propio les corresponde para que sin limitacion, ni embaraso usen de toda su livertad, á cuyo fin, y á mas de este Ynstrumento celevrado a su beneficio mandava, y mando que siendo nesesairo se les dé, á cada uno respectivamente, el documento que lo acredite para que ningun tiemp[o] vuelvan á la esclavitud, y servidumbre, ni á reconocer sovre si Señorio alguno; de lo que queda entendido dicho apoderado; asegurando que de qualesquiera exseso, ó demasia que en el valor de la esclavonia haya tenido la Cede renuncia, y transfiere en el Estado cooperando en el modo que puede á su franquesa, y humanidad, haciendole gracia, y donacion, pura, mera, perfecta, é irrebocable por contrato firme . . . y apartando el Señor, y Dueños de los Esclavos da la acsión de propiedad, dominio, y Señorio que en ellos haya tenido, Consintiendo que de esta escriptura se le dé testimonio que acredite su liveralidad, y compacion, y obligando se por el interesado de Ayotla á la edicion [sic, ebición], Seguridad, y saneamiento de la venta [sic], en toda forma de derecho . . . . En testimonio de lo qual asi lo otorgáron, y firmáron siendo testigos los Ciudadanos Fransisco Antonio Salgado, Vicente Santaella, y Fransi[s]co Aragon, vesinos de esta dicha Capital.

Ramon Ramirez de Aguilar	Manuel Saenz De Enciso	Ante mi, José Ygnacio Salgado

Document 118: 1829—President Vicente Guerrero abolishes slavery[21]

The president [Vicente Guerrero] of the United Mexican States, to the inhabitants of the republic, let it be known:

---

21. *Colección de las leyes y decretos expedidos por el Congreso General de los Estados Unidos Mejicanos en los años de 1829 y 1830* (Méjico: Imprenta de Galvan, 1831), 149–150.

Desiring in 1829 to commemorate the anniversary of independence with an act of justice and national beneficence that would bring about benefit and support to such a laudable good; one that would secure the public peace more and more; that would cooperate in the aggrandizing of the republic; that would reintegrate a disgraced part of its inhabitants in the sacred rights that nature gave them; and that protects the nation by means of wise and just laws, according to what has been disposed in Article 30 of the constitutive act. By using the extraordinary faculties that I am conceded, I have come to decree that:

1. Slavery is abolished in the republic.

2. Those who until today had been considered as slaves, therefore, are now free.

3. When the treasury's circumstances allow it, the slaves' proprietors will be indemnified in accordance with the terms established by the law.

Mexico, September 15, 1829 = to Don José María de Bocanegra

[Spanish transcription]

El presidente [Vicente Guerrero] de los Estados-Unidos Mejicanos, á los habitantes de la república, sabed:

Que deseando señalar en el año de 1829 el aniversario de la independencia con un acto de justicia y de beneficiencia nacional, que refluya en beneficio y sosten de bien tan apreciable; que afiance mas y mas la tranquilidad publica; que coopere al engrandecimiento de la república; y que reintegre á una parte desgraciada de sus habitantes en los derechos sagrados que les dió naturaleza y proteje la nacion por leyes sabias y justas, conforme á lo dispuesto por el artículo 30 de la acta constitutiva; usando de las facultades extraordinarias que me están concedidas, he venido en decretar:

1. Queda abolida la esclavitud en la república.

2. Son por consiguiente libres los que hasta hoy se habían considerado como esclavos.

3. Cuando las circunstancias del erario lo permitan se indemnizará á los propietarios de los esclavos, en los términos que dispusieren las leyes.

Mejico 15 de setiembre de 1829. = A Don José María de Bocanegra

Essay on Sources

This history of slavery and freedom in colonial and early national Mexico is based on abundant source material. The argument that there are not enough documents to conduct research on enslaved and free Mexican communities is simply not valid. These sources do exist. The larger, structural problem consists of gaining access to, translating, and sharing documents on the experiences of enslaved, free, and free-born people.

It is important to recognize, however, that most documents on enslaved people do not reflect their perspectives. This is often a difficult and disappointing revelation. We may glimpse an instant in the life of a sixteen-year-old "Angolan" girl through a bill of purchase, but that document was produced for the people who sold and purchased her. Mexico's archives are full of such dehumanizing documents. They reveal next to nothing about that girl's feelings, memories, and desires. Still, those documents do allow us to chronicle, even if imperfectly, the lives of the enslaved people who existed, survived, forged friendships, and eventually became part of local communities. Perhaps we cannot construct the biographical narrative of a particular coerced Nahua worker in a Toluca textile mill, but through careful research we can begin to assemble a sense of the food that the Toluca mill workers consumed, how frequently they were allowed to leave the mill, or whether they ever became godparents to their co-workers' children. A focus on the communal experiences of free and enslaved people, then, is often a productive way of advancing our understanding of the Mexican past.

In order to recover fragments of the historical experiences of freed and bonded people, many scholars urge us to challenge archival documents: to consider the enslaver's power, the scribe's complicity, and our continued reliance on violent texts. For instance, notarial sources often reduce enslaved people to the status of disposable objects, whereas our intent is to consider their full humanity. Therefore, we must constantly challenge the words, perspectives, and even the tone contained in these primary source documents. This volume encourages students to read against the grain and to carefully imagine the unwritten sights, sounds, and emotions that would have accompanied the production of any document. We must also consider how and why people changed or eliminated their testimonies, identifying labels, and family histories at particular moments. These tensions are rich sources of historical inquiry.

Students interested in pursuing further research on Mexican slavery and freedom—especially at the graduate level—should invest their time in developing their reading comprehension of the Spanish language or, more properly, *castellano*. Without a doubt, the vast majority of archival documents related to enslaved and freed people in Mexico was written in Spanish. Native chroniclers and scribes (especially in central and southern New Spain) certainly wrote accounts that mentioned such bonded and free populations, but Indigenous people were not the primary enslavers in the viceroyalty. Nonetheless, there is also important work still to be done on Mexican slavery through extant Portuguese, Nahuatl, Mixtec, Dutch, and French documents. These eclectic collections are dispersed in archives, museums, and research libraries throughout Mexico as well as in the United States, Spain, France, Portugal, and many other locations. What follows are suggestions for research in some of these physical locations and in digital repositories.

The Archivo General de la Nación (AGN) in Mexico City contains an immense collection of sources on enslaved and free people. The records of the Inquisition, in particular, offer highly detailed information on the daily lives, expectations, and genealogies of people of African, Asian, Spanish, and mixed descent. These investigations focused on unorthodox beliefs and practices that allegedly deviated from Catholic dogma. As such, they offer deeply textured case studies through which to understand the cultural fabric of colonial society. Likewise, the Viceroyalty Miscellany (*Indiferente Virreinal*) holds a vast collection of miscellaneous documents that include everyday complaints, transactions of enslaved people, petitions from free militiamen, and marriage petitions, among many, many more genres of documents. The documentation included about Indians, in the *Indios* collection, often speaks to the concerns of Native communities and individuals who sought protection from Crown officials and tribute collectors, but also from African-descended and mixed individuals. Finally, very interesting information on marriage petitions across ethnic groups can be found in the marriage records (*Matrimonios*) of the *Regio Patronato Indiano*.

An abundance of documents can also be found outside of Mexico City, in regional, municipal, and parish-level archives. At the local level, marriage records for enslaved and freed people can be found in virtually any church office with records for the colonial period. A single city may contain multiple parish offices that reflect different marital patterns among various ethnic communities. In Puebla, for instance, research at the parish or *barrio* level can be conducted in the Archivo del Sagrario Metropolitano, Archivo Parroquial del Señor San José, and Archivo del Santo Angel Custodio (Analco), among other parishes. The same can be said for baptismal registers, which record the name of a child's godparents and the social networks that formed from these unions among families. Researchers have been less attentive to death records (*libros de decesos* or *defunciones*), yet these may provide the basis for microhistorical or even quantitative research. Visiting these parish archives requires spending time in these communities, explaining one's interest in a particular research topic, and earning the trust of the local religious community and its gatekeepers.

Fortunately, several digital platforms now enable students, researchers, and the general public to conduct research in parish registries from afar. For instance, Family Search provides access to an immense cache of Mexican baptismal, marital, and death records for enslaved and free people. These records were compiled and microfilmed by the Church of Latter-day Saints in the twentieth century, before being digitized and uploaded to an online platform (https://www.familysearch.org/en/). Researchers will find these digitized records organized at the parish level, sometimes by caste label (*libro de indios, libro de negros*). The digital files typically follow the chronological order found in the original parish books. This digital database, then, provides a very useful tool by which to reconstruct family and community histories. Because enslaved people were expected to participate in Catholic sacraments, they were not excluded from these parish registers. Anyone interested in the baptismal practices of the free and enslaved families of San Francisco de Campeche, Guadalajara, Zacatecas, or any other colonial Mexican settlement may study these records remotely.

Notarial archives preserve property transactions, last wills, bills of slave purchase, apprenticeship contracts, manumissions, and debt obligations. As such, these protocols, which can be found in most state capitals, are absolutely essential to the study of Mexico's enslaved and free communities. Because most of these archives are uncatalogued, conducting research in them can be quite time-consuming. Nonetheless, they offer very valuable information on everyday interactions and exchanges. Records of individual and collective sales of enslaved people (*cartas de compra-venta*) can be found in these notarial registers and as such may be used to reconstruct a person's dislocation across different ports, cities, and rural settlements. Freedom papers, either as *cartas de libertad* or as excerpts from testaments, are also found in these notarial documents. Researchers interested in free individuals and families may also find rental agreements, records of real estate purchases, and debt contracts, in documents labeled *obligación*. Finally, the testaments of free people also provide us with fascinating windows into their material possessions and into the relationships of trust and friendship that informed their lives.

Fortunately, considerable efforts have been and are still being made to produce search aids for Mexican notarial archives. The 2017 *Catálogo y estudio introductorio de la presencia de las personas de origen africano y afrodescendientes durante los siglos XVI y XVII en el valle de Toluca* provides a priceless guide to the Archivo General de Notarías del Estado de México. For research in central Veracruz, Fernando Winfield Capitaine's *Esclavos en el archivo notarial de Xalapa, Veracruz, 1668–1699* remains an essential text. Building on these efforts, the University of Veracruz has developed a digital portal that now serves as a search tool and virtual archive for the notarial collections of Xalapa, Córdoba, and Orizaba (https://eval.uv.mx/bnotarial/default.aspx). Known as the "Archivos Notariales de la Universidad Veracruzana," these databases are searchable by key terms, dates, and geographical references. The ADABI organization (Apoyo al Desarrollo de Archivos y Bibliotecas de México) has also developed CD-Rom catalogues and search tools for notarial archives in Chihuahua, Toluca, and

Oaxaca. These and other relevant materials can be found in the WorldCat catalogue and requested through InterLibrary Loan services.

The expansion of digital resources has enabled students, professors, and researchers to access ever more detailed information on the experiences of free-born, freed, and enslaved people in Mexico. *Memórica* is a recent digital initiative that brings together texts, images, audio recordings and other media from the Archivo General de la Nación, the Biblioteca Nacional de México (BNM), and several other regional archives and research centers. The portal provides high-resolution images and descriptions of documents from the colonial and early national periods (https://memoricamexico.gob.mx/es/memorica/home#landing). These digitized records currently represent a minuscule fraction of what can be found in the actual archives, but they provide enough sources to develop a research project and may even be used to practice Spanish-language paleography.

Since the viceroyalty of New Spain was an integral part of the global Spanish empire, a vast portion of Mexico's colonial documents can be found in the Archivo General de Indias (AGI) in Seville, Spain. Those pursuing research projects on the transatlantic and inter-American slave trade in the AGI collections will find relevant material in the *Contratación* and *Escribanía* records. Slave ship captains' permissions, debts, and trials contained in these records often reveal connections between Veracruz, Angola, Portugal, Cabo Verde, and other locations. The AGI's *México* records preserve multiple genres of documents that touch on the lives of free and enslaved people. The correspondence between the viceroys of New Spain, the Crown, and the Council of Indies, as well as reports from town councils and the inventories of wealthy individuals' possessions, can all be examined in the search for traces of freedom and slavery.

Anyone interested in conducting research in the AGI's vast collections—either remotely or in person—can make use of the Portal de Archivos Españoles, or PARES. This invaluable website (https://pares.culturaydeporte.gob.es/inicio.html) allows researchers to enter keyword searches for specific individuals, concepts, or locations and to filter them by date. For instance, a researcher interested in examining the social and political context that freed sailors would encounter in Acapulco can simultaneously search the *Filipinas*, *Contratación*, and *México* records. Moreover, PARES serves as the digital repository for eight other archives—including the Archivo Histórico Nacional (AHNE) and the Archivo General de Simancas (AGS)—that hold important documents for colonial Mexican history. Students pursuing research on religious questions, for instance, can search the Inquisition records sent from Mexico to Spain in the AHNE catalogue by way of PARES. Many of these examinations have been fully digitized. The AGS records will especially appeal to scholars interested in eighteenth-century organizations, such as the free militiamen of Campeche, Yucatán, and Veracruz.

Several institutions in the United States have also developed important manuscript collections related to Mexican colonial history. Within the Manuscript Division at the Library of Congress in Washington, DC, the Domingo del Monte, Hans Peter Kraus, and Jay I. Islak collections feature rare books, manuscripts, and microfilms dealing with New Spain. Many of these documents refer directly or indirectly to free and enslaved Mexican communities. The Library of Congress also features astounding holdings of out-of-print books, many of them digitized (https://www.loc.gov/). These materials may be especially relevant for research projects on nineteenth-century slavery and freedom in Mexico. Similarly, the John Carter Brown Library (JCB) in Providence, Rhode Island, holds very large collections of rare printed materials related to New Spain. Students interested in the visual culture of colonial Mexico, especially engravings within book collections, can search the JCB Archive of Early American Images through their Luna Imaging portal (https://jcb.lunaimaging.com/luna/servlet). The University of Texas-Austin's Benson Library also preserves an important corpus of colonial Mexican rare books and manuscripts. Some of these materials have been digitized as part of the LLILLAS Benson Digital Collections (BDC) and Collaborative Digital Initiatives. Finally, the Online Archive of California (OAC) has emerged as an especially powerful search engine by combining the catalogues, search tools, and digitized records of more than three hundred contributing research libraries, museums, and historical societies. Within the OAC platform (https://oac.cdlib.org/), scholars of Mexican slavery and freedom will find useful documents from UC-Berkeley's Bancroft Library, the Huntington Library's *Mexican Inquisition Papers*, and UCLA's Special Collections at Young Research Library (YRL). Evidently, the expansion of digital tools will only further research into free and enslaved communities, but conducting research in physical archives remains absolutely essential.

Bibliography

Archives

AGI	Archivo General de Indias
AGS	Archivo General de Simancas
AGNEM	Archivo General de Notarías del Estado de México
AGNEP	Archivo General de Notarías del Estado de Puebla
AGNM	Archivo General de la Nación (México)
AHEZ	Archivo Histórico del Estado de Zacatecas
AHJP	Archivo Histórico Judicial de Puebla
AHNE	Archivo Histórico Nacional (España)
AHNO	Archivo Histórico de Notarías de Oaxaca
AMP	Archivo Municipal de Puebla
ANUV	Archivos Notariales de la Universidad Veracruzana
APSJ	Archivo de la Parroquia de San José (Toluca)
ASMP	Archivo del Sagrario Metropolitano de Puebla
ASAC	Archivo del Santo Ángel Custodio (Analco)
ASSJ	Archivo del Señor San José (Puebla)
BDC	Benson Digital Collections (University of Texas-Austin, Teresa Lozano Long Institute of Latin American Studies)
BGH	Biblioteca General Histórica, Universidad de Salamanca
BNE	Biblioteca Nacional de España
BnF	Bibliothèque nationale de France
BNM	Biblioteca Nacional de México
FABF	Fondo Antiguo Biblioteca Franciscana
IASTD	Intra-American Slave Trade Database
JCB	John Carter Brown Library
LOC	Library of Congress (Washington, DC)
MEM	Memórica. México haz memoria
OAC	Online Archive of California
PARES	Portal de Archivos Españoles
TASTD	Trans-Atlantic Slave Trade Database
TUL	Tulane University, Latin American Library
YRL	Young Research Library, Special Collections (UCLA)

Works Cited

Alcántara López, Alvaro. *Gobernar en familia: disidencia, poder familiar y vida social en la provincia de Acayucan, 1750–1802*. Ciudad de México: Bonilla Artigas Editores, 2019.

Alegría, Ricardo E. *Juan Garrido: el conquistador negro en las Antillas, Florida, México, y California, c. 1503–1540.* San Juan: Centro de Estudios Avanzados de Puerto Rico y el Caribe, 1990.

Altman, Ida. *Life and Society in the Early Spanish Caribbean: The Greater Antilles, 1493–1550.* Baton Rouge: Louisiana State University Press, 2021.

Amaral, Adela. "The Archaeology of a Maroon Reducción: Colonial Beginnings to Present Day Ruination." PhD diss., University of Chicago, 2015.

———. "Social Geographies, the Practice of Marronage and the Archaeology of Absence in Colonial Mexico." *Archaeological Dialogues* 24, no. 2 (2017): 207–223.

Barba, Paul. *Country of the Cursed and the Driven: Slavery in the Texas Borderlands.* Lincoln: University of Nebraska Press, 2021.

Bennett, Herman L. *Colonial Blackness: A History of Afro-Mexico.* Bloomington: Indiana University Press, 2009.

Bialuschewski, Arne. *Raiders and Natives: Cross-Cultural Relations in the Age of Buccaneers.* Athens: University of Georgia Press, 2022.

Boyd-Bowman, Peter. "Negro Slaves in Colonial Mexico." *The Americas* 26, no. 2 (October 1969): 134–151.

Bristol, Joan Cameron. *Christians, Blasphemers and Witches: Afro-Mexican Ritual Practice in the Seventeenth Century.* Albuquerque: University of New Mexico Press, 2007.

Brooks, James F. *Captives and Cousins: Slavery, Kinship, and Community in the Southwest Borderlands.* Chapel Hill: Omohundro Institute, 2002.

Bryant, Sherwin K. *Rivers of Gold, Lives of Bondage: Governing through Slavery in Colonial Quito.* Chapel Hill: University of North Carolina Press, 2014.

Camba Ludlow, Úrsula. *Imaginarios ambiguos, realidades contradictorias: Conductas y representaciones de los negros y mulatos novohispanos, Siglos XVI y XVII.* México, D.F.: Colegio de México, 2008.

Carroll, Patrick. "Black-Native Relations and the Historical Record in Colonial Mexico." In *Beyond Black and Red: African-Native Relations in Colonial Latin America*, edited by Matthew Restall, 244–269. Albuquerque: University of New Mexico Press, 2005.

———. *Blacks in Colonial Veracruz: Race, Ethnicity and Regional Development.* Austin: University of Texas Press, 2001.

Castañeda García, Rafael. "Santos negros, devotos de color. Las cofradías de San Benito de Palermo en Nueva España. Identidades étnicas y religiosas, siglos XVII–XVIII." In *Devoción, paisanaje e identidad. Las cofradías y congregaciones de naturales en España y en América (siglos XVI–XIX)*, edited by Óscar Álvarez Gila, Alberto Angulo Morales, and Jon Ander Ramos Martínez, 145–164. Bilbao: Servicio Editorial de la Universidad de País Vasco, 2014.

Castañeda García, Rafael, and Juan Carlos Ruíz Guadalajara, eds. *Los afrodescendientes en el México virreinal. Espacios de convivencia, sociabilidad y conflicto.* San Luis Potosí: El Colegio de San Luis, 2020.

Castro Gutiérrez, Felipe. *Nobles, esclavos, laboríos y macehuales. Los nuevos súbditos indianos del rey.* Ciudad de México: Universidad Nacional Autónoma de México, 2021.

Castro Morales, Efraín, ed. *Suplemento de el Libro Número Primero de la Fundación y Establecimiento de la Muy Noble y Muy Leal Ciudad de los Ángeles.* Puebla: Ayuntamiento del Municipio de Puebla, 2009.

Clark, Joseph M. H. *Veracruz and the Caribbean in the Seventeenth Century*. Cambridge: Cambridge University Press, 2023.
Clayton, Lawrence A. *Bartolomé de las Casas: A Biography*. Cambridge: Cambridge University Press, 2012.
Colección de las leyes y decretos expedidos por el Congreso General de los Estados Unidos Mejicanos en los años de 1829 y 1830. Méjico: Imprenta de Galvan, 1831.
Colmenares, Joseph Carlos de. *Ordenanzas del Baratillo de México*. Edited by Guillermo Espinosa Estrada and Éric Ibarra Monterroso. Monterrey: Universidad Autónoma de Nuevo León, 2022.
Conrad, Robert. *Children of God's Fire: A Documentary History of Black Slavery in Brazil*. University Park: Penn State University Press, 1994.
Cope, Douglas R. *The Limits of Racial Domination: Plebeian Society in Colonial Mexico City, 1660–1720*. Madison, University of Wisconsin Press, 1994.
Delgadillo Núñez, Jorge E. "Becoming Citizens: Afro-Mexicans, Identity, and Historical Memory in Guadalajara, 17th to 19th Centuries." PhD diss., Vanderbilt University, 2021.
Del Paso y Troncoso, Francisco. *Epistolario de Nueva España, 1505–1818*. México: Antigua Librería Robledo de J. Porrúa e Hijos, 1939–1942.
Díaz del Castillo, Bernal. *Historia verdadera de la conquista de la Nueva España escrita por el capitan Bernal Diaz del Castillo, uno de sus conquistadores*. Madrid: En la Imprenta del Reyno, 1632.
———. *The True History of the Conquest of New Spain*. London: Hakluyt Society, 1916.
Diccionario enciclopédico hispanoamericano de literatura, ciencias y artes. Barcelona: Montaner y Simón Editores, 1894.
Dufendach, Rebecca. "Nahua and Spanish Concepts of Health and Disease in Colonial Mexico, 1519–1615." PhD diss., UCLA, 2013.
Fitzpatrick Sifford, Elena. "Mexican Manuscripts and First Images of Africans in the Americas." *Ethnohistory* 66, no. 2 (April 2019): 223–248.
Flores García, Georgina et al., eds. *Catálogo y estudio introductorio de la presencia de las personas de origen africano y afrodescendientes durante los siglos XVI y XVII en el valle de Toluca*. Toluca: Universidad Autónoma del Estado de México, 2017.
García de León, Antonio. *Tierra adentro, mar en fuera: El puerto de Veracruz y su litoral a Sotavento, 1519–1821*. México, D.F.: Fondo de Cultura Económica, 2011.
García Montoya, Alejandro. *El esclavo africano en San Luis Potosí durante los siglos XVII y XVIII*. San Luis Potosí: Universidad Autónoma de San Luis Potosí, 2016.
García Rodríguez, Gloria, ed. *Voices of the Enslaved in Nineteenth-Century Cuba*. Chapel Hill: University of North Carolina Press, 2011.
Gerhard, Peter. "A Black Conquistador in Mexico." *Hispanic American Historical Review* 58, no. 3 (August 1978): 451–459.
Gharala, Norah. "'From Mozambique in Indies of Portugal': Locating East Africans in New Spain." *Journal of Global Slavery* 7, no. 3 (October 2022): 243–281.
———. *Taxing Blackness: Free Afromexican Tribute in Bourbon New Spain*. Tuscaloosa: University of Alabama Press, 2019.
González, Anita. *Afro-Mexico: Dancing between Myth and Reality*. Austin: University of Texas Press, 2010.

Graham, Margaret A., and Russell K. Skowronek. "Chocolate on the Borderlands of New Spain." *International Journal of Historical Archaeology* 20 (2016): 645–665.

Gruzinski, Serge. "The Ashes of Desire." In *Infamous Desire: Male Homosexuality in Colonial Latin America*, edited by Pete Sigal, 197–216. Chicago: University of Chicago Press, 2003.

———. "Las cenizas del deseo: Homosexuales novohispanos a mediados del siglo XVII," in *De la santidad a la perversión o de la porqué no se cumplía la ley de Dios en la sociedad novohispana*, edited by Sergio Ortega Noriega, 255–281. México: Editorial Grijalbo, 1985.

Gutiérrez, Ramón A. "The Genízaro Origins of the Hermanos Penitentes." In *Nación Genízara: Ethnogenesis, Place, and Identity in New Mexico*, edited by Moises Gonzales and Enrique R. Lamadrid, 80–117. Albuquerque: University of New Mexico Press, 2019.

Gutiérrez Brockington, Lolita. *The Leverage of Labor: Managing the Cortés Haciendas in Tehuantepec, 1588–1688*. Durham: Duke University Press, 1989.

Heywood, Linda, and John K. Thornton. *Central Africans, Atlantic Creoles, and the Foundation of the Americas, 1585–1660*. Cambridge: Cambridge University Press, 2007.

Jaffary, Nora E., and Jane E. Mangan, eds. *Women in Colonial Latin America, 1526 to 1806: Texts and Contexts*. Indianapolis: Hackett Publishing Co., 2018.

Jiménez Meneses, Orián, and Edgardo Pérez Morales, eds. *Voces de esclavitud y libertad. Documentos y Testimonios: Colombia, 1711–1833*. Popayán: Universidad de la Cauca, 2013.

Katzew, Ilona. *Casta Painting: Images of Race in Eighteenth-Century Mexico*. New Haven: Yale University Press, 2004.

Kellogg, Susan, and Matthew Restall, eds. *Dead Giveaways: Indigenous Testaments of Colonial Mesoamerica and the Andes*. Salt Lake City: University of Utah Press, 2008.

Klein, Herbert, and Ben Vinson III. *African Slavery in Latin America and the Caribbean*. Oxford: Oxford University Press, 2007.

Krögel, Alison. "Mercenary Milk, Pernicious Nursemaids, Heedless Mothers: Anti-Wet Nurse Rhetoric in the Satirical Ordenanzas del baratillo de Mexico (1734)." *Dieciocho: Hispanic Enlightenment* 37, no. 2 (2014): 233–248.

Lara Tenorio, Blanca, and Carlos Paredes Martínez. "La población negra en los valles centrales de Puebla: Orígenes y desarrollo hasta 1681." In *Presencia africana en México*, edited by Luz María Martínez Montiel, 19–77. México: CONACULTA, 1994.

Lecaros Sánchez, José Miguel. *El fenómeno de la esclavitud y del trabajo esclavo: perspectiva histórico jurídica e histórica*. Sevilla: Caligrama, 2019.

Lockhart, James, and Enrique Otte, eds. *Letters and People of the Spanish Indies*. Cambridge: Cambridge University Press, 1976.

Lucena Samoral, Manuel. *Regulación de la esclavitud negra en las colonias de América Española (1503–1886): documentos para su estudio*. Alcalá de Henares: Universidad de Alcalá / Universidad de Múrcia, 2005.

Luis, Diego Javier. "Diasporic Convergences: Tracing Knowledge Production and Transmission among Enslaved Chinos in New Spain." *Ethnohistory* 68, no. 2 (April 2021): 291–310.

———. *The First Asians in the Americas: A Transpacific History*. Cambridge: Harvard University Press, forthcoming 2024.

Martínez, María Elena. "The Black Blood of New Spain: Limpieza de Sangre, Racial Violence and Gendered Power in Early Colonial Mexico." *The William and Mary Quarterly* 61, no. 3 (July 2004): 479–520.

———. *Genealogical Fictions: Limpieza de Sangre, Religion and Gender in Colonial Mexico*. Stanford: Stanford University Press, 2008.

Martínez Vargas, Enrique, and Ana María Jarquín Pacheco. "Sacrificios de negros al inicio de la conquista de México." In *¿Donde están? Investigaciones sobre Afromexicanos*, edited by Emiliano Gallaga Murrieta, 105–134. México: Universidad de Ciencias y Artes de Chiapas, 2009.

McKnight, Kathryn Joy, and Leo J. Garofalo, eds. *Afro-Latino Voices: Narratives from the Early Modern Ibero-Atlantic World, 1550–1812*. Indianapolis: Hackett Publishing Co., 2009.

Molina, Alonso de. *Vocabulario en lengua castellana y mexicana*. México: En Casa de Antonio de Spinosa, 1571.

Müller, Viola Franziska. *Escape to the City: Fugitive Slaves in the Antebellum Urban South*. Chapel Hill: University of North Carolina Press, 2022.

Naveda Chávez-Hita, Adriana. *Esclavos negros en las haciendas azucareras de Córdoba, Veracruz, 1690–1830*. Xalapa: Universidad Veracruzana/Centro de Investigaciones Históricas, 1987.

Newitt, Malyn. *The Portuguese in West Africa, 1415–1670: A Documentary History*. Cambridge: Cambridge University Press, 2010.

Oropeza, Déborah. *La migración asiática en el virreinato de la Nueva España: Un proceso de globalización (1565–1700)*. Ciudad de México: El Colegio de México, 2020.

Otte, Enrique, and Guadalupe Albi Romero, eds. *Cartas privadas de emigrantes a Indias, 1540–1616*. México: Fondo de Cultura Económica, 1993.

Palmer, Colin. *Human Cargoes: The British Slave Trade to Spanish America, 1700–1739*. Urbana: University of Illinois Press, 1981.

———. *Slaves of the White God: Blacks in Mexico, 1570–1650*. Cambridge: Cambridge University Press, 1976.

Paredes Martínez, Carlos. *El impacto de la conquista y colonización española en la antigua Coatlalpan (Izúcar, Puebla) en el primer siglo colonial*. México: CIESAS/Cuadernos de la Casa Chata, 1991.

Pennock, Caroline Dodds. *On Savage Shores: How Indigenous Americans Discovered Europe*. New York: Alfred A. Knopf, 2023.

Proctor, Frank, III. *Damned Notions of Liberty: Slavery, Culture and Power in Colonial Mexico, 1640–1769*. Albuquerque: University of New Mexico Press, 2010.

———. "Gender and the Manumission of Slaves in New Spain." *Hispanic American Historical Review* 86, no. 2 (2006): 309–336.

Reséndez, Andrés. *A Land So Strange: The Epic Voyage of Cabeza de Vaca*. New York: Basic Books, 2007.

———. *The Other Slavery: The Uncovered Story of Indian Enslavement in America*. Boston: Houghton Mifflin Harcourt, 2016.

Restall, Matthew. "Black Conquistadors: Armed Africans in Early Spanish America." *The Americas* 57, no. 2 (October 2000): 171–205.

———. *The Black Middle: Africans, Mayas, and Spaniards in Colonial Yucatan*. Stanford: Stanford University Press, 2009.

———. *When Montezuma Met Cortés: The True Story of the Meeting that Changed History*. New York: Ecco, 2018.

Restall, Matthew, Lisa Sousa, and Kevin Terraciano, eds. *Mesoamerican Voices: Native Language Writings from Colonial Mexico, Oaxaca, Yucatan and Guatemala*. Cambridge: Cambridge University Press, 2005.

Rodríguez Ortíz, Guillermo Alberto. "El lado afro de la Puebla de los Ángeles. Un acercamiento al estudio sobre la presencia africana, 1595–1710." PhD. diss., Benemérita Universidad Autónoma de Puebla, 2015.

Romero, Brenda. "Afro-Mexican Women in the Northern Frontier." In *AfroLatinas and LatiNegras: Culture, Identity, and Struggle from an Intersectional Perspective*, edited by Rosita Scerbo and Concetta Biondi, 207–224. London: Rowman and Littlefield, 2022.

Schwaller, John. "Alcalde vs. Mayor: Translating the Colonial World." *The Americas* 69, no. 3 (January 2013): 391–400.

———. *The Fifteenth Month: Aztec History in the Rituals of Panquetzaliztli*. Norman: University of Oklahoma Press, 2019.

Schwaller, Robert. *Géneros de Gente in Early Colonial Mexico: Defining Racial Difference*. Norman: University of Oklahoma Press, 2016.

Seijas, Tatiana. *Asian Slaves in Colonial Mexico: From Chinos to Indians*. Cambridge: Cambridge University Press, 2014.

Seijas, Tatiana, and Pablo Miguel Sierra Silva. "The Persistence of the Slave Market in Seventeenth-Century Central Mexico." *Slavery & Abolition* 37, no. 2 (January 2016): 307–333.

Sierra Silva, Pablo Miguel. "Portuguese Encomenderos de Negros and the Slave Trade Within Mexico, 1600–1675." *Journal of Global Slavery* 2 (2017): 229–234.

———. "The Slave Trade to Colonial Mexico: Revising from Puebla de los Ángeles, 1590–1640." In *From the Galleons to the Highlands: Slave Trade Routes in Spanish America*, edited by Alex Borucki, David Eltis, and David Wheat, 73–102. Albuquerque: University of New Mexico Press, 2020.

———. "El tráfico de esclavos a la ciudad de Puebla." *El Pregonero de la Ciudad*. Nueva Época 18 (Julio–Septiembre 2018): 11–15.

———. *Urban Slavery in Colonial Mexico: Puebla de los Ángeles, 1531–1706*. Cambridge: Cambridge University Press, 2018.

Smith, Sabrina. "Juana Ramírez, Eighteenth-Century Oaxaca." In *As If She Were Free: A Collective Biography of Women and Emancipation in the Americas*, edited by Erica L. Ball, Tatiana Seijas, and Terri L. Snyder, 207–217. Cambridge: Cambridge University Press, 2020.

———. "The People of African Descent in Colonial Oaxaca." PhD diss., UCLA, 2019.

Stone, Erin Woodruff. *Captives of Conquest: Slavery in the Early Modern Spanish Caribbean*. Philadelphia: University of Pennsylvania Press, 2021.

Sue, Christina A. *The Land of the Cosmic Race: Race Mixture, Racism, and Blackness in Mexico*. New York: Oxford University Press, 2013.

Terrazas Williams, Danielle. *The Capital of Free Women: Race, Legitimacy, and Liberty in Colonial Mexico*. New Haven: Yale University Press, 2022.

Torget, Andrew J. *Seeds of Empire: Cotton, Slavery, and the Transformation of the Texas Borderlands, 1800–1850*. Chapel Hill: University of North Carolina Press, 2015.

Tortorici, Zeb. *Sins Against Nature: Sex and Archives in Colonial New Spain.* Durham: Duke University Press, 2018.

Townsend, Camilla. *Malintzin's Choices: An Indian Woman in the Conquest of Mexico.* Albuquerque: University of New Mexico Press, 2006.

———. "'What in the World Have You Done to Me, My Lover?' Sex, Servitude, and Politics among the Pre-Conquest Nahuas as Seen in the *Cantares Mexicanos*." *The Americas* 62, no. 3 (January 2006): 349–389.

Valdés, Dennis Nodín. "The Decline of Slavery in Mexico." *The Americas* 44, no. 2 (October 1987): 167–194.

Valerio, Miguel. *Sovereign Joy: Afro-Mexican Kings and Queens, 1539–1640.* Cambridge: Cambridge University Press, 2022.

———. "'That There Be No Black Brotherhood': The Failed Suppression of Afro-Mexican Confraternities, 1568–1612." *Slavery & Abolition* 42, no. 2 (2021): 1–22.

van Deusen, Nancy E. "Coming to Castile with Cortés: Indigenous 'Servitude' in the Sixteenth Century. *Ethnohistory* 62, no. 2 (2015): 285–308.

———. *Global Indios: The Indigenous Struggle for Justice in Sixteenth-Century Spain.* Durham: Duke University Press, 2015.

———. "The Intimacies of Bondage: Female Indigenous Servants and Slaves and Their Spanish Masters, 1492–1555." *Journal of Women's History* 24, no. 1 (2012): 13–43.

Velasco Murillo, Dana. "'To Search and Claim': Indigenous Prospectors, Silver Mining, and Legal Practices in Spanish America, 1530–1600." *Colonial Latin American Review* 30, no. 4 (2021): 498–519.

Velázquez, María Elisa. *Mujeres de origen africano en la capital novohispana, siglos XVII y XVIII.* México, D.F.: UNAM/INAH, 2006.

Vinson, Ben, III. *Bearing Arms for His Majesty: The Free-Colored Militia in Colonial Mexico.* Stanford: Stanford University Press, 2001.

———. "The Racial Profile of a Mexican Rural Province in the 'Costa Chica': Igualapa in 1791." *The Americas* 57, no. 2 (October 2000): 269–282.

Vinson, Ben, III, and Bobby Vaughn, eds. *Afroméxico: El pulso de la población negra en México.* Ciudad de México: Fondo de Cultura Económica, 2004.

Walcott, Rinaldo. *The Long Emancipation: Moving toward Black Freedom.* Durham: Duke University Press, 2021.

Wheat, David. *Atlantic Africa and the Spanish Caribbean, 1570–1640.* Chapel Hill: University of North Carolina Press/Omohundro Institute, 2016.

Winfield Capitaine, Fernando. *Esclavos en el archivo notarial de Xalapa, Veracruz, 1668–1699.* Xalapa: Universidad Veracruzana, 1984.

Zavala, Silvio, ed. *Ordenanzas del Trabajo, Siglos XVI y XVII.* México, D.F.: Editorial Elede, 1947.

Index

abolition, 9, 15, 60–61, 98, 332–33
Acámbaro, 224–27
Acapulco, 13–17, 91, 95, 100–107, 258–59, 309
Amatepec, 19, 108–13
Amatlan, 116–17
Amaya, Antonio de, 266–67, 276
Angola: descended from, 23, 55–57, 75–76, 82–83, 180–81, 244–45; governor of, 95; land of, 13, 59, 70
Antonia (convent slave), 185–86, 232, 250
Apache, 18, 149–50
Arara (Ardra), 15, 66
Atlixco, 45, 47, 55, 136, 172, 205, 310
Ayotla, 328–30
baptism, 26n79, 27, 60, 278, 288
Barbados, 15, 60, 85
Benito, Creole, 23–24, 176, 216–17, 231–32
blasphemy, 23, 185–186
bounty hunter, 35–36, 123–25
bozal, 44–45, 64, 66, 83, 86–87, 89–90, 180, 183, 205
branding tools, 6, 29–33, 44–46, 60, 87, 109, 308
brotherhood, 20, 23–24, 176, 184, 187, 211–13, 261, 289. *See also* Franciscan Order; Jesuit Society
burial, 24, 79–80, 187, 260, 274
Caballero, Gertrudis, 285–86
Campeche, 13–14, 24, 76, 205
Cape Verde, 7, 12–13, 63
Caravalí (Calabar), 15, 249
Caribbean, 5–7, 60–89

Carnestolendas (Mardi Gras), 290–91
Carrasco, Juan, 177–79
Cartagena de Indias, 64–65
caste, 20–22, 128, 325
Chichimec, 10, 38–40, 98, 114–15
Chihuahua, 17–18, 148–49, 224–26
Cholula, 55, 96, 239, 254, 256, 310
clothing, 11, 49, 56, 73, 156, 158, 241, 243, 261, 264, 280–81, 296–97
cohabitation, 154, 184, 229, 295
communion, 178, 180–83, 204–5, 217, 229
concubinage, 4, 61, 229
confession, 178, 181, 204–6, 217, 221, 229, 260, 297
confraternity, 21, 176, 207–8, 212–13
Congo, 205
conquistador, 3–8, 30
Constansa (baby), 233–34
convent, 11–12, 185–86, 188, 212–13, 243, 260–61, 268, 270–71, 274, 278, 310, 317
Córdoba, 96–97, 145–46, 309
Cortés, Hernando, 4, 6–8, 30, 32, 34, 136n16
Crax Bomba, 1, 134–38
credit, 76, 88, 281
Creoles, Mexican-born, 24, 44–46, 55, 177–78, 190–95, 228, 231–32, 308
Cruz, Ana de la, 235, 239
Cruz, Clara de la, 246
Cruz, Francisco de la, 20, 128–29, 235
Cruz, Juana de la, 235
Cruz, Micaela de la, 249

dances, 162–63, 190–95, 289, 292, 298
Daza Villalobos, Captain Santiago, 85–87
debt, 41–42, 51–53, 64–65, 75–76, 128–29, 208, 255–87
Díaz del Castillo, Bernal, 7, 32–33
disease, 7, 66, 97, 162–63, 216–17
Fernando VII, King of Spain, 322
Franciscan Order, 142, 176, 178
Francisco, Juan, 166–67, 207
godparent (*madrina, padrino*), 204–5, 221
Gómez, Pedro, 51–53
Guadalajara, 26–27, 80, 98, 115, 315
Guadalupe, Our Lady of, 19, 207–8, 211–13, 325
Guatemala, 2, 204, 219–21
Guerrero, President Vicente, 27–28, 289, 332–33
hacienda, 116–17, 124–25, 142–45, 220, 225, 240–41, 316–17, 320
Hernández, Gaspar, 260–61
Hernández, Luisa, 295
Hispaniola, 5, 205
Huexotzingo, 231, 240–41
Inquisition, Holy Office of the, 23, 164, 168, 177–83, 185–86, 219–21, 278, 299
Isla de Cabezas, 69–70
Izúcar, 251, 320
Jamaica, 70–71, 78
Jesuit Society, 82–83, 278
Loriga, Lorenzo, 184
Louisiana, territorial, 151
Lovillo, Antonio Rodríguez, 121
Manila, 16, 102–3
Manuela, María, 142–43
Manzanedo, Francisco, 294
Mariscal, María Antonia, 250–51
maroons, 116–17, 119–21, 123–25, 130–31, 145–46

marriage, 119, 155, 166–67, 210, 219–211, 224–25, 243, 246, 261, 270, 278, 286
Martín, Juan (Indigenous), 300, 307
Martín, Juan (*mulatto*), 161, 295
Matute, Captain Diego, 144–46
Medina, Juan de, 172–73
Mendoza, Viceroy Antonio de, 9, 19, 109–11, 154–55
Mesa, Simón de, 254–55
Mexico City: armed conflict in, 109–11, 124, 149–50; debts in, 65; draining Lake Texcoco in, 42–43; enslaved in, 128, 154–55, 190–96, 204–6, 216, 308, 320; enslavers in, 70; homosexuality in, 296–310; as an imperial center, 39, 92, 98, 166–67, 172–73, 177–78, 224–25, 285–86, 322; slave market in, 78–79, 94, 101
Michoacán, 136
Mónica, Agustina, 269–71
Montúfar, Friar Alonso de, 60–61
Morelos, José María, 27, 323–26
Mota y Escobar, Bishop Alonso de, 44
Mozambique: ancestors from, 52, 55, 95, 97, 99, 101
Munguía, Sebastián Domingo de, 204–5
music, 190–96, 292, 316–17
Muslims, 92–93
Nuñez Bohorquez, Juan, 64–65
Nuñez Franco, Juan, 79
Oaxaca, 36, 38–39, 228–29, 309, 328–29
Olola, Lucas, 162–63
Pablo, Diego, 165–66
Palomino Arias, Nicolás, 219–21
Pamplona, Captain Diego, 89–90
Peralta, José de, 274
Philip II, 63, 92–93, 232

Philippine Islands: 16, 100–105; ancestors from, 233; arrival of enslaved from, 92–95; enslaved in, 99
Portuguese: 5, 13; descended from a, 205, 307; enslaved by, 44, 77–78, 88; slave trade, 92, 95, 101
Puebla de los Ángeles: 24; burial in, 274; crime in, 156, 165, 169–70, 184–86, 276, 289–92, 295; debt in, 254–59, 264–65; disease in, 158–59; education in, 278; enslaved people in, 41–42, 51, 55, 79, 116–17, 177–79, 204–6; enslavers in, 64, 67–68, 70, 161; freedom from slaver in, 132–33, 142–43, 171, 233–36, 239, 243–45, 247–49; as a government center, 40, 128, 188, 210, 260–61, 266–71, 285–86; homosexuality in, 297, 308–10; religion in, 177–83, 185–86; slave market in, 35–36, 66, 82–83, 89–90, 96–97, 250–51
Puerto, Lorenzo del, 266–67
rebellions, 1, 30, 109–52, 229
Rinconada, 135–38, 149–50
Río Blanco, 119–21, 124–25
Rodríguez, Marta, 187–88
Rodríguez de la Torre, Lázaro, 268
San Benito de Palermo, 23–24, 216–17
San Juan, Catarina de, 247–48
San Juan de Ulúa, 72–73, 124, 232
Santa Efigenia, brotherhood of, 211–13
Santo Domingo, 33, 75–76
Seville, 63, 69, 75, 90, 111, 119
Sheba, 191
Simona, Gertrudis, 144–45
Solomon, 191
Sotomayor, Don Juan Manuel de, 130, 296–97, 299, 306
sugar plantation (*ingenio*), 36, 134–35, 328–29
syncretism, 168–69
Tampico, 12, 39
taxes, 10, 27, 34, 48–49, 63, 67, 72–73, 78, 94, 264, 285–86, 324–25
Tecamachalco, 31, 161
Tehuantepec, 168–69
Tepeaca, 6, 30, 142–43, 161, 294
Terra Nova, Juana de, 258–59
Texas, 18, 151
textile mill (*obraje*), 41–42, 48–49, 51–53, 55–57, 96–97, 158–59, 161, 205, 268
Tlaxcala: cathedral of, 185, 187, 235; Indigenous people from, 30; jurisdiction of, 128, 205, 240–41, 254, 285
Toluca, 176, 211, 212–13
Torre, Juliana de la, 166–67
Upper Guinea: ancestors from, 36, 60, 63, 120, 144
Valle, Lázaro del, 224–26
Vásquez, Hernán, 63
Vega, Juan de la, 296–97, 300, 306
Veracruz: 13–14; crime in, 119; enslaved peoples in, 38–39, 134–37; slave trade in, 69–71, 85, 88, 149, 205; weapons in, 111
Vergara Gaviria, Pedro de, 69, 71, 73
Victoria, Cristóbal de, 299, 306
Yanga, Gaspar, 19, 119–21
Zacatecas: citizens of, 279–82; mines near, 114, 226